IP Routing

Primer Plus

Heather Osterloh

SAMS

201 West 103rd St., Indianapolis, Indiana 46290 USA

IP Routing Primer Plus

International Standard Book Number: 0-672-32210-2

Library of Congress Catalog Card Number: 2001094221

Printed in the United States of America

First Printing: December, 2001

04 03 02 01   4 3 2 1

Trademarks

Warning and Disclaimer

ASSOCIATE PUBLISHER
Jeff Koch

ACQUISITIONS EDITOR
William Brown

DEVELOPMENT EDITORS
Mark Renfrow
Jason Burita

MANAGING EDITOR
Matt Purcell

PROJECT EDITOR
Andy Beaster

COPY EDITOR
Kate Givens

INDEXER
Kevin Broccoli

PROOFREADER
Harvey Stanbrough

TECHNICAL EDITOR
André Paree-Huff

TEAM COORDINATOR
Denni Bannister

INTERIOR DESIGNER
Anne Jones

COVER DESIGNER
Aren Howell

PAGE LAYOUT
Rebecca Harmon

CONTENTS AT A GLANCE

CONTENTS

ABOUT THE AUTHOR

Heather Osterloh has earned industry recognition as a Cisco Certified Network Associate (CCNA), Cisco Certified Network Professional (CCNP), Cisco Certified Design Associate (CCDA), Cisco Certified Design Professional (CCDP), Network Associate Sniffer trainer, Certified Network Expert (CNX) for Ethernet and Token Ring, Novell CNI/ECNE, Microsoft Certified Systems Engineer (MCSE), and Microsoft Certified Trainer (MCT). She also holds her Cisco Certified Internetworking Expert (CCIE), written portion and is currently waiting to take the practical lab exam.

Having spent the past 15 years training and consulting worldwide, Heather is an acknowledged leader in the networking industry. Author of one book, *CCNA 2.0 Prep Kit 640-507 Routing and Switching,* and of several popular Microsoft, Cisco, and Novell video series geared towards the busy professional, Heather continues to produce material that helps educate people about the world of networking.

Heather also has lectured at the University of California, Berkeley; NetuCon's NetWare User Conference in San Jose; and the University of Puerto Rico; and was president of IT Academy, LLC for three years.

Heather lives in Northern California with her husband Kirk and her dogs, Cocoa and Kato.

DEDICATION

This book is dedicated to my biggest fans, Rita and Karl Osterloh.

ACKNOWLEDGMENTS

There are many people I need to thank for supporting me in writing this book. First I would like to thank Sams Publishing and its amazing team of professionals, including William Brown (Sr. Acquisitions Editor), Jason Burita (Development Editor), Mark Renfrow (Development Editor), Andrew Beaster (Project Editor), Kate Givens (Copy Editor), and André Paree-Huff (Technical Editor). There are many more people who contributed to this book, from production and other departments (names unknown to me) who deserve recognition and appreciation for a job well done.

A special thanks to J. DiMarzio, and Michelle Truman who contributed their technical expertise, in the development of several chapters.

To my mom and dad for calling me and giving me words of encouragement throughout the months I spent writing, thank you.

I would like to acknowledge my extended family, the Gass's and Beckmans, for their constant encouragement. Hey grandpa Beckman, you better hurry up and finish reading my first book, because the second one just came out and the third one is on its way.

To my husband and best friend Kirk for putting up with me through the writing of this, my third book. Your love and support mean everything to me and keep me going. Thanks, Honey.

TELL US WHAT YOU THINK!

As the reader of this book, *you* are our most important critic and commentator. We value your opinion and want to know what we're doing right, what we could do better, what areas you'd like to see us publish in, and any other words of wisdom you're willing to pass our way.

As an Associate Publisher for Sams, I welcome your comments. You can fax, e-mail, or write me directly to let me know what you did or didn't like about this book—as well as what we can do to make our books stronger.

Please note that I cannot help you with technical problems related to the topic of this book, and that due to the high volume of mail I receive, I might not be able to reply to every message.

When you write, please be sure to include this book's title and author as well as your name and phone or fax number. I will carefully review your comments and share them with the author and editors who worked on the book.

Fax: 317-581-4770
E-mail: feedback@samspublishing.com
Mail: Jeff Koch, Associate Publisher
          Sams Publishing
          201 West 103rd Street
          Indianapolis, IN 46290 USA

INTRODUCTION

Routing and routing protocols are what make the exchange of information throughout the world possible. Without routers and routing protocols we would be using "SneakerNet" (I don't know who coined the term), which means we would have to deliver messages to recipients by foot.

As a long-time instructor and networking professional, routing seems second nature to me. For those who have a pretty good handle on routing, this book attempts to make routing second nature to you as well. However, I found that some people (usually my beginning students) have only a vague idea of how their e-mail works. They had even less knowledge about specific routing protocols and how data gets from their computer across the Internet to another computer using those protocols. For those who have only a vague idea of routing, this book attempts to take the mystery out of routing. That is, you will learn the intricate details of datagram delivery.

Audience

This books covers IP routing methods and protocols used in small, medium, and large networks in depth. There are three main groups that would benefit from this book: newbies (beginners), intermediate (some exposure to routing), and advanced (experienced routing professionals). For newbies, this book provides an excellent introduction to the world of routing and routing protocols that can be referenced over and over. Those with a fundamental understanding of networking and routing (intermediate level), who may not know some of the specifics of the routing protocols they have been implementing on their networks, will find that this book will enhance their existing skills. Advanced routing professionals who have been working with routers for years will find this book helpful not only as a reference for well-known interior routing technologies, but also as an invaluable tool for those in the process of implementing advanced routing protocols or technologies, such as BGP, QoS, and multicast routing.

Organization

The approach to this book is straightforward, providing clear explanations and examples of how datagram delivery occurs from beginning to end.

The first two chapters of this book start with a discussion of the OSI (Open Systems Interconnection) model, popular LAN and WAN architectures, and IP addressing. They provide the foundation for understanding the infrastructure routing protocols use to deliver datagrams.

Chapters 3 through 9 cover IP routing methods and protocols, starting with a basic discussion of routing principles, and then moving on to specific LAN and WAN routing protocols. Each chapter starts with a brief history, discusses routing protocol operations, calculations, strengths, and weaknesses and ends with a sample configuration.

Chapters 10 and 11 cover timely topics, such as service-level routing (ToS and QoS) and multicast routing protocols and technologies.

All chapters include helpful notes, sidebars, and cautions calling attention to important information or warning of routing issues of which the reader should be aware. Each chapter concludes with a quiz to assist the reader in retention. Chapter quiz answers are included in Appendix G.

CHAPTER 1

OVERVIEW OF INDUSTRY MODELS, STANDARDS, AND TCP/IP PROTOCOLS

You will learn about the following in this chapter:

- The OSI Model
- The DoD Model
- LAN Architectures and Topologies
- Wide Area Network Technologies
- Request for Comments

Overview of the OSI Reference Model

In the early days of networking only proprietary systems and proprietary protocols existed. Operating systems developed by large companies, such as IBM's SNA and Digital Equipment Corporation's DECNet, included proprietary protocol suites. These operating systems and their corresponding protocols primarily facilitated mini- and mainframe network communication; however, these companies made no provisions for interconnection or to allow for communication with outside systems. When IBM developed SNA and Digital Equipment Corporation developed DECNet, no one had anticipated the prevalence of the mixed computing environments that exists today, which meant that only systems using compatible protocols and operating systems could communicate with one another and exchange data.

As you can imagine, these different proprietary systems had a hard time communicating with one another, if they were able to at all. It soon became necessary to create some type of industry standard to enable company systems to communicate and share information with one another. The Department of Defense (DoD) developed an intercommunication model in the early 1970s, which became the source model for the TCP/IP protocol suite. The DoD model consists of four functional layers each with distinct responsibilities. The layers in the model define protocol and hardware functions and the interaction of the layers.

However, this model has been largely replaced with the ISO (International Standards Organization) OSI Reference Model released in the early 1980s. The OSI Reference Model consists of a seven-layer architecture that defines different networking functions that occur at each layer (see Figure 1.1).

FIGURE 1.1
The OSI Reference Model defines the seven layers and their functions.

OSI Model and Functions

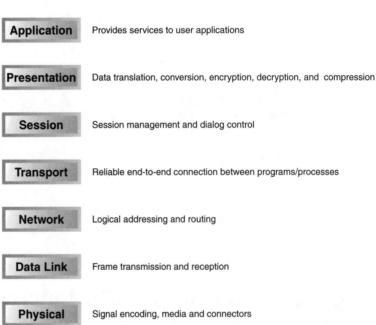

Application	Provides services to user applications
Presentation	Data translation, conversion, encryption, decryption, and compression
Session	Session management and dialog control
Transport	Reliable end-to-end connection between programs/processes
Network	Logical addressing and routing
Data Link	Frame transmission and reception
Physical	Signal encoding, media and connectors

The purpose of the OSI Reference Model is to allow similar and dissimilar systems to communicate seamlessly by providing an architectural framework for hardware manufacturers and software developers to follow when designing products. It makes the implementation of different operating systems, protocols, network architectures, and lower-layered media types possible. Although seamless communication is not always achieved, the OSI Reference Model considers it the primary goal.

Before the OSI model, the protocols in existence did not lend themselves easily to interconnectivity. In most cases retrofitting these protocols would be difficult at best and possibly even infeasible. As such, most protocols and hardware currently implemented by vendors and manufacturers conform to the guidelines of the OSI model. The smooth, swift exchange of data and seamless interconnectivity required in today's mixed computing environments depends on manufacturers and vendors adhering to a standardized reference model.

The OSI model is a *conceptual* framework consisting of seven layers. These layers represent a series of functions and standards vendors follow. The logical layers of the model do not specifically define what needs to be performed at each layer; they simply define what functions should occur at each respective layer and how upper and lower layers logically pass information.

How the functionality occurs at each layer depends on the vendor or the manufacturer that creates or implements the hardware or the protocols. Individual manufacturers have the liberty of interpreting and deciding how closely they wish to adhere to the specifications for a given layer. Because functionality is left up to vendor interpretation the intended result, seamless compatibility between dissimilar devices, is not always achieved. However, this framework and model provides the best resource available for this compatibility.

The OSI model consists of the following seven layers (from top to bottom):

- Application (layer 7)
- Presentation (layer 6)
- Session (layer 5)
- Transport (layer 4)
- Network (layer 3)
- Data Link (layer 2)
- Physical (layer 1)

Overall, each layer has distinct functions that must occur within it to prepare data to go out on the wire to communicate with a remote station. The vendor can determine the specifics within the general functions. That is, the manufacturer or developer defines how those specifics work, so vendors need to concern themselves with only their part of the puzzle. Assuming an organization or vendor follows the guidelines laid out by the ISO organization for a particular layer, the result is a product that can easily integrate with other products that follow the model.

Keep in mind that you use the OSI only when you package data for transmission to connect to a remote host.

The OSI Reference Model and its associated layers are not used when data is being locally accessed on a system, for instance, if you are sitting at your PC using Word and you want to save this file to the local hard disk. The application you are running and the ultimate storage location of the file is local to the PC so there is no need to prepare information for delivery across the network. In this case your PC's internal operating system handles the entire process of saving the file to the local disk by interfacing with the local application.

However, if you want to perform that same function on a remote host, the OSI model and the protocols associated with its layers must be used. The request for remote resources must somehow be prepared and sent from the source host across the network to the other device to access the file, and have that device respond by transferring the data.

To do this, first the request to access the remote file is intercepted by the local PC's redirector, which directs this request to the remote host for processing. The redirector prepares the request for transmission across the internetwork by adding header and control information so the destination knows what to do with the data upon reception and how to respond. Header and control information is discussed later in this chapter.

Overview of the Department of Defense Model

The history of the DoD Model began long before the OSI model, which has since superseded it. Beginning in 1973 the Department of Defense Advanced Research Projects Agency (DARPA) began a program to formulate technologies that could facilitate the interconnection of various kinds of packet networks. This research was called the "Internetting Project" and, as you might surmise from the name, resulted in today's Internet.

The model developed by DARPA as an initial standard by which the core Internet protocols would conform became known as the DoD model. This four-layer model, shown in Figure 1.2, consists of the following (from top to bottom):

- The Process/Application layer
- The Host-to-Host layer
- The Internet layer
- The Network Access layer

In contrast to the OSI, the DoD model consists of four layers, which roughly map to the OSI model from top to bottom as follows:

FIGURE 1.2
The DoD consists of four distinct layers.

DOD Model

Process/
Application

Host to Host

Internet

Network
Access

General Description of OSI Layers

Now that you are familiar with the purpose of the OSI model take a look at each of the layers identifying the functionality expected by each layer.

Remember the OSI model is only necessary when you are attempting to access a resource remotely—that is, a resource located on some host other than your own. When you get ready to send data (this could mean anything from an e-mail message to a request to read a file from a remote host), that request needs to be intercepted by the redirector and packaged for delivery across the network. To do this, the sending system must follow these steps, which are based on the specific functions of the OSI Reference Model:

1. Apply addressing to it.

2. Associate protocols with it.

3. Send it out on the wire.

Each layer within the model logically interfaces with its upper and lower layer. When a system prepares data to be sent out on the wire, starting at the top and moving down through the model each layer adds specific header and control information.

It is important to understand that both the sending and receiving host use this model. The sending host uses the model to prepare the message for transmission. As the message moves down through this model each layer provides header and control information which the receiving host uses to process the message upon reception. The receiving host uses the model in reverse, from bottom to top, stripping each layer's header and control information and passing it up, until finally the user information is exposed. As mentioned earlier, each layer has a distinct role in preparing data to be sent out on the wire to communicate with a peer remote host (see Figure 1.3). All of the steps inherent to these roles appear transparent to the user.

FIGURE 1.3

Each layer of the OSI Model adds header and control information.

Headers and Trailers

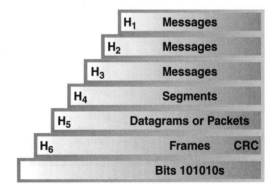

Each layer simply treats everything handed down as generic upper-layer data. This process is similar to an envelope being placed inside another envelope at each layer with each envelope including its own specific sending and receiving address information.

For example, the Application layer places the user data in an envelope, providing header and control information to the peer Application layer at the remote host location. It then passes this envelope down the Presentation layer.

The Presentation layer upon reception simply treats the upper layer's information as data, ignoring both the header and control information, and the data contained within the (Application) layer's envelope. The Presentation layer places the received envelope inside its own envelope adding header and control information for the peer Presentation level at the remote host. In other words, each lower layer (in this case the Presentation layer) ignores everything it receives from the upper layer. It views it as a separate unit, which it disregards. The header, control information, and data are only processed by the corresponding layer at the remote host. Each subsequent layer adds its own header and control information and sends the data down to the next level.

At each layer within the model headers and control information are added. However, once the data reaches the Data Link layer, the system runs an algorithm called a cyclical redundancy check (CRC) (also referred to as FCS, frame check sequence). It then adds the CRC as a trailer to the end of the information to guarantee that the bits being sent match the bits the end host receives. This is the only layer within the model that adds both a header and a trailer. At this layer the message is referred to as a frame because the Data Link fully encapsulates all upper layer information. The term *frame* refers to the logical grouping of information that data undergoes at the Data Link layer. From there the data goes out on the wire as electrical or light signals—1s and 0s—and the intended remote host receives the data (see Figure 1.4).

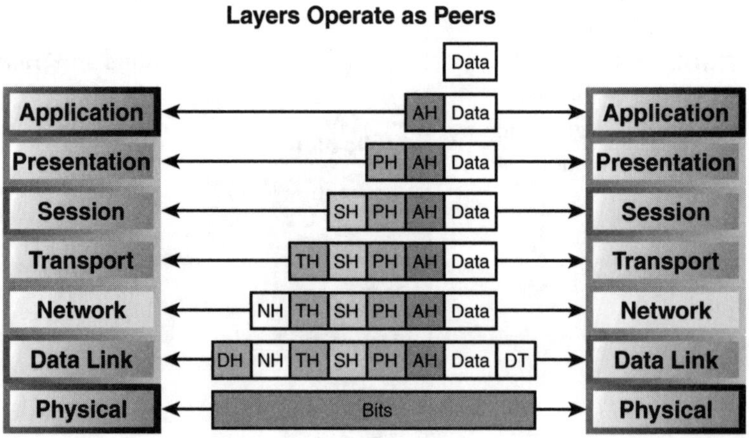

FIGURE 1.4

The receiving host removes headers and trailers before sending the datagram contents up to the next layer.

Layers Operate as Peers

When the host receives the data, the process is reversed. Each corresponding layer removes its header information and passes it up to the next layer, exposing that layer's header and control information and data until it arrives at the Application layer, which strips off its own header and control information and passes the data up. This happens with every single frame that goes out on the wire. Each layer must attach header and control information so the peer layer can identify the upper layer that should receive it next.

Note

By taking a layer approach the OSI model benefits manufacturers and software developers, and network engineers who offer support and troubleshooting. OSI layers compartmentalize the function and responsibilities of protocols within the layers. This eases the development and support burdens that manufacturers and network engineers face. Layering makes troubleshooting a network problem easier, allowing network engineers to use the model to isolate problems. Each layer's function and responsibilities are clearly defined, making problem identification easier.

Application Layer

The top layer of the OSI model can confuse people because they think it refers to user applications such as Word, Excel, PowerPoint, and so on. The Application layer does not refer to the software applications themselves, but rather a portal that facilitates the access of resources between an application and end systems across a network. This portal provides a window to the OSI Reference Model to prepare your data to be packaged and sent out on the wire.

The Application layer enables user applications to send data across the network. It simply affords access to the lower layers, or provides a window to the OSI model. Remember the Application layer's job is to provide an interface to your protocol stack. Unlike the other OSI layers, this layer does not provide services to any of those other layers; rather it provides access for Application layer services only.

Some of the Application layer services include

- Applications with network and internetwork services
- File and print services
- E-mail
- Web access and HTTP
- Telnet access on a remote host
- File Transfer Protocol (FTP) .

Presentation Layer

The Presentation layer provides a common data format across different platforms. It is responsible for the following services:

- Data conversion and translation

- Compression/decompression

- Encryption/decryption

Functionality of the Presentation Layer is generally included in most implementations within the Application layer protocol or program; therefore, the presentation layer is integrated as a component within the upper layer program and is not seen as a separate distinct protocol within the model.

One example of a true Presentation layer protocol is eXternal Data Representation (XDR). Sun Microsystems uses this protocol in its client/server-based Network File System (NFS) implementation. NFS uses XDR to provide platform independence.

Session Layer

The Session layer manages and sets up sessions between two. remote hosts. A session consists of a dialog between Presentation layers on two end systems. This layer also handles the requests for different services between systems and manages the responses to those requests between systems. It also controls the dialog between two applications on different hosts and manages datastreams.

The efficiency of dialog control between hosts in the Session layer depends on whether the communication mode is *half-duplex* or *full-duplex*. In a half-duplex configuration, only one device can communicate or transmit at a time while all others wait in standby mode for their turns. Each side must wait until the other process has finished sending, and then respond with a separate acknowledgement. A full-duplex communication can send and receive at the same time; therefore, it provides a more efficient means of communicating than half-duplex communication. Full-duplexing accomplishes its efficiency by piggybacking, or including data within the same frame.

An example of a Session layer protocol that you might know is the Network Basic Input Output System (NetBIOS). NetBIOS sets up a session between two Windows NT or Windows 95 machines. NetBIOS, a true Session layer protocol used by Microsoft, provides name services and session management between two devices using simple naming.

The Session layer also includes Remote Procedure Call (RPC), developed by Sun, which allows clients to make requests for remote execution. The requests are sent to a remote host for processing and a response, which enables communication between two hosts across a network. NFS uses RPC to send calls and get responses at the session layer, and uses XDR at the presentation layer.

Note

The term "message" is used to describe manipulated information units within the upper three layers (Application, Presentation, and Session) of the OSI model.

Transport Layer

The Transport layer generally is thought to provide guaranteed. reliable delivery of data only between two communicating processes or programs running on remote hosts. However, this holds true only if the vendor decides to implement a connection-oriented protocol, such as the Transmission Control Protocol (TCP), rather than its less reliable counterpart User Datagram Protocol (UDP) within the TCP/IP protocol suite.

The Transport layer does the following:

- Controls end-to-end communication between two processes running on different hosts.

- Provides connection-oriented or connectionless services to upper layers.

- Uses client and server port addresses to identify processes running within a host.

Note

The term used to describe information manipulated at the Transport layer is *segment*. The Transport layer is responsible for breaking up the message or datastream received from upper layers into more manageable pieces and assigning source and destination port addresses to keep track of them.

The Transport layer has the task of identifying which processes are communicating on each host and providing either connection-oriented services or connectionless services to these processes. Connection-oriented service provides for the reliable transmission of data. Connectionless service provides speed of delivery, but no reliability. Both Transmission Control Protocol (TCP) and User Datagram Protocol (UDP) reside at the Transport layer.

The Transport layer handles addressing with *ports.. These* addresses identify which upper-layer program or process is communicating on a particular device. End systems may have many active applications running simultaneously each with a different port address. Port addresses are used to distinguish between different programs running within the system

The term *socket* describes the combination of an end system's logical IP address and transport layer port. The combination uniquely identifies a process running with a specific host. When two end systems are communicating, a socket pair is created. The socket pair includes each end system's IP address and port address. Together they uniquely identify a logical communication channel between remote systems. When a server has many connections to manage, it uses socket pairs to distinguish and keep track of them.

> ### Socket Pairing
>
> When you have end-to-end communication between hosts that involves source and destination IP addresses and ports (also called sockets), the industry refers to this as a *socket pair*.

Client-based and server-based addresses such as TCP or UDP ports are used to identify the process that is running within a host. Client ports fall within a range of 1,024 through 65,536 and are chosen at random whenever a client process is started.

Server ports have a range of 1 through 1,023. Well-known server ports are ports that are recognized industry wide and fall within the range of 1 through 255. Server ports within the range 256 through 1,023 may be used by vendors to identify their own programs or processes. Appendix C contains a comprehensive list of TCP and UDP ports.

It is important to fully understand the nature of connectionless and connection-oriented services and how TCP and UDP function as Transport layer protocols.

All protocols can be categorized as either connection-oriented or connectionless. Connection-oriented protocols provide guaranteed reliable delivery of data between two end systems. Before any meaningful data can be exchanged between two remote systems, a logical virtual connection must be set up. After the connection is established, data transfer can occur over this connection between communicating applications. Throughout the duration of the session all information exchanged is tracked via sequence numbers and acknowledgments for reliability. The process of tracking every piece of information sent requires a lot of resources of the end systems and adds traffic to the network. When data transfer is complete or the communication between end systems is no longer needed the session is torn down.

The amount of resources required by connection-oriented protocols depends on the protocol being implemented. Some protocols sequence each frame, whereas others sequence each byte within the frame. Whatever the method, the purpose is the same: to detect lost frames or data, and recover them by retransmitting the lost data.

When no user data is being exchanged between hosts, the virtual connection must still be maintained. This is accomplished through keepalives. *Keepalives* are essentially packets that do not carry upper-layer data and are only sent to maintain idle connections.

Another attribute of connection-oriented protocols is flow control. When data is being sent too fast, it may overrun the receiving host's buffers, causing frames to be lost. To prevent overrunning another host's buffers, a mechanism to control data flow can be used.

The TCP (Transmission Control Protocol) within the TCP/IP protocol suite is considered a connection-oriented protocol and as such provides guaranteed reliable delivery of data to upper-layer applications and processes.

All TCP connections are set up prior to delivery of data. The establishment of a connection involves a three-way handshake between remote hosts. After the connection is established TCP sequences and acknowledges each byte sent and received to guarantee no data is lost in transit. When the connection is no longer needed the session is torn down.

Note

The BGP (Border Gateway Protocol) discussed in Chapter 7 is the only routing protocol, which utilizes TCP's connection-oriented services at the transport layer.

In contrast, connectionless protocols, such as UDP (User Datagram Protocol), send information but do not require a virtual connection or the verification that information was properly received, making them fast but unreliable. Instead they rely on other protocols to ensure that data sent has been received and is error-free. These protocols are not as reliable as their connection-oriented counterparts, but are very fast and have very little overhead. In most cases only a simple CRC is used to verify that the protocol header has not been damaged in transit. IP is an example of a connectionless protocol, providing fast yet unreliable delivery to upper-layer protocols.

In comparing these two types of service, there are two key considerations: speed versus reliability and overhead. When vendors want fast delivery, they opt for connectionless protocols, such as UDP; when reliability is more important than speed, they prefer connection-oriented protocols, such as TCP. For example, vendors that write printing applications typically use connection-oriented protocols because users don't want to *hope* that their print jobs are printed.

Network Layer

The primary responsibility of the Network layer is to assign logical source and destination addresses and determine the best path for routing data between networks. All network layer protocols are connectionless, providing unreliable yet fast delivery of datagrams. The main network layer protocol within the TCP/IP protocol suite is IP the Internet Protocol.

Note

The terms used to describe the unit information manipulated at the Network layer may be referred to as either *datagrams* or *packets* interchangeably. Each datagram or packet is treated as a separate unit including its own source and destination addressing for delivery.

The Network layer covers the following:

• Logical addressing

• Packet delivery

• Routing

Network layer protocols deal with *logical addressing,* which is distinguished from the Data Link layer Media Access Control (MAC) address associated with a network interface card. Unlike MAC addresses, which are burned in to the network interface permanently assigning an address to a device, network layer addresses are assigned by an administrator either manually or dynamically. We will discuss logical Network layer IP addresses in Chapter 2, "IP and IP Addressing," and refer to them throughout the book.

To achieve the best routing of data, Network layer devices such as routers (also referred to as gateways) utilize *packet switching*. In this process the router identifies the logical destination Network layer address of traffic received in one interface; then the router sends it out on a different interface to its destination.

The following protocols and devices exist at the Network layer:

- RARP, ARP, BootP, DHCP—protocols that perform address resolution or configuration.

- ICMP—diagnostic and control protocol.

- RIP (Routing Information Protocol), IGRP (Interior Gateway Routing Protocol), EIGRP (Enhanced Interior Gateway Routing Protocol), OSPF (Open Shortest Path First)), IS-IS (Intermediate System-Intermediate System), PNNI (Private Network to Network Interface), and BGP (Border Gateway Protocol)—IP routing protocols

- Routers function at this layer

Each of the routing protocols mentioned previously will be discussed later in the book. RIP is discussed in Chapter 4, IGRP and EIGRP in Chapter 5, OSPF in Chapter 6, BGP in Chapter 7, IS-IS in Chapter 8, and PNNI in Chapter 9.

Note

Keep in mind that although routing protocols are considered to be part of the Network layer, some actually run on top of Transport layer protocols, technically making them upper-layer protocols. However, because the function and service they provide is delivery of datagrams utilizing Network layer information, they are classified as such.

Data Link Layer

The Data Link layer's main responsibilities include frame transmission and reception, and physical addressing. The Data Link layer adds both a header at the front and a four-byte trailer at the end of each frame prior to transmission, thereby forming a *frame* around the data. The term *packet framing* refers to the formation of such frame sequences. Only the Data Link layer adds a trailer to the data.

The Data Link layer has the following characteristics and duties:

- Controls access to the medium.

- Adds source and destination hardware addresses.

- Assumes the function of sending and receiving data over the wire.

- Calculates CRC, also referred to as FCS. The industry uses these terms interchangeably.

- Bridges and switches function at this layer.

Note
The data link layer prepares frames for transmission by converting datagrams or packets received from the network layer into frames.

Note
The term used to describe the unit information manipulated at the Data Link layer is *frame*. Each frame includes a Data Link header containing source and destination hardware addresses at the beginning and a CRC at the end.

The Data Link layer's responsibility is to put data on the wire and take it off. Prior to transmitting data the Data Link layer must prepare the information received from its upper layer (the network layer) by framing the data. This process includes adding a header, which includes the source and destination MAC (layer 2) burned in addresses. In addition a trailer is added to the end framing the data. This trailer is referred to as a CRC (or FCS). In reception mode the Data Link layer must buffer the frame, identify its address as the recipient, verify the CRC is good, and if good pass the contents of the frame to its immediate upper layer for further processing. If the datagram is not meant for this system or the CRC is not good the datagram is discarded and no further action is taken.

Layer 2 (Data Link) Addresses

Manufacturers burn in Data Link addresses or MAC addresses on each network interface card. Manufacturers define the numbering sequences when they produce the cards. Each address is six bytes or 48 bits in length, as mandated by the IEEE (Institute for Electrical and Electronics Engineers).

Note
The IEEE (Institute for Electrical and Electronics Engineers) is an organization that develops computer- and networking-related standards. Committees consisting of industry professionals and organizations help develop standards, such as the 802.x series, which deals with Data Link and Physical layer technologies. A result of these committees was the 802.3 (Ethernet) and 802.5 (Token-Ring) specifications, among others.

The first three bytes represent a pre-assigned vendor code identifying the manufacturer of the product. Each vendor is assigned this value by the IEEE. The vendor uniquely assigns the last three bytes. Devices that function at the Data Link layer must have the capability to identify those addresses.

The Data Link layer adds source and destination MAC addresses to the header to identify both the NIC (Network Interface Card) address of the device that sent the frame, and the local device that should receive the frame. Every MAC address must be unique throughout the entire network. Layer 2 devices, such as bridges and switches, use the destination address to decide whether to forward information.

Sending devices perform a Cyclic Redundancy Check (CRC algorithm before transmission. The devices at the Data Link layer add this CRC as a trailer to the end of the data handed down from the Network layer framing the bits. This is why we call them "frames" at the Data Link layer.

CRC does not guarantee delivery of data. It merely verifies that the transmitted bits match the received bits at the receiving host. Receiving hosts use the same algorithm to identify whether the frame remained undamaged during transit. If the CRC does not match, the receiving host simply tosses the frame without notifying the sending station. Stations never pass data up to the next layer unless the frame is good. The sending devices have the responsibility of retransmitting damaged frames.

Basic Switch Operation

Layer 2 (Data Link) devices, such as switches and bridges, forward frames based on MAC addresses. Because they operate at layer 2 of the OSI model, they are not protocol-aware and therefore can forward traffic regardless of the upper-layer protocol (IP, IPX, AppleTalk, NetBIOS, and so on) being carried within the frame. To do this switches must learn which devices are out each port, build a MAC address to port the mapping table, and then forward traffic based on this table.

Switches, unlike routers, do not block broadcast or multicast traffic. When a frame is received with a destination address specifying such an address, the frame must be flooded out all ports except the one it was received through. Flooding frames to all other ports adds additional loads to all other segments on the network. If the destination switch port(s) this traffic is flooded to does not contain hosts that need or care about the flooded frame, this is an unnecessary waste of bandwidth. VLANs can be used to isolate broadcast and multicast traffic to only those switch ports that require the flooded frame. By isolating traffic to specific ports, traffic loads on the network are reduced.

Note

Switches and switch operations are not standardized across vendor platforms. Some switches do not support VLANs. It is a good idea to consult with your vendor as to the specific operation of their switch products.

So how do switches operate? How do they identify where devices are, build their tables, and forward frames? The switching process can be summed up as follows: Switches flood until they learn, and then they forward.

Switches, like bridges initially (when brought online), have an empty MAC address to port mapping table stored in memory. Traffic with unknown or unlearned destination addresses (not in mapping table) are immediately flooded out all ports except the one it was received on (see Figure 1.5).

FIGURE 1.5

Switch with empty MAC address to port mapping table. Switches flood all frames with unknown or unlearned destination MAC addresses.

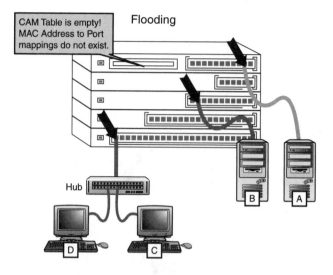

Switches quickly and dynamically build this table (see Figure 1.5) by listening to all traffic received through each port. Every frame received by the switch is inspected, identifying the source MAC address within the Data Link header. Switches assume that the source host sending the frame must be out the port this frame was received through and add this address to its MAC address table, mapping it to the incoming port. By doing this the switch can identify all hosts connected to every port (see Figure 1.6).

FIGURE 1.6

Switches learn and build their MAC address to port mapping table based on source address.

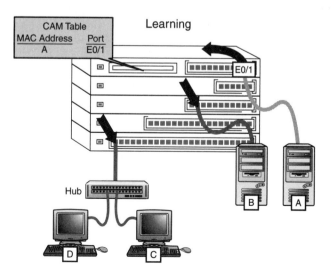

The switch then uses this mapping to deliver a frame to devices. When it receives a frame, the destination MAC address is compared to the switch's table to decide which port to forward the frame en route to its destination. If the destination MAC address is found to belong to the same port the frame was received through, the switch drops the frame and no further action is taken. If the destination address is found within the table, the switch forwards the frame to the appropriate outgoing port or ports (see Figure 1.7).

FIGURE 1.7

The switch has checked its local mapping table and found a MAC address to port mapping and can therefore send the frame directly to the destination port, not requiring it to be flooded.

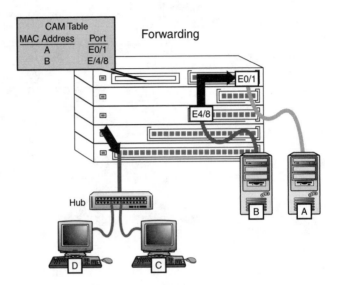

If the switch does not find the destination MAC address within the table (the source MAC address has not been learned), it floods the frame out all ports except the one through which it was received. After the destination host responds, the switch will learn and map the source MAC address of this host to a port and will no longer need to flood for this host. If the destination address is found (within the table) to be mapped to a specific port the switch will forward the frame out the designated port without flooding.

Depending on the switch and its configuration, switches may operate in one of three modes; Cut-through, Fragment Free Cut-through, or Store and Forward (see Figure 1.8). The mode of operation effects the speed at which frames are delivered between switch ports. The fastest mode of switching is Cut-through, offering the lowest latency (delay during transfer). The slowest, but most reliable, mode of switching is Store and Forward. Some switches support all three modes (configurable by an administrator), whereas others only support a single mode.

FIGURE 1.8

Switches operate in one of three modes— Cut-Through, Fragment Free Cut-Through, or Store and Forward.

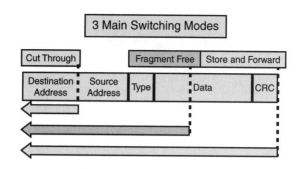

Cut-Through

Switches that operate in Cut-Through make forwarding decisions based on the first six bytes (see Figure D.4) within the frame only (the destination MAC address). Because switches only look at the destination MAC address when making forwarding decisions this is the fastest method of switching. However, being the fastest method does not necessarily mean it is the best.

Because Cut-Through switches only consider the first six bytes of a frame, bad frames (for example, collision fragments) can be forwarded to other segments wasting precious bandwidth. If your network is generally clean this method is great.

Collisions occur when more than one signal exists on the transmission medium. LAN architectures that implement Baseband technology allow only one signal to occupy the transmission channel at a time. If more than one signal is present, a collision occurs.

Collisions cause frames to be truncated. Truncated frames are referred to as runts or fragments. Most frames involved in a collision are truncated somewhere within the first 64 bytes of the frame. Because Cut-Through switches only check the first six bytes are present, frames with damage occurring beyond this are still propagated to other segments.

Fragment Free Cut-Through

This method is slower than Cut-Through, but faster than Store and Forward. Switches implementing this method look at the first 64 bytes of each frame before forwarding frames. This method guarantees that runt frames (collision fragments) are not forwarded. A *runt* is any frame that is less than 64 bytes. Runt frames are generally caused by collisions. Although collisions may occur anywhere within a frame, they usually occur within the first 64 bytes. By verifying that each frame is at least 64 bytes in length prior to forwarding, most damaged frames can be prevented from being propagated to other segments. This method only verifies that each frame is at least 64 bytes in length, but does not perform a CRC check on the contents. This means that frames damaged beyond the 64th byte are still transmitted to other segments.

Store and Forward

This method is the slowest switching method due to the additional processing required. However, it is the most reliable because it does not forward any damaged frames. When a Store and Forward switch receives a frame it fully buffers the frame (hence the term *Store*) and performs a CRC check on the entire contents prior to transmission. By first verifying the CRC is good, switches can determine whether a frame has been damaged by noise or collisions.

If the CRC is not good—that is, it indicates the frame has damage—the frame is discarded and not forwarded. If the CRC is good the switch performs a lookup for the destination address in its MAC address tabled stored in cache and then forwards (if the destination address is unicast) or floods (if the destination address is unknown or a broadcast) out the appropriate port or port.

Vendors make the decisions as to what method their switches will use. Some vendor switches will begin operating in Cut-through cycling between the three methods as damaged frames are encountered. This cycling is dependent on thresholds set on the switch. For example, if very few or no damaged frames are encountered a switch may remain in the fastest mode, Cut-through. If however an unacceptable number of damaged frames are being forwarded to other segments it may dynamically move into Fragment Free Cut-through. If damaged frames are still being forwarded the switch may cycle to Store and Forward. If the level of damaged frames drops below a specified threshold it may go back to Cut-through or Fragment Free Cut-through. Cycling and thresholds are vendor-specific and not covered in this book.

Physical Layer

The Physical layer deals with 1s and 0s—Bits that make up the frame. *Bits* are encoded as electrical or light pulses. This layer also deals with electrical and mechanical characteristics, signal encoding, media, connectors, physical connector specifications and voltage levels. Generally speaking, the Physical layer involves tangible items, that is, "physical" items that you can touch, like cabling and repeaters.

Note

The term used to describe the unit of information manipulated at the Physical layer is *bit*. At the Physical layer data is represented as ones or zeros.

Data Link and Physical Architecture and Topologies

This section is not meant to be a complete discussion of Data Link and Physical layer architectures and topologies, but a refresher. Because our focus is on routing, that is where we will spend our time. However, routing and routing protocols function at layer 3 of the OSI model, but are implemented over various architectures and topologies. We will briefly review some of the most common LAN (Local Area Network) and WAN (Wide Area Network) architectures and topologies in use. The IEEE governs some standards, while others are ANSI specifications.

Note

The ANSI American National Standards Institute is an organization involved in approving computer and communication standards for the U.S.

Local Area Networks are generally small in size and are Networks that involve a single geographic location. Wide Area Networks are networks that span multiple geographic locations and typically include dial up and leased line connections. Dial up links are temporary links that provide access to remote sites for low-volume, infrequent data transfers. Leased lines are permanent links that are used to connect remote sites, providing high-volume data transfer networks. Leased lines are not shared and are always active. That is, there is no setup and teardown of the links connections, which means that it is always available.

Examples of LAN architectures include the following:

- Ethernet version 1 and 2, IEEE 802.3, Fast Ethernet (802.3u), and Gigabit Ethernet (802.3z)

- Token-Ring (IEEE 802.5)

- FDDI (ANSI X3T9.5)

Ethernet and IEEE 802.3

We start with the most popular Data Link architecture, Ethernet technologies, as defined by IEEE within the 802.3 specification. Xerox, credited with inventing Ethernet, actually acquired the original technology (then known as Aloha Net) in the 1970s from the University of Hawaii. Xerox then joined Digital Equipment Corporation and Intel to develop the earliest Ethernet standard, called Version 1, released in 1980. The three companies quickly released a follow-up standard, Ethernet Version 2, in 1982. Version 1 has been obsolete for quite some time.

In the mid-1980s the IEEE 802 committee adopted Ethernet as the 802.3 standard. All current and future development on Ethernet technologies ostensibly build on this base standard. Since its inception, Ethernet has become the most popular LAN standard used throughout the world. Table 1.1 provides a comparison between the three main Ethernet implementations.

TABLE 1.1   Ethernet Versions 1, 2, and IEEE 802.3

Version 1	Version 2	IEEE 802.3
Data Link layer architecture	Includes Ethernet_II frame (the defacto industry frame to carry IP traffic over Ethernet LANs)	Adds jabber control (or jabber inhibit) to detect and disable faulty transceivers
Delivered data at 10Mbps as linear bus topology	Delivers data at 10Mbps as linear bus topology	Expands physical topology support to star configurations

TABLE 1.1 Continued

Version 1	Version 2	IEEE 802.3
Could use only thick coaxial media	Can use only thick coaxial media	Adds media types such as thin coaxial, fiber, and twisted pair
Used unbalanced signaling with ground as reference point (susceptible to noise and EMI)	Uses balanced signaling	Enhancements provide 100Mbps transfer rates (802.3u) and Gigabit transfer rates (802.3z)
Did not support Signal Quality Error (SQE) (also known as heartbeat)	Adds SQE	Supports SQE but is necessary with only external transceivers
Incompatible with Version 2	Incompatible with Version 1	Incompatible with Version 1

The IEEE 802.3 specification was quickly adopted as the standard of choice for most Ethernet implementations. This specification defines the general operation, components, and distance limitations of Ethernet and are the basis for slow (10Mbps), Fast (100Mbps), and Gigabit (1000Mbps) standards.

The 802.3 specification defines all Data Link and Physical layer components, functions, channel access methods, and operations and provides vendors with rules for implementing and developing Ethernet 802.3 LAN technologies.

The IEEE 802.3 specification references 10Base5 as its base standard from which all other 802.3 standards follow with minor variations.

The IEEE 802.3 standard defines a 10Mbps broadcast-based linear network architecture using a contention channel access method known as CSMA/CD (*Carrier Sense Multiple Access with Collision Detection*), which is discussed in the next section.

Channel Access Methods

Various channel access methods exist today (polling, contention, and token passing); the one that is implemented depends on the network architecture. *Channel access methods* describe the rules used by devices that dictate how a device may access, transmit, and then release a channel.

Note

Polling involves a single device controlling access to the medium. This device is referred to as a master and all other devices are slaves. The master dictates when and for how long the slaves may use the medium.

Contention-based networks treat all systems as equals. There are no masters or slaves. When a device wants to transmit it simply senses the channel to see if it is being used. If the channel is free, the system may transmit; if not, it must wait and then try again. Ethernet networks use a contention-based channel access method known as CSMA/CD (Carrier Sense Multiple Access with Collision Detection).

Token passing networks use a token to control transmission. When a device receives a free (unused) token it may transmit. If the token is already being used the system must wait until a free token arrives. Token-Ring networks use the token passing channel access method.

Contention Channel Access Method

All Ethernet networks use a contention-based channel access method, known as CSMA/CD, discussed next. Devices using the CSMA/CD channel access method

- Contend for the right to transmit.

- Can successfully transmit only one at a time.

- Must wait for channel availability to transmit a frame when other devices are using the channel (half-duplex operation).

When devices transmit simultaneously on the same channel, signal collisions occur and frames become corrupted. This contention-based access is called *Carrier Sense Multiple Access with Collision Detection (CSMA/CD)*. Because Ethernet uses silence as the indication to transmit, devices perform a carrier sense to detect that silence. If no frequency exists on the wire, they can access the channel and begin transmission at once. After transmission, devices release the channel and wait at least 9.6[gm] (microseconds) before attempting to access the channel again, thereby giving other transceivers a chance to transmit their frames.

Collision

Collisions are just that—collisions of more than one signal. In a baseband network, more than one signal should not occupy the channel at any one time. The result of more than one signal traversing the wire simultaneously is a collision, which impedes successful transmission. During transmissions a transceiver (transmitter/receiver) encodes the signal on the medium and listens for collisions. If one occurs, the transceiver's internal collision detection circuitry notifies the network adapter card by sending a signal, causing the adapter to abort its transmission. It is the responsibility of the transmitting device to detect and retransmit frames when collisions occur.

Ethernet Frames

There are four different frame types within the realm of Ethernet standards, each designed with a different purpose by a different entity. The four frame types are as follows:

- Ethernet_II (DIX)

- Ethernet_802.3 (Novell proprietary)

- IEEE 802.3

- IEEE 802.3 SNAP (SubNetwork Access Protocol)

DEC, Intel, and Xerox developed the original Ethernet frame known as Ethernet_II (also called *DIX*). Novell developed its own proprietary frame (Ethernet_802.3) exclusively for IPX/SPX traffic. The IEEE developed and named the last two frames. Despite specific companies naming the frame types, the industry and IEEE have different names for the frames. Table 1.2 shows the four Ethernet frame types and compares the naming conventions used by the IEEE and industry; Table 1.3 contains information specific to each frame type.

TABLE 1.2 Ethernet Name Mapping

IEEE Name	Industry
N/A	Ethernet_II (DIX)
N/A	Ethernet_802.3
802.3	Ethernet_802.2
802.3 SNAP	Ethernet_SNAP

TABLE 1.3 Ethernet Frame Types

Ethernet_II -(DIX)	Ethernet_802.3	Ethernet_802.2	Ethernet_SNAP
Designed to carry IP traffic	Designed to carry only IP/SPX traffic	Contains LLC headers using DSAP and SSAP addresses to identify upper-layer protocols	Contains LLC headers using DSAP and SSAP addresses to identify upper-layer protocols
Uses two byte registered Ether-type values to identify protocols; for example, 0800=IP	Uses two-byte Length value that specifies the amount of data included in the frame	Uses two byte Length value that specifies the amount of data included in the frame	Uses two byte Length value that specifies the amount of data included in the frame
Most common frame type in use today	Was de facto frame type for IPX networks prior to Ethernet_802.2	Uses registered SAP to indicate addresses; for example, 06=IP	Specifies special SAP address of AA to indicate SNAP header follows with two-byte Ether-type. Adds a five byte SNAP header after the LLC header to identify the protocol

All four frame types can coexist in a single network but are: not compatible. When stations configured with dissimilar encapsulation types want to exchange information, they must communicate through a router that supports both types. The router performs the conversion between the hosts. Conversion adds unnecessary overhead and delays to the network, so it's best to select and use only one frame type for your network. Figure 1.9 provides a quick reference comparison of the four frame types.

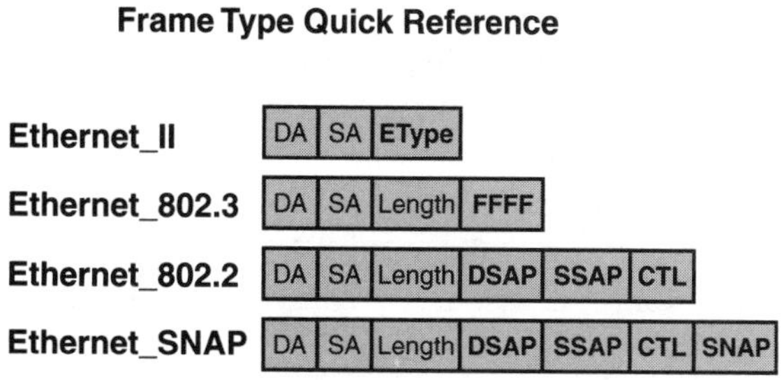

Frame Type Quick Reference

FIGURE 1.9
Use the Frame Type Quick Reference to quickly identify the differences between each frame.

Ethernet_II   DA | SA | EType

Ethernet_802.3   DA | SA | Length | FFFF

Ethernet_802.2   DA | SA | Length | DSAP | SSAP | CTL

Ethernet_SNAP   DA | SA | Length | DSAP | SSAP | CTL | SNAP

Sidebar head??

The Ethernet_II frame is the only frame that includes a 2-byte Ether-type value following the source address used to identify the protocol being carried within the frame.

Ethernet_802.3 is a proprietary frame developed by Novell, which only supports the IPX/SPX protocol suite.

IEEE 802.3 frames, known industry-wide as Ethernet_802.2 and Ethernet_SNAP respectively, include an 802.2 header (referred to as the LLC, Logical Link Control) with DSAP (destination SAP) and SSAP (source SAP) fields. These 1-byte SAP addresses are the equivalent of the protocol type in Ethernet_II, which is used for protocol identification.

The Ethernet_SNAP adds a 5-byte extension header (SNAP) to the 802.2 header. This header includes a 3-byte vendor code followed by a 2-byte Ether-type identifying the protocol being carried.

Slow Ethernet

Slow (10Mbps) Ethernet has been the mainstay of LAN networks since it came out in the mid-1980s. Despite the emergence of standards-defining bodies to provide clear rules for implementing technologies (such as the IEEE's 802.3 specification), desire to exceed limitations drives the industry to ignore many of those rules.

Slow Ethernet specifications include the following:

- **10Base5**—Transmission takes place at 10Mbps using thick coaxial cable on a linear bus.

- **10Base2**—Transmission takes place at 10Mbps using thin coaxial cable on a linear bus.

- **10BaseT**—Transmits 10Mbps over twisted pairs in a physical star configuration.

Fast Ethernet

Fast Ethernet has exactly the same base standards as Slow Ethernet. The difference lies in the additional 10 clauses of the IEEE 802.3u addendum, released in 1995. These clauses define the standard for three different 100Mbps implementations known generally as 100BaseX. Table 1.4 illustrates a comparison between the Slow and Fast Ethernet configurations.

TABLE 1.4   Fast Versus Slow Ethernet Comparison

	Fast	Slow
CSMA/CD channel access	X	X
Same min/max frame sizes	X	X
Supports same frame types	X	X
Supports cat 3, 4, and 5	X	X
Supports fiber	X	X
Supports physical star	X	X
Full-duplex/half-duplex	X	X
Coaxial bus topology support		X
Manchester signal encoding		X
100BaseX hardware required	X	
Component and timing changes	X	

100BaseX Standards

All three 100BaseX standards define 100Mb baseband technologies over twisted pair or fiber. Distance and limitations vary within each standard based on physical layer characteristics. There are three types of 100BaseX standards:

- **100BaseTX**—Defines 100Mbps over a minimum Category 5 UTP, implementing the same two pairs as 10Mbps Ethernet.

- **100BaseFX**—Defines 100Mbps transfers over fiber-optic media.

- **100BaseT4**—Uses four unshielded twisted pair for transmission; three pairs for transmission and reception and one pair for collision detection.

Gigabit Ethernet

The Gigabit Ethernet standard enables transmission speeds of up to 1000Mbps using Category 5 UTP cabling. You will often find Gigabit Ethernet abbreviated as GE. The task force specification is the IEEE 802.3z, which uses 802.3 Ethernet frame formats, and the CSMA/CD access method. Note that the continuing use of the 802.3 standard supports backward compatibility with the 100BaseT and 10BaseT technologies.

Token-Ring and IEEE 802.5

IBM released the technology to the IEEE, whose 802.5 subcommittee developed and released the 4Mbps Token-Ring standard in 1985. The IEEE 802.5 specification defines the MAC sublayer and the Physical layer specification, using the 802.2 specification at the LLC (Logical Link) layer for protocol identification.

Note

The IEEE divided the OSI model's Data Link layer into to distinct sublayers, known as the MAC (Media Access Control) and LLC (Logical Link Control). These layers clearly separate the responsibilities of Data Link protocols within these layers. MAC layer (lower sublayer of the Data Link) protocols are only concerned with media access (frame transmission and reception) and are protocol-independent, relying on the upper sublayer, the LLC to identify the protocol being carried within the frame. The LLC's main responsibility is protocol identification. By subdividing the Data Link into two layers this allows for media and protocol independence. Media and protocol independence allows multiple protocols, such as IP and IPX, to be carried simultaneously over a single network interface. Prior to this subdivision Data Link implementations were protocol- and media-dependent. For example, you could only run one protocol at a time over an interface.

In 1989 the IEEE released an enhancement to the 802.5 standard that defines 16Mbps Token-Ring operations.

Token-Ring uses a unidirectional transmission, with each device always receiving from its upstream neighbor and sending to its downstream neighbor. It utilizes token-passing ring topology that passes frames with no collision risk because only one device can transmit at a time. However, devices can access the medium and transmit upon reception of a free token, which is a 3-byte signal that propagates around the ring.

Token-Ring exhibits these important characteristics:

- All devices connect serially, transmitting a signal in one direction.

- Each device's transmit pair connects through to its downstream neighbor's receive pair.

- Signal transmission is unidirectional.

- Each device directly connects in a physical star formation through central hubs known as *Multi-Station Access Units* (MSAUs) (see Figure 1.10). The MSAU's objective is to keep the ring functional by electrically bypassing a non-functional device or port when end devices are either turned off or fail.

- Each device's network card operates as a fully functional unidirectional repeater, completely regenerating the signal and bit repeating it on to the next system on the ring.

- Operates at either 4Mbps or 16Mbps but not both, as determined by the configuration of the network card.

- All devices must agree on the speed of the ring.

Token–Ring

FIGURE 1.10
Token-Ring transmission is unidirectional. Each system transmits to its downstream neighbor (through its transmit circuit TX) and receives from it upstream neighbor (through its receive circuit RX).

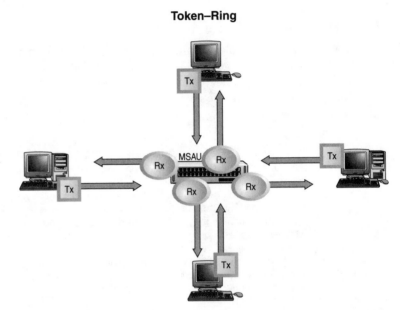

Bit Repeating
The industry uses the term *bit repeating* to describe the amplification and regeneration of a received signal that is repeated out all other interfaces.

Token Passing Channel Access Method

Token-Ring devices access the channel using a token-passing method. When a device has information to transmit, it waits for a free token, a 3-byte frame that traverses the ring and provides access to the medium. When it receives a token, it can convert it to a frame.

Stations send their frames around the ring hoping to find the destination host. All other devices on the ring check the destination address of the frame to determine whether it is for them; then bit repeat the signal on. Each network interface card acts as a repeater, amplifying, retiming, and bit repeating the signal. The responsibility of stripping its frame and releasing a new token belongs to the sending device.

Token-Ring Frames

The two types of Token-Ring frames are token and data/command. Figure 1.11 shows an example of a token frame. In Figure 1.11, stations identify the signal as a free token by looking at the status of the token bit within the AC field. If the bit contains a 0 in the AC field, it is a token frame. SDs and EDs simply mark the beginning and end of a frame.

Token Frame

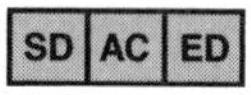

FIGURE 1.11

A 3-byte signal circles the ring providing attached devices with access to the channel.

SD = Start Delimiter
AC = Access Control bytes
      indicates whether this is
      a Token or Data/Command
      frame
ED = End Delimiter

Figure 1.12 shows an example of a Token Ring frame used to transmit data and commands. Note that the MAC/LLC field following the SA (source address field) indicates whether the frame is a command (MAC) or data frame (LLC) .

Token–Ring Frame

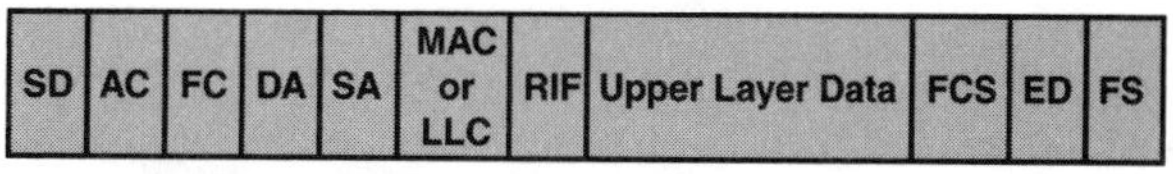

FIGURE 1.12

Token-Ring frames can command MAC or data (LLC) frames. If the frame is a MAC frame it does not carry user data. If the frame is an LLC, it carries upper layer protocols and user data.

SD	AC	FC	DA	SA	MAC or LLC	RIF	Upper Layer Data	FCS	ED	FS

SD = Start Delimiter for frame
AC = Access Control byte indicates whether this is a Token or Data/Command frame
FC = Frame Control indicates whether frame is a Data (LLC) or Command (MAC) frame
DA = Destination Address
SA = Source Address
MAC or LLC = MAC frames carry MAC data. LLC frames contain 802.2 header for
                        protocol identification
RIF = Route Information Field, only exist when Source Route Bridging is being used.
Upper Layer Data = Headers for upper layer protocols and User Data
FCS = Frame Check Sequence, similar to CRC
ED = End Delimiter for frame
FS =   Frame Status byte used to identify whether receiving device recognized and copied
         a frame

FDDI and ANSI X3T9.5

Fiber Distributed Data Interface (FDDI) is a type of media access defined by the American National Standards Institute (ANSI) X3T9.5 specification. Although FDDI also uses a MAC addressing scheme, it differs from Ethernet and Token-Ring. The difference is that instead of referring to the MAC address in terms of a 6-byte address (like other topologies), FDDI uses 4-bit symbols to refer to the MAC addresses.

FDDI incorporates token passing in a dual-ring physical topology, which provides a self-healing redundancy. If there is a problem with the primary ring, the secondary ring serves as a backup. If a break occurs, it reroutes the data from the primary ring to the secondary ring at two or more locations, known as a *ring wrap*.

FDDI was once a favorite standard for network backbones because it enables transmission speeds of up to 100Mbps and, unlike copper, is immune to EMI and RFI. In fact, fiber-optic cabling has many advantages over conventional copper cable, including the following:

- Speed at which data can travel

- Signal distance achieved before attenuation

- Immunity to EMI and RFI

- Redundancy in having counter-rotating rings

Note

Note that FDDI was once a favorite standard for backbones, but now most places have replaced FDDI with the cheaper Fast or Gigabit Ethernet.

Token Passing Channel Access Method

For its channel access method, FDDI uses a token passing channel access method for transmission of packets. FDDI communications access the physical medium (the ring) through the token being passed around the ring. When a node wants to transmit, it simply grabs a token, sends its transmission, and then releases a new token on the ring. Note that unlike Token-Ring, which allows only one token to circulate at a time, FDDI allows multiple tokens to circulate at any given time.

Note

Although Token Ring vendors did implement something called "early token release" to allow for multiple transmissions on the ring at a time, only one token is allowed.

Wide Area Networking (WAN) Technologies

WAN (Wide Area Network) technologies use transmission facilities provided by common carriers, such as service providers or telephone companies, to provide a data path to networks covering a broad geographical area. WAN technologies operate at the lowest two levels of the OSI model— the Physical and Data Link layers (see Figure 1.13).

FIGURE 1.13

Mapping the OSI model
to WAN protocols.

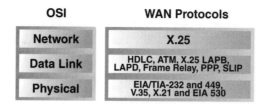

WAN connection types allow a company to connect remote sites to extend their network. Most companies that have remote sites over a large geographical area require some sort of WAN connection types. Which connection type they choose depends on a company's specific needs. Three WAN connection types can be used to transfer data across a service provider's network:

- **Leased (dedicated) line**—The leased line, also known as a point-to-point or dedicated line, employs a synchronous serial connection through a service provider.

- **Circuit-switched**—Circuit-switched has a dedicated circuit path and employs an asynchronous serial connection through a telephone company.

- **Packet-switched**—Packet-switched uses a synchronous serial connection through a service provider.

Table 1.5 explains the three connection types.

TABLE 1.5 WAN Connection Types, Layer One

Connection Type	Description
Leased Line (also known as point-to-point or dedicated)	Provides a single, existing WAN communications path through a service provider network, from a customer to a remote network.
	Service providers reserve the connection and bandwidth for a client's private use.
	Guarantees bandwidth is available.
	Has the drawback of being expensive because connection is always active even if it's unused.
	Employed over synchronous serial connections up to E3 speeds, 45Mbps.
	Supports PPP, SLIP, and HDLC Data Link encapsulations.

TABLE 1.5   Continued

Connection Type	Description
Circuit-switching	Dedicated circuit or path is built on-the-fly for each session and must exist between sender and receiver for the duration of the transmission.
	Commonly used in environments that require only minimal or infrequent WAN usage.
	Used to provide asynchronous serial connections over standard telephone lines or ISDN connections.
	Supports PPP, SLIP, and HDLC encapsulations.
Packet-switching	WAN switching method. Network devices share common point-to-point links to deliver packets from a source to a destination across a service provider's network.
	Establishes temporary virtual circuits (VCs) to provide an end-to-end connection between source and destination.
	Switching devices establish the virtual circuit and use multiplexing devices to provide customers with shared access to the circuit.
	Less expensive because the circuit is not dedicated.
	Employed over a serial connection with speeds ranging from 56Kbps to E3.
	Supports X.25, ATM, and Frame Relay encapsulation.

A leased line, known as a *dedicated line*, provides a single existing WAN communication path through a service provider network, from a customer to a remote network (see Figure 1.14). Figure 1.15 shows a path being built on-the-fly for a WAN circuit-switched connection. Figure 1.16 shows an example of packet-switching.

Leased Line

FIGURE 1.14
Leased lines tend to be expensive because the connection remains active even when not in use.

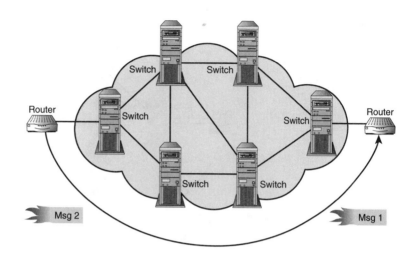

Circuit Switching

FIGURE 1.15
Circuit-switching requires that a connection be set up and torn down for each session between the sender and receiver.

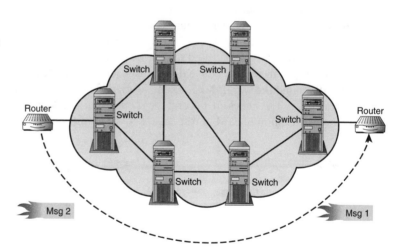

Packet Switching

FIGURE 1.16
Packet-switching relays packets from node to node, occupying the channel only for the duration of transmission.

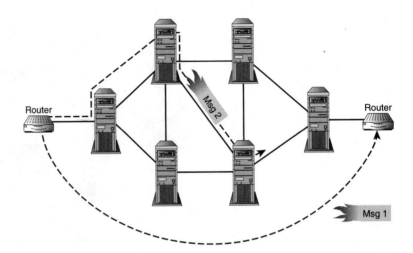

Telephone companies and service providers provide most of the WAN connections today. You can use routers to access servers providing circuit-switched dial-up connections through standard analog modems or ISDN lines. You can configure dedicated leased line connections to support consistently high volumes of traffic over synchronous serial connections. Packet-switched connections, such as X.25, ATM, and Frame Relay, require that Multiplexer/Demultiplexer (MUX/DEMUX) devices be used to provide devices with shared access to the same circuit. You can use any of these methods to deliver data across a service provider's network to remote sites all around the world. X.25, Frame Relay, and ATM are Data Link layer WAN switching technologies. The topics are beyond the scope of this book and will not be discussed further, with the exception of ATM in respect to PNNI routing, which is covered in Chapter 9.

Note

X.25 and Frame Relay are very similar. Both are packet-switching technologies, which transfer data in variable length frames between remote points across a WAN connection. X.25 was the first packet-switching WAN architecture developed over 20 years ago. X.25-enabled devices establish and maintain connection-oriented sessions sequencing and acknowledging each packet transmitted. This slows down the transfer process, but makes it very reliable. Frame Relay is basically X.25, but without the overhead of sequencing and acknowledgments. Frame Relay is connectionless and is therefore faster, yet unreliable. Frame Relay relies on other protocols to detect the loss of datagrams and recover them. A simple CRC is used to verify a frame has not been damaged in transit. ATM, unlike X.25 and Frame Relay (frame-based) transfers data in cells. ATM cells are fixed in length (53 bytes). With fixed length cells instead of variable length frames, ATM switches do not have to determine when a cell ends or how long it will be, they know the exact length. This allows switches to switch cells at a much faster rate increasing the transfer time cells.

WAN Encapsulation Protocols

WAN encapsulation is a way of wrapping a packet to enable it to traverse a mesh of distance-separated networks. The Internet is based on many different types of WAN connections, including dedicated and non-dedicated. On each WAN connection local LAN data must encapsulate into frames before crossing the WAN link. You need to know the proper protocol to configure the appropriate Data Link layer encapsulation type. The protocol depends on the WAN technology being used; your service provider should provide you with the specific configuration information to connect to their network successfully.

Several options can provide an interface to a service provider's network. These options all are variations of the High-Level Data Link Control (HDLC) protocol—the widely used standard introduced by the ISO, which was patterned after IBM's Synchronous Data Link Control (SDLC) protocol. These protocols operate at the Data Link layer of the OSI model, providing Data Link layer connection-oriented and connectionless services to upper-layer applications and user data across the WAN.

Most WAN protocols come from descendents of HDLC. Vendors have several implementations of HDLC and not all are compatible. For instance, Cisco has its own proprietary HDLC implementation, which is incompatible with other HDLC protocols. IBM's SDLC protocol, used in its Systems Network Architecture (SNA), is very similar in functionality and provides connection-oriented, reliable delivery between IBM minis, mainframes, and their clients. Other protocols, such as X.25's LAPB, ISDN's LAPD, and even LLC2, all are subsets of HDLC. Table 1.6 shows the primary WAN encapsulation protocols.

TABLE 1.6   Primary WAN Encapsulation Protocols

Protocol Type	Description
Frame Relay	Establishes multiple virtual logical paths or virtual circuits.
	Two encapsulation types: Cisco's Proprietary encapsulation or the IETF Frame relay standard encapsulation
(RFC 1490 standard encapsulation)	Operates at the Data Link and Physical layers. More efficient than X.25 because it does not establish connections and does not employ error correction or recovery. Assumes most networks are physically reliable and have low error rates. Relies on upper-layer protocols for error detection and recovery. Frame relay supports congestion control.
ISDN (Integrated Services Digital Network)	Uses existing telephone lines to transmit data, voice, and other source traffic. Uses two types of channels: D and B. D channel carries signaling and control information. B carries data. There are two main types of ISDN services: BRI (Basic Rate ISDN) and PRI (Primary Rate IDSN). BRI supports total bit rate of 144Kbps, and PRI supports 1.544Mbps (in the U.S., Canada, and Japan) or 2.048Mbps (in Europe).

TABLE 1.6 Continued

Protocol Type	Description
X.25 LAPB (Link Access Procedure, Balanced) encapsulation for signaling channel	LAPB is the Data Link layer protocol in the X.25 protocol stack. Derived from HDLC, it is a connection-oriented protocol that provides error detection and recovery at layer 2. Extremely reliable but slow because of the high overhead involved in connection maintenance. Good to use if your WAN link is prone to error. Has been generally replaced by Frame Relay and other WAN standards.
HDLC (High-Level Data Link Control)	Connection-oriented protocol at the Data Link layer introduced by ISO Does not support data compression or authentication. ISO's HDLC can't identify the type of protocols being carried inside HDLC encapsulation. Therefore, only one protocol can be carried over HDLC at a time. Vendor implementations vary.
PPP (Point-to-Point)	Provides a communications path from the customer over an established WAN asynchronous connection, and a synchronous connection over a carrier network to a remote network. Supports multiple protocols, such as IP, IPX, and AppleTalk. Supports data compression authentication, error detection, and multilinking.
Serial Line Internet Protocol (SLIP)	Older protocol supporting point-to-point serial connections using TCP/IP. Replaced by PPP.
Asynchronous Transfer Mode (ATM)	International standard for cell-based switching and multiplexing technology.Supports multiple service types (voice, video, and data) through fixed-length (53-byte) cells. Fixed-length cells reduce processing overhead and transit delay. Supports high-speed transmissions over copper or fiber lines with data rates ranging from 1.544Mbps (T1 service) up to 622Mbps (OC-12).

Request for Comments (RFCs)

No one owns the TCP/IP technologies, nor can one obtain information in the form of documentation, policies, protocols, and standards from a vendor. However, you can find this type of documentation online at no charge in the form of Request for Comments (RFCs). Although vendors do publish documentation on the implementation of these technologies, RFCs provide the base standards, describing protocol functions, rules, and methods of implementation; vendors interpret these standards.

RFCs provide documentation in the form of a series of technical reports written by committees, individuals, and corporations for the development of various protocols, policies, implementations, and so on. The RFCs appear in chronological order; revised RFCs supersede earlier documents and are assigned new numbers. We recommended that you be careful to obtain the latest RFC when researching. RFCs vary from technical documentation of a protocol to suggestions for changes to proposals for new protocols and can range from dry and academic to humorous in tone. In this book we will refer to RFCs as a reference. We also provide a categorized list of RFCs in Appendix A. You can access RFC through the Web at `http://www.faqs.org/rfcs/`.

Internet Versus Intranet

Throughout this book we will use the term *Internet* to describe the collection of networks and systems owned by different organizations, universities, government agencies, and individuals which make up what is referred to as the networking "Superhighway." No particular organization governs or controls the Internet. To forward traffic successfully through the Internet, cooperation is necessary. Cooperation by many different organizations, such as ISPs, is needed to ensure that paths to networks throughout the world are available. Companies providing transit for Internet traffic must work together to achieve the common goals of delivering data fast and reliably.

The term *intranet* is used to refer to a specific organization's networking environment. A company's intranet may include many end systems, routers, and geographic locations. However, administrative control is the responsibility of only that organization or institution.

In this book you will learn how data is forwarded by routers within an intranet and across the Internet and the various routing protocols that make that happen.

Summary

The OSI Reference Model was created to enable both similar and dissimilar systems to communicate seamlessly by providing an architectural framework for vendors and manufacturers. It consists of seven layers: Application, Presentation, Session, Transport, Network, Data Link, and Physical.

The OSI model benefits manufacturers and software developers, and network engineers who offer support and troubleshooting. By compartmentalizing each layer's function, it narrows the scope of each layer's responsibilities. This eases the development and support burdens that manufacturers and network engineers face.

The four-layer model developed by the DARPA (referred to as the DoD model) as an initial standard for the core protocols within the TCP/IP suite consist of Process, Host-to-Host, Internet, and Network Access layers.

Many LAN and WAN standards exist today. The most popular was and still is the IEEE 802.3, which describes the standards and specifications for slow, fast and gigabit transmission. Other LAN technologies exist, such as Token-Ring and FDDI, defining various channel access methods and frame types. WAN standards provide connectivity between remote sites. Three main WAN connection types exist—Leased, Circuit-switched and Packet-switched.

Chapter Quiz

1. Name the seven layers of the OSI model.

2. Which layer of the OSI Model is responsible for logical source and destination addressing and routing of datagrams?

3. Which layer of the OSI Model identifies programs or processes with port addresses?

4. At what layer do bridges and switches function and what type of address do they use to forward data?

5. Name the four Ethernet frame types using the industry names.

6. Name the two main protocols that function at the Transport layer.

7. What type of channel access method is used by all Ethernet specifications?

8. What is the channel access method for Token-Ring?

9. Name the network architecture defined by ANSI as X3T9.5.

CHAPTER 2

IP AND IP ADDRESSING

You will learn about the following in this chapter:

- IP protocol and function
- Binary-to-decimal conversion
- IP addressing

- IP subnetting
- Network Address Translation (NAT)

The Internet Protocol (IP)

The Internet Protocol or IP is the best-known protocol within the TCP/IP suite. It provides for fast but unreliable movement of individual packets or datagrams from source to destination end systems. It provides the address and delivery mechanism for all TCP/IP-related traffic. IP does not concern itself with reliability; rather, it lets the upper-layer protocols handle that aspect of transmission. The Internet Protocol is the heart of the TCP/IP protocol suite, one that all other protocols rely on for addressing, fragmentation/reassembly, and connectionless delivery of datagrams.

IP's primary responsibility is to provide logical network layer addressing of datagrams. This layer identifies the IP address of the sending and receiving hosts within the datagram. Routing protocols use the destination or receiving host's network layer IP address to forward datagrams. As a network layer protocol, IP performs the following functions:

- Logical addressing
- Connectionless packet delivery
- Fragmentation and reassembly

Logical Addressing

Network layer protocols, such as IP deal with logical addressing, which is distinguished from the Physical layer MAC (Media Access Control address associated with a network card. Unlike physical addresses, logical addresses are not permanently assigned by a manufacturer; instead, they are assigned by an administrator manually or dynamically.)

Unique logical addresses are assigned to systems (hosts, servers, routers, and so on). These addresses facilitate the identification and location of a device within and between networks. Logical addresses are protocol-dependent and vary based on the network layer protocol implemented. For instance, IP addresses are 32 bit (4 byte) addresses represented in dotted decimal notation (191.16.1.1), whereas Novell's IPX (Internetwork Packet Exchange) addresses are represented as network.node (100.000c00112222). Regardless of protocol logical addresses are necessary to facilitate communications between different systems. Logical addresses generally identify two pieces of information, the network to which a device is attached and the unique address of that device on that network. Detail about the specific construction of IP addresses will follow later in this chapter. For now let's address how IP addresses can be given to systems. The first method (not necessarily the best) is manual.

In the early days of networking when IP was but a twinkle in everyone's eyes and only a few hundred hosts existed out in the Internet the only method of address assignment was manual. This meant that every system participating in the Internet or using TCP/IP for that matter had to be manually configured with this information. If hosts were moved to another location this information needed to be changed. Manual intervention was required to configure and maintain all IP addresses adding a lot of management overhead and the potential of erroneously configuring two devices with the same address. Although manual configuration of critical devices, such as routers, servers, and so on is highly recommended, end-host configuration has shifted to dynamic methods.

Most implementations of TCP/IP these days make use of dynamic protocols to quickly and efficiently provide end systems with logical IP addresses. By utilizing dynamic assignment, manual intervention and management is minimized. Duplicate address assignments are less likely to occur and as systems are moved from one location to another, addresses can be dynamically given reflecting the new location.

The dynamic assignment of IP addresses is achieved through the use of protocols such as RARP (Reverse Address Resolution Protocol), BootP (Boot Parameter) or DHCP (Dynamic Host Configuration Protocol). Although a discussion of these protocols and how they perform IP address assignment is beyond the scope of this book, a brief explanation is necessary. As mentioned earlier, the first method of address assignment was manual. As more and more organizations began implementing TCP/IP within their networks and with the emergence of the Internet it became apparent that this approach was impractical. The first dynamic protocol introduced was RARP, which provides MAC (physical) address to IP (logical) resolution. RARP is implemented as a service running on a host (referred to as a RARP server). RARP servers are configured by administrators with static MAC to IP address mappings. RARP is a client/server based protocol, where RARP clients broadcast a request out on their local segment requesting

IP address configuration from any RARP server. Servers hearing this would check their local table for an entry mapping this hosts MAC address to an IP address. If one exists a response is sent back to the client including the IP address configuration. At this point the client adopts the assigned address and becomes an active IP host on the network. RARP requests and responses are sent as broadcasts. Broadcasts are not forwarded by routers and are therefore limited to a single segment only. Because of this limitation RARP implementations require that at least one RARP server be located on each network segment. This limitation was addressed by the next generation protocol known as BootP.

BootP is basically the same as RARP except that request and response messages can be forwarded by BootP-enabled routers or relay agents. The goal with BootP was to provide the same functionality, but avoid having to place a server on each and every segment. BootP, like RARP, has a static mapping table, which requires manual update and management. However, BootP is implemented over UDP (transport layer) utilizing ports 67 (BootP Server) and 68 (BootP Client) to carry requests and responses. Routers can be configured to forward UDP port 67 and 68 traffic allowing clients and servers to be located on different segments. However, allowing routers to forward broadcasts for these ports adds unnecessary traffic to networks and undermines the general purpose of routers, which is to isolate broadcast traffic. Relay agents offer a compromise by allowing a local host or router, configured as a BootP relay agent, to intercept local broadcast requests, convert the request to a directed (unicast) datagram, and send it to the remote BootP server on behalf of the client. The response from the server would upon return to the agent be relayed back to the client. BootP eliminated the need to locate a resolution server on every segment allowing them to placed strategically around the network. The latest and most popular resolution protocol is DHCP. DHCP, like its predecessors, is a service that may be implemented on a server or router configured with valid IP address ranges identifying subnetworks (referred to as *scopes*) and other IP configurations necessary for hosts to participate on an IP network.

DHCP builds upon BootP technology, utilizing the same UDP ports and relay agents to allow requests and responses to be forwarded by routers. However, unlike BootP, DHCP does not require a static mapping table. Although static mappings are supported, IP addresses are generally assigned from a predefined range. Hosts are given IP addresses for a specific period of time (defined by a lease). When the lease expires this address may be given to another host. When an unconfigured host comes online, that is, a host without an IP address and information necessary to function as a host on the network, it may request this information from a DHCP server. DHCP servers receive this request and provide the host with the configuration information requested. Once this is received by the new host, it completes the initialization process and can begin to communicate with other hosts on the network. IP addressing is discussed in detail later in this chapter.

Connectionless Packet Delivery

As discussed in Chapter 1, "Overview of Industry Models, Standards, and TCP/IP Protocols," there are two main categories of protocols: connection-oriented or connectionless. IP is considered connectionless and as such offers best effort delivery of datagrams. IP packages information it receives from upper-layer protocols into smaller units referred to as packets or datagrams. Each datagram is treated as a separate, independent entity individually addressed with a logical source and destination IP address as well as other IP header and control information. IP provides connectionless delivery of these datagrams relying on other protocols to detect lost datagrams. It is not encumbered by overhead involved in the sequencing and acknowledgment of datagrams. All TCP/IP protocols run on top of IP utilizing its datagram address and handling services. Vendors can choose to enhance datagram reliability by using the TCP transport layer protocol.

Fragmentation and Reassembly

Units of information at the network layer of the OSI model are referred to as packets or datagrams. Each datagram packaged and addressed for delivery by IP must be no greater than the legal size (for example, Ethernet's maximum frame size is 1518 bytes) of network media being accessed. Datagrams exceeding this maximum must be broken down into more manageable portions prior to transmission.

While the goal is to maximize the amount of data sent over the media, any frame deemed too large for any medium on the network automatically undergoes fragmentation to reduce the frame to an acceptable size. In any given network, the maximum frame size can only equal the capacity of the smallest medium between end systems. *Fragmentation*, as the name implies, is the process of breaking information up into smaller pieces. *Reassembly* is the process of putting these pieces back together.

The source end system or an intervening device, such as a router, may perform the function of fragmentation. The receiving end system or destination host reassembles the data and passes it up to the higher layers. Although routers are capable of fragmentation, this is not the optimal solution. Routers are meant to forward data as quickly and efficiently as possible. When routers perform other duties, like fragmentation, this adds overhead, potentially causing delay in normal traffic forwarding. It is always best to configure routers not to fragment oversized datagrams, but to alert the sending system to adjust the datagram size appropriately. This way the router simply forwards the datagram normally, preserving precious resources. Ideally the originating system's IP process will perform fragmentation of datagrams, sizing them such that they are no larger than the acceptable frame size along the path to the destination (see Figure 2.1). Reassembly is only performed at the final destination.

> **Note**
>
> Datagram size depends on the underlying network architecture in use. For instance, Ethernet supports a maximum frame size of 1,518 bytes, while 16Mbps Token-Ring can support much larger frames (up to 17,600 bytes). When mixed architectures exist end systems communicating across them must adhere to the smallest supported frame size.

FIGURE 2.1

Host A performs
fragmentation prior to
transmission. Each data-
gram sent is no larger
than the maximum frame
size of the local Ethernet
segment. The intervening
router forwards and Host
B reassembles.

Fragmentation

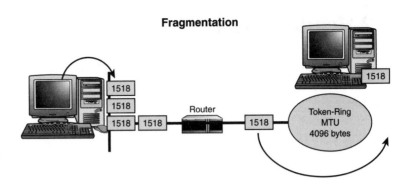

Using Figure 2.1 as an example, assume you (Host A) want to transfer 1MB of data from your end system located on an Ethernet segment supporting a maximum transmission unit (MTU) of 1,518 byte frames to an end system (Host B) located on a Token-Ring (configured to support an MTU of 4,096 bytes) segment across a router. The entire message obviously cannot be sent within a single datagram. It must be broken up by IP into smaller chunks, addressed separately and framed for transmission. Each chunk cannot exceed the maximum transmission unit of the local segment to which the source host is attached, which in this case is 1,518 bytes (the maximum Ethernet frame size).

As each datagram is received by the router, the router inspects the destination address to determine which interface should be used to forward the datagram on to its destination. Because the destination end system is attached to a segment directly connected to the router and the datagram does not exceed the Token-Ring MTU size, it's is simply forwarded onto that segment. The destination host receives and buffers all related datagrams, reassembling them into logical framework before sending them up to the next higher layer protocol for processing.

When routers receive datagrams exceeding the MTU size of the medium the router plans to use to forward this datagram one of two things will occur. If the "may fragment" bit has been set by the source, the router may further fragment the datagram to the appropriate size prior to transmission on the medium. If the source sets the "don't fragment" bit the router will discard the frame and generate an ICMP message back to the source indicating the datagram exceeds the MTU size allowed. It is then up to the source host to resize the datagram. The "may and don't fragment" bits used to control fragmentation are discussed within the next section. The ICMP protocol is an integral part of IP. ICMP messages are used to notify systems of problems with datagram transmission as well as a diagnostic and troubleshooting tool.

IP Header and Fields

The fields within the IP header (see Figure 2.2) are used to control and manage the movement of datagrams. Table 2.1 gives a description of the various fields shown in the figure.

FIGURE 2.2

Example of an IP header.

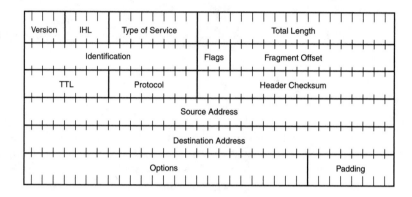

TABLE 2.1 IP Header Fields

Field	Function
Version	Identifies the current version of IP. Currently this is version 4.
IHL	Internet Header Length describes the size of the IP header.
ToS	Different Types of Service can be used to deliver data based on application requirements such as reliability, low delay, throughput, and cost.
	This 1-byte field is divided into three parts: 3-bit Precedence, 4-bit ToS, and 1-bit Reserved fields. The precedence field is used to provide an eight-level priority-based forwarding indicator used by routers. Datagrams with higher priorities (such as 5) are forwarded before lower priority datagrams (priority 4) and so on. This priority scheme allows IS managers to manipulate the forwarding of individual packets hop by hop, giving precedence to specific types of traffic. Precedence values range from 0 to 7, with 7 being the highest priority.
	The next 4-bit field identifies the type of service level a packet will receive by a router as it forwards the datagram to its destination. ToS bits must be recognized by the receiving router to forward datagrams, when multiple paths exist, along the path supporting the desired service level. For instance, when multiple paths to a destination exist with varying characteristics, such as link capacity and transfer rates, routers must select the best path possible for forwarding. Applications may assist routers in this selection by setting

TABLE 2.1 Continued

Field	Function
	one of the ToS bits indicating to the router its preference for a particular type of service level. With this information the router will forward traffic along the path with the desired ToS level.
	The last bit is reserved and currently not in use.
Total Length	Identifies the entire length of the datagram.
ID	The identification field is used by IP for fragmentation and reassembly of datagrams. The sending end system assigns each datagram an ID. Related datagrams are given the same ID. This allows the receiving host to identify all datagrams as part of the same datastream. Because datagrams can be sent via different paths and be received out of order, it is important for the receiver to be able to identify all related datagrams. Identifying related datagrams allows the receiving host to reassemble any datagrams received out of order.
Flag	The flag field will be at least one of four options. The first two are used to control the fragmentation of datagrams by routers. The last two work in conjunction with the IP ID field to indicate whether this is the only datagram or one belonging to a stream containing the same IP ID.
	Don't Fragment indicates to receiving systems that this datagram should not be fragmented (see Figure 2.3).

FIGURE 2.3

Four Ethernet segments exist; all except one support 1,518 byte frames. The source host has set the DF bit and initially transmits a datagram to router one. This datagram reaches router two, which trashes it, sending an ICMP message back to the source. The source host resizes the datagram to 1,024 bytes and resends it. This time it makes it through all three routers.

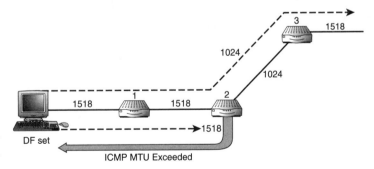

Datagrams marked as don't fragment are prohibited from being resized by the receiving host. With this bit set routers do not forward datagrams out interfaces where the datagram exceeds the maximum frame size allowed. Routers receiving datagrams with this bit set trash the datagram and transmit an ICMP (Internet Control Message Protocol) message back to the source end system alerting it of the problem. When this message is received, the source host must resize the datagram prior to attempting retransmission. End systems may also use this bit to automatically discover the MTU size possible across a network. First the end system prepares a datagram for transmission, sets this bit, and sends it out. If the destination host it is trying to reach is across two routers, the datagram is sent to the first router. If the first router supports the datagram size and is able to forward it without resizing it, it is successfully sent out the interface en route to the next router. If the second router receives the datagram but is unable to resize it to fit onto an attached segment, the datagram is trashed and an ICMP message is transmitted back to the source indicating this. With this information the source end system resizes the datagram and attempts this process again. This time the data-gram is forwarded successfully by both routers reaching the destination end system. By allowing the source end system to discover the appropriate MTU size, not involving the router in the fragmentation process, routers are not encumbered by additional overhead of resizing datagrams. This allows routers to efficiently and quickly forward datagrams to their destination.

May Fragment	Allows intervening devices like routers to fragment frames that are too large for a particular segment.
More Fragments	Indicates to the receiving host that this is not the only datagram in the stream and more fragments, bearing the same IP ID, should follow. This helps the receiving host reassemble discontinuous datagrams.
Last Fragment	Tells the receiving host that a particular fragment is the last in a datastream and not to expect more.
Fragment Offset	Indicates where a datagram belongs within the overall stream and is set by the source end system.

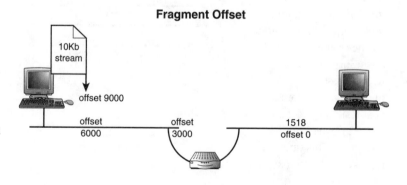

Fragment Offset

FIGURE 2.4

Station A performs fragmentation of a 10Kb datastream, breaking it up into 1,518 bytes frames. Each frame is assigned a fragment offset within the IP header to tell the receiver how to reorder the datagrams.

For example in Figure 2.4, the sending host sends 10Kb of data that needs to be broken up into legal size datagrams based on the maximum media frame size allowable. If sent on Ethernet, whose max frame size is 1,518, the 10Kb datastream must be broken into 1.5Kb datagrams before transmission. Each datagram bears the same IP ID because they belong to the same stream. The first datagram will have a starting offset value of zero, the next datagram will receive an offset of 1,500 and the next will receive an offset of 3,000, and so on. The receiver can now tell that the datagram with a zero offset should be first if it receives the frames out of order. The receiving system buffers all datagrams reassembling them by comparing the IP ID and offset values. Once all datagrams within a stream are received the reassembled stream is passed to the upper layers for processing.

TTL	The Time To Live value is a timer represented in seconds that determines the maximum lifetime a datagram can exist on a network. Routers decrement this value by at least 1 (one second) based on how long the router takes to process and forward a datagram. When the TTL value reaches zero, routers discard the datagram. Although forwarding by routers never takes more than one second, rules dictate that routers must decrement this value by one when processing and forwarding datagrams. Therefore each TTL second may also be associated with a single hop. The TTL value range is 0 through 255 seconds (or hops).

Most routing protocols have a maximum hop count value that defines the maximum distance a datagram may travel before being discarded. Destination networks that exceed this maximum hop count are considered unreachable by this routing protocol. Typically, this hop max count is much lower than the TTL value and is reached prior to the TTL expiration, resulting in the frame being discarded. When the TTL timer expires, routers drop the frame to prevent a frame from continually traversing the network.

Protocol	Identifies the immediate upper layer protocol as either TCP or UDP by using protocol IDs; TCP = 06 and UDP = 17.
Header checksum	Because IP is a connectionless protocol, there is no guarantee of delivery. IP uses a checksum within the header to at least guarantee that the bits within the IP header have not been damaged during transit.
Source Address	Identifies the logical IP address of the sending host.
Destination Address	Identifies the logical IP address of the receiving host.
Options	Used by vendors adding additional features.

Understanding Binary-to-Decimal Conversion

No IP book would be complete without a discussion of IP addressing. Before you can understand the derivation of IP addresses you must have a basic understanding of decimal and binary numbering, and how to convert from one to the other. For those unfamiliar with binary and decimal numbers, the base-10 numbering system is referred to as the decimal numbering system. Decimal numbering consists of the numbers 0,1,2,3,4,5,6,7,8, and 9. This comprises the 10 unique digits of 0 through 9.

Computers use the binary numbering system, which consists of only two unique numbers, 0 (zero) and 1 (one). Computers recognize only the uncharged 0 and charged 1. Unlike decimal numbering, binary numbering uses powers of 2 rather than powers of 10 (see Figure 2.5).

FIGURE 2.5

The binary numbering system uses the base-2, not base-10, system.

Binary (Base-2)

- The Binary Number System uses 2 values to represent numbers
- 0 and 1

8 Bits = 1 Byte

1 0 1 1 0 1 0 0

To understand binary numbers convert them to the decimal numbering system. A byte (also called an *octet*), which measures storage and memory, is composed of 8-bit positions, with possible values ranging from 0 (all bits being zeros) to 255 (all bits being ones). Binary numbering uses powers of 2 for each bit position. As shown in Figure 2.6, moving from right to left, beginning with the number 1 and moving to 2, each position is equivalent to the value squared of the previous position. The last position on the left is equal to 128. To convert a number from binary to decimal, assign the decimal value to each corresponding bit position; then add them together. Remember that the computer recognizes only the number in the on position, represented by 1; the highest possible total is 255 if all bits are in the on position or ones (128+64+32+16+8+4+2+1). To convert 172 to its binary equivalent, place a 1 under the bits (turning them on) until the total equals 172. That is, 128+32+8+4 = 172 or in binary numbers, 10101100.

Note

Remember when you convert binary to decimal, add only the numbers in the on position. The "on" position is represented by the number 1 and is the only number that the computer recognizes.

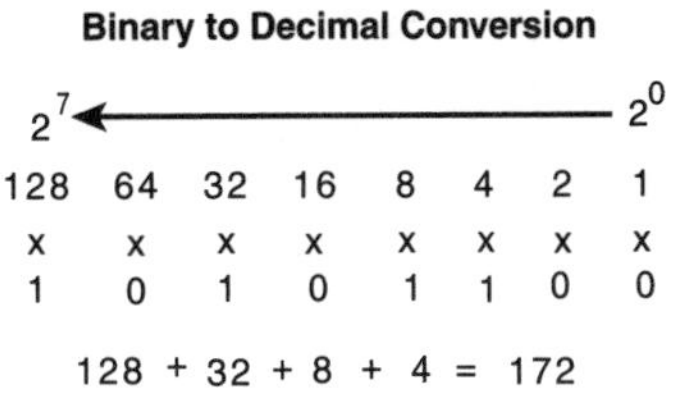

FIGURE 2.6

Note that the number 1 indicates that the bit is in the on position.

Binary to Decimal Conversion

$2^7 \longleftarrow\hspace{3cm} 2^0$

128	64	32	16	8	4	2	1
x	x	x	x	x	x	x	x
1	0	1	0	1	1	0	0

128 + 32 + 8 + 4 = 172

Now use Figure 2.7 and the number 176 as an example. In binary, 176 is represented by placing a 1 under the 128 at the far left. Again, 128 is the largest number within our numbers (to the power of 2) in our byte (eight bits). As 128 is the largest number, you build upon it for any numbers larger than 128.

If you place a number 1 (on position) under the 64, the sum (64+128) adds up greater than the value of 176, so you place a zero (off position) under the number. Next place a 1 under the number 32 for a total of 160. You need a sum of 16 to reach 176, which means you place a 1 under the 16, giving you a total of 176. You then place zeros under the remaining numbers. Your binary number is 10110000.

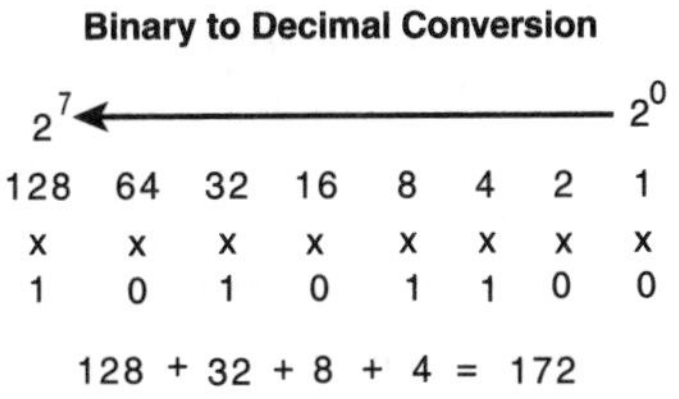

FIGURE 2.7

The ones represent the numbers the computer recognizes.

Binary to Decimal Conversion

$2^7 \longleftarrow\hspace{3cm} 2^0$

128	64	32	16	8	4	2	1
x	x	x	x	x	x	x	x
1	0	1	0	1	1	0	0

128 + 32 + 8 + 4 = 172

IP Addressing

Now that you understand basic binary-to-decimal conversion let's begin our discussion of addressing. In Chapter 1, I discussed Data Link layer or MAC addresses, and how those permanent addresses uniquely identify devices on a network. You now move up one layer in the OSI model to the Network layer. As you recall, the Network layer controls logical addressing of source and destination end systems and the routing or datagrams between systems. Those routing decisions rely on the 4-octet, or 32-bit, destination IP address contained within the IP header described earlier in this chapter. The parameters for a unique 32-bit value to define both the network and host portions with a 2-level hierarchical structure.

Note

The IP addressing hierarchy is defined in the 1985 publication Request for Comment (RFC) 950.

Its purpose is to logically divide the IP address into at least two parts, identifying the network and device, such as a router, and maybe even a third part that describes a subnetwork (referred to as subnet) within the network. A subnet is an extension of the IP addressing scheme and I will discuss subnetting later in this chapter.

The hierarchy differentiates the network address and subnetwork within the network from the node address. A node address uniquely identifies an individual device on a given subnet or network, and that the network is assigned to a company identifying the major network as a whole. Think of the logical network assigned to an organization as a city, the subnet as a street within the city, and each unique logical host portion of the address as a specific house.

Each logical address consists of network, optional subnetwork, and node address that identifies where the host belongs:

- The Network Address—The first part of the logical address identifies the city or major network. This address is assigned by a governing body and unique throughout the Internet.

- The Subnetwork Address—Each organization's network address represents an intranet, which may contain one or more subnetworks or streets. If an organization is small it may only consist of a single network segment with attached nodes and therefore no subnetworks or streets exist. In this case no subnetwork address would be necessary. If more than one segment exists, that is, multiple segments connected through routers, unique street names or subnetwork addresses must be given to each to distinguish them within the major network or city. All hosts attached to the same segment will share the same subnetwork or street name. Each street within the city is named uniquely so that the mailman can successfully deliver the mail. If more than one street within a city were to have the same name, the mailman (router) would be confused.

- The Node Address—The logical network layer address is used to identify the host uniquely. In keeping with the postal example, imagine if once the postman got to your unique street, there were two houses with the same address. This would be a problem. Think of the node address as the house number. Once the mailman has found the street, it is easy to find the exact house by using the node address.

Routers and routing protocols utilize the services of IP. Routers forward datagrams between and within cities by reading the destination logical network layer address (street name) and locating the shortest, fastest path possible, just like the U.S. Postal service.

Like the postal service many post offices (organizations) exist each with separate jurisdiction over the delivery of mail throughout a city (if it is quite small) or sub-area of a city. Within the postal system mailmen (routers) facilitate the actual delivery of mail by sorting mail based on where it is going, not where it came from. Knowing where mail is destined is more important than who sent it, unless it gets lost or is undeliverable. And just like the post office the delivery of mail is not guaranteed, that is, it is connectionless. In later chapters each of the IP routing protocols will be discussed.

Address Classes

When the Internet community developed the hierarchical addressing scheme they did so by dividing the 32-bit or 4-byte addresses into classes based on predicted use. They defined these addresses as *classful* because they clearly differentiate the classes in predefined boundaries. There are five major classes of network addresses, three of which are for public Internet use: Classes A, B, C, D, and E. Classes A, B, and C are assigned to organizations for public Internet use. Class D supports multicasting, which allows stations to support group level broadcasts, and Class E is reserved for future use. You may obtain registered public Internet addresses through ARIN (American Registry for Internet Numbers), which assigns them based on your network size or class. The ARIN organization makes these assignments to individual companies and Internet service providers based on the size of network defined by the class type.

The Internet community originally defined the classes to address networks of varying sizes designated by their high-order bits, and with specific ranges. Table 2.2 exhibits this information for Classes A, B, and C.

TABLE 2.2 Attributes of Public Addresses

Attributes	Class A (Slash /8)	Class B (Slash /16)	Class C (Slash /24)
Size	Meant to define the relatively few networks such as government, university, military, and research facilities in which a vast number of hosts exist.	Encompasses large numbers of networks with equally large numbersof hosts, as inmedium-sized companies.	Intended to tackle the needs of small networks by providing a very large number of network addresses with a minimal number of hosts per network.
Bit designations	Begin with zero (0) as their first bit.	Begin with 10 as their first two bits.	Begin with 110 as their first three bits.
Value range	1–126	128–191	192–223
Assigned network bytes	1 byte	2 bytes	3 bytes
Assigned default mask	255.0.0.0	255.255.0.0	255.255.255.0
Available host bytes	3 bytes	2 bytes	1 byte

TABLE 2.2   Continued

Attributes	Class A	Class B	Class C
	(Slash /8)	(Slash /16)	(Slash /24)
Number of networks	126	16,384	2,097,152
Number of hosts	16,777,214	65,534	254

Classes D and E addresses have special uses and are not assigned to mainstream networks. Class A network 127 is reserved as a loopback address (127.0.0.1) used for testing purposes.

Note

Class A addresses support a small number of networks with potentially millions of hosts. Class B addresses were designed for medium-sized networks and Class C were intended for small organizations with a maximum of 254 hosts. This hierarchical addressing scheme was developed to address the vast number of networks based on class type (size). It was assumed that there would only be a few (no more than 126) very large networks (Class A), thousands of medium sized (Class B), and millions of small (Class C) networks.

Designation bits within the first byte are used to define the class of network address, or NetID. Class A addresses always begin with a leading bit of 0 within the first octet, making the highest possible range of the remaining bits 1 through 127 inclusive. However, the value 127 in this octet is reserved as a loopback address. The valid range of addresses for Class A consists of 1 through 126. ARIN assigns these 7 bits within the first byte to assign Class A addresses, with the remaining 24 bits or (3 bytes) available to organizations to define multiple subnetworks and uniquely identify hosts within the network if the network has been subdivided. If you have not subdivided the network, the remaining bits within the last three bytes may only be used to define hosts.

Class B addresses always begin with a starting 2-bit value of 10 within the first byte and use the remaining 14 bits within the first and second bytes as the NetID. You can use the second two bytes to define additional subnetworks (if you have subdivided the network) or hosts. Following this pattern, Class C addresses always begin with a 3-bit value of 110, using the remaining 21 bits to identify the ARIN-assigned NetID. You can use the last byte to define subnetworks and hosts on these subnetworks. Figure 2.8 shows the structures of Classes A, B, C, D, and E addresses.

FIGURE 2.8

Note that only A, B, and C are for public use.

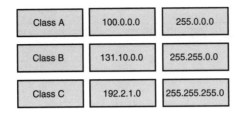

Class A	100.0.0.0	255.0.0.0
Class B	131.10.0.0	255.255.0.0
Class C	192.2.1.0	255.255.255.0

Each of the preceding address classes defines major classful boundaries (or major networks). If each of these major networks represents a city and you are the city developer you would want to further subdivide these address classes to allow for streets (or subnetworks) within the city rather than the chaos of having no streets to subdivide the many houses within the city. This subdivision requires that you allocate the leftover bits—(host bits) anything not assigned by ARIN—to networks (Class A, B or C).

I discuss the topic of subnetting later in this chapter. For now let's keep it simple: Assume the assigned network has not been subnetted and all leftover bits are host bits only. This is a representation of a pure classful addressing scheme, in which only the major class-based network address defines the network and all other bits are host bits. That is, there is only one city, no streets, with many houses. This may be okay for a very small network, but for larger networks subdivision is necessary and achieved through subnetting.

Class A

Class A networks, or Slash 8 (8-bit registered addresses) begin with the first (high order) bit of zero, followed by another seven bits that define the network number, and 24 variable bits that can define host addresses for that network. Slash 8 describes the total number of bits within the subnet mask that indicate the network portion of the address. Keep in mind the first bit is always 0. With seven bits allocated for network addresses within the first byte, a total of 126 possible networks may be assigned within this class. Many methods can be used to arrive at this value. One method takes into consideration the total number of bits available for network assignment, which is 7, represented as a power of two (2^7) results in a total possible bit values of 128. Two of these values, 0 and 128, are not valid because zero is an illegal network and all ones (bits one through seven being on) are the equivalent of a broadcast address. Therefore, always subtract 2 (2^7-2) from the total. The end result is 126 possible Class A network addresses. Class A networks have an address range of 1.xxx.xxx.xxx through 126.xxx.xxx.xxx. Here's an even easier method, not requiring any complicated math on your part. Using the calculation chart in Figure 2.9 you will come to the same conclusion.

FIGURE 2.9

The IP calculation chart is helpful when calculating the number of subnets and hosts. Always use the chart from right to left, covering bits until you see a value at least two greater than the number of hosts or subnets you require. Subtract two from the uncovered number to your immediate left to arrive at the value.

IP Calculation Chart

16777216	8388608	4194304	2097152	1048576	524288	262144	131072	65536	32768	16384	8192	4096	2048	1024	512	256	128	64	32	16	8	4	2	1
X	X	X	X	X	X	X	X	X	X	X	X	X	X	X	X	X	X	X	X	X	X	X	X	X

Use this chart to determine how many bits are required for subnets and hosts

Now using the same example, starting from right to left with your hand or a piece of paper cover seven bits. Look at the uncovered number just to the left of the covered portion, which should be 128, and subtract two (this takes into consideration the two unusable values). Your total should be 126. This chart can be used to calculate the number of networks, subnetworks, and hosts and will be used throughout this chapter as a reference.

In keeping with our two methods, you will now determine the maximum number of hosts within a standard Class A address. Again you can use powers of two to achieve our result; $2^{24}-2$, which equals a total of 16,777,214 hosts per network. Again, you subtract 2 because an address of all ones within this 24-bit range indicates a broadcast to all hosts on the network, and an address of all zeroes is not a valid host address. Using the IP calculation chart in Figure 2.7 cover 24 bits, take the value immediately to the left or the 25th bit, and subtract two. With 24 variable host bits Class A networks have a valid host range of A.0.0.1 through A.255.255.254.

Class B

Class B, or Slash 16, networks follow the same basic formula as Class A in that the first 14 bits, with the first two bytes, assigned by ARIN are the network ID. Slash 16 describes the total number of bits within the subnet mask that indicate the network portion of the address. Remember the first two bits will always be 10. Using the calculation chart you find after covering 14 bits and subtracting two, the maximum number of networks is 16,384. Class B networks have a possible address range value of 128.0.xxx.xxx through 191.255.xxx.xxx. This leaves the second two bytes available for the host ID. To identify the number of hosts, go back to the chart. With 16 bits left over for hosts, you can assign a total of 65,534 (16 bits covered) hosts per network. Class B networks have a valid host range of B.B.0.1 through B.B.255.254.

Class C

Class C, or Slash 24, networks have the value 110 for their first three high-order bit designations, leaving 21 network bits. Slash 24 describes the total number of bits within the subnet mask that indicate the network portion of the address. Following the same calculation chart, if you cover 21 bits, you get 2,097,152 networks, with a valid range of 192.0.0.x through 223.255.255.x. You can easily identify Class C addresses if the value within the first byte falls in the range of 192 to 223. With eight host bits left over, class C networks have a valid host range of C.C.C.1 through C.C.C.254.

Classes D and E

As previously noted, the public cannot use Classes D and E. ARIN reserved Class D addresses for multicast addresses, and is not for use by individual hosts on a network. The Class D address range is between 224 to 239. ARIN has reserved the Class E address for future use. Its address range falls between 240 and 247.

Reserved Addresses

Reserved addresses can be used for a variety of special purposes. These specific addresses and address ranges remain reserved and have restricted uses; they include

- **255.255.255.255**—An entire IP address set to all ones, such as this one, signifies a network-wide message sent to all nodes and all networks. Used for broadcast purposes.

- **0.0.0.0**—An IP address set to all zeros represents an unknown network or host, and typically is used to define a default gateway of last resort.

- **127.0.0.1**—This is a special Class A address used for internal loopback testing. It designates the local node and will not generate any network traffic.

Although IP address 255.255.255.255 is considered a network-wide flooded broadcast, routers do not forward this type of broadcast. Routers isolate broadcasts to subnets. To broadcast to all hosts on a subnet or network, set all host bits to ones. For example, to send a broadcast to all hosts on a Class B network 131.107.0.0 with a standard mask of 255.255.0.0, you would specify the destination address as 131.107.255.255.

Private Addresses

Private addresses defined with RFC 1918 may be used internally by private networks:

Note
RFC 1918 defines private addresses, which are not routable through the Internet and should not be used other than internally to maximize an organization's addressing capabilities. Companies implementing these addresses must use some form of NAT (Network Address Translation) with registered IP addresses when communicating with the outside world. NAT is discussed later in this chapter.

- Class A—10.0.0.0-10.255.255.255

- Class B—172.16.0.0-172.31.255.255

- Class C—192.168.0.0-192.168.255.255

You cannot use the nonregistered private addresses on the Internet. Companies commonly use them internally within a company's network.

Many companies use the 10.x.x.x private network because it offers internal addressing flexibility. With three bytes available for subnetworks and hosts, it provides more than enough bits to handle any company's IP addressing needs. With registered IP addresses becoming scarce, it is common to use inside private addressing schemes with address translation mechanisms allowing one or two outside registered addresses to be used for Internet access.

Translation between inside private addresses and outside registered addresses is defined as NAT (network address translation). Typically, a gateway (router) or firewall connecting a company's network to the outside world or Internet, where private addresses are not allowed, is responsible for the NAT process. I discuss NAT in further detail later in this chapter.

Network and Subnet Masks

Network and subnet masks are an integral part IP's addressing hierarchical scheme. They are used to mask off a portion of an IP address to delineate the network and subnetwork from the host address. The capability to identify which portion of the address is the network is particularly important to end systems and routers. You know from previous discussions in this chapter that devices attached to the same segment must share the same network or subnet address. Generally speaking, when two devices do not share a common network or subnet address, they reside on entirely different networks.

Two systems on the same network do not need a router's assistance when they want to exchange information. However, two systems on different networks require a router to forward communication. IP hosts do not instinctively know whether a destination host is on the same network or not. It must discover this prior to transmission. This is where the mask comes in.

End systems and routers use masks to determine whether to *shout* or *route* traffic to forward datagrams to a destination host. You then might ask, "What do *shouting* and *routing* mean?" The short answer is that if a sending end host knows a destination host resides on the same *local* segment, it can shout a local Address Resolution Protocol (ARP) broadcast to resolve the logical Network layer IP address to a MAC address and deliver the datagram without assistance. Conversely, if the sending host determines the receiver resides on a *remote* subnet or network, the sender has to route the frame by sending it to a local gateway router. A sending host uses its local mask to determine whether to shout or route.

> **Note**
>
> ARP is a broadcast-based address resolution protocol used to resolve logical (IP) addresses to physical (MAC) addresses. ARP assists devices in determining the local MAC address to be used for the delivery of datagrams. This address may be of the destination host or local router used to reach a remote host. ARP clients broadcast an ARP request asking "Does anyone recognize the IP address x.x.x.x," and hoping to get a response. If a host or router exists on the segment with this address it replies including its MAC address. The sending host uses this address, adding it to the data link header's destination address)field.

Each of the three classful network types comes with a corresponding default classful mask. As previously mentioned, Class A addresses use an eight-bit default mask of 255.0.0.0 or Slash 8 (/8). Class B addresses use a 16-bit default mask of 255.255.0.0 or Slash 16 (/16). In this case, notice that the first 16 bits have been masked off by turning on each of the eight bits within each of the bytes. If you add up the value of all the bits within each masked octet, you come up with a maximum value of 255. The last 16 bits remain unused (and are not defined for network purposes), thus all are zeros and remain available for subnets and hosts.

Class C addresses have a 24-bit default mask of 255.255.255.0 or Slash 24 (/24), indicating that the first three bytes of this address definitely are part of the network. This leaves the last eight bits unmasked and available for subnets and hosts.

For example, host 166.3.22.1 (note the Class B address) wants to establish a connection to a remote Telnet server 151.10.5.2 (another Class B address). It's important to understand that sending hosts have absolutely no idea where the destination host really resides. That is, the IP address of the destination host alone does not tell the sender where or how get to that host, or even if it resides on the local segment.

For the sending host to determine whether the destination host resides on the same local segment, the sender compares its local mask to the destination host's IP address. If the sender finds that the receiving host resides on the local subnet it knows that it can shout (send) a local ARP to resolve this logical address to a MAC address and deliver datagrams without the assistance of a router.

The source host must determine whether the destination host resides on the same subnet by performing and internal process known as *bitwise ANDing*, which compares the destination host's IP address to the sending host's subnet mask. Until it conducts bitwise ANDing, the source host has no idea whether this host is local or remote. (I will discuss bitwise ANDing later in this chapter.) If the sender determines that the host does not reside on the local segment (remote), it knows that sending a local ARP will not reach the remote host. The sending host now knows it must route the frame by sending it to a local gateway router. To get the datagram to the router for forwarding, this host must know the MAC address of the local gateway. Typically end systems are preconfigured with the IP address of a local gateway. And hopefully the end system has already gone through the process of resolving the gateways IP address to a local MAC address and still has this information in cache. If not, the sending host must send a local ARP to resolve the gateway's IP address to a MAC address before it sends datagrams for forwarding (see Figure 2.10).

FIGURE 2.10

The sending host sends a local ARP to resolve the gateway's IP address to a MAC address.

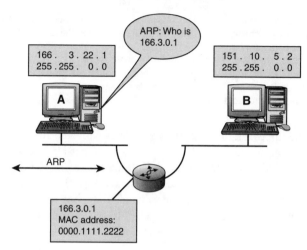

Local ARP for Gateway

Note

It is important to note that an improperly configured subnet mask could cause an end host to *shout* (send out a local ARP broadcast for the end host) when it should *route* (send out a local ARP broadcast for the gateway), and vice versa.

Bitwise ANDing

Bitwise ANDing is the process of comparing the destination host's IP address (see Figures 2.11 and 2.12) to the sending host's subnet mask, governed by a set of rules. Before beginning the process of ANDing, you must convert the 32-bit addresses to their binary forms so you can understand how the comparison occurs. Bitwise ANDing has the following rules:

- If both values are one, the result is one.
- If one of the values is zero, and the other is one, the result is zero.
- If both of the values are zero, the result is zero.

FIGURE 2.11

Note that during Bitwise ANDing the number remains one only if both values are one.

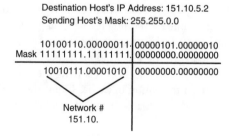

Destination Host's IP Address: 151.10.5.2
Sending Host's Mask: 255.255.0.0

```
            10100110.00000011.00000101.00000010
Mask 11111111.11111111.00000000.00000000
            10010111.00001010 00000000.00000000
```

Network #
151.10.

Using Figure 2.10 as an example, determine whether the destination host resides on the same local network as the sending host. To determine this

1. Compare the destination host's IP address with the sending host's mask. The destination host's IP address is 151.10.5.2; the sender's mask is 255.255.0.0.

2. Convert the IP address and mask to binary.

3. Draw a line vertically to separate the masked area (which represents the network address) from the unmasked area (which represents the host portion).

4. Consider any values within the IP address falling within the masked portion on the left to be part of the network. In this example, the first two bytes have been masked off and represent the network: (151.10) or 151.10.0.0.

5. Any values to the right of the vertical line represent the host address with the last two bytes being 5.2. Remember routers only care about the network and subnet in terms of routing traffic to a destination.

Using Figure 2.10 as an example, determine whether the sending host resides on the same network as the destination host. To determine this

1. Compare the IP address of the sending host with its local mask.

2. With an IP address of 166.3.22.1 and a standard Class B mask of 255.255.0.0, convert both the IP address and mask to their binary equivalents to identify which part of this address represents the network or subnet.

3. Draw a line vertically to separate the masked area (which represents the network address) from the unmasked area (which represents the host portion).

4. Consider any values within the IP address falling within the masked portion on the left to be part of the network. In this example, the first two bytes have been masked off and represent the network: (166.3) or 166.3.0.0.

5. Any values to the right of the vertical line represent the host address with the last two bytes being 22.1.

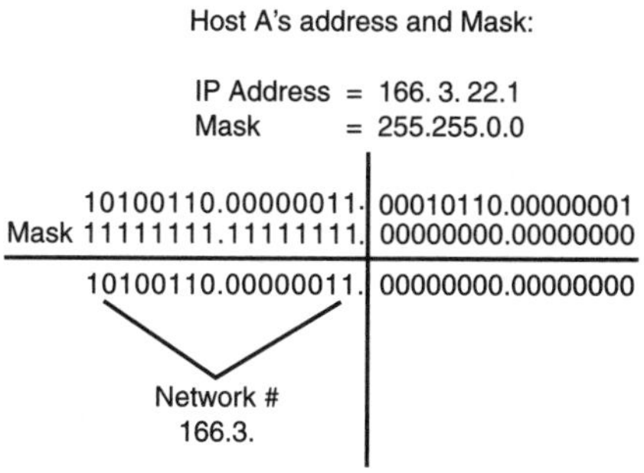

FIGURE 2.12

To compare the mask of the sending host to its IP address, convert the decimal value into binary.

Host A's address and Mask:

IP Address = 166. 3. 22.1
Mask   = 255.255.0.0

```
        10100110.00000011. 00010110.00000001
Mask 11111111.11111111. 00000000.00000000
        10100110.00000011. 00000000.00000000
```

Network #
166.3.

Note that host 5.2 on network 151.10 does not reside on the same network with host 22.1 on network 166.3, listed in Figure 2.9. As a result, Host A must send the frame to its local gateway instead of directly to Host B.

IP Subnetting

Going back to the analogy of our postal system described earlier in the chapter, network addresses represent major areas like cities. Within each city, houses must be organized by adding streets with each house having a unique address on that street. A city without streets would make it impossible to deliver the mail. Not to mention the traffic congestion caused by automobiles aimlessly traversing the city looking for a particular house.

IP address designers developed a hierarchical scheme to facilitate the division of networks into subnets to organize hosts within these subnets and limit the amount of traffic throughout the network. By subdividing the major network, traffic exchanged between hosts on the same segment would not affect hosts on other subnets within the network. When hosts on different subnets want to communicate, routers facilitate this by forwarding traffic between subnets, working much like the postal service. Routers must have a clear picture of the city and its streets to efficiently forward datagrams.

Each IP network address is assigned a default classful mask. This IP network represents a city or major network boundary within the Internet. The address assigned is four bytes (or 32 bits) in length, with the first byte determining the class type. Depending on the class type either one, two, or three bytes will be assigned. This portion of the 32-bit address cannot be modified in any way. The remaining unassigned bits within this 32-bit address may be used any way you wish, in terms of subnetwork and host assignment.

As an example, if you have been assigned a network address of 130.57.0.0 with the default mask of 255.255.0.0, you have a Class B address with a network capable of supporting more than 65,000 hosts. You probably won't need a network with more than 65,000 hosts; instead you'll want to subdivide your network (city) into smaller, more manageable pieces called subnets (streets) connected through gateways. Before you begin the subdivision process you need to consider four things:

- How many subnets are presently required for the organization?
- How many additional subnets will need to be provided for in the future?
- What is the number of hosts in the network's largest subnet?
- What is the anticipated size of the largest future subnet on the network?

Subnetting a network involves borrowing from the host bits and adding them to the network side. For example, say you need 254 subnetworks within a Class B network. At this point you have been preassigned a constant two-byte network address of 130.57.0.0, which leaves 16 bits to play with any way you like. To subdivide this network into 254 subnetworks, you would need to borrow eight of the host bits (within the third byte) and use them for subnets within network 130.57.x.0 (x represents the 8-bit byte you are borrowing).

To understand how I arrived at eight bits, refer to the IP calculation chart (refer to Figure 2.7) used earlier in this chapter. Whenever you want to determine how many bits you will need for x number of hosts or subnetworks, cover the bits starting from right to left, look at the number immediately to the left, and subtract two. With eight bits covered you see the value 256 to the left. Subtract two to take into consideration the illegal value of 0 and the broadcast value; this leaves 254 valid addresses.

You can continue to borrow unassigned bits to increase the number of subnets and decrease the number of hosts. Once you determine how many bits you must borrow from the host side, you must then extend the classful mask to include these bits as part of the network portion of the address. Remember the purpose of the mask is to identify which portion of the address is network or subnetwork. This changes your mask of 255.255.0.0 to a subnet mask of 255.255.255.0. Notice that after borrowing eight bits from the third byte, this still leaves eight bits within the last byte available for hosts addresses. Changing the default classful mask to a variable length to include subnetworks is referred to as VLSM (Variable Length Subnet Masking).

Note

It is important to note that some routing protocols do not understand subnetting. That is, they only understand classful addresses with standard masks. Forwarding of datagrams within networks that have been subnetted with VLSMs poses a problem because they do not understand subnetworks.

In Figure 2.13 the network 130.57.0.0 has been broken up into several subnetworks by borrowing all eight bits within the third byte and masking them off.

FIGURE 2.13
A Subnetted Class B network.

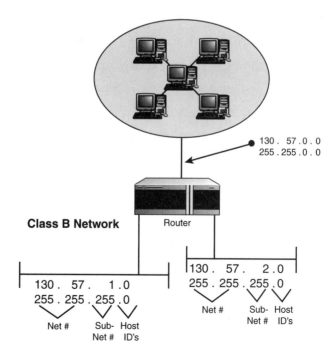

From there, you need to identify the network IDs for each new subnet such as 130.57.1.0. Now instead of one network, you have a total of 254 usable subnets. Although this example shows only two subnets, network 130.57.0.0 now can support a total of 254 subnets, providing for future growth. With one byte (8 bits) left over for hosts, each of these subnets could support up to 254 hosts.

Now you are going to subnet a Class C address. For this example, you need 13 additional subnets for a Class C network address of 192.3.1.0 with a default mask of 255.255.255.0. To calculate the number of bits required for a specific number of subnets, use the calculation chart in Figure 2.17.

To determine the number of bits to borrow

1. Start from the right.

2. Cover bits with a your hand or a piece of paper until you reach a value that is at least two greater than the number of subnets you need.

3. Take that number and subtract 2 (subtracting 2 from the number eliminates 2-bit values that are all ones and all zeroes, which are invalid).

4. The resulting value represents the number of subnets you get if you borrow the bits you covered.

For instance, for 13 subnets

1. Cover the following bits from right to left 4, 2, and 1.

2. You should see a value of 8 in the next bit position.

3. Subtract 2 from 8, which equals 6; with three bits you do not get enough subnets.

4. Cover one more bit so you have covered four bits total.

5. Look at the next value, 16 (this is at least two greater than the 13 subnets you need).

6. Subtract 2 from 16, which equals 14.

7. You now have enough for the required 13 subnets (see Figure 2.7).

You can use the same calculation chart and method to calculate the number of bits necessary for hosts.

Note

Note that when you have a finite number of bits to be shared between subnets and hosts, bits you use for one cannot be used for the other. For example, if you have 16 bits available and you borrow 7 bits for subnets, you have only 11 bits for hosts. If you borrow 12 bits for subnets you have only 4 bits for hosts. It's simple math.

Now that you have determined you need 4 bits to have 13 subnets, you need to extend the network mask to include the subnets, that is, the 4 subnetted bits (subnet mask). You know the default classful mask for network 192.3.1.0 is 24 bits in length or 255.255.255.0, so you leave these bits alone. To determine the VLSM mask

1. Start from the leftmost bit within the last byte (the 25th bit, and so forth).

2. Count from left to right four bit positions.

3. Add up the bit values of the four bit positions you counted off: 128+64+32+16 = 240 (see Figure 2.13).

4. The subnet mask for 14 subnets equals 240. The standard Class C network mask changes to include subnets within the last octet, making your new network and subnet mask 255.255.255.240. You now have 14 usable subnet addresses with four bits left over for hosts on each of the subnets.

FIGURE 2.14

To figure the VLSM mask, add up the masked bits to calculate the mask value.

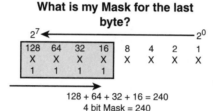

What is my Mask for the last byte?

128 + 64 + 32 + 16 = 240
4 bit Mask = 240

You also need to identify the available subnet range within the 240 subnet mask:

1. Use the lowest value in the masked range (16, the start of the range) as your base value. This represents the first valid subnet. You can figure all other subnets with this base value.

2. Continue to add 16 (the difference between each range) to these numbers until you reach the highest value below the mask. These numbers create your subnet range.

    For example, add 16 to 16 (32). Add 16 to 32 (48). Your next subnet range should equal 64 (see Figure 2.14).

You now must figure the number of hosts per subnet. Different classes and different number of bits borrowed affect the number of hosts per subnet. Because you borrowed four of the eight bits within the last byte for subnets, you have only four bits left over for host assignment. You already know the calculation for four bits; it is the same calculation you did for subnets. To figure the number of hosts per subnet

1. Start from the low order bit and move to the left. Cover the four bits you have left to use for hosts.

2. Look at the next uncovered value (16).

3. Subtract 2 to find out how many hosts you get with the remaining four bits. Of course you already know the answer to this question because you did the math for subnets (16–2 = 14 hosts per subnet).

4. For valid host IDs on each subnet, add 1 to each starting subnet range (for example, 16+1) and subtract 2 from the next value in the subnet range (for example, 32–2).

5. Continue this process for each subnet range to get the values of the valid hosts for each subnet.

6. You should have 17–30, 33–46, 49–62, 65–78, 81–94, 97–110, 113–126, 129–142, 145–158, 161–174, 177–190, 193–206, 209–222, and 225–238 as your valid ID ranges (see Figure 2.16).

What is the Subnet Range?

FIGURE 2.15
The subnet range is found by using the lowest value within the mask as a base.

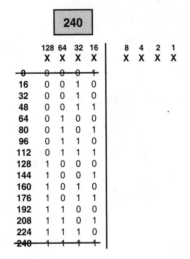

	128	64	32	16	8	4	2	1
	X	X	X	X	X	X	X	X
0	0	0	0	1				
16	0	0	1	0				
32	0	0	1	0				
48	0	0	1	1				
64	0	1	0	0				
80	0	1	0	1				
96	0	1	1	0				
112	0	1	1	1				
128	1	0	0	0				
144	1	0	0	1				
160	1	0	1	0				
176	1	0	1	1				
192	1	1	0	0				
208	1	1	0	1				
224	1	1	1	0				
240	1	1	1	1				

Hosts and Broadcast Addresses per Subnet?

FIGURE 2.16
The valid host and broadcast addresses for each subnet.

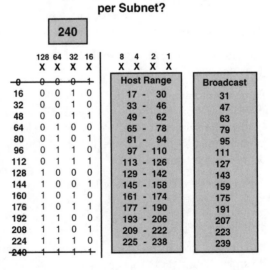

	128	64	32	16	8	4	2	1	Host Range	Broadcast
	X	X	X	X	X	X	X	X		
0	0	0	0	1						
16	0	0	1	0					17 - 30	31
32	0	0	1	0					33 - 46	47
48	0	0	1	1					49 - 62	63
64	0	1	0	0					65 - 78	79
80	0	1	0	1					81 - 94	95
96	0	1	1	0					97 - 110	111
112	0	1	1	1					113 - 126	127
128	1	0	0	0					129 - 142	143
144	1	0	0	1					145 - 158	159
160	1	0	1	0					161 - 174	175
176	1	0	1	1					177 - 190	191
192	1	1	0	0					193 - 206	207
208	1	1	0	1					209 - 222	223
224	1	1	1	0					225 - 238	239
240	1	1	1	1						

Note that the broadcast value for each subnet is one less than the next valid subnet value. For example, the broadcast address for subnet 16 would be 31 (32–1, as 32 is the next subnet).

As previously mentioned, class type affects the number of host bits available for borrowing. The good news is the calculation procedure does not.

Take a look at a Class B address. For a Class B address with a standard 16-bit network mask (255.255.0.0) with an additional four subnetted bits, you can see that you have 12 host bits available to borrow. You already did the math on four bits. You know that four bits will get you 14 (subnets or hosts), depending on what you are using the bits for.

With that information you know how many bits you need to extend the Class B default mask: four additional bits to include the subnets. That changes the mask to 255.255.240.0. You have extended the mask to include four bits within the third byte as subnetted bits. This means you have 12 bits left over within the third and fourth bytes to assign hosts. Use the calculation chart to find out how many hosts you will get per subnet with 12 bits. Cover all 12 bits with a piece of paper and look at the next uncovered value, which should be 4,096. Subtract 2 (4,096–2 = 4,094) to determine the number of hosts per subnet (see Figure 2.17).

FIGURE 2.17

The Class B network 130.100.0.0 has been further divided into subnets by masking off four of the host bits within the third byte (240).

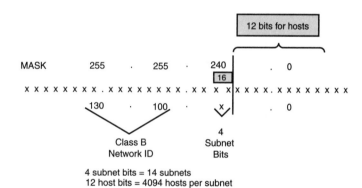

Earlier you learned how to derive the subnet range from a Class C network with four subnet masked bits. With four subnetted bits you get this subnet range: 16, 32, 48, 64, 80, 96, 112, 128, 144, 160, 176, 192, 208, and 224, respectively. These 14 numbers represent your sub-network addresses. Now that you know the subnet range, you identify the valid host IDs and broadcast address on each subnet. This is where you deviate from the previous method. With a Class C example, as previously used, you had only eight bits to worry about; now you have 16 bits to deal with.

With a Class B network, when you cross over an 8-bit boundary, such as this example (network 130.100.0.0 255.255.240.0 mask, representing the four subnetted bits in the third byte) in which the host bits straddle the third and fourth bytes, the calculations get a little more complex in calculating the host ranges. The best method of tackling this is to use binary. To calculate the host range

1. Take the first subnet within network 130.100.16.0 (the lowest subnet within the mask) and convert it to binary.

2. Start with the lowest possible value within the host ID bits. This gives you the first valid host within the subnet.

3. Identify the highest possible value (which represents the broadcast for the subnet). By doing this you can easily back into the highest valid host range within the subnet (which is always one less than the broadcast).

4. When you cross over an octet boundary, you add the values in each octet separately. Remember to add only the charged bits within each byte.

3rd byte					4th byte											
							4 bit mask 240									
128	64	32	16	|	8	4	2	1	.	128	64	32	16	8	4	2	1
0	0	0	1	|	0	0	0	0	.	0	0	0	0	0	0	0	1

5. To identify the first valid host address on subnet 16, place 0s in all host bit positions except the rightmost bit, which is a 1. This represents the lowest possible host value available within this subnet. Remember you cannot have all 0s in the host portion (invalid host ID).

6. Take each byte separately and add the charged bits within the byte. The third byte contains only one charged bit, 16; therefore, the value within that byte equals 16.

7. The fourth byte contains only the last byte charged bit, which has a value of 1. Your first valid host IP address for subnet 16 on network 130.100 would be 130.100.16.1 (see Figure 2.18).

What is the First Valid Host for each Subnet?

FIGURE 2.18
Calculate the first valid host for each subnet.

240

Sub nets	128	64	32	16	8	4	2	1	•	128	64	32	16	8	4	2	1	First Valid Host
	X	X	X	X	X	X	X	X		X	X	X	X	X	X	X	X	
16	0	0	0	1	0	0	0	0	•	0	0	0	0	0	0	0	1	16.1
32	0	0	1	0	0	0	0	0	•	0	0	0	0	0	0	0	1	32.1
48	0	0	1	1	0	0	0	0	•	0	0	0	0	0	0	0	1	48.1
64	0	1	0	0	0	0	0	0	•	0	0	0	0	0	0	0	1	64.1
80	0	1	0	1	0	0	0	0	•	0	0	0	0	0	0	0	1	80.1
96	0	1	1	0	0	0	0	0	•	0	0	0	0	0	0	0	1	96.1
112	0	1	1	1	0	0	0	0	•	0	0	0	0	0	0	0	1	112.1
128	1	0	0	0	0	0	0	0	•	0	0	0	0	0	0	0	1	128.1
144	1	0	0	1	0	0	0	0	•	0	0	0	0	0	0	0	1	144.1
160	1	0	1	0	0	0	0	0	•	0	0	0	0	0	0	0	1	160.1
176	1	0	1	1	0	0	0	0	•	0	0	0	0	0	0	0	1	176.1
192	1	1	0	0	0	0	0	0	•	0	0	0	0	0	0	0	1	208.1
208	1	1	0	1	0	0	0	0	•	0	0	0	0	0	0	0	1	224.1
224	1	1	1	0	0	0	0	0	•	0	0	0	0	0	0	0	1	

Now go to the opposite extreme to derive the broadcast address. Change all 12 host bits to ones; then add the charged bits within the third and fourth bytes separately (see Figure 2.19).

3rd byte									4th byte							
									4 bit mask 240							
128	64	32	16	|	8	4	2	1 .	128	64	32	16	8	4	2	1
0	0	0	1	|	1	1	1	1 .	1	1	1	1	1	1	1	1

What is the Broadcast address for each subnet?

FIGURE 2.19
The broadcast address is indicated by all ones in the hosts' bits.

240

Sub nets	128	64	32	16	8	4	2	1 •	128	64	32	16	8	4	2	1	Subnet Broadcast
	X	X	X	X	X	X	X	X	X	X	X	X	X	X	X	X	
16	0	0	0	1	1	1	1	1 •	1	1	1	1	1	1	1	1	31.255
32	0	0	1	0	1	1	1	1 •	1	1	1	1	1	1	1	1	47.255
48	0	0	1	1	1	1	1	1 •	1	1	1	1	1	1	1	1	65.255
64	0	1	0	0	1	1	1	1 •	1	1	1	1	1	1	1	1	79.255
80	0	1	0	1	1	1	1	1 •	1	1	1	1	1	1	1	1	95.255
96	0	1	1	0	1	1	1	1 •	1	1	1	1	1	1	1	1	111.255
112	0	1	1	1	1	1	1	1 •	1	1	1	1	1	1	1	1	127.255
128	1	0	0	0	1	1	1	1 •	1	1	1	1	1	1	1	1	159.255
144	1	0	0	1	1	1	1	1 •	1	1	1	1	1	1	1	1	175.255
160	1	0	1	0	1	1	1	1 •	1	1	1	1	1	1	1	1	191.255
176	1	0	1	1	1	1	1	1 •	1	1	1	1	1	1	1	1	207.255
192	1	1	0	0	1	1	1	1 •	1	1	1	1	1	1	1	1	223.255
208	1	1	0	1	1	1	1	1 •	1	1	1	1	1	1	1	1	239.255
224	1	1	1	0	1	1	1	1 •	1	1	1	1	1	1	1	1	

Broadcast 130.100.31.255—You get this by adding all charged bits within the third byte; then the fourth byte. You have 16+8+4+2+1 = 31 in the third byte. From here you can easily determine that highest possible valid host ID, which is always one less than the broadcast address for the subnet. To determine this, just change the rightmost bit to a 0; then add them up again. You have 130.100.31.254 as your last valid host range (see Figure 2.20).

3rd byte									4th byte							
									4 bit mask 240							
128	64	32	16	|	8	4	2	1 .	128	64	32	16	8	4	2	1
0	0	0	1	|	1	1	1	1 .	1	1	1	1	1	1	1	0

What is the Last Valid Host for each Subnet?

FIGURE 2.20
As you can see, the last valid host within a subnet is always one less than the broadcast, indicated by a value of 0 in the rightmost (value of 1) bit position.

	240																
Sub nets	128 X	64 X	32 X	16 X	8 X	4 X	2 X	1 X	•128 X	64 X	32 X	16 X	8 X	4 X	2 X	1 X	**Last Valid Host**
16	0	0	0	1	1	1	1	1	•1	1	1	1	1	1	1	0	31.254
32	0	0	1	0	1	1	1	1	•1	1	1	1	1	1	1	0	47.254
48	0	0	1	1	1	1	1	1	•1	1	1	1	1	1	1	0	65.254
64	0	1	0	0	1	1	1	1	•1	1	1	1	1	1	1	0	79.254
80	0	1	0	1	1	1	1	1	•1	1	1	1	1	1	1	0	95.254
96	0	1	1	0	1	1	1	1	•1	1	1	1	1	1	1	0	111.254
112	0	1	1	1	1	1	1	1	•1	1	1	1	1	1	1	0	127.254
128	1	0	0	0	1	1	1	1	•1	1	1	1	1	1	1	0	159.254
144	1	0	0	1	1	1	1	1	•1	1	1	1	1	1	1	0	175.254
160	1	0	1	0	1	1	1	1	•1	1	1	1	1	1	1	0	191.254
176	1	0	1	1	1	1	1	1	•1	1	1	1	1	1	1	0	207.254
192	1	1	0	0	1	1	1	1	•1	1	1	1	1	1	1	0	223.254
208	1	1	0	1	1	1	1	1	•1	1	1	1	1	1	1	0	239.254
224	1	1	1	0	1	1	1	1	•1	1	1	1	1	1	1	0	

Supernetting, Summarization, Aggregation, and CIDR

The networking industry throws around the terms supernetting, route summarization, route aggregation, and CIDR (class interdomain routing) on a regular basis as if they were completely different technologies. These terms do not merit a distinction as separate technologies. In reality they all describe a method of reducing route update traffic and routing tables by condensing a group of contiguous IP addresses into a single address representative of the entire group.

Whichever term you decide to use, it enables routers to advertise a subset of routes reducing the number of route updates that need to be sent and reducing the size of route tables. I'm most comfortable with the term "summarization," so I'll use it throughout this section and book in describing the process.

Even though summarization might seem like a foreign concept, believe it or not you're probably implementing it in your network already. If you have a network that has been assigned a registered IP address to connect to the Internet, the address ARIN or your upstream service provider assigned to you represents the summarization of your company's network to everyone in the Internet.

The ARIN organization through its classful addressing scheme deliberately defined Class A, B, and C addresses which, if defined with one summarized address and assigned to a company, represent the company (city) and all of the internal subnets (streets). Of course you could advertise to the entire world all of your internal subnets through the Internet; however, I do not advise this for two reasons: It's an obvious security issue, and it's not necessary.

You would not need or want to advertise all internal subnets because to get to your network and its subnets, the other routers within the Internet need to know only how to get to your major unique classful network assigned by ARIN. Once traffic destined for network reaches your local gateway, this gateway takes care of the rest. Consider the additional route update traffic that would be required to advertise all of your routes, and the resources it would take for all routers on the Internet to keep track of all networks and subnets for every network in existence. This is why summarization is so important.

You also can implement summarization within your company's routing infrastructure to reduce the amount of route update traffic and routing table sizes. Typically you perform summarization on routers connecting to a company's core, where link congestion and bandwidth capacity are important issues. By summarizing multiple IP addresses into a single address before this information is sent into the core you can reduce update traffic, conserving precious bandwidth.

CIDR

The industry tends to use the term "CIDR" to describe route summarization performed on contiguous Class C addresses. This type of summarization typically is done by ISPs or service providers, which have been assigned a group of contiguous Class C addresses—which they in turn have given to their downstream clients.

ISPs and Service Providers

Most of the time the terms *ISP* and *service provider* can be used interchangeably. However, the term *ISP* describes a company that provides Internet service (thus, the name Internet Service Provider) and only Internet service. A service provider can provide Internet service (an ISP) as well as other services that an ISP does not provide, such as Frame Relay and WAN connections.

The provider knows the Class C address of each client representing its network. The ISP can advertise each of the Class C network addresses out to the Internet or a subset of them. It might summarize several of these addresses into a single address to reduce the route information it passes to other gateways on the Internet.

Summarization of a group of addresses can be performed only when the addresses being summarized are contiguous and can only be summarized on a power of 2 boundary. Take the following IP addressing example and perform summarization: You have a Class B network address assigned to your organization (130.100.0.0, default mask 255.255.0.0) with many internal subnets. Look at a subset of these subnets for simplicity. You have x number of IP addresses that are contiguous; instead of advertising each of these separately, you want to group them and advertise the summarized route.

You would

1. Convert the IP addresses in question to binary (see Table 2.3).

2. Start from left to right.

3. Look for the longest binary match (or common bit pattern) within each address; this represents the IP address for summarization.

TABLE 2.3   Route Summarization

IP Address	Mask	Binary Representation							
		128	64	32	16	8	4	2	1
130.100.16.0	255.255.255.0	0	0	0	1	0	0	0	0
130.100.17.0	255.255.255.0	0	0	0	1	0	0	0	1
130.100.18.0	255.255.255.0	0	0	0	1	0	0	1	0
130.100.19.0	255.255.255.0	0	0	0	1	0	0	1	1
130.100.20.0	255.255.255.0	0	0	0	1	0	1	0	0
130.100.21.0	255.255.255.0	0	0	0	1	0	1	0	1
130.100.22.0	255.255.255.0	0	0	0	1	0	1	1	0
130.100.23.0	255.255.255.0	0	0	0	1	0	1	1	1
130.100.24.0	255.255.255.0	0	0	0	1	1	0	0	0
130.100.25.0	255.255.255.0	0	0	0	1	1	0	0	1
130.100.26.0	255.255.255.0	0	0	0	1	1	0	1	0
130.100.27.0	255.255.255.0	0	0	0	1	1	0	1	1
130.100.28.0	255.255.255.0	0	0	0	1	1	1	0	0
130.100.29.0	255.255.255.0	0	0	0	1	1	1	0	1
130.100.30.0	255.255.255.0	0	0	0	1	1	1	1	0
130.100.31.0	255.255.255.0	0	0	0	1	1	1	1	1

You really don't need to do a binary conversion to determine whether the first two bytes match because it is obvious that each address starts with 130.100, so the binary match would be identical. In this case only the third byte is in question. Now that you have the list of binary values for each subnet, it's clear that all of these subnets have the first four bits in common, in addition to the 16 bits within the first and second bytes. This means you can summarize all of these subnets with a single IP address of 130.100.16.0 using a 20-bit mask (16 networks bits plus four subnet bits) or 255.255.240.0 or /20.

Remember the point of summarization is to reduce route updates. You might have recognized that a subset within this group all contain further matches. Only those addresses that matched exactly can be summarized and only to the longest match. You could group the subset of matches and summarize them separately; however, this would mean you would need to advertise that group separately. Because all 16 of the previously mentioned networks have four common bits you can group and summarize all 16 of them with a single address. Summarizing a subset proves less efficient and unnecessary.

Network Address Translation (NAT)

The term *network address translation* describes the process of translating nonregistered private IP addresses (listed earlier in this chapter) to a single registered valid IP address or range of addresses to be used when communicating with hosts in the Internet. Remember that ARIN is responsible for assigning registered IP addresses to organizations for use out in the Internet. However, the 32-bit addressing scheme it developed way back when cannot support the millions of Internet hosts in existence today. The original IP addressing hierarchy did not take into consideration the massive Internet craze, requiring registered IP addresses for all participating hosts.

With the exhaustion of available addresses looming something had to be done. NAT addresses the issue of dwindling IP addresses and the exponential growth of Internet hosts.

> **Note**
>
> Although the networking industry proposed one solution—known as IPv6 meaning version 6 to change the current IP addressing scheme, increasing the number of Network layer bits from 32 to 128, making more addresses available, it has largely been ignored. The current and de facto version of IP is version 4. Implementing IPv6 would require all Internet participants to redesign and deploy their addressing schemes. In addition, adjustments would have to be made to current routing protocols, and so on, to effectively implement it. Meanwhile, other solutions have emerged that enable us to continue using the existing addressing structure of IPv4, such as NAT.

NAT provides address translation between private and public IP addresses. The main purpose of NAT is to allow companies to implement private addressing internally, maximizing their IP addressing capacity while using registered Internet addresses when communicating with the outside world. To use NAT an administrator must enable and configure a router or server with the NAT service. Routers supporting NAT basically convert inside private addresses, such as 10.x.x.x, to a registered outside IP address, when a host within the private network attempts to communicate with a host on the Internet. NAT has three types of implementation:

- Static (see Figure 2.21)
- Dynamic (see Figure 2.22)
- Combination of static and dynamic

FIGURE 2.21

A one-to-one (static) mapping of the inside to the outside address.

Static Mappings

NAT Table	
Inside	Outside
10.1.1.2	36.1.2.3
10.1.1.3	36.1.2.4

Dynamic Mappings

FIGURE 2.22
Multiple private addresses mapping to the same outside registered address using different port numbers (dynamic).

Inside NAT Table		Client Port
Inside Local	Inside Global:	
10.1.1.2	36.1.2.3	1004
10.1.1.3	36.1.2.3	6002

Static

Think of static NATs as one-to-one network translations—each inside address is mapped to a unique outside address. Administrators must manually create the static mapping on the router performing the translation. With this type of NAT you must have as many outside addresses as inside, which makes the use of NAT seem useless. Figure 2.23 is an example of static NAT mapping configuration from a Cisco router.

Static NAT Configuration

FIGURE 2.23
Static NAT maps each inside private address to a registered outside address.

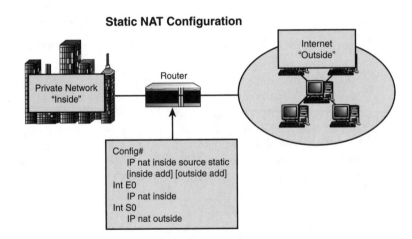

```
Config#
    IP nat inside source static
    [inside add] [outside add]
Int E0
    IP nat inside
Int S0
    IP nat outside
```

Dynamic

Think of dynamic NATs as many-to-one or many-to-few network translations—multiple inside addresses mapped to a single outside address or small pool of addresses. Administrators typically define a small pool of registered addresses to be used when translating any inside address. Because a single IP address or small pool of addresses is used to translate all inside addresses, an administrator must implement a method of uniquely identifying each inside host.

To identify each inside host uniquely, even though they map to the same outside address, the source host's Transport layer port (identifying the process or program) is appended to the outside address. The industry uses this type of NAT the most. With this type of NAT, you need only one or a small pool of outside addresses, making the most efficient use of the registered addresses.

Routers performing NAT maintain mapping tables to keep track of the mapped addresses. When an inside host wants to send a datagram to a host outside the private address, it sends the datagram to the gateway for forwarding. The router maps the inside address to a registered outside address using one of the methods previously mentioned and forwards the datagram. It then holds the mapping in memory for later use (see Figure 2.24).

Network Address Translation

FIGURE 2.24
The NAT process.

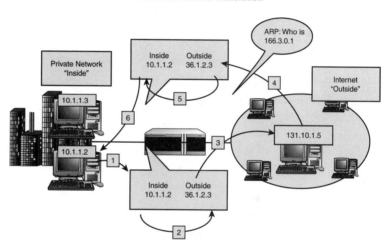

After the router has mapped the inside address to an outside address, it uses this address within the IP header of the datagram, indicating the source or sending host. The destination host does not know that the sending host's address is actually a translated address, nor does it care. When the destination host responds to the source host, the router remaps the outside address to the inside address and delivers it to the original host. Because translation is transparent, you can effectively hide your inside network hosts and infrastructure from the outside world and still allow them to communicate.

ICMP

Routers use the ICMP (Internet Control Message Protocol), defined by RFC 792, as a control, messaging, and diagnostic protocol. ICMP is considered an integral part of the IP protocol. As such, it utilizes the services of IP for its delivery of messages.

> **Note**
>
> Most people are familiar with the Ping and Trace route utilities, which allow the testing of network layer connectivity between IP hosts. Both of these utilities utilize ICMP messages.

Routers on occasion need to inform a source host of delivery problems, test connectivity to that host, ask for transmission to slow down and so on. These messages allow a source host to learn and recover from some (not all) of the problems that may occur on an internetwork. Although these messages inform a host of problems with the delivery of datagrams, ICMP does not guarantee a solution to these problems.

ICMP Header and Message Formats

ICMP messages are identified within an IP header by protocol type 1. Information contained within ICMP messages vary depending on the message type being sent. ICMP messages can be categorized as a query, error, or reply messages:

- Query—Sent for various reasons, such as to check time, retrieve a subnet mask, or test connectivity between hosts among other things.

- Error—Sent to alert devices of problems

- Reply—Sent in response to query messages

The type field identifies the type of the message sent by the router. Table 2.4 lists the all of the ICMP message types.

TABLE 2.4   ICMP Message Type

Type	Description ICMP Message Types
0	Echo Reply (reply)
3	Destination Unreachable (error)
4	Source Quench (error)
5	Redirect (error)
8	Echo Request (query)
9	Router Advertisement (reply)
10	Router Solicitation (query)
11	Time Exceeded (error)
12	Parameter Problem (error)
13	Timestamp Request (query)
14	Timestamp Reply (reply)

TABLE 2.4 Continued

Type	Description ICMP Message Types
15	Information Request (obsolete)(query)
16	Information Reply (obsolete)(reply)
17	Address Mask Request (query)
18	Address Mask Reply (reply)

Since each of the ICMP message headers vary depending on which one is sent, we will discuss each type separately, identifying the corresponding code fields, if applicable, as we go.

Types 8 and 0—Echo Request and Reply

We discuss the ICMP Echo request Type 8 and Echo Reply Type 0 because ICMP uses these messages in tandem. The Ping utility is used to test network layer connectivity between two IP hosts. When a user executes the Ping utility, an ICMP echo request is sent with the expectation that the destination host will respond with a corresponding echo reply.

Figure 2.25 shows an example of an echo request and Figure 2.26 shows an example of an echo reply.

FIGURE 2.25

This is an example of an echo request and reply generated as a result of user executing the Ping utility. In frame one host 36.53.0.202 sends an echo request to test the connectivity with host 36.28.0.1. Note the detail pane indicates a type 8 value stating this is an echo request.

FIGURE 2.26

In frame two, host 36.53.0.202 returns the echo reply to host 36.28.0.1. The ICMP message type 0 indicates this is a reply.

In Figure 2.25, a user sitting at host 36.53.0.202 has executed the Ping command to test the connectivity between this host and remote host 36.28.0.1. As you can see from the output screen of the Sniffer protocol analyzer, the ICMP message type sent is 8 (Echo). This host is expecting a reply from the remote host, which it gets (see Figure 2.26). In the reply (Figure 2.26) host 36.28.0.1 sends an ICMP message type 0 to host 36.28.0.1. Typically multiple ICMP (five) replies are returned to the source host. The receipt of these reply messages indicates network layer communication between source and destination hosts is functioning properly. If no ICMP replies are received by the source host this indicates a problem exists at the network layer or some lower layer within the OSI model.

Type 3—Destination Unreachable

ICMP type 3 message, destination unreachable sent by a router to alert a source host of delivery problems encountered while trying to reach the destination. For example, this message may be sent by a router to a source host indicating that the router is unable to forward a datagram, because it can not find the destination network, host or process. This may occur is the destination does not exist, has failed or has no route to this network. In other words, the router can not deliver or forward an IP datagram to the destination network.

Type 4—Source Quench

A receiving host generates this message when it can not process datagrams at the speed requested due to a lack of memory or internal resources. This message serves as a simple flow control mechanism that a receiving host can utilize to alert a sender to slow down its transmission of data. A router generates this message when in the process of forwarding datagrams, it has run low on buffers and can not queue the datagram for delivery.

Type 5—Redirect

A router sends a redirect error to the sender of an IP datagram when the sender should have sent the datagram to a different router or directly to an end host (if the end host is local). The message assists the sending host to direct a misdirected datagram to a gateway or host. Note that a gateway receiving a misdirected frame does not trash the offending datagram if it can forward it. The gateway forwards the frame, sends an alert message to the source and hopes the source host will properly direct future frames to the designated host or gateway indicated in the message.

Types 9 and 10—Router Advertisement and Solicitation

ICMP type 9 and 10 messages may be used dynamically discover routers. Routers send ICMP advertisements to announce their presence, while both hosts and router may send solicitation messages to discover routers.

Type 11—Time Exceeded

The time exceeded message occurs when a router receives a datagram with a TTL (Time To Live) of 0 or 1. IP uses the TTL field to prevent infinite routing loops. A router can not forward a datagram that has a TTL of 0 or 1. Instead, it trashes the datagram and sends a "time exceeded" message. The traceroute utility also uses the TTL to discover the path or route to a destination host or network.

Type 12—Parameter Problem

The parameter problem message indicates that a host or gateway received and could not interpret an invalid or misunderstood parameter. A host or gateway can also send this message when no other ICMP message covering the problem can be used to alert the sending host. In this respect, it is a "catchall" message.

Types 13 and 14—Timestamp Request and Reply

Timestamp request and reply messages work in tandem. You have the option of using timestamps. When used, a timestamp request permits a system to query another for the current time.

Types 15 and 16—Information Request and Reply

Although ICMP message list information request and reply as a potential ICMP message type, they actually do not occur, thus obsolete. When used a host can request information, such as what network it was attached to.

Types 17 and 18—Address Mask Request and Reply

Address mask request and reply messages work in tandem. Although we rarely use this message today, its original design supported the function of dynamically obtaining a subnet mask. Host may use the ICMP address mask request to acquire its subnet mask during bootstrap from a remote host.

Throughout this book the ICMP messages mentioned in this chapter are referenced as they apply to routing and datagram delivery problems.

Summary

The Internet Protocol provides for connectionless delivery of packets or datagrams between source to destination end systems. Its primary responsibilities include addressing, fragmentation/reassembly, and connectionless delivery of datagrams. Binary and decimal conversion is an important part of understanding IP addressing. The base-10 numbering system, known as decimal numbering, consists of the numbers 0, 1, 2, 3, 4, 5, 6, 7, 8, and 9. Computers use the binary, or base-2, numbering system. To understand binary numbers, you convert them to the decimal.

IP addresses are 4 byte or 32 bit values assigned by a governing body known as ARIN or ISP. The major network address identifies a company within the Internet community. Subnetworks within the network are used to divide the major network into more manageable pieces.

There are five major address classes: A, B, C, D, and E. The public uses only Classes A, B, and C.

Subnet masks help routers and end hosts determine how to route datagrams. If the destination host resides on the same local segment, it can send an ARP broadcast to resolve the logical Network layer IP address to a MAC address. If the destination is remote, it routes the datagram to a local gateway router.

The process of comparing the destination host's IP address to the sending host's subnet mask is called bitwise ANDing.

Summarization is a method used by routers to combine contiguous IP addresses sharing common bit boundaries into one or more route advertisements. This reduces the size of the routing tables and the number of route updates that need to be sent.

NAT is a translation process performed by routers or servers. This process allows inside private addresses to be mapped to outside registered addresses usable on the Internet.

ICMP is a network layer control and messaging protocol used by routers to alert other devices of problems encountered with the delivery of datagrams among other things. There are three main message types; query, reply and errors. ICMP messages do not fix the problem, they simply serve as problem notification.

Quiz

1. What are the various IP address classes and their ranges?

2. Name the responsibilities of the Internet Protocol.

3. Name the address class type that defines IP multicasting.

4. What is the default Class A mask?

5. What is the decimal value equivalent of binary 10000011?

6. With a network address of 195.5.2.0 and a subnet mask of 255.255.255.220, how many subnetworks are available and how many hosts per subnet?

7. If you have a /27 subnet mask, what would the decimal representation of the subnet mask be?

   Answer: 255.255.255.224

8. What is the correct number of subnets and hosts that are available on a Class B network with a subnet mask of 255.255.255.128?

9. On a Class C network, how many bits would you need to borrow if you needed 60 hosts?

10. On a Class B network, how many bits would you need to borrow if you needed 2000 hosts?

11. What is static NAT?

12. What is dynamic NAT?

CHAPTER 3

IP ROUTING

You will learn about the following in this chapter:

- Basic routing principles
- Static routing
- Default routing

- Dynamic routing
- Distance Vector protocols
- Link State protocols

Nonroutable Versus Routable Protocols

Some protocols can be routed and others cannot. Nonroutable protocols, such as DEC's LAT (Local Area Transport) and NetBEUI (Network Basic Input/Output System), do not contain network layer addressing information. Without the network layer addressing information, routers lack the information they need to determine how to decide for which network or host traffic is destined. Therefore, these protocols need to be bridged or switched using layer 2 information such as a MAC address.

As a general rule nonroutable protocols are broadcast-based, which adds overhead and traffic to a network. For this reason, you usually install a router to isolate the traffic from propagating through an entire internetwork.

However, on some occasions, you may find it necessary to allow this traffic to be forwarded to other segments. You can accomplish this by replacing the router with a layer 2 device (like a bridge or switch) or by configuring the intervening router to forward the nonroutable traffic without determining the specific route this traffic will take.

Note

Routers configured to bridge traffic are referred to as Brouters, allowing the router to bridge traffic using the layer 2 address like a bridge. Routers can transparently bridge, source route, or combine the two methods, depending on your needs and the architectures supported, such as Ethernet or Token-Ring. How a router bridges traffic is determined by the layer 2 implementation you have in place.

Routable protocols are protocols that can be forwarded by a router. Any protocol that has layer 3 logical network addressing can be routed, like IP, IPX, and AppleTalk. Because IP, IPX, and AppleTalk all supply the network layer addressing information and any protocol, application or service that runs on top of these protocols may also be routed. Routers forward traffic based on network layer logical destination addresses; without it routing would not be possible. We discussed IP and logical network layer IP addresses in Chapter 2, "IP and IP Addressing."

Basic Routing Concepts

Routing involves the delivery of datagrams between end systems located on different networks. Without routers and routing protocols, end host communication would be limited to only those systems on the same physical segment (see Figure 3.1).

Single Segment

FIGURE 3.1
All hosts are attached to the same segment. There is no need for routers and routing protocols for these hosts to communicate with each other.

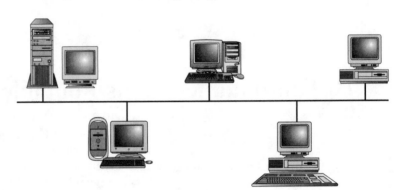

Routers provide the physical connection between networks. Routers must be configured with some type of routing mechanism to enable communication between hosts beyond their local segments (see figure 3.2).

Multiple Subnets

FIGURE 3.2
Routers connect multiple subnets together allowing remote hosts to communicate. The router forwards traffic between hosts on subnets 1 and 2.

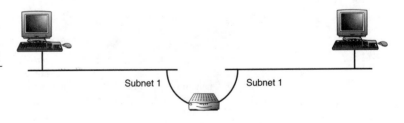

Subnet 1   Subnet 1

These routing mechanisms are either static or dynamic in nature. Static means manual configuration is necessary. Dynamic mechanisms involve routing protocols that facilitate the exchange of information, allowing routers to learn and adapt to changes in a network's topology. Static and dynamic routing protocols will be discussed later in this chapter.

Whether a router is configured statically or dynamically or a combination of both the objective is the same, to facilitate communication between remote hosts. For hosts to communicate with other hosts located on different networks, end systems must be configured with the IP address of at least one local router (also referred to as the *default router*). Hosts may be statically configured or dynamically discover their local router's or router's IP address(see Figure 3.3).

Note

The terms gateway and router are used interchangeably within the industry to describe a router. For clarity's sake, the term router will be used from now on. When a hosts wants to communicate with hosts outside its local subnet it sends the datagram to the local router for forwarding.

FIGURE 3.3

Host A is configured with the IP address (131.107.1.1) of the Default router located on its subnet.

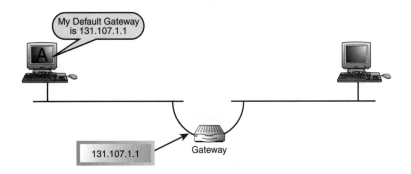

The local router (131.107.1.1) in figure 3.3 is the exit and/or entry point connecting the network and its local hosts to the outside world. Whenever Host A wants to communicate with a host or hosts not connected to its local segment, it must send the datagram to the local router for forwarding. Specific configuration of end hosts is not discussed in this book.

The reference to the "outside world" does not necessarily mean the Internet. Remember that hosts are limited to communicating with hosts connected to the same network unless a router is present. The outside world could simply be a single network on the other side of this router or it could be a series of networks connected through multiple routers leading out to the Internet (see Figure 3.4). The point is that whenever a host wants to go outside of its local segment, it must send datagrams to a local router for delivery.

FIGURE 3.4

A typical network with multiple internal subnets may contain a router providing a connection to the Internet. The router providing access to the Internet has one interface connected to the inside network and one connected to the outside world.

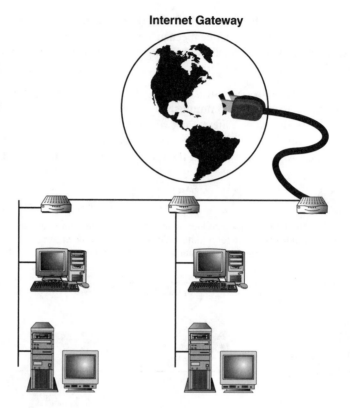

Internet Gateway

Let's relate routing to the postal service analogy used in Chapter 2, "IP and IP Addressing," which discussed a network as a "city" and subnetworks as "streets" within a city. The city represents the major classful address (class A, B, or C). The street represents the subnetworks within the major network used to organize and divide the houses within the city. Now let's consider the U.S. postal service as the routing entity that makes delivery of mail within and between cities possible.

First consider a single street without postal service. If you want to send a note to a neighbor who lives on the same street you do, you would probably save yourself the cost of a stamp and deliver the mail yourself, without involving the postal service. In this case you would address the letter as follows: Your name and return address complete with city, street, and house number. You would also indicate the destination address of the intended recipient.

However, if you wanted to send a note to a friend who lives on a different street within your city or in some other city or state, you would most certainly rely on the postal service for the delivery of this message. The U.S. Postal service provides a delivery infrastructure for mail throughout the entire U.S. and interfaces with other delivery services outside the U.S. to facilitate the delivery of mail throughout the world. Standard delivery of mail is best effort, which means there is no guarantee other than trust in the service that your mail will actually get to its final destination.

Now consider yourself the end host on a single segment. And just like an end host you must be able to identify the entry or exit point (router) to use to delivery mail outside of your local street. In this case your mailbox (router) would be considered your entry and exit point outside your local street(see Figure 3.5).

FIGURE 3.5

A host's entry and exit point (mailbox) in and out of its subnet is its local router.

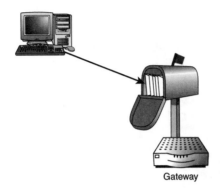

Gateway

Somehow when you were young you were taught the basics about mail. Perhaps you learned how to address a letter and what to do with it when you want the postal service to handle delivery outside your local street. Placing a letter in your mailbox is second nature.

However, what happens to your mail once it gets picked up by the mailman is not. That is the mysterious magic of routers and routing protocols. We will discuss how routers and routing protocols handle the delivery of mail in a moment, but for now let's continue with our analogy.

Your letter is in the mailbox; now what? For your letter to arrive at its destination it must travel through the massive delivery infrastructure developed by the postal service. This infrastructure consists of postmen, postal offices, trucks, planes, and so on that through coordinated efforts receive, sort, and deliver the mail.

The first point of contact with your mail is your local postal carrier, who knows to check your mailbox (router) for outgoing mail and take it to the local post office. At that point all mail received at this office is examined. This process involves identifying the address of the destination (end system) or recipient.

Identifying the destination and the path to that destination is key to proper delivery. The postal service has many different options for delivering mail: air, sea, land, and so on. To determine what delivery paths are available and to select the "best path," information about the physical postal infrastructure is either known or needs to be learned (for a router, this function is performed by static or dynamic routing protocols). The postal service's delivery options and best paths to destinations may be in the form of a map or table, similar to the local route table stored by a router. This information is most likely posted at the local post office for all postal workers to use when determining the best path to deliver the mail to its destination.

After identifying the destination address and potential delivery paths by consulting the postal infrastructure map (route table), the most efficient path is chosen. The mail is then sent to the next post office (router) along this path closest to the destination where similar procedures are performed. This continues until it reaches the post office (router) responsible for delivering mail for the destination city (network) and street (subnet) (see Figure 3.6).

FIGURE 3.6
An example of the delivery of mail from one city to another. Routers serve as the entry, exit, and intermediate delivery points between and across cities (networks) facilitating the delivery of mail (datagrams) between houses (end systems).

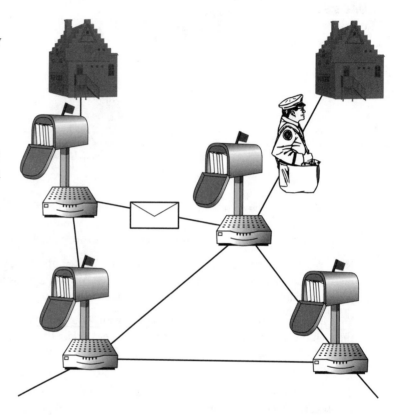

The mail is then given to a postman (router) who knows the exact location of the street and house. The postal service (any router involved with delivery) is not concerned with the sender's address or name, unless the destination (end system) is unreachable for some reason. In this case the postal service may return mail marked Undeliverable to the sender.

The delivery and decisions based on the delivery of mail center around the destination address. At no time does the postal service (any router) change the address of the sender or recipient. However, routing markers are added as mail transits from one postal office to another. These markers are used as indicators throughout the postal infrastructure to identify the distribution centers mail has passed through. These markers can be likened to Data Link addresses in that they specifically identify each entity that handled the mail along the path end to end. These markings are not significant outside of the postal delivery system.

Routers represent the physical delivery system of the postal service. Router interfaces connect cities (networks) and streets (subnets) and serve as the entry (mail box), exit (mail box) for end systems (houses) within these cities and streets. Static or dynamic routing protocols build and maintain local route tables. These route tables represent the physical network infrastructure (similar to the postal infrastructure) identifying paths to networks and subnets. Routers after identifying the destination address, use these route tables to determine the best path between source and destination. Route tables are discussed next.

Route Table

All routers must have a local route table. Routers use different routing mechanisms to build and maintain a table known as a *route table* (also referred to as a *forwarding database*). Several routing mechanisms exist (directly connected, static, default and dynamic). These mechanisms serve as route table input sources providing a router with network and subnet information necessary to build and maintain the route table. Routing methods and mechanisms are discussed in more detail later in this chapter. Similar to the postal service infrastructure map, these tables are used by routers to determine the best path between source and destination when forwarding datagrams. Route tables include a list of all cities (networks) and streets (subnets) known to a router and the address of the post office (the IP address of the next hop router) used to reach that city or street, among other things.

Route tables are built through several input sources, such as directly connected networks, static, default, and dynamic routes. No matter what the source the end result is the same, the router builds a table that identifies known cities (networks) and streets (subnets).

When a router receives a datagram, the destination address is determined and then compared to each route within the route table until an exact or best route match is found. If an exact match is found within the route table, the router readdresses the datagram using its MAC address as the source and the next hop routers address as the destination. It does not change the logical network layer addresses within the datagram. It then sends the datagram out the local interface connected to the link leading to the next hop router.

When the routers does not find a specific match within its route table, the default route (if one exists) is used or the datagram is discarded and an ICMP error is sent to the originator. ICMP is covered in Chapter 2 of this book.

If multiple paths exist to a destination, more than one route may be included in the route table. Typically, when more than one path to a destination exists, one path needs to be selected (as the best path) by the routing protocol and placed in the route table. This would be the primary (active) path the router would use to forward the traffic to that destination. However, some routing protocols support load balancing across multiple paths. Both paths would become active for the destination and placed in the route table. Both active paths could then be alternately used by routers to forward, balancing the traffic load across these paths.

Once a router has built its route table, it must accurately maintain the information. Maintenance might include manual configuration of routes by an administrator or learned route information through the use of dynamic routing protocols. Whatever the method, accuracy is key to a router's capability to successfully forward traffic. The contents of the route table are only as good as the information entered into the route table. Successful communication between remote systems depends on the maintenance of this information. Bad information leads to bad forwarding decisions. Good information leads to good path selection.

Datagram Forwarding

Datagram forwarding begins when an IP host wants to communicate with another system. Routers and routing protocols provide the delivery infrastructure when source and destination systems are not on the same segment. To send a datagram to another host, the sender must first identify whether the destination host is local or remote. To do so it compares its local mask to the destination hosts IP address to determine whether they are on the same or different subnets (streets). If both hosts reside on the same (local) street, there is no need to involve a router. If not, the source host must route the datagram by sending it to its local router for delivery. The addressing of such a datagram includes the network layer IP addresses of the source and destination hosts. However at the Data Link layer MAC addresses are of the source host and the local router (or mailbox) that will be used to deliver the datagram.

So what happens when a router receives a frame in one of its interfaces?

1. It strips off the Data Link header and trailer and passes the datagram to the upper layer routing process.

2. The router examines the logical destination address, conducting a BITwise ANDing comparison against its local mask to determine the destination network address (city and/or street).

3. The router checks its local cached route table to see if it has a specific route to the destination network, subnet, or end host and which local interface should be used to reach the destination.

   • If the destination network address matches a directly attached network or subnet, the router uses a local interface in an attempt to locate the recipient (end system) on that subnet using the end host's IP address.

   • If the router determines that the destination network is not local, the router identifies the local interface and IP address of the next hop router it will use to reach this destination.

   • If however, a route to the specific destination network does not exist in the route table, the router looks to see if a default route is present. A default route is a route used as a last resort when no other route to a destination exists within the route table.

   • If there is no default route specified, it sends a routing error in the form of an ICMP Destination Unreachable message to the originating host. ICMP was discussed in Chapter 2.

4. Once the IP address of either the destination end system or the next hop router has been identified, the router must resolve this address to a MAC address for delivery.

   • The router accomplishes IP-to-MAC resolution by examining its local ARP (the Address Resolution Protocol is a broadcast-based protocol used to resolve IP addresses to MAC addresses) cache first to see if it has resolved the address recently for the destination host or next hop router. If an IP address to MAC address mapping resides in cache, the resolution is complete.

   • If the IP address does not exist in the local ARP cache, the router broadcasts a local ARP request to resolve the network address to a physical address.

5. Once the IP address has been resolved, the router then uses this information to re-encapsulate the Data Link portion of the datagram. Re-encapsulation does not change the logical IP addresses of the source and destination hosts. The router does however add its own MAC address (of the outbound interface) and the destination host or next hop router's MAC address to the Data Link header. The router also calculates a new CRC, adding this to the end of the datagram as a trailer.

Note

Although routers do not modify the source and destination IP address information they do modify some parameters within the IP header. For instance, the TTL timer (previously mentioned in Chapter 2) is decremented by at least 1 second/hop by each forwarding router. Because changing the TTL value is a modification to the datagram the IP header checksum value must be recalculated.

6. After re-encapsulation, it sends the frame out the local interface either directly to the destination host or to the next hop router for forwarding.

7. The next hop router then performs the same process until the datagram reaches the final destination network.

Autonomous Systems and Routing Domains

Most routing occurs within logical boundaries referred to as Autonomous Systems (AS), or routing domains. Up until recently these terms were used interchangeably within the industry to describe a collection of related networks, subnets, and routers that use the same routing protocol and share information within the common area controlled by a single administrative entity. However, that is not necessarily the case these days, and most companies do not operate in this manner. Take an organization's network that spans a large geographic area. It might deploy several different routing protocols (for example, RIP and OSPF) within each geographic location. Each location might have a separate IT (Information Technology) department (administrative body) controlling it. In this example, RIP and OSPF would be considered separate routing domains. Each routing domain consists of the routing protocol (RIP or OSPF) and the networks, subnets, and routers within this domain. The organization's network as a whole, regardless of the number of routing protocols operating within it, is considered a single Autonomous System.

Presently it is more common to use the term *routing domain* when referring to routers and networks sharing a common routing protocol. Figure 3.7 shows a routing domain with a collection of networks and routers running a single routing protocol. The term AS is now used to describe a group of routing domains (see Figure 3.8). For example, an organization running two routing protocols, such as RIP and IGRP, would be considered to have two separate routing domains within a single Autonomous System (logically representing the organizational entity and the routing protocols within it as a whole).

Routing Domain

FIGURE 3.7

An example of a RIP routing domain. A routing domain refers to a collection of networks and subnets associated with routers running the same routing protocol.

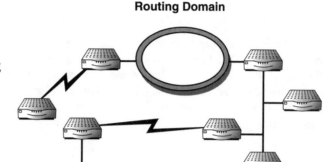

Autonomous with Multiple Routing Domain

Autonomous System

FIGURE 3.8

An Autonomous System consists of multiple routing domains. In this example, there are three separate routing domains RIP, EIGRP and IGRP.

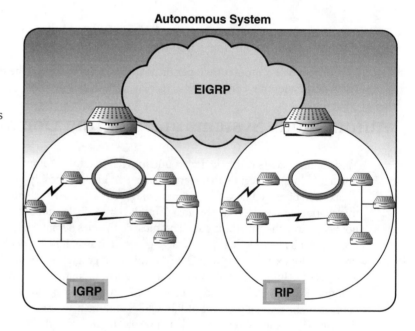

The distinction between routing domain and AS is not always clear because the industry uses these terms sometimes interchangeably. In addition routing protocols, such as IGRP, EIGRP, and OSPF, refer to their routing domains as AS. The Internet community has adopted the term AS to describe major logical network boundaries (for example, ISP or organizations). Each of these AS' may implement any number of internal routing domains, each running a different routing protocol. Routing between and across these AS is handled by an Inter-AS routing protocol, known as BGP. Each of the above referenced protocols will be discussed later in the book.

Routing Mechanisms

How does a router learn about paths (routes) to destinations? There are several routing mechanisms that may be used as input sources to assist a router in building its route table. Typically, routers use a combination of the following routing methods to build a router's route table:

- Directly connected interface

- Static

- Default

- Dynamic

Although there are specific advantages and disadvantages for implementing them, they are not mutually exclusive.

Directly Connected Interface

Directly connected interfaces are routes that are local to the router. That is, the router has an interface directly connected to one or more networks or subnets. These networks are inherently known through the routers configured interface attached to that network. These networks are immediately recognizable and traffic directed to these networks can be forwarded without any help from routing protocols (see Figure 3.9).

In Figure 3.9 each of the routers shown is directly connected to three links. For instance, Router A connects to networks 199.10.1.0, 199.10.2.0, and 199.10.3.0. Because Router A has a direct connection to these networks and the interfaces attached are appropriately configured, they are immediately learned and placed within the router's local route table. Datagrams received by Router A destined for any of these attached networks will be forwarded without assistance.

However, datagrams destined for networks not directly connected to Router A, such as 192.10.4.0, 192.10.5.0, and 192.10.6.0 will not be forwarded as Router A has not learned about those networks (there is no route in the route table) and does not have a directly connected interface (see Figure 3.10). In this case the datagram will be discarded and an ICMP message will be sent back to the source indicating that the destination network or host is unreachable.

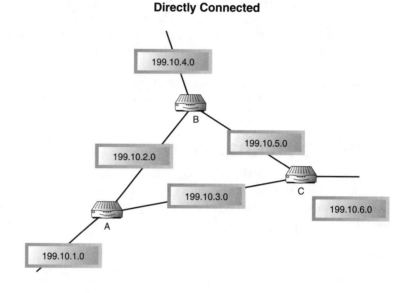

FIGURE 3.9
This network has three Routers (A, B, and C). Each router has three directly connected networks. For example, Router A is directly connected to networks 192.10.1.0, 192.10.2.0, and 192.10.3.0 through local interfaces.

FIGURE 3.10
Route table showing only networks directly connected (indicated by a C in the leftmost column) to Router A. Routes to remote networks are not known.

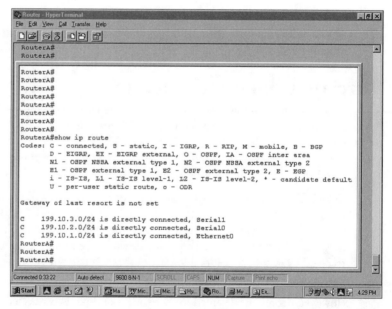

Directly connected routes are always the best method of routing because the router knows the network this datagram is destined for firsthand and does not rely on some other means to learn this route, such as static or dynamic routing protocols. However, when traffic is destined to networks beyond a routers locally attached links help is needed.

Static Routing

Static routes are routes to destination hosts or networks that an administrator has manually entered into the router's route table. Static routes define the IP address of the next hop router and local interface to use when forwarding traffic to a particular destination.

Because this type of route has a static nature, it does not have the capability of adjusting to changes in the network. If the router or interface defined fails or becomes unavailable, the route to the destination fails.

This type of routing method has the advantage of eliminating all traffic related to routing updates. Static routing tends to be ideal where the link is temporary or bandwidth is an issue, so you want to use this method for dial-up networks or point-to-point WAN links. You can implement static routes in conjunction with other routing methods to provide routes to destinations across dial backup links when primary links implementing dynamic routing protocols have failed.

You would not want to design an entire network with only this method because you would have to enter a static route on every router for each network they are not directly attached to, thus highly impractical. In addition, if a link or a router within the internetwork fails or is added, you would have to reconfigure each router, removing the failed route or adding a new route. Meanwhile, routers obviously cannot forward traffic to that destination because the original path has become invalid. Static routing can have an extreme amount of overhead in the form of intense administrative hours spent getting the network up and keeping it going.

You want to implement static routes in very small to small networks, with perhaps as little as 10 to 15 links total. Even then, dynamic routes offer so much more versatility.

Note

Static routes conserve bandwidth because they do not cause routers to generate route update traffic; however, they tend to be time consuming because a system administrator has to manually update routes when changes occur in the network.

Static routes are also ideal for a stub network providing a single dedicated point-to-point WAN connection outside the network to an upstream ISP (Internet Service Provider) providing Internet access. Generally there is no reason to advertise your company's internal subnetworks out to the world through this connection, as most companies are concerned about having their network hacked into by intruders. The connection should only provide internal users access to Internet resources and traveling users with the capability to access network resources and e-mail via the Internet. Probably the only outsider entry you want is someone accessing the corporate Web site. This situation provides a perfect example of where static routing is needed. You can configure a "default route" directed at the upstream router, which keeps your company's internal subnetworks from being advertised while still providing inside users with a way out. Default routes are discussed later in this chapter.

Configuring Static Routing

The network diagram shown in Figure 3.11 shows the IP addresses of router interfaces connecting Routers B and C to A. It also shows Router A's interface types, such as S0 and S1 (Serial 0 and Serial 1), which indicates the specific interfaces on Router A connected to these links. Although the specific configuration of a router's interfaces is beyond the scope of this book, it's important to know which interface a Router must use to reach the next hop.

Note

Configuration examples in this book relate specifically to routing, not to interfaces or other router configurations.

Static Routes

FIGURE 3.11

Router A is connected to two routers through serial connections, one to Router B (Serial 0) and the other to Router C (Serial 1).

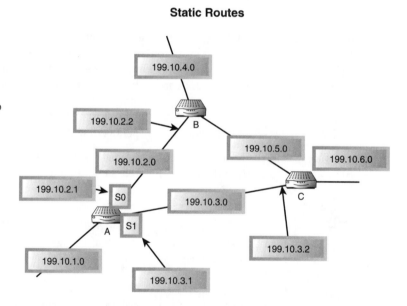

In Figure 3.11, Router A has three directly connected networks. Because they are directly connected to this router, they are immediately known to Router A. The other three networks in this diagram (199.10.4.0, 199.10.5.0, and 199.10.6.0) are remote and therefore unknown to Router A. For Router A to forward datagrams to these remote networks, it must be configured with routes to these networks. Three static route entries must be added to Router A's route table—for example, one route entry pointing to Router B as the next hop router en route to networks 199.10.4.0 and 199.10.5.0 and one route entry pointing to Router C as the next hop to 199.10.6.0. The purpose of these entries is to inform Router A of each remote network (see Figure 3.12).

FIGURE 3.12

Three static routes have been added to Router A.

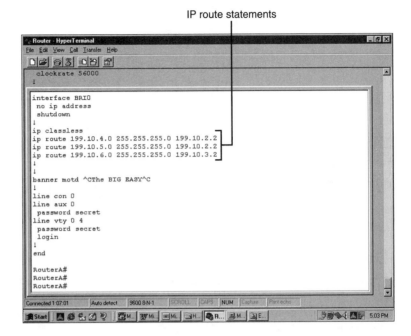

The output in Figure 3.12 is a view of the configuration of Router A (a Cisco router). As you can see Router A has been configured with three static routes using the `ip route` command. The first two statements indicate that to get to network 199.10.4.0 and 199.10.5.0 with the mask 255.255.255.0, use 199.10.2.2 as the next hop router. The last statement says that to get to network 199.10.6.0, mask 255.255.255.0 use 199.10.6.2 as the next hop router. After configuration, Router A now has a path to each of these networks. To verify the routes were entered properly we will view the route table (see Figure 3.13).

Keep in mind that communication is two way. That is, for two devices to have a conversation there must be a path in both directions (forward and reverse). Therefore to complete the configuration each of the other routers (B and C) in the diagram would need to also be configured with static routes to all networks they are not directly connected to. For example, Router B would need three static routes—one each to network 199.10.1.0, 199.10.3.0, and 199.10.6.0—and Router C would need routes to 199.10.1.0, 199.10.2.0, and 199.10.4.0. After all routers are configured with specific paths to all remote networks they would be able to forward traffic to and between them. In addition, as new routes become available or routes fail adjustments to each router would need to be made adding or removing routes to reflect these changes.

FIGURE 3.13

Three static routes have been added to the router's route table (indicated by an S in the leftmost column).

```
Router - HyperTerminal
File  Edit  View  Call  Transfer  Help

RouterA#
RouterA#

RouterA#
RouterA#
RouterA#
RouterA#show ip route
Codes: C - connected, S - static, I - IGRP, R - RIP, M - mobile, B - BGP
       D - EIGRP, EX - EIGRP external, O - OSPF, IA - OSPF inter area
       N1 - OSPF NSSA external type 1, N2 - OSPF NSSA external type 2
       E1 - OSPF external type 1, E2 - OSPF external type 2, E - EGP
       i - IS-IS, L1 - IS-IS level-1, L2 - IS-IS level-2, * - candidate default
       U - per-user static route, o - ODR

Gateway of last resort is not set

C    199.10.3.0/24 is directly connected, Serial1
C    199.10.2.0/24 is directly connected, Serial0
C    199.10.1.0/24 is directly connected, Ethernet0
S    199.10.6.0/24 [1/0] via 199.10.3.2
S    199.10.5.0/24 [1/0] via 199.10.2.2
S    199.10.4.0/24 [1/0] via 199.10.2.2
RouterA#
RouterA#
RouterA#
RouterA#
RouterA#

Connected 1:08:13    Auto detect    9600 8-N-1    SCROLL  CAPS  NUM  Capture  Print echo

Start                                                                    5:04 PM
```

Default Routing

Every IP host needs to have a default route either manually configured or dynamically learned. Default routes provide end hosts a way out of their local subnet and routers with a router of last resort if no other route (specifically relating to the destination) exists in the routers route table.

End hosts, although capable, do not usually maintain their own local route tables, they rely on local routers to forward traffic to remote hosts. For an end host to communicate with hosts beyond their local segment, an administrator at a minimum must configure it with an IP address of a router (known as the Default Router). You can, depending on the vendor implementation, configure end hosts to send datagrams to an alternate router if the first one on the list becomes unavailable. If an end host does not have a default router configured, it limits this host to communicating to hosts on its local segment only.

Routers use default routing as a last resort when all other methods (directly connected, static, or dynamic) have been exhausted. Routers inspect received datagrams to identify the logical Network layer address of the ultimate destination. If a directly connected static or dynamic route exists within the router's route table, it forwards the datagram.

If the destination remains unknown, that is, no method of routing has resulted in a learned route, it forces the router to use a default route. Typically, administrators implement default routes on point-to-point (a link with only two routers) or dial-up connections, linking a company's network to the outside work.

You may implement dynamic or static routes within the company's network to facilitate the learning of route information of local links. You could then use a default route to direct all traffic outside your network regardless of destination. This provides a good method because somewhere near 80,000 plus routes exist on the Internet and it would overwhelm routers if they had to learn and maintain each one of these routes. By implementing a default route the router simply directs all traffic to unknown destinations through the default path, typically serviced by an ISP.

Default routes are static routes that are used to define a route to an unknown destination. Typically you won't need to configure a default route on a router because the router should already know how to route a frame to a destination by consulting their route table for a known path. However, if the router has no learned path, it uses the default route statement (also known as the router of last resort).

Figure 3.14 shows the configuration of a default route on a Cisco router.

IP route

FIGURE 3.14
The values for the destination network and subnet mask fields are all zeros. The zeros represent any unknown destination.

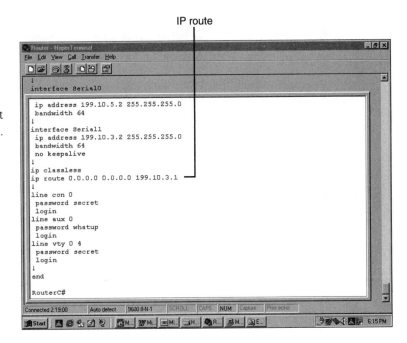

In Figure 3.14 a default route statement has been added to a router. The default route specifies that to get to any unknown network, with any mask, the router should use 199.10.2.1 as its Default Router. Figure 3.15 shows a router's route table with a default route.

FIGURE 3.15

An output screen of a router's route table with a default route configured.

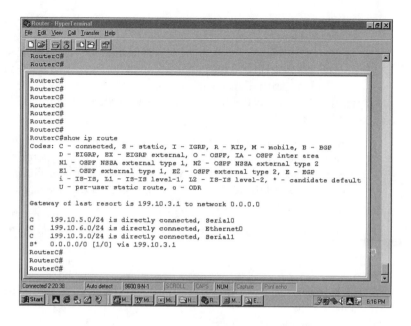

Router output screens vary from vendor to vendor, figure 3.15 shows a sample route table taken from a Cisco router. In this example, the S (in the leftmost column) indicates the route has been statically entered. The * signifies that this route is a candidate for default routing. Also note that the Gateway of last resort is now set, indicating this route will be used when no other route exists in the table.

Interior Versus Exterior Routing Protocols

Routing protocols fall into two categories, Interior and Exterior. Interior protocols called IGPs (Interior Gateway Protocols), refer to any routing protocol used exclusively within an Autonomous System, providing Intra-AS routing. Each IGP represents a single routing domain within the AS. Multiple IGPS may exist within an AS. Exterior protocols called EGPs (Exterior Gateway Protocols) are routing protocols that facilitate routing between and across different AS'. EGPs provide Inter-AS routing. IGP and EGP are discussed later in this chapter.

IGP (Interior Gateway Protocols)

The term *IGP* (Interior Gateway Protocol) is used to describe any routing protocol operating as a separate routing domain within an AS. IGPs learn about routes to networks that are internal to the AS, hence the name *Interior*.

Within an organization's network there may be one or more routing protocols (IGPs) keeping track of the routes to subnets within the AS. Routers running a single IGP (routing protocol) only share route information with other routers running the same routing protocol. Routers running more than one IGP, like RIP and OSPF, are participants in two separate routing domains. These routers are referred to as border routers, that is, they sit on the border between two IGP routing domains. Some examples of IGP protocols are: RIP, OSPF, and IGRP. Individual routing protocols will be discussed throughout this book.

Note

Routing protocols that reside within an organization's AS are considered IGPs. Each IGP, consisting of subnets and connected routers, represents a separate routing domain.

IGPs are responsible for building and maintaining route information within a single Autonomous System (see Figure 3.16).

FIGURE 3.16
There are two IGPs (RIP and IGRP) running within a single Autonomous System. The router connecting the IGPs is a border router, running both RIP (on its lower interface) and IGRP (on its upper interface).

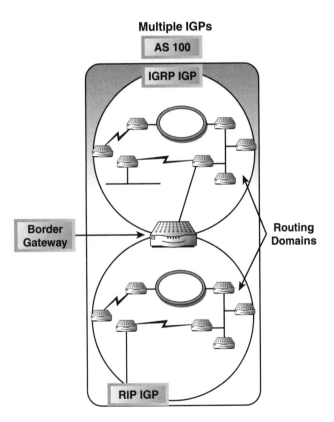

In Figure 3.16, two IGPs exist within the AS. All routers running RIP will learn about networks and subnets within their routing domain only. Routers in the IGRP domain will only learn routes from this domain. The router in the middle of the diagram is a border router, running more than one routing protocol (RIP and IGRP) and will therefore learn about routes from both routing domains.

EGP (Exterior Gateway Protocols)

Exterior Gateway Protocols, such as BGP (Border Gateway Protocol), are designed to serve as a conduit for communication between autonomous systems. BGP is the most popular inter-autonomous system (or Inter-AS) routing protocol used throughout the Internet community. EGP protocols connect separate AS' together providing a transit path between and through these AS' to facilitate traffic forwarding across the Internet (see Figure 3.17).

FIGURE 3.17
Multiple AS' (AS 1 and AS 2) are connected by border routers running both IGP and EGP routing protocols. The EGP protocol used in this example is BGP (Border Gateway Protocol).
    EGP protocols only

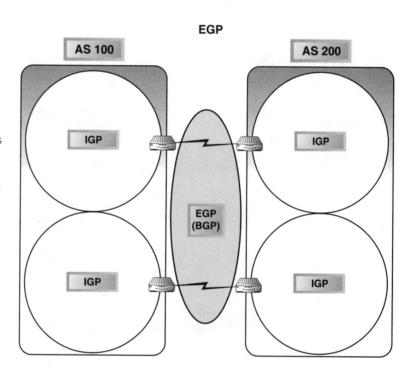

recognize the AS within the routing hierarchy, ignoring the IGPs. Border routers from different AS' typically run some type of IGP over the interfaces within their home AS and BGP or some other EGP over the external interface used to connect this AS to a remote AS. A full discussion of BGP and inter-autonomous system routing can be found in Chapter 7, "Border Gateway Protocol (BGP)."

Note

Routers running multiple routing protocols for the purpose of connecting routing domains or AS' are referred to as *Border* routers.

Routing Metrics and Costs

Metrics are cost values used by routers to determine the best path to a destination network. Several factors help dynamic routing protocols decide which is the preferred or shortest path to a particular destination. These factors are known as metrics and algorithms.

Metrics are the network variables used in deciding what path is preferred in terms of these metrics. For some routing protocols these metrics are static and may not be changed. For other routing protocols these values may be assigned by a network administrator. The most common metric values are hop, bandwidth, delay, reliability, load, and cost.

Hop

A hop is a metric value used to measure distance based on the number of networks a datagram traverses. Each time a router forwards a datagram onto a segment this counts as a single hop. Routing protocols that observe hops as their primary metric value consider the best or preferred path (when multiple paths exist) to a destination to be the one with the least number of network hops (see Figure 3.18).

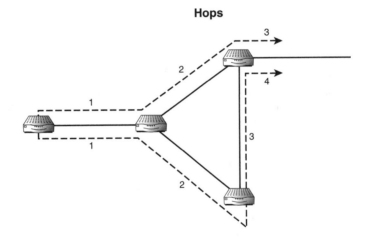

Hops

FIGURE 3.18
The upper path to network X is preferred because it involves only three hops.

In Figure 3.18, the upper path consists of three network hops, whereas the lower path has four hops. The assumption of the hop metric, is that the path with the least number of hops is the always the best route.

Routing protocols that only reference hops as their metric do not always select the best path through a network. Just because a path to a destination contains fewer network hops than another does not make it best. The upper path may contain a slower link, such as 56Kb dial-up link along the second hop, whereas the lower path may consist of more hops but faster links, such as gigabit Ethernet. If this were the case, the lower path would undoubtedly be faster than the upper. However routing protocols that use hops do not consider other metric values in their routing decisions.

Bandwidth

Protocols that consider the capacity of a link use this).metric. Bandwidth is measured in terms of bits per second. Links that support higher transfer rates like gigabit are preferred over lower capacity links like 56Kb. These protocols determine and consider the bandwidth capacity of each link along the path end to end. The path with the overall higher bandwidth is chosen as the best route (see Figure 3.19).

Bandwidth

FIGURE 3.19
The lower path is longer (in terms of hops), but preferred because the bandwidth capacity end to end is greater than the upper path.

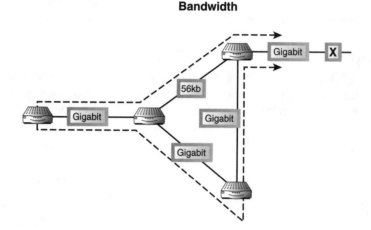

In Figure 3.19, the upper path consists of three hops. The first and last are gigabit Ethernet, the second is low-speed 56Kb link. The lower path is four hops, with all hops offering gigabit capacity. Although the lower path is longer in terms of hops, it is much faster in terms of bandwidth capacity end to end.

Delay

Delay is measured in tens of microseconds (the symbol μ is used to indicate this). Delay represents the amount of time it takes for a router to process, queue, and transmit a datagram out an interface. Protocols that use this metric must determine the delay values for all links along the path end to end, considering the path with the lowest (cumulative) delay to be a better route (see Figure 3.20).

Although the lower path in Figure 3.19 is obviously longer in terms of hops, it is faster in terms of delay. The lower path has an overall delay time of 30 microseconds end to end, while the upper path has a delay of 60 microseconds. The lower the delay time the better the path.

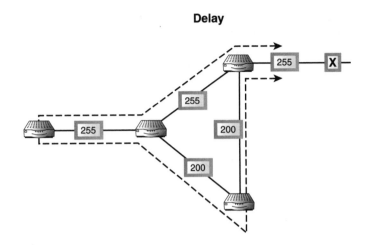

FIGURE 3.20
The upper path has an end to end delay of 60μ. The lower path has a delay of 300μ, making it the preferred path.

Reliability

Although this metric may be configured as a fixed value by an administrator, it is generally measured dynamically over a specific time frame, such as five seconds. Routers observe attached links, reporting problems, such as link failures, interface errors, lost datagrams and so on. Links experiencing more problems would be considered less reliable than others making them less desirable paths—the higher the reliability the better the path. Because network conditions are constantly changing, link reliability will change. This value is generally measured as a percentage of 255, with 255 being the most reliable and 1 being least reliable (see Figure 3.21).

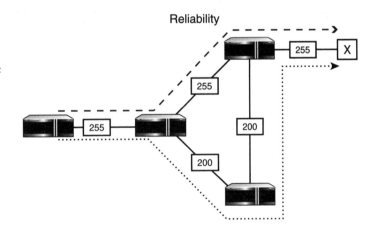

FIGURE 3.21
The lower path contains links that are less reliable than the upper path.

In Figure 3.21 two of the links along the lower path have been experiencing intermittent problems. Because of these problems, the reliability factor for this path are lower (200) than the upper path. The upper path has not experienced any link or datagram delivery problems and therefore has a history of providing more reliable data delivery.

Load

Load is a variable value, generally measured over a five-second window indicating the traffic load over a specific link. Load measures the amount of traffic occupying the link over this time frame as a percentage of the link's total capacity. The value 255 is equivalent to 100% utilization or load—the higher the value the higher the traffic load (bandwidth utilization) across this link.

As traffic increases, this value increases. Values approaching 255 indicate congestion, while lower values indicate moderate traffic loads—the lower the value, the less congested the path, the more preferred (see Figure 3.22). This value may be manually configured as a static value by an administrator or it may be dynamically tracked allowing it to adjust as traffic patterns within the network change.

Load

FIGURE 3.22
The upper path contains three links. The last two show a 128 load value, which represents 50% bandwidth utilization. The lower path has lower load values and is the preferred path.

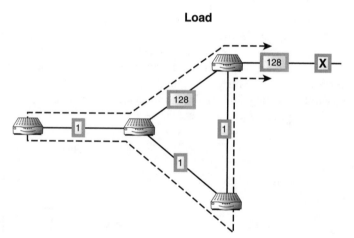

It is important to remember that as traffic increases load across a link will increase. This value changes as traffic patterns change. Routing protocols using this value can recognize when a path is becoming congested and use an alternate path during that time.

Cost

Network administrators can affect the way routers make path decisions by setting arbitrary metric values on links along the path end to end. These arbitrary values are typically single integers with lower values indicating better paths.

Distance Vector Routing

Routing protocols fall into two main categories, Distance Vector or Link State. Generally speaking Distance Vector protocols determine best path on how far the destination is, while Link State protocols are capable of using more sophisticated methods taking into consideration link variables, such as bandwidth, delay, reliability and load. We will discuss Distance Vector protocols and their characteristics first and then move on to Link State protocols. We will address specific routing protocols in later chapters.

Distance Vector protocols judge best path on how far it is. Distance can be hops or a combination of metrics calculated to represent a distance value. The following lists the IP Distance Vector routing protocols still in use today and the metric that they use for determining the best path:

- RIP v1 (hops)

- RIP v2 (hops)

- IGRP (combined metric, bandwidth and delay)

The best known and most popular Distance Vector protocol to date is IP RIP (Routing Information Protocol). There are two versions IP RIP, one and two. IGRP was originally developed by Cisco Systems and also supports the routing of IP traffic. You will find a detailed discussion about IP RIP v1 and v2 in Chapter 4 and IGRP in Chapter 5.

Route Updates

All routing protocols exchange information about networks and subnets through route updates. Route updates carry the reachability information routers need to build and maintain their route tables. Some routing protocols transmit these updates as broadcasts to everyone on the subnet while others send them out as multicasts (addressed to devices belonging to a multicast group).

Broadcasts are addressed to 255.255.255.255 and are received and processed by all hosts and routers on the local subnet. This adds unnecessary overhead and processing to hosts that do not function as routers. For instance, IP RIPv1 and IGRP both use broadcasts to exchange route information. RIPv2 addresses these issues by multicasting route updates. Multicast routing is discussed in Chapter 11, "IP Multicast Routing." All of the routing protocols mentioned here use period timers to time the transmission of their updates.

Upon initialization, all routers (regardless of routing protocol) send out their entire route tables to neighbor routers. Thereafter updates (depending on routing protocol) are either sent using periodic timers or sent when an event, such as a change in the network occurs causing (triggering) the update to be sent. Routing protocols that send periodic updates, send them even though no change has occurred in the network, wasting bandwidth. When a new route becomes available or one fails, the entire table is sent.

The constant broadcasting of route information adds unnecessary traffic to the network and wastes bandwidth. Multicasts are in essence broadcasts in that everyone on the subnet receives them. However, only those devices that belong to the multicast group fully process the datagram and therefore multicasts reduce the overhead hosts incur by processing datagrams they do not care about.

Metrics

Metric values were discussed earlier in this chapter. Metrics are values routing protocols use to determine the best path to a destination, when multiple paths exist. The metric(s) used depends on the routing protocol implemented. For instance, IP RIP v1 and v2 both use hops as their distance value. IGRP uses a combined metric value consisting of bandwidth and delay. While IGRP is capable of using bandwidth, delay, reliability and load, it generally is not configured to do so.

VLSM

If you recall from our discussion of IP addressing and VLSM in Chapter 2, VLSMs are the extension of standard classful masks (A, B, and C) to include subnets. Some routing protocols understand subnetting through the use of VLSMs, while others do not. Routing protocols that carry the subnet mask within their route updates are able to recognize subnets and forward datagrams within networks that have been subnetted. Routing protocols that do not carry these masks are considered classful routing protocols; that is, they only understand major classful networks (A, B, and C).

By including the subnet mask within a routing update, the receiving router not only knows what network is being advertised, but the exact subnet mask to use with this mask. If you recall from our Chapter 2 discussion, the subnet mask is used to determine which part of an IP address is the network or subnet. If no mask is included, this information is unknown and only the classful major network can be assumed. This causes problems when a classful routing protocol is implemented within a network that has been subnetted.

ToS

Routing protocols that are ToS-capable are able to make routing decisions based on the bits contained within the ToS filed of the IP header. These bits are set by end systems requesting a specific level of datagram forwarding.

The Type of Service bits contained within the IP header of datagrams were discussed in Chapter 2. Chapter 10, "Type of Service and Quality of Service Routing," has also been devoted to further exploring ToS and QoS. Please refer to those chapters for more detailed information.

Load Balancing

Load balancing is a feature a router can employ when multiple paths exist to a destination. There are two main types of load balancing, equal and unequal. When both paths have equal cost (for example, both are two hops away) datagrams may alternately be forwarded across both paths evenly distributing the traffic load.

All dynamic routing protocols support this type of load balancing. However, when unequal cost paths exist there must be a configured threshold by which a routing protocol can determine whether the variance between the paths is similar enough to justify or even perform load balancing across them. Some routing protocols can support load balancing across two to six active paths simultaneously.

Maximum Network Diameter

Distance Vector networks such as RIP are limited in scope (diameter). These routing protocols were not designed to operate in medium to large internetworks with hundreds of links and routers connecting hundreds or even thousands of hosts. The maximum network diameter specifies the distance a datagram may travel (for example, the maximum number of hops) before the destination is considered unreachable, causing the datagram to be discarded. This maximum distance is measured in hops from transmitter to receiver. You can think of the maximum rule as "No two devices can communicate through more than x hops."

Note
IP RIP v1 and v2 both have a maximum hop count of 15, which means anything beyond that is unreachable. IGRP's maximum is 255 hops.

As datagrams traverse the network routers forward them and increment the hop count by one before passing it on to the next hop router. Using RIP as an example, when a datagram reaches the 15th router, that router must discard the datagram because a value of 16 or greater is considered too far by RIP. The router discarding the datagram generates an ICMP message back to the source indicating that the destination is unreachable.

Routers also use this maximum hop count value to maintain their route tables. When a network link fails, the router sends news of this failure in its next route update. It relays this news by applying a hop count one higher than the maximum (16 for RIP and 256 for IGRP) to the failed link, which indicates the distance to this network as infinity (unreachable). Routers receiving this news know to remove this route from their route table.

Authentication

Routing updates can easily be intercepted by unauthorized routers placed on the network. Some routing protocols do not have any means of authenticating a neighbor router before giving up route information. Others have simple clear text passwords, which offer some security but can be learned by hackers scanning the network with any protocol analysis tool. More sophisticated routing protocols can be configured to use clear text or encrypted authentication. The configuration and use of authentication varies. However, when used, all routers must share the same password to exchange route information.

Convergence

Convergence is achieved when all routers within a routing domain agree on reachability information. Distance Vector routing protocols require that each router send its entire route table to all of its neighboring routers. Timers control how often updates are sent. When the router receives updates, it must recompute all routes and update their route tables before they can forward traffic.

Distance Vector routing protocols are slow in converging and therefore are highly susceptible to routing loops. Routing loops and loop avoidance mechanisms will be discussed later in this chapter.

The time that elapses before all routers have processed route updates and modified their tables is called convergence time. Convergence is an important concept because when a link or a router fails, no data passes within the internetwork until all the router's tables are fully updated.

Distance Vector Characteristics

In the previous sections we discussed Distance Vector routing characteristics. Table 3.1 provides a quick list comparing the characteristics of RIP v1, RIP v2 and IGRP. As a network engineer implementing a routing protocol, it is necessary to be familiar with the characteristics of the routing protocols you are evaluating prior to implementation. For example, if IP hosts on your network are separated by more than 15 subnets, RIP v1 or v2 would not be your choice. RIP v1 and v2 are limited to a maximum distance (hop count) of 15, whereas IGRP supports up to a maximum of 255 hops.

TABLE 3.1   Distance Vector Characteristics

Characteristic	Routing Protocol		
	RIP v1	RIP v2	IGRP
Route Updates:			
Broadcasts	X		X
Multicasts		X	
Includes entire route table	X	X	X
Periodic timer	30 seconds	30 seconds	90 seconds
Metrics:			
Hops	X	X	
Combined Metrics:			
Bandwidth and Delay			X
VLSM		X	
ToS			X

TABLE 3.1   (continued)

Characteristic	Routing Protocol		
	RIP v1	RIP v2	IGRP
Load balancing:			
Equal Cost	X	X	X
Unequal Cost			X
Maximum network diameter	15 hops	15 hops	255 hops*
Authentication		X	

Although IGRP observes a maximum network diameter of 255 hops, it does not use this as a distance value in path selection.

In the previous sections each routing characteristic was discussed. This chart is meant to summarize the characteristics supported by RIP v1, v2 and IGRP.

Routing Loops and Remedies

One of the main problems inherent with Distance Vector routing protocols is routing loops. Routing loops occur in networks when old (bad) route information exists in a route table. The problem stems primarily from the periodic scheduled route updates that result in slow convergence.

For example, IP RIP updates are broadcast every 30 seconds by default. This allows enough time to elapse, causing slow convergence. Because of the intervals between the periodic route updates, routers may not learn about topology changes in a timely manner. In this case, they may be relying on outdated or incorrect route information. Slow convergence can result in routing loops, causing datagrams to bounce between routers endlessly if not detected, causing the routers to start a count to infinity. Routing protocols can take advantage of one or more loop avoidance mechanisms to minimize the impact a loop has on the network.

These techniques, or combinations of these techniques, can minimize routing loops passing on incorrect routing information. The different techniques are count to infinity, split horizon, poison reverse and holddown timers.

- Count to infinity (maximum hop count, see Figure 3.23)
- Holddowns
- Split horizon (see Figure 3.23)
- Poison reverse (see Figure 3.24)

Implementations vary based on vendor support and routing protocol.

Count to Infinity

Count to infinity is a loop avoidance mechanism that sets a maximum hop count value, that, when exceeded, equates to infinity hops (or destination unreachable). The maximum hop count for RIP is 15 and IGRP is 255. Any value above this is considered infinity (unreachable).

To understand this mechanism you need to understand how routers handle datagrams when forwarding them. As a router processes and forwards a datagram, it decrements two values within the IP header, the TTL timer and increment the hop count. TTL was discussed in Chapter 2. Each router assumes, from its perspective, the destination network exists one hop further than the router that sent them the datagram.

If a loop exists in the network, this process would go on forever without some way of controlling it. Luckily, Distance Vector routing protocols specify an infinity value (RIP = 16 and IGRP = 256) that, when reached, causes an endlessly circulating datagram to be dropped.

If for some reason datagrams continue to be forwarded after the maximum hop has been exceeded (infinity has been reached), then a fall back method, the TTL timer, deals with the vigilante datagram. When the TTL timer within an IP header reaches zero, the router trashes the datagram. With an infinity value and TTL timer providing a backup, this combination provides a viable remedy to most routing loops.

Count to Infinity

FIGURE 3.23

Distance-vector protocols limit the distance (hops) a datagram may traverse. If a route loop exists within the topology, the router automatically trashes the datagram when it exceeds the maximum hop (for RIP the maximum is 15, for IGRP the maximum is 255), stopping the count to infinity.

Split Horizon

Split horizon prevents information being sent back in the direction from which that information was received (see Figure 3.24). When a change occurs in the network, routers only advertise that change in one direction, which means that they send the update out to all other ports except the one from which it was learned.

With split horizon, any router is the starting point. split horizon sends only information learned from other ports. Split horizon never sends information out the same port it learned it from.

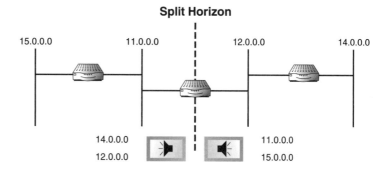

FIGURE 3.24

Routing information learned from an interface is never advertised back out that same interface

The split horizon rule states that "route information learned through an interface may not be transmitted out that same interface." In Figure 3.23, the middle router learns about networks 12.0.0.0 and 14.0.0.0 from the interface on the right and can only propagate this information out the opposite interface. It learns about networks 11.0.0.0 and 15.0.0.0 from the interface on the left and can only propagate this information out the opposite interface.

Poison Reverse

Poison reverse allows routers to break the split horizon rule by advertising information learned from an interface out the same interface. However, it can advertise routes learned from an interface out the same interface with a 16 hop count, which indicates a destination unreachable, "poisoning" the route. Routers with a route with a better metric (hop count) to the network ignore the destination unreachable update.

Poison reverse prevents updates with inconsistencies from spreading. Routers poison a route by sending out a broadcast with an infinity hop count, or destination unreachable. While the other routers slowly converge, the router maintains the poisoned route in its table and ignores updates from other routers about better routes to the network.

Poison reverse when implemented takes precedence over split horizon. When a router learns that a route has become unavailable, it overrides split horizon by advertising the failed route with an infinity hop count (destination unreachable) out all the interfaces including the one it was received on (see Figure 3.25). This allows a router to advertise out the same interface it learned information on, but poisons the route by using a value greater than the maximum hop count. Routers receiving this advertisement assume the destination network is unreachable.

FIGURE 3.25

A router advertising information out the same interface it learned the information from with an infinity hop value, indicating the route is unreachable.

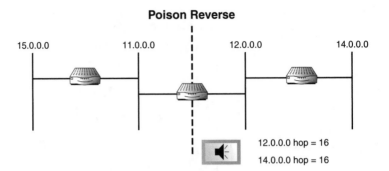

Holddown Timers

Another technique typically used in combination with route poisoning is holddown timers. Holddown timers start as soon as a router receives an update from a neighbor indicating that an attached network has gone down. Until the timer elapses, the router ignores updates regarding this route from other routers unless it receives an update from the neighboring router that initially informed the network of the downed link. The timer stops if it receives a message from the neighboring router. At that point, the network is marked as reachable again and the route table is updated. .

Routers use holddown timers after they have learned that a route is unavailable to ensure that this route will not be mistakenly reinstated by an advertisement received from another router that has not yet learned about this route being unavailable. Typically this timer is greater than the total convergence time, providing time for accurate information to be learned, consolidated, and propagated through the network by all routers.

The holddown timer causes the router to ignore any new updates to invalid destination routes that contain a similar or less favorable metric value than its own. This prevents an unavailable route from being reinstated inadvertently. Routers accept and reinstate invalid routes if it receives a new update with a better metric than their own or the holddown timer has expired.

Link State Routing

Link State Routing protocols provide greater flexibility and sophistication than their Distance Vector counterparts. They reduce overall broadcast traffic and make better decisions about routing by taking characteristics such as bandwidth, delay, reliability, and load into consideration (see Table 3.3), instead of basing their decisions solely on distance or hop count.

Examples of Link State Routing protocols are OSPF and IS-IS which only supports IP traffic, and Novell's NLSP (NetWare Link State Protocol), which only supports IPX. Other than mentioning NLSP here, it will not be discussed further. OSPF is covered in Chapter 6 and IS-IS is covered in Chapter 8.

TABLE 3.3   Link State Characteristics

Characteristic	Routing Protocol	
	OSPF	IS-IS
Route Updates:		
Multicasts	X	X
Triggered Updates	X	X
After initial route table exchange.	X	X
Only sends changed route information		
Databases and Tables:		
Neighbor (Adjacency)	X	X
Topology Map(Link State)	X	X
Route (Forwarding)	X	X
Metrics:		
Various. Link State protocols do share		
common values.		
OSPF uses Bandwidth only. Refer to Chapter 6.		
IS-IS may use Default, Delay, Expense, and/or Error		
(refer to Chapter 8).		
VLSM	X	X
ToS	X	X
Load balancing:		
Equal Cost	X	X
Unequal Cost	X	X
Authentication	X	X

General Link State Operation

Link State Routing protocols reduce broadcast traffic because they do not send out periodic broadcasts or send out their entire tables with each broadcast. Link state routing protocols exchange a complete copy of their route tables upon initialization. Thereafter route updates are multicast only when a change has occurred (triggered by a change in the topology), including only the change in the update not the entire table. Changes are flooded immediately and computed in parallel. If no changes occur, they do not generate an update.

Triggered updates improve convergence time by requiring routers to send an update message immediately upon learning of a route change. These updates are triggered by some event, such as a new link becoming available or an existing link failing.

When these changes do occur, they only propagate to and affect routers within the same logical area. In addition link state protocols support VLSM (Variable Length Subnet Masks), which allows routers to recognize and forward traffic to subnets within a network. Unlike most distance vector routing protocols, link state updates include the subnet mask, which allows a router to clearly identify the exact subnet to forward traffic to. This is also referred to as classless routing, which means that the routing protocol does not assume a specific default class type address and mask are being used.

All Link State protocols must build and maintain three separate tables (also referred to as databases): The neighbor table (also known as Adjacency database), Topology Map (also known as Link State database) and Route Table (also known as Forwarding database). Before traffic can be forwarded certain things must happen.

1. All routers attached to the same network must identify themselves and their neighbors, establishing a relationship with one another (referred to as adjacency). Adjacent routers form this relationship through the exchange of hello messages. From these hellos each local router builds its first table (the neighbor). Figure 3.26 shows the neighbor hello exchange and 3.27 shows a routers neighbor table. If this first stage fails, routing will never occur.

Note

Within hello messages routers announce themselves, identify the links they are directly attached to and the state of these links (up or down), among other things.

2. Once the adjacency relationship is intact, route information may be exchanged by flooding updates throughout the routing domain. Unlike Distance Vector routing protocols, which must receive, process, and wait for their periodic timer to expire before sending route updates on. Any change in the network triggers Link State protocols to immediately flood route updates to all segments except the one from which it was received, with all routers processing these updates in parallel. This speeds up convergence as routers can virtually receive and process updates simultaneously.

3. From received route updates routers build and maintain local Topology Maps (also known as Link State database) of the entire routing domain. Unlike distance vector protocols, which do maintain a complete picture of the network, Link State protocols have first-hand knowledge of all networks and subnets within their area and the paths to reach these networks.

4. Each router then builds a logical tree structure placing itself in the root position, with all networks and subnets emanating from this root.

5. All Link State routing protocols derive their route table by running Dijikstra's SPF (Shortest Path First) algorithm against the tree (topology map or Link State database) placing lowest cost paths to destinations in the route table (also known as Forwarding Database).

FIGURE 3.26
Link state routers
exchange hello messages.

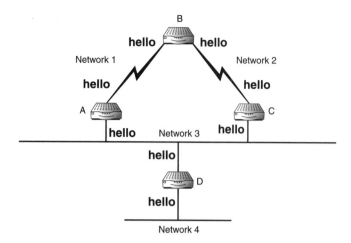

FIGURE 3.27
Router D has discovered
two neighbors on
network 3.

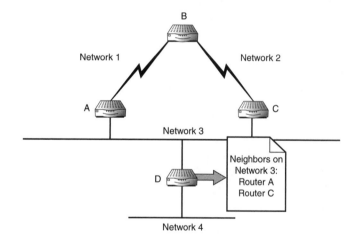

The main drawbacks to Link State protocols are the amount of CPU overhead involved in calculating route changes and memory resources that are required to store neighbor tables, route tables, and a complete topology map.

Summary

Some protocols are routable and others are nonroutable. Nonroutable protocols are typically broadcast-based, which adds overhead and traffic to a network. Nonroutable protocols do not contain network layer addressing information that routers need to determine the destination of network or host traffic. However, any protocol that has layer three logical network addressing can be routed.

Routers serve as traffic forwarders for remote end systems. Routing protocols and mechanisms are needed to build and maintain route information. To forward traffic, routers need to know the destination address, from which source it can learn the path to a given destination, the best path, and a way of verifying the most current path upon which to take. When a router receives a frame, it identifies the destination network address and checks its route table to determine the best path. Routers use a combination of the following routing methods to build a router's route table: directly connected interface, static, default, and dynamic.

The term IGP (Interior Gateway Protocol) describes any routing protocol operating as a separate routing domain within an AS. EGPs (Exterior Gateway Protocols), such as BGP (Border Gateway Protocol), serve as a conduit for communication between autonomous systems.

Routing protocols fall into two main categories, Distance Vector or Link State. Distance Vector protocols determine best path on how far away the destination is (distance) while Link State protocols can use more sophisticated methods to determine the best path. Link State can take into consideration link variables, such as bandwidth, delay, reliability, and load. When determining the best path, Distance Vector protocols use hops or a combination of calculated metrics that represent a distance value.

Chapter Quiz

1. Name the four ways routers can learn about networks and subnets.

2. What is the name of the mechanism referred to as the router of last resort?

3. What metric is used by both IP RIP v1 and v2?

4. What is IGP?

5. What is EGP?

6. Describe an AS.

7. What is a Routing Domain?

8. Name the four main loop remedies.

9. What two metric values does IGRP use by default?

10. What is the purpose of hello messages in Link State routing?

CHAPTER 4

RIP V1 AND V2

You will learn about the following in this chapter:

- RIP v1 and v2 operation and functions

- Similarities and differences of RIP v1 and v2

- Advantages and disadvantages of RIP

- RIP timers

- RIP v1 and v2 headers and fields

- How end hosts and servers support RIP

RIP (Routing Information Protocol)

RFCs 1058 (version 1) and 2453 (version 2) define the RIP (Routing Information Protocol). Both versions of the RIP protocol were originally designed around Xerox's XNS protocol suite and the routeD program integrated into the Berkeley implementation of Unix.

The RIP protocol may run on end hosts or routers. Although it runs on top of UDP (transport layer) and IP (network layer), utilizing UDP port 520, it is classified as a Network layer protocol because its function and operation are based on the forwarding of network layer datagrams. Functioning as an IGP (Interior Gateway Protocol), RIP provides route determination within an Autonomous System. RIP works best when implemented on small-sized networks because of its limitations, which we discuss later in this chapter.

RIP exhibits the following characteristics:

- Broadcast–based—Routers on the same segment exchange route updates through broadcasts.

- IGP—RIP is best used as an IGP interior routing protocol. IGP routing protocols keep track of routes internal to an organization's internetwork.

- Works best on small-sized networks—Because RIP implements broadcasts and is limited in diameter it is not suitable for medium to large networks.

- Distance-vector routing protocol—RIP uses hops as its distance metric for making best path selection to a destination.

- Metric value is hops—A hop is the unit of distance used by RIP routers. Each network a datagram traverses is considered a single hop. The maximum number of hops is 15.

- Periodic updates—RIP routers use periodic update timers to control route broadcasts. The periodic update timer is 30 seconds.

- Sends out the entire route table, whether or not changes have occurred within the network—Routers broadcast route updates to neighbor routers at regular intervals, including all (changed and unchanged) route entries from their route table.

- Limited to a maximum network diameter of 15 hops—The maximum number of networks a datagram may traverse is 15 (hops). Any value above this is considered unreachable.

As a distance-vector based routing protocol, RIP implements the Bellman-Ford (also referred to as Ford-Fulkerson) algorithm to determine best path selection. RIP bases best path selection to a destination by the shortest distance, measured in hops with a maximum distance of 15. Updates are sent out using periodic updates, including all information in the route tables, even when no changes have occurred in the network. Although many other routing protocols exist today with more intelligent and efficient route selection, RIP v1 remains the most popular protocol in use.

As previously mentioned in this chapter, two versions of RIP exist, version 1 and 2. We will begin with a full discussion of version 1, and then discuss the differences between the two. Version 1 remains the most widely used routing protocol in the world today because of its simplicity. RIP v1 has the advantage of being easy to understand and implement. Although versions 1 and 2 have similarities, version 2 has added extensions, which overcome some of the limitations of the version specification. We will discuss version 2 later in this chapter.

RIP v1 Operation

End hosts or routers may implement RIP to keep track of routes to destinations, such as hosts, networks, subnets, and default routes. End hosts or routers learn routes to destinations via route updates that devices exchange dynamically on the local segment via periodic broadcasts. Although end hosts are capable (if configured) of running RIP, they generally do not, instead relying on routers to keep track of route information.

When RIP is enabled on an end host or router a local UDP port is activated for the routing process. All devices running RIP listen on UDP (transport layer) port 520 and transmit from the same UDP port. On broadcast-based networks, such as Ethernet or Token Ring, all devices receive these broadcast datagrams, but only those listening on UDP port 520 process these datagrams.

As discussed in Chapter 3, "IP Routing," routers must build and maintain a local route database (known as a route table) listing all locally connected networks as well as both statically and dynamically learned networks (which in this case would be RIP).

Initially the route table only includes entries for local or directly connected networks, but after exchanging dynamic RIP updates with its neighbors, a router modifies this table to include remote routes learned from its neighbors. The route table includes the following information:

- The IP address of the destination host, network, subnet, or default route (0.0.0.0)

- The IP address of the next hop router en route to this destination

- The metric (or cost) value expressed as an integer between 1 to 15 hops. This value states how far the destination (network, subnet, or host) is from this router (or host)

- The local interface this device uses to forward the datagram to the destination

Each RIP-enabled device listens to updates and builds its database by adding one entry to its route table for each destination learned.

Routes to destinations are learned through the exchange of dynamic RIP updates. These updates are broadcast periodically (every 30 seconds) whether or not changes have occurred in the network. Each router maintains its own clocking mechanism, which controls when it sends updates. The router includes all known routes in its updates in addition to the distance in hops to each destination. Figure 4.1 depicts a small, 2-router network running RIP.

FIGURE 4.1
Routers 1 and 2 are
RIP-enabled routers.
Each router is directly
connected to three
networks.

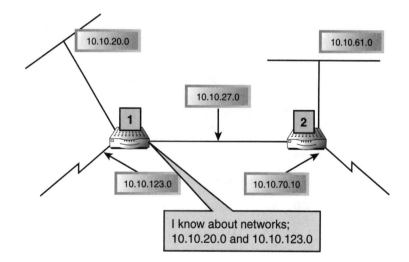

In Figure 4.1, Routers 1 and 2 exchange RIP updates to build their local route tables advertising networks with the mask 255.255.255.0 (or /24). Both routers are connected to one common network, 10.10.27.0. In addition, each router has two other network connections. For router 1 those networks are 10.10.20.0 and 10.10.123.0. Router 2 has connections to 10.10.61.0 and 10.10.70.0. Router 1 will advertise its networks to router 2 and vice versa. Note that although Router 1 also knows about network 10.10.27.0 it does not advertise it to Router 2. This is because the split horizon rule states that information learned from one interface should never be advertised out the same interface. In addition, this would be pointless, because Router 2 is also connected to this network and already knows about it. Split horizon was discussed in detail in Chapter 3.

Now let's take a look at the sample route tables for router 1 and router 2 as a result of this exchange (refer to Figure 4.1 for the diagram and the following sample route tables). The routing table for both routers should include five routes. Three entries for directly connected routes (indicated by a "C") and two RIP-routes learned from the neighboring router through the Ethernet0 interface connected to the common subnet (preceded by "R"). The following route table shows the routes existing on Router 1:

```
Codes: C - connected, S - static, I - IGRP, R - RIP, M - mobile, B - BGP
       D - EIGRP, EX - EIGRP external, O - OSPF, IA - OSPF inter area
       N1 - OSPF NSSA external type 1, N2 - OSPF NSSA external type 2
       E1 - OSPF external type 1, E2 - OSPF external type 2, E - EGP
       i - IS-IS, L1 - IS-IS level-1, L2 - IS-IS level-2, * - candidate default
       U - per-user static route, o - ODR

Gateway of last resort is not set

     10.0.0.0/24 is subnetted, 5 subnets
C       10.10.27.0 is directly connected, Ethernet0
C       10.10.20.0 is directly connected, Ethernet1
R       10.10.61.0 [120/1] via 10.10.27.2, 00:00:01, Ethernet0
R       10.10.70.0 [120/1] via 10.10.27.2, 00:00:01, Ethernet0
C       10.10.123.0 is directly connected, Serial0
```

In this route table two RIP routes exist. The first route points to the destination network 10.10.61.0 with a hop distance of 1 (hop count is the value on the right within the parenthesis [120/**1**]). The next hop router en route to this destination is 10.10.27.2. The second route points to the destination 10.10.70.0, with a 1 hop value through 10.10.27.2. Now let's look at the routing table for the next router (Router 2). The routing table for Router 2 also consists of five routes:

```
Codes: C - connected, S - static, I - IGRP, R - RIP, M - mobile, B – BGP
       D - EIGRP, EX - EIGRP external, O - OSPF, IA - OSPF inter area
       N1 - OSPF NSSA external type 1, N2 - OSPF NSSA external type 2
       E1 - OSPF external type 1, E2 - OSPF external type 2, E – EGP
       i - IS-IS, L1 - IS-IS level-1, L2 - IS-IS level-2, * - candidate default
       U - per-user static route, o - ODR

Gateway of last resort is not set

     10.0.0.0/24 is subnetted, 5 subnets
R       10.10.20.0 [120/1] via 10.10.27.1 00:00:06, Ethernet0
C       10.10.27.0 is directly connected, Ethernet0
C       10.10.61.0 is directly connected, Ethernet1
C       10.10.70.0 is directly connected, Serial 0
R       10.10.123.0 [120/1] via 10.10.27.1, 00:00:06, Ethernet0
```

Router 2's route table shows two RIP learned routes 10.10.20.0 and 10.10.123.0. Both routes are one hop away from this router as indicated by the one value on the right in the parenthesis [120/1]. The IP address of the router to be used as the next hop to reach these destinations is 10.10.27.1.

Routers learn and build their route tables through the exchange of route updates (broadcast every 30 seconds). These route updates are limited in size. A RIP-enabled router can only include up to 25 route entries in each update broadcast. If the router has more than 25 routes to advertise, it must broadcast another update including the remainder of the entries. Each one of these route updates is received by neighbor routers and processed, waiting for their (30 second) update timer to expire prior to generating their own updates. Because RIP routers must fully process updates received and wait for their timer to expire before sending route information to their neighbors, convergence time is slow. Convergence, which was discussed in Chapter 3, is the time it takes for all routers within a routing domain to receive, process, and build their route tables.

The broadcast nature of RIP, and the fact that one route update may not be enough to advertise all routes, adds additional network overhead and traffic. Not to mention the fact that routers broadcast their entire table every 30 seconds regardless of whether any of the route information has changed. When a router receives a route update, the following happens:

- It adds all newly learned routes to its local route table and increments the hop count value by one.

- It replaces previous routes (more hops) with routes with lower metrics (less hops) where applicable.

- It removes failed or unreachable routes (16 hops).

- It prepares to advertise this information to its neighbors on adjacent segments.

Just as you might call friends on your cell phone to tell them about traffic conditions (which routes are available and how far away the route is), a router also advertises routes available to destinations. When a router advertises a route, it states two things, the IP address of the destination and the distance in hops. Receivers listen to these advertisements and learn from them, incorporating the information into their local route table. When routers incorporate this route in their route table, they always increment the distance (hop) value by one. This indicates that the destination learned lies one more hop away from this router than the router from which it learned the route. Once it includes this information in its route table, it advertises the routes contained within its route table to all other neighbors connected to local broadcast segments and point-to-point links.

Both versions of RIP have a maximum distance limitation of 15 hops, which equals the number of routers a datagram may traverse. RIP considers a destination of 16 or more hops away too far, or "unreachable." If a datagram traverses 15 routers, the 16th router discards the datagram and returns an ICMP message "destination unreachable" to the sender. We discussed ICMP messages in Chapter 2, "IP and IP Addressing."

Path Selection

RIP uses distance as the base metric that determines the best route—the shorter the distance, the better the route. When multiple routes exist to a destination, routers running RIP choose the route with the shortest distance (measured in hops) as the best route, installing it in the route table. The route table is then used to forward future datagrams. Just like when you look up directions on the Web, you hope the Webmaster has chosen the shortest route.

However, RIP's simplistic single metric approach to path selection doesn't always instate the best route to a destination. For example, assume two routes to a destination exist (see Figure 4.2). One of the paths is four hops away and consists of three 100Mbps Ethernet links and one gigabit link. The other path is three hops away and consists of two 56Kbps WAN links and a gigabit link.

FIGURE 4.2

The shortest distance measured in hops is not always the best path. In this case, the best path is the four-hop (lower path) route, which has a better overall transfer rate than the route with three hops (upper path).

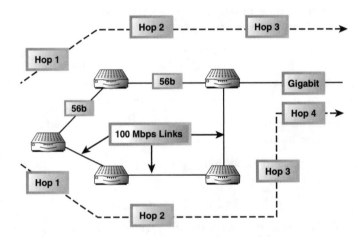

Because RIP uses strictly distance to determine the best path, RIP chooses the path with three hops in Figure 4.2, instead of the best path, the four-hop route that has a higher end-to-end overall transfer rate.

If both paths had three hops, RIP would only consider the fact that both paths have the same number hop count. In this case RIP would try to load balance across these two paths, sending datagrams along both links. In this situation, due to the unequal transfer rates across these links, datagrams sent across the 56Kbps links (the upper path) will slow the transmission process between remote hosts and may even cause connections to timeout and fail.

Unlike Link State Routing protocols, RIP does not take into consideration other factors, such as

- Bandwidth capacity of a link
- Reliability
- Load
- Delay

RIP makes decisions based on a limited amount of data— distance. As you may have experienced or guessed, this can pose a problem. Use your commute as a parallel example. Your commute consists of two main paths, one is the freeway (two hops door to door) and the other consisting of 10 side streets end to end. If RIP were controlling route decisions it would always choose the freeway as the best route, not taking into consideration commute traffic (bandwidth and load) and accidents (reliability). The freeway could have an accident (delay) and it might take four times as long to get to your destination. With RIP, you never know because it doesn't concern itself with any data other than distance when determining the best path.

As humans we can apply logic to our decisions prior to making them. When you took the job and began commuting to work you tested both routes and found that the freeway, although technically the shortest path, was the slowest and least reliable method of getting to work on time. Taking the 10 side streets is by distance a longer commute, but you arrive on time to work so it becomes your preferred path. You came to this conclusion by considering distance, the number of stop lights, and overall time it takes you to get from your home to work.

Link State routing protocols can apply relevant link status information, such as bandwidth, delay, reliability, and load, making more intelligent path selection based on changing traffic (network) conditions. Link State routing was discussed in Chapter 3.

RIP v1 Header and Fields

RIP enabled devices use two different message types to facilitate the exchange of route information. The first message is used to exchange route update information. The second message type is used to request route update information from other routers.

Both message types use the same general header format, starting with a fixed header and followed by a list of network and distance pairs. The length of a RIP header depends on the number of network and distance pairs within the datagram. However, RIP datagrams cannot exceed a maximum of 512 bytes or a maximum of 25 route entries. Maximum size does not include the Data Link, IP, or UDP headers. Figure 4.3 shows the format of a RIP v1 message. We will describe each field contained in the header after the figure.

All RIP messages begin with the same three fields within the header, command, version, and an unused field. The route and distance information fields repeat depending on the number of routes being advertised. For example, if a router advertises five routes, the IP Address, two unused and metric fields repeat five times, one for each advertised route. The RIP datagram can carry up to 25 route entries within each datagram.

FIGURE 4.3
Route entries follow the
common RIP header.
Each route entry pair
includes the address of
the destination and hop
value.

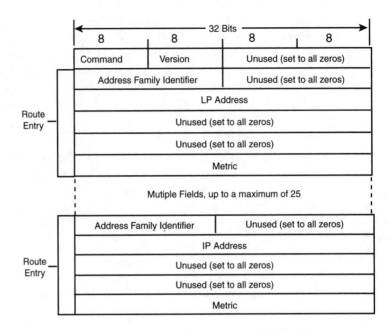

Command—1 Byte

This field identifies what the intended purpose of the frame is, such as a RIP request versus a
response. Eight different commands exist, depending on the kind of RIP message sent. Table
4.1 describes the different commands and their meanings.

TABLE 4.1   RIP's Command Messages

Command	Meaning
1	A request sent by a host or router upon initialization (or after the local route table has been cleared) requesting from all neighbors responses carrying all routing information
2	A response sent by a host or a router in response to a RIP request providing route information, or a regular periodic update sent every 30 seconds advertising a host's or router's routes to its neighbors
3	Turn on trace mode (obsolete)
4	Turn off trace mode (obsolete)
5	Reserved for Sun Microsystems internal use
9	Update request (used with demand circuits)
10	Update response (used with demand circuits)
11	Update acknowledgement (used with demand circuits)

Version—1 Byte

The version field identifies the RIP version as 1 or 2. RIP hosts and routers must agree on which version type to use. If both RIP v1 and v2 exist on the network, version 1 devices do not support the extensions implemented by version 2 and may cause interoperability problems. Version 1 does not support the following:

- VLSM

- Authentication

- Multicasting

However, version 2 hosts or routers support the version 1 specifications and in a mixed environment they use the fields and values recognized by the lowest common denominator (version 1) to exchange route information with version 1 devices.

You can configure RIP v2 routers to support version 1 or version 2 on a per interface basis. If one interface connects to a segment where mixed version 1 and 2 devices exist, you must configure for version 1 support on that interface. If another interface connects to a segment where only version 2 devices exist, you can configure for RIP v2.

Although RIP versions 1 and 2 have almost identical features, the version 2 extensions not supported by version 1 make them incompatible. :

Unused—2 Bytes

Version 1 has several fields that it does not use. These fields always contain zeros and repeat depending on how many routes the datagram carries.

Address Family Identifier—2 Bytes

Although RIP technically may support various Network layer protocols, this field only contains the value 2, which represents IP.

IP Address—4 Bytes

The IP address field identifies the address of the destination host, network, subnet, or default being advertised by the router.

Metric—4 Bytes

This value represents the cost in hops representing the distance to reach this network from the host or router advertising the route. The field should have a value between 1 and 15. If the field contains a value of 16, RIP considers the advertised route unreachable, due to a network link or router failure. Figure 4.4 shows a screen shot taken from a protocol analyzer of a RIP advertisement sent by a router.

FIGURE 4.4

This is a route broadcast (111.255.255.255) to all routers, on network 111.0.0.0. There are 24 route entries included this update message.

In Figure 4.4 router 111.1.54.139 is sending a RIP v1 broadcast containing 24 route entries. Due to a lack of space only four of the entries appear in the bottom half of the screen. As you can see this router is advertising network 1.0.0.0 with a metric hop count of 2 and networks 65.0.0.0, 35.0.0.0, and 192.6.100.0 with hop counts of 7, 4, and 5 hops respectively. The advertising router is basically telling all other routers about the networks it knows about and how far in hops these networks are from this router.

RIP v1 Disadvantages

Despite being one of the most popular protocols in use today, RIP has the following disadvantages:

- Broadcast-based

- Sends out the entire table even when no changes occur

- Slow convergence due to periodic timers

- Maximum distance limitation of 15 hops

- Prone to routing loops

- Classful routing protocol (does not support VLSM)

Because version 1 is broadcast-based, routers broadcast their entire table every 30 seconds even when no changes occur. This adds unnecessary traffic to the network with no new or viable information. Other routing protocols, such as Link State, use multicast advertisements and only send updates when a change has occurred on the network. The timer-based control slows convergence and the response to problems, such as routing loops.

When a router learns of a change in the network, such as the addition of a new link or notification of a failed link, it goes through the following process:

1. The receiving router incorporates the new information into its table and increments the hop count by one. This indicates that this router resides one hop further than the router from which it learned the route.

2. If the router learns of a failure, it updates the entry with a hop count of 16 and gets ready to remove the route.

3. The router waits for its periodic timer to expire prior to advertising, causing this router to send out this information with its regular updates.

If the network has many routers and segments, new information can take quite a while to reach all routers throughout the network. In the meantime these routers operate with outdated and incorrect information.

In addition, the maximum distance between any two communicating devices on an internetwork is 15 hops, which

- Limits the diameter of the network

- Makes RIP an unacceptable routing protocol for medium to large networks

Routers cannot forward datagrams that have traversed or been forwarded through more than 15 routers. When a router receives a datagram that has traversed more than 15 hops, it sends an ICMP Destination Unreachable message back to the sender, alerting it of the problem.

RIP, like other Distance Vector routing protocols, has a propensity for routing loops. Routing loops and loop avoidance mechanisms were described in Chapter 3. RIP implementations may employ a combination of routing loop prevention mechanisms, such as

- Count to infinity

- Holddowns

- Split horizon

- Poison reverse

Implementations vary based on vendor support and your configuration of RIP.

Remember from Chapter 3, the maximum hop count for RIP-enabled networks is 15. Anything above that is considered unreachable (or infinity). Holddown is a timer set by routers when a route is considered invalid. Once set, a router ignores route updates pertaining to the invalid route until the timer expires. Split horizon dictates that a router or RIP-enabled host cannot advertise route information out the same interface that the information came from. Poison reverse allows routers to break the split horizon rule by advertising information learned from an interface out the same interface. However, it can advertise routes learned from an interface out the same interface with a 16 hop count, which indicates a destination unreachable, "poisoning" the route. Routers with a route with a better metric (hop count) to the network ignore the destination unreachable update.

RIP v1, considered a classful routing protocol, only recognizes classful IP addresses, such as class A, B, or C (classful routing was discussed in Chapter 2). It does not understand subnets and cannot identify subnets within a network because route advertisements do not include the subnet mask. Because route advertisements do not include the subnet mask of the destination being advertised, receiving routers can only assume the default mask based on the address class being advertised (see Figure 4.5).

Classful Routing

FIGURE 4.5
Router A only advertises the classful address 172.16.0.0 (not subnets 1, 2 and 3). Router A, a RIP v1 router, does not include the subnet mask in its update.

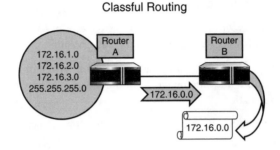

For example, Routers A and B are RIP v1 routers as shown in Figure 4.5. Router A knows about three subnets (1, 2, and 3) within the classful network 172.16.0.0. Because RIP v1 is being used, Router A only advertises the classful network not including the subnet mask (255.255.255.0) to Router B. Without the subnet mask information Router B (not directly connected to the remote subnets being advertised) can only assume that this route is a class B destination with a default mask of 255.255.0.0. Because of this Router B thinks there are no subnets. This is of course incorrect, but without the correct mask, it cannot make any other conclusion.

RIP Timers

RIP-enabled devices have timers that can be changed by administrators to control route updates. When changed they effect how often routers broadcast their route tables, the amount of time a router should maintain a route in its table that it has not heard an advertisement for, and how long a router will ignore route updates for an invalid route.

- Periodic update—30 seconds
- Invalid—180 seconds
- Holddown—180 seconds

RIP sends a periodic update every 30 seconds. It broadcasts its entire routing table whether any change has occurred or not.

RIP uses its invalid timer every 180 seconds. If a router does not receive a route advertisement that relates to a route in its route table within 180 seconds, it considers this route invalid and marks it as such.

RIP uses its holddown timer every 180 seconds. After a router marks a route invalid because it detects a link failure or receives a lack of updates, the router starts the holddown timer. This suspends the reception of updates relating to this route until the timer expires. During the hold-down period, this router does not listen to any advertisements from other routers to reinstate this route. After the timer expires, this router either flushes (discards) or reinstates this route. If it does not receive an advertisement from another router stating that the route is valid, it discards it. If it receives an advertisement from another router stating that the route is valid, it reinstates it.

Controlling Route Update Traffic

Some implementations allow an administrator to control the amount of RIP update traffic generated on a network. Implementations vary so you should consult your vendor for specific application and configuration parameters. You can use the following to control RIP update traffic:

- Adjust the RIP timers

- Configure routers on a broadcast network with neighbor statements

- Configure route update filters

You can adjust RIP timers on RIP-enabled devices, such as the periodic update timer from 30 seconds to a greater value. Increasing the interval between updates cuts down on the amount of broadcast traffic on a network, but slows convergence times. If you increase the interval, it increases broadcast traffic but reduces convergence times.

It is extremely important to note that all RIP-enabled hosts and routers must agree on timer values for convergence to occur. On non-broadcast networks, such as point-to-point or multi-point WAN links, each router must know the IP address of all other routers with which this router will exchange RIP updates.

Although seldom implemented, you can configure routers on a broadcast network, such as Ethernet or Token-Ring, with neighbor statements, which will cause the routers to exchange updates as directed datagrams instead of broadcasts. However, this means if your network adds or removes a router, you have to manually change these statements to facilitate route information exchange.

Probably the most common and effective way of minimizing route update traffic is to configure route update filters on RIP-enabled devices to filter inbound or outbound updates on an interface. Filters typically consist of permit or deny statements that allow or disallow route information from being received or propagated. Because each RIP datagram can only include a maximum of 25 routes, a router with 27 routes to advertise must send two RIP broadcasts. If you could filter two of the 27 routes, you could effectively cut the number of broadcasts in half. Implementation of filters is vendor-specific.

RIP Operation on Demand Circuits

Demand circuits or WAN links such as ISDN or X.25 provide bandwidth by establishing a link between remote sites when they need to forward data and terminate the link when they no longer need the transfer of data. These types of links prove ideal when low volume or infrequent data transfers occur between remote sites or as a backup link in case of primary link failure.

Because demand circuits only activate when you need them and terminate when you do not, they conserve resources and reduce costs. However, the temporary nature of demand links does not work well with dynamic routing protocols. If a link goes down, routers cannot exchange periodic updates, which means they lose their routing information. Without this information, routers cannot exchange data between sites.

Typically, an administrator enters permanent entries using static or default routing as the type of routing method on demand circuits. When the link initializes, routers immediately know how to route data. This method adds no extra traffic to the link from broadcast or multicast route advertisements.

Modifications to the RIP routing protocol makes the use of dynamic protocols possible on these types of links. RFC 2091 defines this modification to the RIP protocol to support dynamic routing over demand links. In RFC 2091, it defines the use of triggered updates. *Triggered* means that an event triggers the router to send an update, not a timer.

Routers also use triggered updates. As mentioned earlier in this chapter, the use of neighbor configuration on each router connected to the link supports route update exchange. By specifying each router's neighbor, it can send directed route updates to the router at the other end of the link without broadcasting. With demand links the following events trigger RIP routers to send updates:

- A router initializes and requests route update information—Entire route table exchanged

- A change occurs in the network—Only changes in the network are sent

- Link status transitions from up to down state or vice versa—Possibly due to a router powering up due to demand

Some vendor implementations also add mechanisms that allow remote routers connected to demand circuits to permanently or semi-permanently store route information learned while the circuit is up. For example, Cisco implements "Snapshot" routing. As the name implies, routers connected to the link take a snapshot of the route table after they exchange route information. They then use this snapshot of the network to route traffic, maintaining this information statically while the link remains down. This allows routers to learn about remote networks and routes to those networks. Snapshots allow routers to keep information even with unavailable links.

Demand Circuit Packet Types

Triggered update support across demand circuits requires the use of three additional RIP packet types and an extended 4-byte update header. Both RIP v1 and RIP v2 support all three packet types and the extended 4-byte header.

Figure 4.6 shows the header format of the three additional RIP packet types that support triggered update support across demand circuits. Table 4.2 gives an explanation of the three packet types.

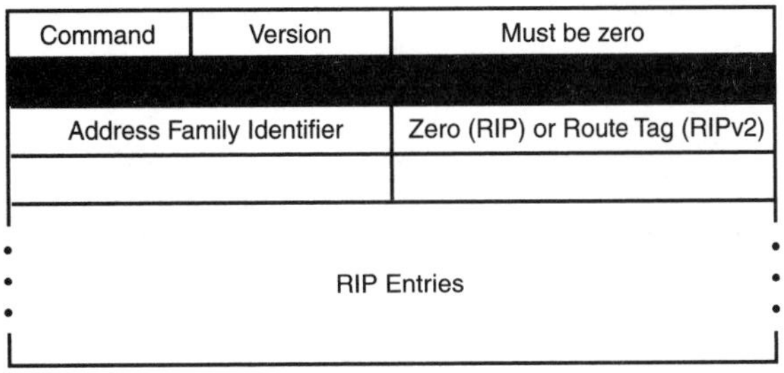

FIGURE 4.6
Note that demand circuit packet types extend the RIP header by four bytes.

Command	Version	Must be zero

Address Family Identifier	Zero (RIP) or Route Tag (RIPv2)

RIP Entries

TABLE 4.2 Demand Circuit Packet Types

9 = request	Sent by routers to request update information
10 = response	Sent in response to a request including either the entire route table or changed routes, depending on the initial request
11 = acknowledgement	Sent to acknowledge receipt of update information contained within a response datagram

Unlike the connectionless LAN-based broadcasts, sequencing and acknowledgements help track demand circuit route exchanges. All RIP responses (type 10) carry sequence numbers. Each response increments these sequence numbers by one. Routers receiving these responses must acknowledge receipt of route information carried within the response datagram by sending an acknowledgement with a matching sequence number. Routers assume that unacknowledged datagrams are lost and will be retransmitted.

RIP Version 2

RFC 2453 defines the version 2 specification of RIP as an extension to the original specification of version 1 (RFC 1058). Version 1 and version 2 perform similarly in operation.

Designed to address some of the limitations of version 1, Version 2 adds some enhanced features to support authentication and VLSM capability. Other routing protocols, such as Link State OSPF, have been developed that address version 1's limitations and offer much better route selection criteria, reduced bandwidth consumption, faster convergence, and so on. With more intelligent routing protocols and the inherent limitations of RIP, version 2 has been overlooked in most corporate network implementations. However, there are several devices that support RIP v2, such as Windows 2000 platform and various Firewall platforms such as the Cisco PIX and Checkpoint Firewall.

RIP still exists in many smaller network implementations. Administrators comfortable with RIP version 1, having worked with it on Unix implementations for years, can easily migrate hosts and routers to a routing protocol that supports VLSM and stronger authentication. RIP retains its popularity because it is probably the easiest method of incorporating dynamic routing that a network administrator has available. Table 4.3 compares and contrasts RIP v1 and RIP v2.

TABLE 4.3   RIP v1 Versus RIP v2

Version 1	Version 2
Broadcast only	Broadcast or multicast
No authentication	Authentication
Classful routing	Classless routing
Distance-vector protocol	Distance-vector protocol
Metric–Hops	Metric–Hops
Maximum Distance 15	Maximum Distance 15
IGP	IGP

Figure 4.7 shows the format of RIP v2 header.

FIGURE 4.7

Note that RIP v2 header contains a subnet mask and next hop field, which were previously zeros (unused) in version 1.

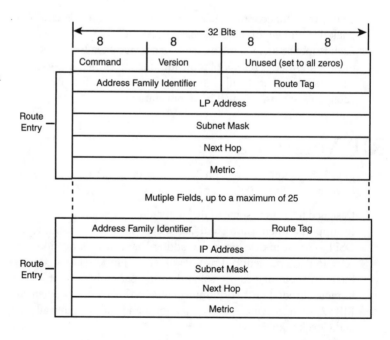

The RIP v2 header follows the same general format as the RIP v1 header. In Figure 4.7 you can see that several previously unused fields within the RIP v1 header are now used to support VLSM. Note the inclusion of the subnet mask and next hop fields. Both of these are key to providing support for subnetting.

Broadcast or Multicast

Version 2 routers exchange route information with each other using multicast rather than broadcast advertisements using 224.0.0.9. When RIP version 1 and 2 routers exist, support for broadcast capability allows for interaction.

Authentication

Unlike version 1, which does not support any type of authentication, version 2 allows assignment of a plain text password. An administrator must manually configure passwords on RIP v2-enabled routers. Passwords allow low-level security to be implemented between routers exchanging information. Figure 4.8 shows the format of an authenticated RIP v2 packet.

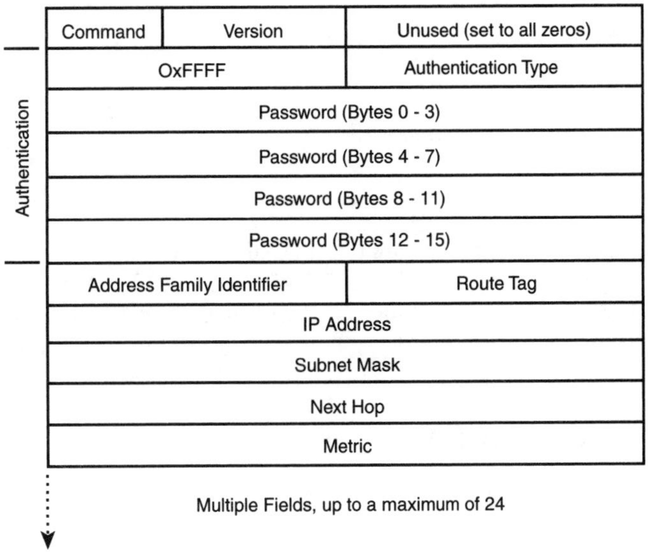

FIGURE 4.8
The address family identifier field within an authentication messages contain the value FFFF (hexadecimal). The route tag field is used to identify the authentication type.

Command	Version	Unused (set to all zeros)
OxFFFF		Authentication Type
Password (Bytes 0 - 3)		
Password (Bytes 4 - 7)		
Password (Bytes 8 - 11)		
Password (Bytes 12 - 15)		
Address Family Identifier		Route Tag
IP Address		
Subnet Mask		
Next Hop		
Metric		

Multiple Fields, up to a maximum of 24

When password authentication is used within RIP v2 messages the Address Family Identifier is replaced by FFFF as expressed in Figure 4.8. The authentication type used must be specified by the sending router followed by the specific password to be used for authentication. Only routers sharing the same password will be able to exchange route information.

Classless Routing

Including subnet mask information within route advertisements allows for classless routing. When a version 2 router advertises its route information to neighbors, it includes not only the networks it knows about but also the subnet mask of that network and next hop router (see Figure 4.9). With this information the receiving router can determine whether the network has been subnetted.

Version 2 does not limit itself, as version 1 does, to the recognition of classful addresses. VLSM (Variable Length Subnet Mask) support allows a classful address and its subsequent subnets to easily be determined and advertised.

Classless Routing

FIGURE 4.9
Router A, a RIP v2 router, advertises networks and subnets including the subnet masks within its update.

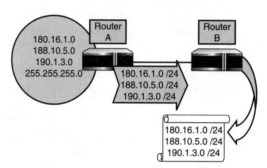

In Figure 4.9 both routers are running RIP v2. Router A knows about subnets within three Class B networks, 180.16.1.0, 188.10.5.0, and 190.1.3.0, with a 24 bit subnet mask (255.255.255.0 or /24). Router A advertises each of these routes to Router 2, including the subnet mask within its updates. Router 2 learns of the three routes, understanding from the mask that these Class B networks have been subnetted.

Compatibility with Version 1

Version 2 is considered to be backward-compatible with version 1 routers. However, to allow them to exchange information, the router must use the lowest common denominator, which means the following:

- Broadcasts only
- No authentication
- Classful addressing only

This, of course, negates the benefits of version 2. If you have RIP v1 and v2 implemented on the same subnet, version 2 devices must adhere to version 1 standards and limitations. If, on another interface, the same device connects to a subnet with v2 peers, it may use v2 out of that interface. Configuration of v1/v2 support varies depending on vendor specifications, but typically you configure on a per interface basis. Although compatible with v1, v2 is seldom seen or used because other protocols (Link State) far surpass its features and limitations, making implementing v2 on an internetwork moot. This may account for the reason RIP v2 is largely obsolete.

Host Support for RIP

There are many end hosts and operating systems that are capable of supporting RIP version 1 and 2, allowing them to build and maintain their own local route tables. All Unix, Microsoft NT, and Windows 2000 hosts support both versions (1 and 2) of the RIP protocol. End hosts (with only one network interface card) generally operate in passive mode, receiving but not advertising RIP routes. Servers running RIP with multiple interface cards installed operate as routers forwarding datagrams between segments. We will discuss how network servers support the RIP protocol next.

Note

Devices operating in passive mode do not generate route broadcasts. They only listen and receive route updates from other devices.

It is typical for a host to listen passively to routes when there are multiple routers available to that host.

A router can be a router or a RIP-enabled server (like a Windows NT, 2000, NetWare, or Unix host), with multiple interfaces (multihomed) that is acting as a router. Routers or servers acting as routers advertise their entire route table via RIP updates.

Note

Although various vendor operating systems support RIP and the routing of datagrams, it is always recommended that traditional routers be used for this purpose. A server's primary responsibility is to provide file, print, and application services to end hosts, not routing. Having a server process and route datagrams in addition to its primary tasks may severely hamper its ability to perform these functions. In small networks, where cost is a factor and congestion is not a problem, this type of implementation may be fine.

Windows NT/2000 Servers and RIP

Microsoft's Windows NT and 2000 server operating system products are capable of supporting RIP. These servers may create and maintain routing tables on a *static* or *dynamic* basis. The system software automatically creates static routing tables when you install multiple network interface cards (configuring the host as a multihomed). Static routing tables don't change in response to network conditions. Regardless of link status or network load, static routes remain the same until a systems administrator changes them. Using RIP allows the server, functioning as a router, to create and maintain dynamic routing tables.

Windows NT and 2000 both support RIP. It is common to put multiple network cards into an NT or 2000 server and use it to route packets from one network to another in a small network. These RIP-enabled devices function as routers in a single routing domain. Table 4.4 is a sample routing table for a server that connects two LANs together.

The NETSTAT command line utility allows you to view the routing table of an NT or 2000 server acting as a router.

TABLE 4.4 Sample Routing Table for an NT Server Connected to Two Networks

Network Address	Netmask	Gateway Address	Interface	Metric
0.0.0.0	0.0.0.0	192.168.10.1	192.168.10.1	1
0.0.0.0	0.0.0.0	192.168.22.1	192.168.221	1
127.0.0.0	255.0.0.0	127.0.0.1	127.0.0.1	1
192.168.10.0	255.255.255.0	192.168.10.1	192.168.10.1	1
192.168.10.2	255.255.255.255	192.168.10.1	192.168.10.1	1
192.168.10.255	255.255.255.255	192.168.10.1	192.168.10.1	1
192.168.22.0	255.255.255.0	192.168.22.1	192.168.22.1	1
192.168.22.2	255.255.255.255	192.168.22.1		
192.168.22.255	255.255.255.255	192.168.22.1	192.168.22.1	1
224.0.0.0	224.0.0.0	192.168.10.1	192.168.10.1	1
224.0.0.0	224.0.0.0	192.168.22.1	192.168.22.1	1
255.255.255.255	255.255.255.255	192.168.10.1	192.168.10.1	1
255.255.255.255	255.255.255.255	192.168.22.1	192.168.22.1	1

Table 4.4 was taken from an NT server enabled with RIP. This server is multihomed (it has two network interfaces) connecting directly to two networks (192.168.10.0 and 192.168.22.0). The first two route entries in lines 1 and 2 are default routes used to forward datagrams to unknown networks. The network (127.0.0.0) in line 3 refers to the local host's loopback address (127.0.0.1). Address 127.0.0.1 (discussed in Chapter 2) is used to test internal TCP/IP functions. Lines 4 through 6 and 7 through 9 refer to the local networks 192.168.10.0 and

192.168.22.0 respectively. This server (which is acting as a router) will forward packets between these two networks, forwarding datagrams to unknown destinations via the default routes. Lines 10 and 11 are entries supporting multicast routing on the local subnets. IP multicast routing is discussed in Chapter 11, "IP Multicast Routing." The last two lines (12 and 13) support broadcasting to the all hosts (or everyone) address (255.255.255.255).

Note that each line references the gateway address (next hop router), interface, and metric value for the route. The gateway address column specifies the IP address of the router to be used to deliver the datagram, which in this case is one of the local server's (router) interfaces. The interface address specifies the IP address of this server's local interface to be used to reach the next hop router en route to its destination. The metric column indicates the number of hops away the target network is from the server (router).

Windows NT only supports version 1 of the RIP protocol, while Windows 2000 supports both versions (1 and 2), with version 2 as the default routing protocol. Most implementations of RIP typically default to version 1 when RIP is turned on. If you have multiple versions of RIP running, your routers probably won't be able to exchange routing information without some adjustment. RIP version 2 supports features that RIP version 1 does not, such as multicast updates. RIP version 1 doesn't use multicasts, and therefore never receives announcements from RIP version 2 routers. Compatibility requires manual configuration. It is possible to set up RIP on either a router or a Windows 2000 server to advertise and listen to both version 1 and version 2, depending on neighboring router requirements.

Unix and RIP

There are two ways routing is usually configured on a Unix host: statically or dynamically. Static routes are set using the **route** command by the initialization scripts during system boot. The most common configuration uses a default router to which all traffic not destined for hosts on the local subnet is directed. It is the function of the default router to figure out how to route the packets to their destination. This would be used for a standalone Unix host with a single router for outgoing packets.

Dynamic routing under Unix means that the *routeD* (referred to as route D) routing process is actively running on the system. routeD uses the RIP routing protocol (described below) to do dynamic route discovery.

Note

Processes or programs in a Unix environment are referred to as daemons (pronounced demon). Routed (also known as Route D) is the routing process daemon used by Unix hosts to route build and maintain route information.

The following (Table 4.5) is a sample routing table from a Linux server acting as a router between two networks. This output was obtained by using the **netstat** command. The **r** argument sends the routing table output to the screen while the **n** option specifies that IP addresses be displayed instead of hostnames.

TABLE 4.5   Sample Routing Table for a Linux Server with Two Host Routes, Three Local Routes, and One Default Route

		Kernel IP routing table					
Destination	Gateway	Genmask	Flags	MSS	Window	irtt	Iface
10.100.1.1	10.100.1.1	255.255.255.255	UH	0	0	0	eth1
172.16.172.245	135.170.172.245	255.255.255.255	UH	0	0	0	eth0
172.16.172.0	135.170.172.245	255.255.255.0	U	0	0	0	eth0
10.100.1.0	10.100.1.1	255.255.255.0	U	0	0	0	eth1
127.0.0.0	127.0.0.1	255.0.0.0	U	0	0	0	Lo
Default	135.170.172.1	0.0.0.0	UG	0	0	0	eth0

The first column specifies the address of the destination network, subnet, or host. The gateway column identifies the IP address of the next hop en route to the destination followed by the mask (in the Genmask column). The fourth column is the Flags column. This column is used to specify the status of the route and how it was learned and placed in the route table. It can have one or more of any of the following five different flags:

U	Signifies that the route is up.
G	Signifies that the route is to a router (router). If this flag is not present, then it means that the destination is directly connected.
H	Means that the route is set to a host—that is, the destination address is a complete host. If this flag is set then the destination address is the complete host address, else it means that the destination address is a network address.
D	Means that the route was created by a redirect.
M	Means that the route was modified by a redirect message.

The last column specifies the local interface to be used (by this host) to reach this destination. Configurations of Unix hosts and specifics are not covered further within this book.

For instance, (referring to the Table 4.5) the first line of the output says that for the destination (host) 10.100.1.1, the gateway (router) to send the packet to is 10.100.1.1.

RIP Configuration

One of the major benefits of RIP is the ease with which it can be configured. There are basically two steps for configuration. The first is to enable the RIP process; the second is to specify which networks RIP should advertise. On many systems the second step may not even be necessary. On systems where the second step is not performed RIP when enabled immediately begins sending and receiving updates for all networks out every active interface. The sample configuration enables RIP version 1, and then advertises three classful networks; 192.1.1.0, 192.1.2.0, and 192.1.3.0. The commands used in these examples are taken from a Cisco router.

```
Router1(config)#Router rip
Router1(router-config)#version 1
Router1(router-config)#network 192.1.1.0
Router1(router-config)#network 192.1.2.0
Router1(router-config)#network 192.1.3.0
```

In the first line, `Router rip` enables the RIP routing process on the router. The second line enables version 1 updates. Cisco routers use send and receive version 1 updates by default. Lines three through five identify the networks RIP should advertise.

The next example illustrates the implementation of both RIP version 1 and 2 on a single router. If you recall from our earlier discussion RIP v1 and v2 updates are not compatible. Although both versions of RIP may coexist on the same network version 2 routers must be able to send and receive both version 1 and version 2 updates. Take a network that is running both RIP versions 1 and 2. There are several routers within the RIP domain. But to keep things simple, we will focus on a single router (Router 1). Router 1 has two interfaces, one Ethernet and one Serial WAN interface. Router 1 must communicate with version 1 RIP routers through its Ethernet interface. Across the serial connection there are both RIP v1 and v2 routers. There Router 1's serial interface must be configured to send and receive both version 1 and 2 updates. Because Router 1 supports updates for version 1 and 2 it is compatible with both versions of RIP. The following sample configuration shows two interface configurations, Ethernet and Serial:

```
interface Ethernet 0
ip rip send version 1
    ip rip receive version 1

!
interface Serial0
    ip rip send version 1 2
    ip rip receive version 1 2
```

In this example the `ip rip` command has been used at the interface level to specify what type of RIP update (version 1 or 2) should be received or sent. As you can see, the Ethernet interface is configured to only send and receive version 1 updates, whereas the serial interface will send and receive both. Because Router 1 supports updates for version 1 and 2 it is compatible with both versions of RIP.

Summary

RIP is classified as a Network layer protocol. Both RIP version one and two were based around Xerox's XNS protocol suite and the routeD program. Both versions of RIP exhibit the following characteristics: broadcast–based, IGP, work best on small-sized networks, distance-vector routing protocol, use hops as their metric, use periodic updates, send out the entire route table, and have a maximum network diameter of 15 hops.

Version 1 (RFC 1058) and version 2 (RFC 2453) perform similarly in operation. Version 2 was developed to enhance some of version 1's limitations. Version 2 has the following enhancements: it can use broadcast or multicast, authentication, and classless routing. However, other routing protocols, such as OSPF, have addressed version 1's limitations and offer a better routing solution than version 2. RIP version 1 has maintained its popularity because it is probably the easiest method of incorporating dynamic routing.

Many end hosts and operating systems (including Unix, Microsoft NT, and Windows 2000) can support both versions of RIP, allowing them to build and maintain their own local route tables. End hosts (with only one network interface card) generally operate in passive mode. Servers running RIP with multiple interface cards installed (multihomed) operate as routers forwarding datagrams between segments. Typically, the host listens passively to routes when the host has multiple routers available. Routers, or servers acting as routers, advertise their entire route table via RIP updates.

RIP has the advantage that it is very easy to configure. RIP has two basic configuration steps: enable the RIP process and specify which networks RIP should advertise.

Chapter Quiz

1. RIP is considered to be what type of routing protocol, Distance Vector or Link State?

2. What metric do both RIP v1 and RIP v2 use to determine the best path to a destination?

3. How often do RIP-enabled routers broadcast route updates?

4. How many route entries can RIP include in a single route update?

5. What is the maximum number of networks a datagram must traverse before the destination is considered unreachable?

6. Name three features RIP v2 supports that RIP v1 doesn't.

7. What is the purpose of authentication within RIP v2 updates?

8. How does RIP v2 support classless routing?

9. What various mechanisms does RIP employ to avoid routing loops?

10. Explain why RIP v2 is considered obsolete.

CHAPTER 5

IGRP AND EIGRP

You will learn about the following in this chapter:

- IGRP and EIGRP operation
- Sample IGRP and EIGRP configurations

An Introduction to Cisco IP Routing Protocols

Many industry professionals are familiar with Cisco Systems, Inc., considering it the industry leader in the manufacturing of network routing and switching hardware. However, you may not know that in addition to networking equipment, Cisco has developed several proprietary routing protocols. The two routing protocols are IGRP (Interior Gateway Routing Protocol) and the enhanced version known as EIGRP ('E' referring to Enhanced). IGRP is considered a Distance Vector routing protocol, while EIGRP is referred to as a hybrid (a mixture of Distance Vector and Link State) routing protocol. Although these protocols were originally only supported by Cisco routers, other vendor platforms now support both.

In this chapter we will discuss both protocols, beginning with IGRP, and then moving on to EIGRP. We will discuss their operations and functions as well as advantages and disadvantages. Both IGRP and EIGRP support IP routing but vary drastically in their methods. One unique feature of EIGRP is its support for the routing of multiple upper layer protocols, such as IPX, IP, and AppleTalk. Networks running more than one protocol suite usually require one routing protocol for each protocol suite. With EIGRP, a single routing protocol may be used to build and maintain route information.

IGRP (Interior Gateway Routing Protocol)

Interior Gateway Routing Protocol (IGRP) was developed in the mid-1980s by Cisco Systems, Inc. Cisco sought to create an internal gateway protocol that would be more robust than RIP for routing within an *autonomous system* (AS) or routing domain. Cisco also wanted to allow for more flexible path selection on networks with more complex topologies, which might have links with different bandwidth capacity and delay characteristics. This protocol must be capable of distinguishing between a 10Mbps Ethernet connection and a 64Kbps serial link, rather than determining best path based solely on a single metric (hops). Each AS is a routing domain or a collection of networks under common administration that share a common routing strategy (IGRP). An IGRP AS is typically given a unique number that identifies all members of that routing domain.

At the time of IGRP's development, the most popular IGP or interior gateway protocol for routing was the *Routing Information Protocol* (RIP). RIP is a very simple protocol that relies on a single metric value based on distance (measured by hop count) to determine best path between source and destination through a network. RIP still is more than adequate for small networks with few routing nodes and similar media types. However, most corporation networks have grown and expanded in geography pushing the implementation of RIP to its limits. The most glaring example of RIP's limitations is distance a datagram can travel. RIP has a hop count limitation of 15 nodes, in essence capping the diameter of a given network. Any network with a diameter greater than 15 (16 or more hops) is considered "unreachable." This maximum distance limitation restricts the growth and expansion of network size severely. In addition, a hop is a hop, no matter the media type, bandwidth, or performance of that hop. A 100Mbps Ethernet (LAN) link would be considered no better or worse path than a T1 (WAN) link offering only 1.5Mbps. RIP, when faced with multiple paths offering differing bandwidths to a given destination, would select the path with the least number of hops, not considering the capacity of each of the paths. RIP was covered in Chapter 4, "RIP v1 and v2."

When IGRP was introduced by Cisco, the adoption rate was fairly high as network administrators quickly moved to take advantage of IGRP's more flexible metric calculations and expanded capabilities for dealing with networks consisting of more than 15 hops.

Cisco's initial IGRP implementation worked only in *Internet Protocol* (IP) networks using registered protocol value 9. IGRP was originally designed to run in any network environment, however, and Cisco soon ported it to run in *Open System Interconnection* (OSI) *Connectionless Network Protocol* (CLNP) networks. CLNP is discussed in Chapter 8, "IS-IS."

Cisco developed Enhanced IGRP in the early 1990s to improve the operating efficiency of IGRP and integrate support for multiple protocols, such as IP, IPX, and AppleTalk. Our discussion begins with IGRP. Enhanced IGRP is discussed in detail later in this chapter.

IGRP Routing Operation

IGRP is a *Distance Vector* interior gateway protocol. Distance Vector routing protocols call for each router to broadcast all of its routing table entries in routing update messages at regular intervals (periodic) to each of its neighboring routers. As routing information reaches a router, that router must stop to process the information, update its route table, and then wait for its periodic update timer to expire prior to sending this new information on to other routers.

IGRP, like most Distance Vector routing protocols (except RIP v2) advertises and learns routes to destinations through broadcasts. Upon initialization IGRP routers send route requests (to build their table) and broadcast their entire route table to all neighbor routers (attached to the same segment). Thereafter, broadcasts are controlled by a periodic update timer. Each IGRP router maintains its own internal clock and timer. Route updates are broadcast by all IGRP when their local timer expires. The update timer value for IGRP is 90 seconds. This means that every 90 seconds an IGRP router must send out the entire contents of its local route table, including all entries. This happens whether or not a change has occurred in the network adding, like RIP (discussed in Chapter 4), unnecessary overhead to the network. Figure 5.1 shows a router sending a route request upon initialization and Figure 5.2 shows a router broadcasting a route update.

FIGURE 5.1

Router 172.30.100.1 is broadcasting a route request to all routers.

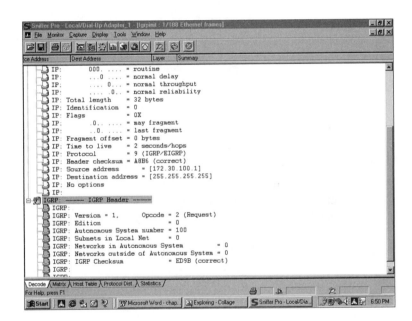

In Figure 5.1 router 172.30.100.1 has just initialized and is broadcasting (255.255.255.255) a route request to all routers within AS 100. Initially routers do not have route entries within their route table other than directly connected links. This information is learned through the exchange of route updates. This router has not learned of any subnets, networks, or external networks. This is indicated by the zero values within subnets in local net, networks in AS, and networks outside of AS fields.

FIGURE 5.2

Routers broadcast route updates every 90 seconds advertising known networks.

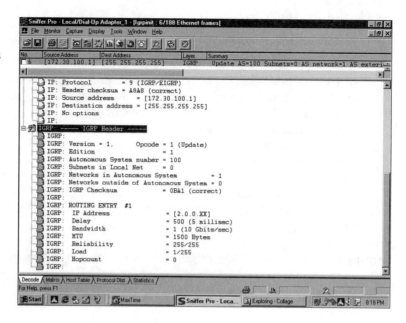

Router 172.30.100.1 in Figure 5.2 is advertising the network 2.0.0.0 in AS 100. All routers within AS 100 will receive this information and update their route tables.

IGRP Metrics

Distance Vector routing protocols call for each router to broadcast all of its routing table entries in routing update messages at regular intervals (periodic). These messages are broadcast out all local interfaces to neighboring IGRP routers. As routing information reaches a neighbor router, that router must stop to process the information, update its route table, and then wait for its periodic update timer to expire prior to sending this new information on to other routers.

The Distance Vector–based routing protocol IGRP enables routers to build their routing tables by exchanging information with adjacent routers (referred to as *neighbors*). The routing information contains a summary about the rest of the network, which helps IGRP make decisions about the best path choice. Unlike RIP, which bases its path choice on hops only, IGRP (despite being considered a Distance Vector protocol) can use a combination of metrics when making route decisions. IGRP routers consider several metric components to calculate a single *composite metric* for the destination path. The composite metric combines the weighted values of the various metric components into a single number, which represents the best cost. IGRP then selects the best route based on the smallest composite metric or cost. The cost values include the following:

- **Bandwidth**—Configurable value that represents the transfer rate (or capacity) of the link in kilobits. The higher the bandwidth the better the path. IGRP uses the link with lowest bandwidth value to a destination as its base value.

- **Delay**—Measures the time (in microseconds) it takes for a router to queue, process, and transmit a datagram out a specific interface. Links that have less delay end to end are preferred. IGRPs use the cumulative delay values of all links to a destination in its route calculation.

- **Reliability**—A percentage value (255 equals 100%) representing the reliability of the link in terms of transmission errors. The more reliable the link, the better the path. A link with a reliability factor of 255 is 100% reliable (no transmission errors have been encountered).

- **Load**—A variable value that adjusts based on the utilization of the link. The range varies between 1 and 255, with 255 representing a network that is 100% utilized (congested). Links with lower loads are preferred over links that are experiencing higher loads.

Although IGRP can technically support and combine any of these cost values, it uses only the bandwidth and delay values by default. Table 5.1 shows common IGRP bandwidth and delay values.

TABLE 5.1   Default IGRP Bandwidth and Delay Values Used for Common Links with Scaled Values

Link Type	Bandwidth Capacity	Scaled Value (10^7/BW)	Delay in microseconds	Scaled Value (Delay/10)
Gigabit Ethernet	1,000,000Kbps	10	10	1
Fast Ethernet	100,000Kbps	100	100	10
Slow Ethernet	10,000Kbps	1,000	1,000	100
Token-Ring	16,000Kbps	625	630	63
FDDI	100,000Kbps	100	100	10
56K Link	56Kbps	178,571	20,000	2,000
T1	1,544Kbps	6,476	20,000	2,000
64K	64Kbps	156,250	20,000	2,000

IGRP calculates its composite metric only taking into consideration the bandwidth and delay values. Consider a simple example involving only a single (T1) link. In this case the composite calculation is as follows:

1. First the bandwidth value (based on the link type) is scaled using a factor of 10^7. For example, consider a single T1 link with a bandwidth of 1.544Mbps. The calculation to scale bandwidth by with the factor is 10^7/1544 or 6476.

2. Next the delay value (measured in microseconds) is considered. The delay value for the router interface connected to the T1 link is 20,000 microseconds. This value is scaled by a factor of 10. The calculation is 20,000/10 or 2000.

3. The two scaled values 6476 (bandwidth) and 2000 (delay) are then added together to arrive at the composite metric for the link.

```
Metric = (scaled BW) + (scaled Delay)
```

In this case the metric value would be 6476 + 2000 metric 8476.

The previous example only takes into consideration a single link. The calculation would change slightly when multiple links exist along the path to a destination. When multiple links must be traversed the bandwidth factor only considers the lowest bandwidth value for the entire path. That value is determined by the link with the lowest configured bandwidth value. This number is then used as the base for bandwidth scaling. Delay is calculated as the sum of the delay values for all outbound interfaces along the path between source and destination scaled by a factor of 10. Using the diagram in Figure 5.3 as an example we will calculate the metric cost value from Router C to the destination network 199.10.4.0 (connecting Routers A and D).

FIGURE 5.3

The path between routers C and A includes one Ethernet link and one WAN link. The Ethernet link is a 10Mbps link with a delay of 1,000 (microseconds) and the WAN link is 64Kbps with a delay value of 20,000 (microseconds).

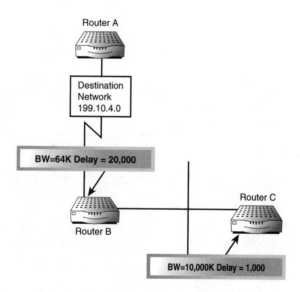

The metric cost value for the destination network 199.10.4.0 from Router C in Figure 5.3 is calculated by taking the lowest bandwidth value associated with any link along the entire path end to end and using this as the base value for bandwidth scaling. In this example the lowest value is 64Kbps (WAN link bandwidth). Using a scaling factor 10^7, divide by 64K to arrive at the scaled bandwidth value for the path end to end $(10^7/64K)= 156,250$. Now calculate the scaled delay value. To do this we take the sum of all delay values for the entire path (1,000 Ethernet + 20,000 64Kbps link) = 21,000 and then divide this by the factor 10 to arrive at the scaled value 2,100. Now take the scaled bandwidth value and add it to the scaled delay value and you will have the metric cost 156,250 (scaled bandwidth) + 2,100 (scaled delay) = 158,350. Take a look at the route table output of Router C, which shows a route table entry (see Figure 5.4).

FIGURE 5.4

Router C's route table has a route entry to network 199.10.4.0 with an IGRP metric cost value of 158,350.

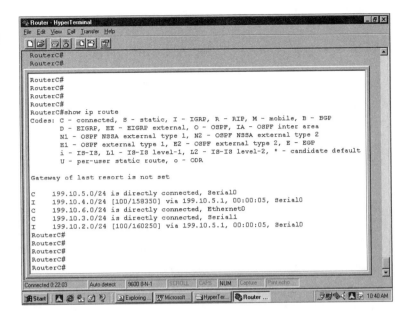

```
Router - HyperTerminal
File  Edit  View  Call  Transfer  Help

RouterC#
RouterC#

RouterC#
RouterC#
RouterC#
RouterC#
RouterC#show ip route
Codes: C - connected, S - static, I - IGRP, R - RIP, M - mobile, B - BGP
       D - EIGRP, EX - EIGRP external, O - OSPF, IA - OSPF inter area
       N1 - OSPF NSSA external type 1, N2 - OSPF NSSA external type 2
       E1 - OSPF external type 1, E2 - OSPF external type 2, E - EGP
       i - IS-IS, L1 - IS-IS level-1, L2 - IS-IS level-2, * - candidate default
       U - per-user static route, o - ODR

Gateway of last resort is not set

C    199.10.5.0/24 is directly connected, Serial0
I    199.10.4.0/24 [100/158350] via 199.10.5.1, 00:00:05, Serial0
C    199.10.6.0/24 is directly connected, Ethernet0
C    199.10.3.0/24 is directly connected, Serial1
I    199.10.2.0/24 [100/160250] via 199.10.5.1, 00:00:05, Serial0
RouterC#
RouterC#
RouterC#
RouterC#
RouterC#

Connected 0:22:03   Auto detect   9600 8-N-1   SCROLL  CAPS  NUM  Capture  Print echo
```

Figure 5.4 is an output screen of Router C's (a Cisco router) route table. IGRP learned routes are indicated by the route code "I" in the leftmost column. As you can see there is a route entry for network 199.10.4.0 in the table. Router C has learned the route to this network is via 199.10.5.1 and the metric cost value associated with this path is 158,350 through interface serial 0.

Caution

Bandwidth and delay are metric cost values used by IGRP routers when determining best path between source and destination. These values can be artificially manipulated by an administrator to affect an IGRP router's path selection. Typically bandwidth follows the data transfer rate of the link, whereas delay measures the time it takes for a router to process, queue, and transmit a datagram out an interface.

Exercise caution when changing these values as they may negatively affect the forwarding decision a router makes. Routing decisions are only as good as the information the routing protocol has available to it. If you have an incorrect value, routing protocol might select suboptimal paths for forwarding based on that incorrect value.

For example, imagine you have multiple T1 (1.544Mbps) links connecting two sites. If both links have identical bandwidth capacities and interface delays (20,000 microseconds), each of the links should be configured with matching values. With matching values both links could be used to load balance traffic between sites.

If however, one of the links was a 19.2Kbps link and the bandwidth value was artificially set on this link to 1.544Mbps, both links would (incorrectly) appear to the router as having the same bandwidth capacity. In this case IGRP would consider both paths for load balancing, sending datagrams over both links. Some datagrams would be sent over the slow link while others are sent over the faster link. This situation could seriously degrade and even cause connections to fail.

In addition to the bandwidth and delay metric values, IGRP keeps track of the number of hops (networks) a datagram has traversed as it is forwarded to its destination. IGRP routers do not have a 15-hop limit as does RIP. Instead, IGRP supports a maximum hop count of 255, with an infinity value of 256 (destination unreachable). Although IGRP routers keep track of the hop count value of datagrams they do not use this information in the cost calculation.

Because IGRP supports a much larger number of hops than RIP it can technically support networks of greater size (in terms of hops). As a router forwards a datagram it increments the hop value by one. When the hop count has exceeded the maximum (255 hops) it is trashed (not forwarded). An ICMP message is sent back to the source notifying it that the destination network or host is unreachable. ICMP messages were discussed in Chapter 2, "IP and IP Addressing."

IGRP Timers

As discussed earlier in this chapter, IGRP includes several control timers that dictate the operation of IGRP's route updates:

- **Update interval**—Used to determine how often IGRP route updates are sent. The default update interval is 90 seconds.

- **Invalid timer**—Routes are marked as invalid after three consecutive route updates have not been received for a specific destination. The default invalid timer is 270 seconds.

- **Holddown timer**—Used to control how long a router will ignore route updates sent by other routers for a route marked as invalid. The default holddown timer is 280 seconds.

- **Flush timer**—Specifies when an invalid route is removed from the route table. The default flush timer is 630 seconds.

These timers control route propagation and expiration. Although the timers have default settings, you can set different time constants.

Caution

It is important to note that although these timers may be manually changed by an administrator all routers must have the same settings or problems will occur. If one router has an update value of 120 seconds and all other routers are using the default (90 seconds), this router will not be able to exchange route update information with the other routers within the same routing domain.

Table 5.2 shows the different timers and their functions.

TABLE 5.2 IGRP Timers

Timer	Function/Default Setting
Update	Defines the interval between route updates.
	Default every 90 seconds.
Invalid	Specifies how long a router should wait in the absence of a routing update message before declaring that route invalid.
	Default 270 (three times the Update Timer)
Holddown	Specifies the holddown period for an unreachable destination. At this point, the router does not accept updates for the same destination during the holddown period.
	Default 280 seconds (three times the update timer plus ten seconds)
Flush	Indicates how much time should pass before it removes a failed route from the routing table.
	Default 630 seconds (seven times the update timer)

IGRP routers expect to receive route updates every 90 seconds from neighbor routers. Upon reception the route information within the update is processed and routes are entered into the route table. If a router does not receive a route update for a previously learned route within three route update cycles that route is marked as invalid. The router marking this route as invalid sets the timer for 270 seconds. If no further route updates are received for this route within this time frame this route will be flushed from the route table within 630 seconds. If however a router sets the invalid timer and then subsequently receives a route update for the marked route, the route will be reinstated within the route table as active (valid).

Routers detecting failed links will mark the route as invalid, set the holddown timer and advertise the failed route with an infinity value of 256 hops to its IGRP neighbors. The router setting the holddown timer will not accept route updates from other routers for the invalid destination until this timer expires. By placing the route in holddown and ignoring route updates for this destination, this router prevents the inadvertent reinstatement of the failed route.

Load Balancing

IGRP also allows for multi-path routing, providing the means to send packets in balanced fashion across multiple paths. When redundant paths to a destination exist both equal cost paths can be used to forward traffic. With load balancing, datagrams are typically sent over one path and then the other, alternating so as not to congest a single link. These redundant paths also offer fault tolerance to failures. If a primary path fails the alternate path can take over providing continuous service by accepting all traffic.

IGRP supports both equal and unequal cost load balancing. Equal cost load balancing means both paths to a destination have the same metric cost values, such as bandwidth (see Figure 5.5). When multiple paths exist with equal costs they are automatically used to forward traffic.

Note

Most vendor implementations support automatic load balancing across two paths without configuration. Some allow load balancing across up to six redundant paths, but this generally requires configuration.

Equal Cost Paths

FIGURE 5.5
Two equal cost paths exist between Routers A and B.

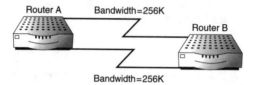

In Figure 5.5 multiple paths exist between two routers, A and B. Both links support the same bandwidth value of 256Kbps. Destinations on the other side of these routers may be load balanced across these links automatically because the bandwidth values are identical.

If the metrics for the paths are different (unequal) IGRP provides for something called *variance*. The IGRP variance feature allows an administrator to set a second path as a particular value (variance) in relation to the first (best) path. For example, if the first path is three times better than the second path, because its metric is three times lower, the first path will be used three times as often (see Figure 5.6). Only routes with metrics that are within a certain range of the best route are used as multiple paths. *Variance* defines that range. Without configuring unequal cost load balancing, IGRP balances traffic across equal cost paths only.

Unequal Cost Paths

FIGURE 5.6
Router A and B have redundant unequal cost links connecting them.

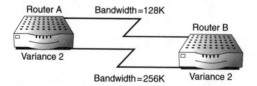

In Figure 5.6 two routers, A and B are maintaining redundant unequal cost paths for destinations on either side. The upper path has a bandwidth value of 128Kbps, while the lower path supports up to 256Kbps. The variance is a multiplier: traffic will be placed on any link with a metric (multiplied by the variance) that is less than or equal to the best path. To load balance over these two paths, a variance multiplier of two could be used for the upper path, $128 \times 2 = 256$, which is within the variance of the lower path. The variance acts like a ratio such that if per-packet balancing is being used, the router sends two packets over the upper path, and one packet over the upper path, and so on. Assuming an administrator has configured both routers with a variance factor of 2, both links can be used to forward traffic. With a value of two, load balancing will occur as long as the path variance is not greater than 2 (metric cost of the lower path). In this example the lower path has a greater bandwidth capacity (256Kbps) making it the better path. This link becomes the primary for which the variance is measured against. The upper path (128Kbps) has half the bandwidth capacity

Caution

This link becomes the secondary path for load balancing. Be very careful when configuring load balancing across unequal cost paths. If the variance (difference in costs) between the paths is too drastic it could hurt your network performance and even cause connections across these links to time out and fail.

IGRP Packets, Headers, and Fields

There are two types of IGRP packets—request and update. Requests are sent by IGRP routers when they come online (their route table is empty) to receive updates from neighbor routers. Route requests do not contain route entries. Route updates are sent to advertise all route information within a router's route table or respond to a request. Both types of IGRP packets begin with the same 12 byte header and fields (see Figure 5.7). Each of the common fields within the packet is discussed following the figure.

All IGRP packet types have a common 12 byte header, which include the following eight fields:

- **Version**—This value identifies the IGRP version number. The version number for IGRP is one.

- **Operation Code**—Identifies the IGRP packet as a request (type 1) or update (type 2). When a request is sent there no route entries will be included.

- **Edition**—This is set and incremented by the source IGRP router in update packets to alert the receiver of the current revision level of this update packet.

- **Autonomous System Number**—This value is the Autonomous System number of the router sending the update. Only routers within the same AS can exchange route information.

- **Number of interior routes**—This value specifies how many subnets of directly connected networks exist. For example, if a router is advertising three local subnets within the route entry portion of the packet below, this value will be 3.

- **Number of system routes**—Specifies the number of summarized routes being advertised below.

- **Number of exterior routes**—Specifies the number of external routes being advertised below. External routes are routes that are not IGRP originated (they exist outside of the IGRP AS).

- **Checksum**—The sending router calculates the checksum value prior to transmission. The receiving host uses this to verify the contents of the IGRP header have not been damaged in transit. :

FIGURE 5.7

All IGRP packets have a 12-byte common header and may contain up to 104 route entries.

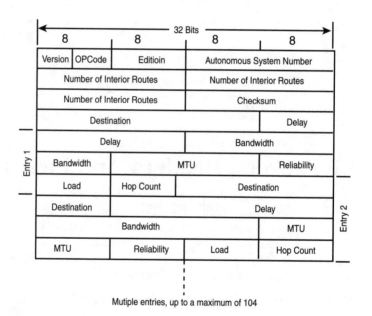

Mutiple entries, up to a maximum of 104

IGRP Request Packet

IGRP request packets are sent when a router's IGRP route table is empty or it is requesting specific route information. Request packets do not carry route entries, they are simply used to obtain route information from neighbor IGRP routers. Figure 5.8 is an IGRP route request.

As you can see in Figure 5.8 the OpCode value is 2, indicating this is a request broadcast to all routers (255.255.255.255) within AS 100. All other settings are zeros (unknown).

FIGURE 5.8

IGRP requests contain the common 12-byte header with no route entries.

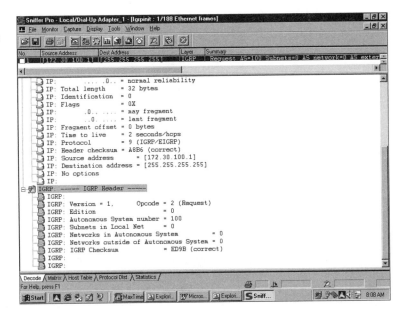

IGRP Update Packet

IGRP routes learn of destinations and build their route tables through the exchange of update packets. IGRP routers send these updates upon initialization to advertise their local routes and thereafter every 90 seconds (based on the update interval). In addition they may transmit an update packet in response to an IGRP request packet received from a neighbor (see Figure 5.9). Update packets start with the 12 byte standard header and fields, followed by up to 104 route entries describing destination networks and metric cost values. The route entry fields listed below repeat depending on the number of routes being advertised by the IGRP router.

- **Destination**—Identifies the network layer address of the destination being advertised (network, subnet, or host).

- **Delay**—Specifies the scaled delay value for the route.

- **Bandwidth**—Specifies the scaled bandwidth value for the route.

- **MTU**—Specifies the maximum transmission unit that may be used to reach this route.

- **Reliability**—Specifies the current reliability of the path to the destination. This value is generally measured over a five-second time frame. Paths with higher error rates will have a lower reliability value. Paths with lower error rates will have a higher reliability value. The reliability value range is 1 to 255, with 255 being the most reliable and 1 being the least reliable.

- **Load**—Specifies the load along the path to the destination as a percentage between 1 and 255 (255 being 100% loaded).

- **Hop Count**—Specifies the number of network hops to reach the destination. This can be any value from 0 to 256. A zero indicates a directly connected network. The maximum hop count for IGRP is 255. A value of 256 indicates the destination being advertised is unreachable.

FIGURE 5.9

IGRP routers broadcast route updates every 90 seconds advertising routes to neighbors.

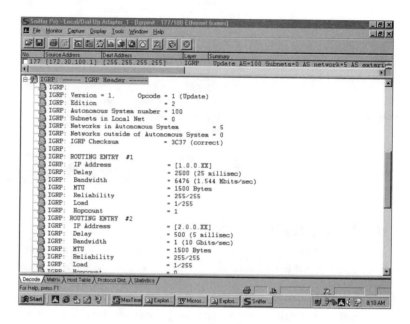

Router 172.30.100.1 in Figure 5.9 is advertising five routes within this update packet. Only two routes (1.0.0.0 and 2.0.0.0) are seen because the output has been truncated. Note the OpCode is type 1 indicating this is an update, not a request.

EIGRP (Enhanced Interior Gateway Protocol)

EIGRP is an enhanced version of IGRP. EIGRP is considered a hybrid routing protocol incorporating may of the same Distance Vector characteristics, while adopting enhanced Link State characteristics. The same Distance Vector technologies found in IGRP, like maximum hop count, are also used in EIGRP, and the underlying metrics remain unchanged. However, the operating efficiency and convergence properties of IGRP have been improved significantly following the behavior of Link State routing protocols. This allows for improved routing capabilities while retaining the existing investment in IGRP.

The Distributed Update Algorithm (DUAL) is the algorithm used by EIGRP to obtain a loop-free routing topology at every stage of a route computation. This provides for an environment in which all routers involved in a topology change are able to synchronize at roughly the same time. The best part is that routers that are not affected by topology changes are not involved in the re-computation. The convergence time of DUAL is therefore extremely fast and efficient.

Another notable feature change is EIGRP's network layer independence. EIGRP has been extended to support multiple network layer protocols, thereby allowing DUAL to support other routed protocols such as IPX and Appletalk in addition to IP. EIGRP uses the registered IP protocol value 88.

EIGRP Operation

EIGRP combines the advantages of Link State protocols with the advantages of Distance Vector protocols. Because EIGRP combines the advantages of both protocols, it is considered a balanced hybrid protocol.

Some of the characteristics of EIGRP include the following:

- Faster convergence by sending triggered, partial updates

- EIGRP routers belong to an AS routing domain

- EIGRP routers build and maintain three databases; Adjacency, Topology, and Forwarding

- Multicast and unicast

- VLSMs, includes subnet masks in updates

- Supports multiprotocol, including IP/IPX/AppleTalk

- Uses cost-based metrics similar to IGRP

- Maintains backup paths when multiple routes exist

Each one of these characteristics will be discussed throughout this chapter.

Fast Convergence

Unlike IGRP, which broadcasts route information using periodic updates to unknown neighbors, EIGRP relies on triggered and partial updates to propagate routing table changes quickly and reliably throughout the network, increasing convergence times. IGRP routers do not wait for timers to expire to propagate route information when a change occurs. Instead they immediately (trigger) generate an update message to EIGRP neighbor routers including only the changed route (partial update), not the entire table. This decreases bandwidth use, which results in better efficiency and performance.

EIGRP AS

EIGRP defines its routing domain (which includes all EIGRP-enabled routers and the networks within the domain) with an AS (Autonomous System) number similar to IGRP. Only EIGRP routers sharing the same AS number may exchange information (considered part of the same domain). EIGRP Autonomous Systems with different AS numbers may not exchange information. You arbitrarily assign the AS number by enabling and configuring EIGRP on the first router within the domain. After you have assigned an AS number, all other routers within the AS must share this same value.

EIGRP routers within the same AS must first discover their neighbor routers, that is, routers directly connected to the same local segment or WAN link. By identifying their neighbors, routers can detect unavailable neighbor routers, thereby quickly detecting failures in the network. This allows them to quickly respond to the failure and adjust their path selection.

EIGRP Databases

All EIGRP routers within the same AS must build and maintain three separate databases; Adjacency (also known as Neighbor Table), Topology, and Forwarding (also known as Route Table). The first database built is the Adjacency. This database is built through the exchange of hello messages between EIGRP neighbor routers. The Adjacency database contains a list of all EIGRP neighbors. After the Adjacency database is built routers can begin to exchange route information, building a Topology database (or map) of the entire network. The Topology database stores routes and metrics to every network and subnet throughout the AS. The EIGRP routing algorithm is then run against this map to derive the best routes, which are placed in the router's Forwarding database (or route table). Each of these databases as well as the routing algorithm is discussed next. We will discuss them in the order they are built, beginning with the Adjacency (or neighbor table), and then moving on to the Topology and Forwarding databases.

Adjacency Database

EIGRP routers attached to the same segment within the same AS routing domain must successfully form an adjacency (neighbor relationship) in order for route information to begin. EIGRP routers become neighbors when they see each other's hello packets on a common network. When an EIGRP router goes through its initial startup it must discover and establish a neighbor relationship with all other EIGRP routers on the same segment. This is called the neighbor discovery process and involves the exchange of hello messages. Routers transmit hello messages to discover and subsequently maintain these relationships. Each router builds a local Adjacency database from the exchange of hello messages keeping track of all of its neighbors and their statuses. If a router does not receive a hello message from a neighbor router for several hello intervals that router is considered dead and is removed from the table. EIGRP message types will be discussed later in this chapter.

Building and Maintaining a Topology Database

All EIGRP routers must build and maintain a complete Topology database. The database is a map of the entire AS, identifying all networks, subnets, and metrics for each destination. The process of building and maintaining the Topology database is achieved through the exchange of route information. Route information exchange begins upon completion of the neighbor relationships(adjacency). Once a router knows its neighbors it begins the process of building its map. EIGRP routers use route queries, route updates, and replies to ask for, exchange, and respond to route information requests. When an IGRP router comes online it has no topology map (topology database) and an empty route table (no Forwarding database). EIGRP routers initially receive a complete copy of their neighbor's route tables. EIGRP prevents routing loops by referring to copies of neighboring routing tables and using the detailed topology map. EIGRP routers use the route information within the Topology database, running the Diffusing Update Algorithm (DUAL) against it to calculate changes and avoid routing loops. The Topology database is a map of the entire EIGRP routing domain including all networks and subnets within the AS. The Topology database contains information that is used to build and maintain the forwarding database. This information includes a list of all paths to destination (networks and subnets) and the composite metric to reach that destination.

Listing 5.1 shows sample output taken from a Cisco router showing the EIRP Topology database for AS 100.

LISTING 5.1   IP-EIGRP Topology Table for AS(100)/ID(131.108.4.4)

```
Codes: P - Passive, A - Active, U - Update, Q - Query, R - Reply, r - Reply status

P 10.0.0.0/8, 1 successors, FD is 128256
        via Summary (128256/0), Null0
P 10.10.40.0/24, 1 successors, FD is 128256
        via Connected, Loopback0
P 10.10.46.0/24, 1 successors, FD is 3845120
        via Connected, Serial0
P 10.10.50.0/24, 1 successors, FD is 2195456
        via 10.10.64.6 (2195456/281600), Serial1
        via 10.10.46.6 (3870720/281600), Serial0
P 10.10.64.0/24, 1 successors, FD is 2169856
        via Connected, Serial1
P 10.100.1.0/24, 1 successors, FD is 281600
        via Connected, Ethernet0
P 10.10.200.0/24, 1 successors, FD is 2221056
        via 10.10.64.6 (2221056/307200), Serial1
        via 10.10.46.6 (3896320/307200), Serial0
```

The output in Listing 5.1 is the Topology database (or map) built from the exchange of EIGRP route updates. As you can see there are six known subnets (10.**10.40**.0, 10.**10.46**.0, 10.**10.50**.0, 10.**10.64**.0, 10.**100.1**.0, and 10.**10.200**.0). These subnets are part of the private Class A network 10.0.0.0 in the EIGRP routing domain identified as AS 100. Some of these routes have only one path, indicated by a single `via` entry below it. Others have multiple paths that can be used to reach the destination (routes with more than one `via` entry). For example, 10.**10.46**.0 is a local subnet, directly connected and reachable via this router's local serial 0 interface. The EIGRP composite metric cost for this route is 3845120. Because there is no better path than a local connected one this router does not show another one. This route is the primary (or best path) to this network and is referred to as the successor.

Several subnets listed here have show more than one `via` entry below the destination. This means there are multiple ways to reach this subnet. EIGRP keeps track of primary and backup paths when multiple paths exist to a destination, listing all of them in the Topology table with their corresponding composite metrics. There are two paths to 10.**10.50**.0, one via the next hop router 10.10.64.6 with a metric cost of 2195456 through interface Serial1 and the other via 10.10.46.6 with a metric cost of 3870720 through Serial0. The route with the lowest metric cost is considered the best path (or successor) and is listed as the first `via` entry below the route. Successor routes are considered the best route to a destination, while feasible successor routes are backup paths for that destination. Successor and feasible successor as well as how EIGRP calculates its composite metric are discussed later in this section.

Note

EIGRP routers running multiple protocols (IP, IPX, and AppleTalk) must maintain one topology database for each network layer protocol it is performing routing for.

Forwarding Database (or Route Table)

The Forwarding database (or route table) is derived by running. the DUA1 algorithm against all route information stored in the Topology database. Once this is done the best path to each destination is selected and placed in the router's local route table. EIGRP is capable of maintaining backup routes in case of primary route failure. These routes are automatically used when the primary route fails or for whatever reason becomes unavailable. EIGRP primary routes are referred to as successor routes, while backup paths are referred to as feasible successors. Successor and feasible successor routes are discussed later in this chapter.

Multicast and Unicast

Unlike IGRP routers, which use only broadcasts for their communications, EIGRP routers can use a combination of multicast and unicast messages to exchange route information. Broadcasts are datagrams address to everyone requiring all systems to stop and process them. Multicasts are datagrams directed to a group, and unicasts are used for one-to-one communication between systems. The multicast group address used by all EIGRP routers is 224.0.0.10.

Only devices belonging to this group (EIGRP routers) will process these datagrams. By using a combination of multicast and unicast datagrams EIGRP reduces the overall traffic load caused by broadcasts. In addition EIGRP datagrams can be reliably sent. Cisco has developed an underlying reliability mechanism they refer to as the reliable transport protocol, which tracks the delivery and reception of EIGRP datagrams containing route information. Reliability is achieved through the inclusion of sequence numbers and acknowledgments. When an EIGRP datagram containing route information is multicast or unicast to a neighbor a sequence number is added by the originating router. The receiver replies, acknowledging receipt of the previously sent sequence number. Only EIGRP datagrams that contain route information are sequenced. EIGRP datagrams that do not carry route information are always sent unreliably without sequencing. EIGRP messages are discussed later in this chapter.

Note

Although EIGRP is not connection-oriented, it does attempt to guarantee the delivery and receipt of update information by employing sequencing information within the EIGRP header portion of the datagram. Receivers must acknowledge the receipt of route information. If the receiver sends no acknowledgement, the sender retransmits the route update. The sending device keeps track of the revision or sequence numbers previously sent to ensure that all acknowledged updates are accounted for.

VLSM

Unlike IGRP, which is a classless routing protocol, EIGRP is classless. This means that EIGRP understands subnetting and can distinguish them when forwarding datagrams throughout an internetwork. This is accomplished through the inclusion of subnet masks within route updates. By including the subnet mask when advertising a destination, the receiver has enough information to determine which part of the address is the network (classful address) and which part is the subnet.

Multi-Protocol Support

Cisco's EIGRP protocol offers a single routing protocol solution for organizations by supporting multi-protocol networks. This gives companies an advantage if they use multiple protocols, such as IPX, IP, and AppleTalk.

Support for multiple protocols does not mean that there is only one EIGRP route process running within a router. You still need a separate EIGRP process for each network layer protocol supported (IPX, IP, and/or AppleTalk). In addition each route process sends route updates and maintains separate route tables for each protocol. The advantage of having a single routing protocol allows organizations to standardize on a single dynamic routing protocol within the routing domain. Otherwise, each protocol would require a different routing protocol, like RTMP (Routing Table Maintenance Protocol) for AppleTalk, perhaps OSPF for IP, and RIP for

IPX. By adopting a single routing protocol, you can take advantage of EIGRP's advanced routing methods such as incremental updates, fast convergence, and diverse metrics. All EIGRP routers within the same AS must maintain three separate databases for each protocol family they route for. If an EIGRP router uses IP, IPX, and AppleTalk, the router will have nine databases, three for each protocol, the Adjacency database, Topology database, and Forwarding database.

The only disadvantage to implementing the EIGRP protocol is that it typically requires you use only Cisco routers. EIGRP is a Cisco proprietary protocol and is not supported by all vendors.

EIGRP metrics

EIGRP, like IGRP, considers the same cost components to calculate a single *composite metric* for each destination path. However, EIGRP scales composite metric by 256 to arrive at a single number, which represents the cost to a destination. EIGRP then selects the best route based on the smallest composite metric or cost. The cost values fp0r EIGRP are the same as IGRP and include

- Bandwidth
- Delay
- Reliability
- Load

The composite calculation for EIGRP is as follows:

1. First the bandwidth value (based on the link type with lowest value end to end) is scaled using a factor of 10^7. The calculation is 10^7/lowest bandwidth value. For example, if three links exist to a destination with the following bandwidth values (56Kbps, 1.544Mbps, and 10Mbps) the link with the lowest value (or 56K) would be used in the calculation. The calculation to scale bandwidth would be 10^7/56 or 178,571.

2. The delay values for all links along the entire path (measured in microseconds) are summed then scaled by a factor of 10. The calculation is delay(sum)/10. For instance, if three links exist each with a delay value of 20,000 microseconds the calculation would be (20,000 + 20,000 +20,000)/10 resulting in a scaled delay value of 6,000.

3. The two scaled values (bandwidth and delay) are then added together and multiplied by 256 to arrive at the composite metric for the destination.

   Composite Metric = ((scaled BW) + (scaled Delay)) * 256

   The scaled values from steps one and two are summed, and then multiplied by 256 (178,571 + 6,000) * 256 for a composite metric of 47,250,176.

Using the network diagram in Figure 5.10 we will learn how the EIGRP composite metric for a destination network is calculated. Router A is determining the best path to destination network 10.10.200.0 /24. There are currently two advertisements for this network: one through Serial 0 to Router B with a minimum bandwidth of 768Kbps and a total delay of 2200 microseconds; and the other through Serial 1 to Router B, with a minimum bandwidth of 1.544Mbps (or 1544Kbps) and a total delay of 1200 microseconds. Router A chooses the path with the lowest composite metric, which would be through Serial 1.

FIGURE 5.10
EIGRP calculates the
total metric by scaling
the bandwidth and delay
metrics and multiplying it
by 256.

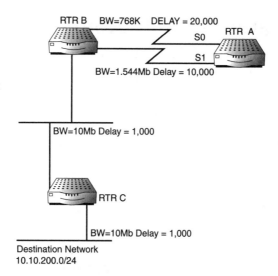

In this example, the total cost to network 10.10.200.0/24 through Serial 0 is

Minimum bandwidth: 768Kbps
Total delay: (20,000 + 1,000 + 1,000)/10 = 2200
Composite metric: [(10,000,000/768) + 2,200] × 256 = (13,021 + 2,200) × 256 = 15,221 × 256 = 3,896,576

And the total cost through Serial 1 is

Minimum bandwidth: 1,544Kbps
Total delay: (10,000 + 1,000 + 1,000)/10 = 1,200
Composite metric: [(10,000,000/1,544) + 1,200] × 256 = (6,477 + 1,200) × 256 = 7,677 × 256 = 1,965,312

So to reach Network 10.10.200.0/24, Router A chooses the route through Serial 1 to Router B (the lower route) as the best path.

Load Balancing

EIGRP, like IGRP, can send traffic across redundant paths, splitting the traffic stream across equal or non-equal cost links. This allows you to maximize the use of the bandwidth to a destination site and provide a failover mechanism when a primary link is unavailable. Equal cost load balancing is supported without configuration. Configuration of the variance command is required to control load balancing and load sharing across unequal cost paths.

Successor and Feasible Routes

EIGRP can maintain multiple routes within the route table for a single destination. The best route (the route with the lowest cost path based on Bandwidth and Delay by default) is referred to as the *successor*, and the second or backup route is referred to as the *feasible successor*.

EIGRP routers learn successor and feasible successor routes by running DUAL against the topology map built after the neighbor discovery process. EIGRP routers first discover their neighbors, and then exchange update information to build their Topology map. Once they have a map of the network, they run the DUAL algorithm against all routes to destinations identified within the map to build their local route table, listing the following information (see Figure 5.11):

- Successor and feasible successor routes
- The local interface
- The next hop router address to forward traffic to the destination.

By keeping a backup path in the route table, EIGRP routers can quickly promote the backup path to successor when that route becomes unavailable. This allows the router to continue routing traffic to that destination. Meanwhile, the router can actively query its neighbors for a new feasible (backup) path to use. This allows EIGRP routers to quickly detect and adjust around failed paths.

FIGURE 5.11

EIGRP successor routes represent the best path to a destination.

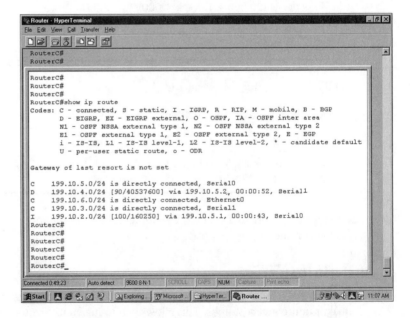

In Figure 5.11 (output from a Cisco router) a single EIGRP route has been learned and placed in the route table. The EIGRP learned route is indicated with a route code of D in the leftmost column. This is the best (successor) and only route to network 199.10.4.0. Note the next hop router and interface to get to this network is 199.10.5.2 using the local serial 1 interface.

EIGRP Packet Types

EIGRP exchanges five different packet trips so that routers can communicate with other routers about the state of their AS. EIGRP uses the following five packet types:

- Hello/Acks
- Updates
- Queries
- Replies
- Requests

Hello

Sent as multicast advertisements, IGRP routers use Hello packets to build the adjacency table (see Figure 5.12). Hello messages are sent to the destination multicast group address 224.0.0.10 (All EIGRP routers). Hello messages are always transmitted unreliably because they do not contain route information.

The exchange of Hello packets controls the process of discovery. Neighbor routers discover all other local routers building and maintaining a neighbor or adjacency table that lists all routers it has learned of. After routers build a neighbor table, they can begin to exchange route information with their neighbors.

FIGURE 5.12

Routers send hello messages to announce their presence to other EIGRP routers.

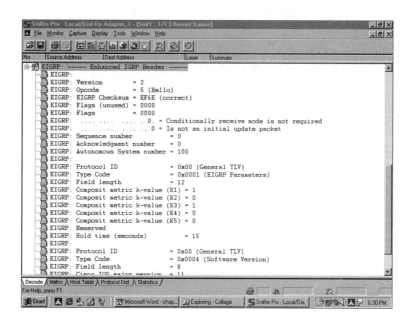

Figure 5.12 is a hello message sent by a router within AS 100. Hello messages do not carry route information. They are used to build and maintain the local Adjacency database. After EIGRP routers exchange hello messages they become neighbors and can begin to build their Topology database for all routes within the AS. They continue to transmit hello messages at regular intervals to maintain their neighbor status.

EIGRP sends hello packets every five seconds on high bandwidth links and every 60 seconds on low bandwidth multipoint links.

- 5-second hello

  Broadcast media, such as Ethernet, Token Ring, and FDDI

  Point-to-point serial links, such as PPP or HDLC leased circuits, Frame Relay point-to-point subinterfaces, and ATM point-to-point subinterfaces with high bandwidth (greater than T1) multipoint circuits, such as ISDN PRI and Frame Relay

- 60-second hello

  Multipoint circuits T1 bandwidth or slower, such as Frame Relay multipoint interfaces, ATM multipoint interfaces, ATM switched virtual circuits, and ISDN BRIs

EIGRP Ack messages are in essence hello messages that do not contain data. Ack messages are acknowledgements sent in response to updates or queries. Acknowledgement messages are unreliably sent within unicast datagrams.

EIGRP Update Packets

Routers send update packets to exchange route information. They use the information gained in this exchange to build a topology map of the internetwork (see Figure 5.13). Updates always include sequencing numbers. The router sends update packets as multicasts to the destination multicast group address 224.0.0.10 (all EIGRP routers). Route updates use the reliable transport protocols connection service, allowing routers to guarantee delivery by sequencing datagrams sent to neighbors.

In Figure 5.13, one route is being advertised (network 172.20.0.0 with a 16-bit subnet mask). The route being advertised also includes the cost values associated with the route. The route update bears the sequence number 3, set by the sender and used by the receivers to keep track of updates.

Query

When routers are converged and routing, this is referred to as *passive mode*. In passive mode routers have an active successor to a destination in their route table. If multiple paths exists to a single destination EIGRP routers will also have a feasible successor route in their route table. Routers send query packets to all neighbors when they have no feasible or successor route available or they need to choose a new one (see Figure 5.14). When a router is querying its neighbors for a new feasible route, the router is said to be in 'active' mode for the route it is querying for. Routers send query packets as a multicast or unicast datagram depending on whether the query goes to all neighbors (multicast 224.0.0.10) or a specific neighbor (unicast). Query messages are always sent reliably.

FIGURE 5.13
Route updates are used to advertise routes to destinations.

FIGURE 5.14
Router send queries to learn of an alternate feasible (backup path) route when a previously learned feasible route to a destination is unavailable.

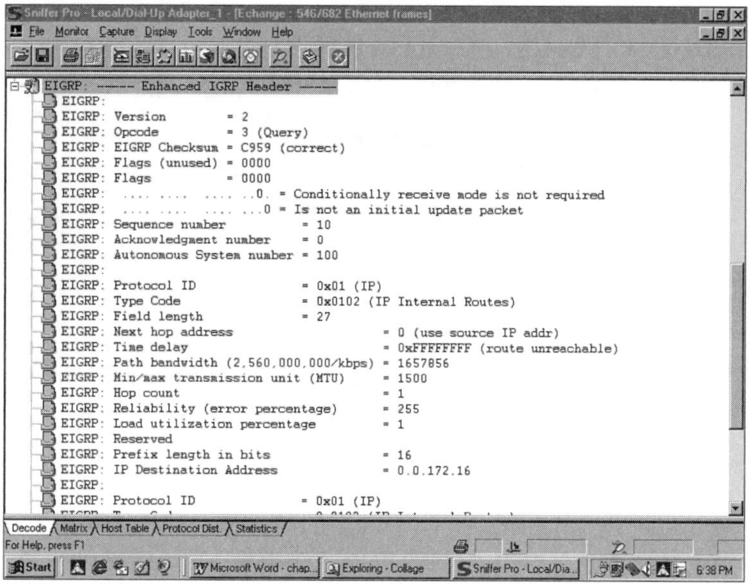

The previously learned backup path in Figure 5.14 to 172.16.0.0 has been lost, indicated by the `route unreachable` in the time delay field. This query message is sent to all local EIGRP routers requesting a new backup path to the destination.

Reply

Routers send reply packets in response to a previous query from a neighbor. Routers always send a reply as a unicast datagram. Reply messages include route information and therefore are always sent reliably.

Request

Routers may send a request packet to all neighbors when they first come online, requesting a complete list of all destinations to build its route table. Or they may send a request for specific information to a particular neighbor. Depending on the request type a router can send this message as a multicast (224.0.0.10) or unicast datagram. Most EIGRP implementations do support or use this message.

Sample Configurations

This section shows you some examples of IGRP and EIGRP configurations using Cisco routers. The first example demonstrates the steps needed to enable the IGRP and EIGRP route processes and configure the networks to be advertised. The second example shows the use of the variance command to configure unequal cost load balancing for EIGRP router.

Enable IGRP or EIGRP and Configure Networks

The steps to enable IGRP or EIGRP and configure the networks to be advertised are as follows:

1. The command to start the route process for IGRP or EIGRP is the same; `Router (IGRP or EIGRP) AS#`.

   For example, if you are enabling EIGRP for AS 100 you would enter **Router EIGRP 100**.

2. Specify the routes IGRP or EIGRP should advertise.

   The command to do this is `network [destination to advertise]`. If a router has two networks 172.20.0.0/16 and 172.30.0.0/16 the command would be entered twice, once for each network to be advertised.

   ```
   Network 172.20.0.0
   Network 172.30.0.0
   ```

After the route process is enabled and the advertised networks are defined the router will immediately begin sending route updates if it is IGRP. If this is an EIGRP router it must first discover its neighbors and form adjacencies through hello messages. Then it can exchange route information.

Configure Unequal Cost Load Balancing

IGRP is capable of load balancing over two equal cost paths without configuration, while EIGRP will, by default, install up to four routes of equal cost in the routing table. Using the variance command, as described earlier, IGRP and EIGRP can also load-balance over unequal cost links.

In the following router output you will see the effect of the variance command. Refer to the diagram in Figure 5.15 for network topology.

FIGURE 5.15

Router A has two paths to the network 10.10.200.0/24, one through serial 0 (S0) interface and the other through serial 1 (S1).

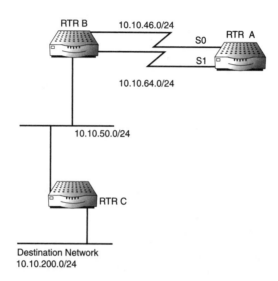

Router A has two local interfaces, serial 1 and serial 2, in Figure 5.15. Either path may be used to reach network 10.10.200.0/24 when unequal cost load balancing is configured.

The serial links connected to these interfaces have different bandwidth values. The cost values for serial 0 and serial 1 are shown in the following listing 5.2. The output is taken from a Cisco router. The bandwidth and delay values have been highlighted for easy comparison.

LISTING 5.2   Interface Metrics Taken from a Cisco Router

```
Interface serial 0
Serial0 is up, line protocol is up
  Hardware is HD64570
  Internet address is 10.10.46.4/24
  MTU 1500 bytes, BW 768 Kbit, DLY 20000 usec,
      reliability 255/255, txload 1/255, rxload 1/255
  Encapsulation HDLC, loopback not set
  Keepalive set (10 sec)
  Last input 00:00:04, output 00:00:00, output hang never
  Last clearing of "show interface" counters 10w0d
  Input queue: 0/75/0 (size/max/drops); Total output drops: 0
  Queueing strategy: weighted fair
```

LISTING 5.2   *Continued*

```
     Output queue: 0/1000/64/0 (size/max total/threshold/drops)
  Conversations  0/4/256 (active/max active/max total)
     Reserved Conversations 0/0 (allocated/max allocated)
  5 minute input rate 0 bits/sec, 0 packets/sec
  5 minute output rate 0 bits/sec, 0 packets/sec
     1541374 packets input, 94717913 bytes, 0 no buffer
     Received 708695 broadcasts, 0 runts, 0 giants, 0 throttles
     0 input errors, 0 CRC, 0 frame, 0 overrun, 0 ignored, 0 abort
     1700619 packets output, 129512232 bytes, 0 underruns
     0 output errors, 0 collisions, 197 interface resets
     0 output buffer failures, 0 output buffers swapped out
     168 carrier transitions
     DCD=up  DSR=up  DTR=up  RTS=up  CTS=up

Interface serial 1
Serial1 is up, line protocol is up
  Hardware is HD64570
  Internet address is 10.10.64.4/24
  MTU 1500 bytes, BW 1544 Kbit, DLY 20000 usec,
     reliability 255/255, txload 1/255, rxload 1/255
  Encapsulation HDLC, loopback not set
  Keepalive set (10 sec)
  Last input 00:00:01, output 00:00:02, output hang never
  Last clearing of "show interface" counters 10w0d
  Input queue: 0/75/0 (size/max/drops); Total output drops: 0
  Queueing strategy: weighted fair
  Output queue: 0/1000/64/0 (size/max total/threshold/drops)
     Conversations  0/3/256 (active/max active/max total)
     Reserved Conversations 0/0 (allocated/max allocated)
  5 minute input rate 0 bits/sec, 0 packets/sec
  5 minute output rate 1000 bits/sec, 0 packets/sec
     303370 packets input, 18174875 bytes, 0 no buffer
     Received 267876 broadcasts, 0 runts, 0 giants, 0 throttles
     0 input errors, 0 CRC, 0 frame, 0 overrun, 0 ignored, 0 abort
     341711 packets output, 30578466 bytes, 0 underruns
     0 output errors, 0 collisions, 361 interface resets
     0 output buffer failures, 0 output buffers swapped out
     111 carrier transitions
     DCD=up  DSR=up  DTR=up  RTS=up  CTS=up
```

Notice that the bandwidth value for Serial 0 is 768Kbps, while Serial 1 has a T1 link with a bandwidth value of 1.544Mbps. The delay value across both links is the same (20,000 microseconds or 2,000 milliseconds, which is 20,000 scaled by a factor of 10).

The basic configuration for Router A is listed as follows:

```
router eigrp 100
  network 10.0.0.0
```

The following output (in Listing 5.3) shows what Router A's route table looks like prior to any changes to the configuration. Notice Router A initially only has one path to the destination network 10.10.200.0 /24 in its table. This is through serial 1, which has the lower composite metric than the path through serial 0.

LISTING 5.3   Router A's IP Route Table

```
Codes: C - connected, S - static, I - IGRP, R - RIP, M - mobile, B – BGP,
➡D - EIGRP, EX - EIGRP external, O - OSPF, IA - OSPF inter area ,
➡N1 - OSPF NSSA external type 1, N2 - OSPF NSSA external type 2,
➡E1 - OSPF external type 1, E2 - OSPF external type 2, E – EGP,
➡i - IS-IS, L1 - IS-IS level-1, L2 - IS-IS level-2, * - candidate default,
➡U - per-user static route, o - ODR, P - periodic downloaded static route,
➡T - traffic engineered route

Gateway of last resort is not set

     10.0.0.0/8 is variably subnetted, 7 subnets, 2 masks
D       10.0.0.0/8 is a summary, Null0
C       10.10.40.0/24 is directly connected, Loopback0
C       10.10.46.0/24 is directly connected, Serial0
D       10.10.50.0/24 [90/2195456] via 10.10.64.6, Serial1
C       10.10.64.0/24 is directly connected, Serial1
C       10.100.1.0/24 is directly connected, Ethernet0
D       10.10.200.0/24 [90/2221056] via 10.10.64.6, Serial1
     131.108.0.0/32 is subnetted, 1 subnets
C       131.108.4.4 is directly connected, Loopback1
```

Now the variance command (with a value of 2) has been added to the EIGRP process for Autonomous System 100 on Router A. This will encourage router A to use the second path through serial 0 as well:

```
router eigrp 100
   variance 2
   network 10.0.0.0
```

After the variance command has been added to the routing process the redundant path through serial 1 can also be used. Take a look at the route table output (see Listing 5.4) from Router A after this command was added.

LISTING 5.4   Router A's IP Route Table

```
Codes: C - connected, S - static, I - IGRP, R - RIP, M - mobile, B – BGP,
➡D - EIGRP, EX - EIGRP external, O - OSPF, IA - OSPF inter area,
➡N1 - OSPF NSSA external type 1, N2 - OSPF NSSA external type 2,
➡E1 - OSPF external type 1, E2 - OSPF external type 2, E – EGP,
➡i - IS-IS, L1 - IS-IS level-1, L2 - IS-IS level-2, * - candidate default,
➡U - per-user static route, o - ODR, P - periodic downloaded static route,
➡T - traffic engineered route

Gateway of last resort is not set

     10.0.0.0/8 is variably subnetted, 7 subnets, 2 masks
D       10.0.0.0/8 is a summary, Null0
C       10.10.40.0/24 is directly connected, Loopback0
C       10.10.46.0/24 is directly connected, Serial0
D       10.10.50.0/24 [90/2195456] via 10.10.64.6, Serial1
                      [90/3870720] via 10.10.46.6, Serial0
```

LISTING 5.4   Continued

```
C       10.10.64.0/24 is directly connected, Serial1
C       10.100.1.0/24 is directly connected, Ethernet0
D       10.10.200.0/24 [90/2221056] via 10.10.64.6, Serial1
                       [90/3896320] via 10.10.46.6, Serial0
     131.108.0.0/32 is subnetted, 1 subnets
C       131.108.4.4 is directly connected, Loopback1
```

The router now has two paths of unequal cost to load balance traffic when trying to reach network 10.10.200.0/24.

Summary

Cisco has developed several proprietary routing protocols with the two most prominent being IGRP (Interior Gateway Routing Protocol) and EIGRP (Enhanced Interior Gateway Routing Protocol). IGRP is considered a Distance Vector routing protocol, while EIGRP is considered a hybrid (a mixture of Distance Vector and Link State) routing protocol. Originally, only Cisco routers supported EIGRP and IGRP, but now other vendor platforms support both protocols.

Cisco developed IGRP in the mid-1980s because it wanted to create an IGP that was more robust than RIP for routing within an AS or routing domain. In addition, Cisco needed a protocol that provided more flexible path selection for networks that had a greater complexity in their topologies. To address RIP's limitations, Cisco developed IGRP to take into consideration other metrics, such as links with different bandwidth capacity and delay characteristics, and extended the hop count to 255. These improvements allow for greater network growth and network expansion size.

Cisco developed Enhanced IGRP in the early 1990s to improve the operating efficiency of IGRP and integrate support for multiple protocols, such as IP, IPX, and AppleTalk. EIGRP was a significant enhancement to the existing IGRP protocol. It brought incremental updates and faster convergence, which greatly aided in the routing performance of networks with slower serial link speeds. EIGRP also scales much better to large network implementations and is used in some of the largest corporate networks today. EIGRP's only real drawback is that it is completely proprietary and was never introduced as a standard for other vendors to implement.

Chapter Quiz

1. Name the metrics both IGRP and EIGP use to make routing decisions.

2. What's the maximum hop count support by IGRP? What are the various IGRP timers and what are their functions?

3. How often does IGRP send out its route updates?

4. What unique feature does EIGRP have that no other routing protocol supports?

5. What is the significance of successor and feasible successor routes?

6. Name the three databases stored by each EIGRP router.

7. Name the different EIGRP packets types.

8. What two metrics does EIGRP use by default?

9. What type of routing protocol is EIGRP, classful or classless?

10. How do EIGRP routers announce their presence and learn of neighbor routers?

CHAPTER 6

OSPF

You will learn about the following in this chapter:

- OSPF operation
- Single and multiple area OSPF
- Link State advertisements
- Sample OSPF configuration

OSPF

The OSPF (Open Shortest Path First) Link State routing protocol is described in RFC 1583. As previously mentioned in Chapter 3, "IP Routing," OSPF uses a Link State routing algorithm, and as such, makes more intelligent path selection than Distance Vector routing protocols. When determining the best path to a destination, OSPF, like all Link State routing protocols, may consider any or all of the following metrics: bandwidth, delay, reliability and load. Each of these metrics was discussed in Chapter 3. We will discuss how OSPF uses these metrics in its path selection later in this chapter.

All OSPF routers, networks, and subnets are logically grouped into areas. OSPF networks may consist of a single area or multiple areas organized hierarchically. Whether a single area or multiple areas exist the entire OSPF internetwork is referred to as one routing domain (or AS). This hierarchical division isolates changes and route update traffic to areas and reduces overhead involved with maintaining large route tables and route table recalculations when changes occur.

As a Link State routing protocol OSPF has many advantages over Distance Vector routing protocols. For example, OSPF uses multicasts instead of broadcasts to disseminate route information to neighbor routers. Route updates are triggered, which means they are only sent when a change occurs in the network (not periodically). Triggered updates are flooded to all OSPF routers, increasing convergence time. In addition, each update only includes the changed route information, not the entire table. Route updates are isolated to only the routers in the OSPF area in which the change occurred. OSPF is, unlike Distance Vector protocols, such as RIP and IGRP, capable of supporting medium to large networks because it does not have a hop count maximum limiting its diameter. These are just a few of the features OSPF offers, making it the preferred routing protocol in many corporate IP internetworks. We will discuss each of these features and more in this chapter.

OSPF Features

OSPF has the following features:

- **Multicast**—224.0.0.5 for all OSPF routers and 224.0.0.6 for designated router/backup designated router

- **Fast convergence**—When an event, referred to as trigger, occurs (like a new link or failed link is detected), routers immediately flood updates without waiting for a periodic timer and compute calculations in parallel

- **Classless routing**—Supports VLSMs

- **Supports various routing metrics**—Bandwidth, Reliability, Load, and Delay

- **QoS (Quality of Service)**—Allows OSPF routers to forward datagrams to a destination based on the level of service required by the application

- **Authentication**—Routers can utilize password protection, allowing them to only exchange information with authorized routers

- **Equal and unequal cost routes**—Routers can forward datagrams across redundant equal and unequal cost paths to a destination balancing the load of traffic

- **Areas**—Can implement OSPF in a single area or divided in multiple areas

OSPF Multicasts

OSPF routers do not send updates and advertisements as broadcasts (to everyone). Instead they transmit updates using multicasts (addressed to a group). IP multicast routing is discussed within Chapter 11, "IP Multicast Routing." By exchanging route updates and advertisements via multicasts instead of broadcasts, the number of systems required to process these updates and advertisements is reduced. This saves precious resources. Only systems (OSPF-enabled devices) belonging to the OSPF multicast group fully process the datagram.

There are two main OSPF multicast group addresses: 224.0.0.5 (which includes all OSPF routers) and 224.0.0.6 (used by the Designated router). After OSPF is enabled on a router it automatically becomes a member of the multicast group 224.0.0.5, listening to multicasts sent to this destination. On each broadcast network, such as Ethernet or Token-Ring, one router will assume the role of DR (Designated Router) and another will become a BDR (Backup Designated Router). Both of these routers will immediately, upon assuming these roles, become members of the multicast group 224.0.0.6, listening to multicasts sent to that address. DRs and BDRs will be discussed later in this chapter.

Fast Convergence

Two main factors contribute to OSPF's fast convergence time: triggered updates and flooding. As mentioned earlier, OSPF routers do not use periodic update timers. When a router detects a new or failed link, this event triggers the router to immediately pass this information on to all other routers within the same area through a process referred to as flooding. By not waiting to

Note

Two versions of OSPF exist, version 1 and 2. Version 2 is the most current OSPF version. Version 1 is rarely seen and is considered obsolete. Because of this our discussions will be limited to version 2 only.

Designed as an IGP, OSPF can support medium to large networks within a single Autonomous System. OSPF Autonomous Systems within the context of this discussion refer to a single or multiple OSPF areas and the routers within these areas used within an organization's internetwork.

Note

THE IETF (Internet Engineering Task Force) originally developed OSPF version 1, which was defined within the RFC 1247. This version was later replaced by OSPF version 2 defined within the RFC 1583. Both versions of OSPF only support the routing of IP datagrams, and is identified by the IP protocol type 89.

OSPF routers detect and adjust to route failures (or a new link) allowing them to adapt quickly to changes in the network. When a router detects a link failure or new link, this triggers an update (without waiting for periodic timers to expire). The router detecting the change immediately floods the update to all routers within the same OSPF area, notifying them of the change.

This differs from Distance Vector routing protocols, which wait for their periodic timers to expire before sending an update. In addition, Distance Vector routing protocols send these updates whether changes have occurred in the network or not. This constant broadcasting of route information adds lots of unnecessary overhead to the network. In contrast OSPF routers generate a multicast route advertisement upon initialization or when a change has occurred (triggered event) in the network. This update is then flooded out all OSPF ports except the one it was received through, notifying all routers within its area of the downed or new link. All routers then compute route changes in parallel, speeding convergence times. The immediate notification (triggered) and flooding of link state changes within an area results in very fast convergence within an OSPF area.

Caution

It is also important to be aware that rapid convergence implies that areas must be kept to a small size. If there are a large number of routers within an area (greater than 50), the link state updates can quickly flood the network and cause severe congestion and delays. This can be overcome by dividing up a single OSPF AS with one area into multiple OSPF areas.

We will discuss the operation of OSPF version 2 as it relates to a single area, and then move on to a more complex AS, implementing multiple areas in a hierarchical structure.

send updates when a change occurs, OSPF routers can react quickly to changes in their environment. The faster a router learns of a change, the faster a router can update its route table and get on with its primary function of forwarding datagrams. With all routers receiving the flooded update and computing the change in parallel convergence, time is dramatically decreased.

Classless Routing

As discussed in Chapter 2, "IP and IP Addressing," classless routing protocols are protocols that recognize and understand subnetting. Classless routing protocols support subnetting through the inclusion of subnet masks within the updates. These subnet masks may contain any variable number of masked bits (VLSM), identifying both the major network and subnet address. As a classless routing protocol, OSPF not only advertises the destination network or host, but includes the subnet mask within the route update, allowing the receiver to identify subnetted networks.

OSPF Metrics

OSPF supports several metrics used in determining the best path between source and destination when multiple paths exist. Unlike Distance Vector RIP, which only takes into consideration a single metric distance (or hops), OSPF can make use of one or more of the following metrics: bandwidth, reliability, load, and delay. Most vendor implementations do not take advantage of every metric. The most common implementation is OSPF using only bandwidth as the metric cost value for path selection.

We discussed each of the previously mentioned metrics in Chapter 3. You may recall from our discussion that bandwidth represents the transfer capacity of the link. For example, if the link is a Fast Ethernet segment, it may have a bandwidth capacity of 100Mbps. Reliability refers to the stability of the link in terms of lost datagrams. An unstable path may result in dropped datagrams, making it less desirable. Load is a variable value that changes based on the utilization of the link. As utilization rises a link is experiencing more traffic and may be less desirable than a less congested link. The final metric delay measures the time in microseconds it takes for a router to process, queue, and transmit a datagram out an interface.

QoS

OSPF supports Quality of Service(QoS) routing, allowing OSPF routers to forward datagrams to destinations based on the level of service set by an administrator or requested by an application. QoS is an emerging service-level datagram forwarding architecture. QoS allows intelligent deterministic delivery of data between end systems across the Internet.

For example, when multiple paths exist to a destination, offering different types of service, OSPF routers with QoS enabled, place the QoS routes within their route table, one for each service level supported. An application or administrator can then specify the type of QoS route its datagrams should take to reach the destination. If the OSPF router has a route with the requested QoS level, datagrams are sent along this path. If not, the router simply sends the datagram over the next best path. QoS and QoS protocols are discussed in Chapter 10.

Authentication

OSPF Authentication is a configurable feature. When implemented, OSPF routers sharing the same password may exchange route information. Password authentication may be clear text or encrypted depending on the authentication type chosen by the administrator.

Load Balancing

When multiple paths exist to a destination with the same or similar costs (metric values), routers can use both routes to forward datagrams, referred to as *load balancing*. OSPF routers place both (equal cost) routes in their local route table. Equal cost refers to the fact that both paths have the same metric value, which in OSPF, is bandwidth by default. Two links connecting two remote networks with bandwidth T1 (1.544Mbps) values would be considered equal cost paths, making them eligible for load balancing. Load balancing across equal (same) cost paths happens automatically (without configuration). Load balancing across unequal cost paths requires manual configuration of OSPF.

OSPF Areas

A single OSPF AS with one area is generally sufficient for small networks (10 to 15 routers). As the number of segments and routers increase, so does the traffic. In medium to large networks consisting of geographically separate networks with many routers, the amount of routes to maintain and OSPF updates to traffic may overwhelm a single area. An OSPF AS can be hierarchically subdivided into multiple areas, reducing the amount of update traffic routers receive and the number of SPF (Shortest Path First) calculations performed. We discuss OSPF areas in more detail later in this chapter.

OSPF Databases

All OSPF routers maintain and build three separate databases: Adjacency, Link State and Forwarding. The first database, the Adjacency (or Neighbor Table), is used to keep track of OSPF routers connected to a common network segment. The next database (the Link State or Topology Map) is used to keep track of all networks, subnets, and destinations within an OSPF area. The last database, known as the Forwarding (or Route Table), stores the best paths to OSPF networks, subnets, and destinations.

Adjacency Database (Neighbor Table)

For OSPF routers to exchange and learn about routes, they must first form an adjacency with their directly connected neighbors on the local segment. If they do not form this relationship, they cannot participate in OSPF routing.

When an OSPF router first comes online, it must discover and establish its adjacency with all other local OSPF routers. Upon completion of the discovery process, each router will have built its Adjacency database. This database is also referred to as the neighbor table, in that it is really a list of all OSPF neighbor routers. As each router is discovered, it is added to this table and adjacency is formed. Each OSPF router goes through the following events to achieve successful adjacency with its neighbors:

1. It transmits hello packets out on the local wire identifying itself to its neighbors. This message is multicast to the destination address 224.0.0.5.

2. Receiving OSPF routers add the new router to their Adjacency database and respond to the hello with their own hello, identifying themselves.

This provides a simplistic view of the process because we assume that all required parameters within the hello message match and are agreed upon by neighbors. If this is not the case, they will not form an adjacency. At this point all neighbors should know about each other and have theoretically formed a neighbor relationship. We will discuss the hello and all other packets types later in this chapter.

Link State Database (Topology Map)

OSPF routers build the Link State database (also referred to as the Topology Map) after the Adjacency database, called *neighbor discovery*. After the OSPF routers know which routers to exchange information with, they can build a complete map of the internetwork topology within their OSPF area, identifying every network and subnet and the path to each. From this database each router creates a tree structure identifying itself as the root connected to each destination through the shortest path.

Forwarding Database (Route Table)

Each router uses the information contained within the Link State database to derive the Forwarding database (or route table). After each router has a complete topology map, it runs the SPF algorithm against the map to derive the "best route" to all known destinations. It then places these routes in its local route table to forward data.

OSPF Operation

OSPF can support various Data Link layer architectures, such as. LAN and WAN connections. How adjacencies and database exchanges take place depend on the architecture OSPF runs over. For the purposes of our discussion, we focus on LAN-based (broadcast) architectures. We describe other architectures later in this chapter.

We begin by discussing OSPF operation within a single area. When only a single area exists, the OSPF Autonomous System and Area are one in the same. All routers within an OSPF area maintain a copy of the same Link State database (see Figure 6.1). When multiple areas exist, routers connected to both areas maintain separate databases for each area.

FIGURE 6.1

In a single area OSPF implementation only one area exists. All routers within the area maintain three databases: a topology map, a neighbor table, and a routing table.

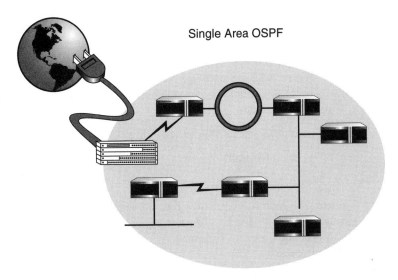

Single Area OSPF

OSPF has six different Link State Advertisements (known as LSA packets) grouped into three categories:

- Intra-area
- Inter-area
- External

Each describes the type of Link State advertisement and where its propagation occurs. Table 6.1 shows the six different LSA packet types. Each of these is discussed in more detail later in this chapter.

TABLE 6.1 Link State Advertisement Packet Types

LSA Type	Advertisement Name	Description
1	Router link	Describes the router's directly connected network and state of the interfaces
2	Network link	Identifies all routers connected to the local network
3	Summary link	Summarizes their subarea to a network outside the area
4	Summary link	Summarizes routes to external non-OSPF networks outside the AS
5	AS external link	Describes a route to a destination in another AS
7	AS external link	Carries route information through a NSSA (Not So Stubby Area) stub network. Areas and stub networks will be discussed later in this chapter.

Intra-Area Advertisement

Routers send intra-area advertisements within an area. These advertisements only propagate within the area of origination. These advertisements describe local router links and networks within an area. Routers flood type 1 (originated by all routers) and 2 (originated by Designated Routers only) advertisements throughout a single area only. Designated Router (or DR) is discussed later in this chapter.

Two types of intra-area LSAs exist, including

- Type 1 (router link)

- Type 2 (network link)

Routers send router-link, LS type 1 advertisements to the destination multicast 224.0.0.6 (Designated Router and Backup Designated Router multicast group address). These advertisements describe their directly connected networks and the state of the interfaces connected to these networks.

On LANs (broadcast) networks the Designated Router sends a network-link, LS type 2 advertisement to the destination multicast address 224.0.0.5, the multicast group address for all OSPF routers. These advertisements identify all routers connected to the local network.

Figure 6.2 shows an example of a type 1 (router link) intra-area LSA and Figure 6.3 shows an example of a type 2 (network link) int ra-area LSA.

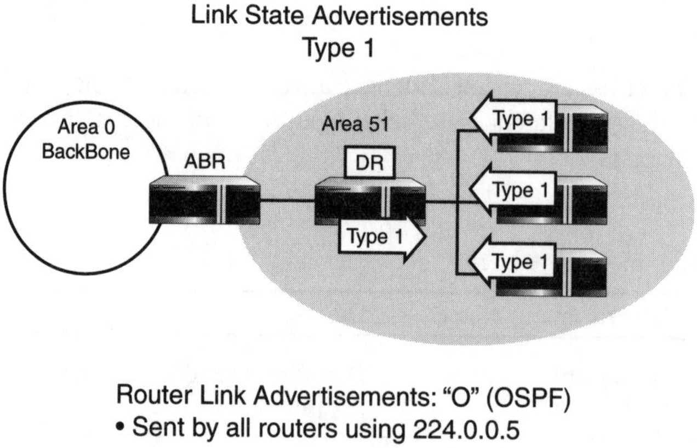

FIGURE 6.2

All routers send LSA type 1 intra-area router link advertisements to the destination multicast address 224.0.0.5.

Link State Advertisements
Type 1

Router Link Advertisements: "O" (OSPF)
• Sent by all routers using 224.0.0.5

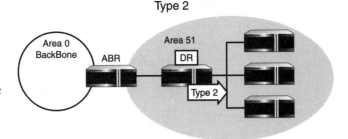

FIGURE 6.3

Only the DR sends LSA type 2 intra-area network link advertisements to all routers (224.0.0.6) on the same segment.

Inter-Area Advertisement

ABRs (Area Border Routers) send inter-area advertisements between directly connected OSPF areas (when multiple areas exist). Typically ABRs connect subareas to the backbone (Area 0), the main transit area for all Inter-Area traffic. These advertisements summarize the routes within an OSPF subarea. ABRs sends these advertisements into Area 0, where other ABRs learn and then propagate this new inter-area information to their own area.

Two types of inter-area LSAs exist, including

- Type 3 (summary link)
- Type 4 (summary link)

ABR routers also send summary link LS Type 3 advertisements to summarize their subarea into Area 0 (backbone). ABRs also use these advertisements to advertise summarized routes from other subareas learned through Area 0 into their own subarea.

ABR routers send summary link LS Type 4 advertisements to identify ASBRs (Autonomous System Boundary Routers) that provide access to external non-OSPF networks outside this AS.

Figure 6.4 shows examples of types 3 and 4 inter-area advertisements.

External Advertisement

Only ASBR routers send external advertisements. These advertisements propagate throughout the entire OSPF AS, except stub areas, which we describe within the multiple area section of this chapter. These advertisements describe external non-OSPF routes outside the AS (OSPF routing domain). An example of an External route would be a RIP route that is being injected (redistributed) into OSPF to be advertised within the AS. Because RIP is not OSPF, OSPF considers this information foreign and advertises it as such. External route injection is beyond the scope of this book and its configuration varies based on vendor implementation. In this book we will simply refer to external routes as any route that is not natively learned by OSPF.

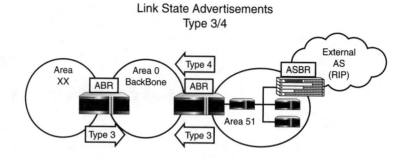

FIGURE 6.4

ABR routers send LSA type 3 and 4 inter-area summary link advertisements.

Summary Advertisements: "IA" Inter-Area
- Type 3: Sent by ABRs into Area 0 summarizing their local area
- Type 4: Used to identify route to ASBRs

Two types of external LSAs exist, including

- Type 5 (external link)
- Type 7 (external link)

Only ASBRs—routers that are running more than one routing protocol, such as OSPF and RIP, IGRP, EIGRP, static routing, and so on—send external link, LS Type 5, advertisement. An administrator can configure OSPF ASBRs to take non-OSPF routes and inject them into the OSPF environment. The LS type 5 advertisements allow foreign routes to be advertised throughout the AS, making them known to all other OSPF areas and routers.

Only ASBRs connected to a NSSA (Not So Stubby Area, described later in this chapter) running more than one routing protocol, such as OSPF and RIP, IGRP, EIGRP, static routing, and so on, send an external, LS Type 7, advertisement. You can configure OSPF ASBRs to take non-OSPF routes and inject them into the OSPF NSSA environment as Type 7, a special LSA type used to carry this route information through the stub network. An ABR connected to area 0 converts this LSA type to Type 5 prior to passing this information into the backbone.

Figure 6.5 shows an example of a type 5 external advertisement and Figure 6.6 shows and example of a type 7 external advertisement.

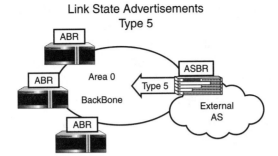

FIGURE 6.5
ASBR routers send type 5 LSAs to advertise external non-OSPF routes.

AS External Advertisements: "E1 & E2"
• Sent by ASBR; used to identify routes to external autonomous networks

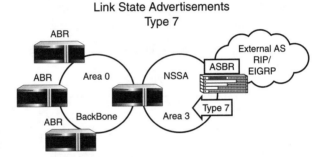

FIGURE 6.6
Similar to type 5 advertisements, ASBRs use type 7 advertisements to send external route updates describing non-OSPF routes through a NSSA area to reach Area 0.

AS External Advertisements:
• Sent by ASBR only within NSSA area to advertise external AS routes

Link State Advertisement Header

Each LSA (Link State Advertisement) header has the same format, containing the identical fields. Each LSA header contains 20 bytes. Figure 6.7 shows the format of an OSPF Link State Advertisement header and fields.

FAll link state advertisements share the same 20-byte header. This header has the following eight fields:

- **LS Age**—Contains a value measured in seconds and indicates the time that has passed since the originating router sent this LSA.

- **Options**—Contains the same option values described in the hello packet.

- **LS Type**—Defines the type of LSA being sent as either intra-area (1 or 2), inter-area (3 or 4), or external (5 or 7).

- **Link State ID**—Identifies either the IP address of the originating router (LSA type 1 and 4) or IP address of the network being advertised (LSA type 2, 3, 5, or 7). This varies based on LSA type. Table 6.2 shows the following Link State IDs that exist.

- **Advertising Router**—Identifies the router that originated this advertisement.

- **LS Sequence Number**—Guarantees the delivery and receipt. of DD packets. Each time an OSPF router sends an advertisement, the originator includes a sequence number identifying the advertisement. The receiver uses the sequence number to keep track of the DD packets received.

- **LS Checksum**—Verifies the contents of the OSPF DD packet has not been damaged in transit. The sending OSPF router calculates this value using an algorithm, placing the results within this field. The receiver recalculates the algorithm, then compares the results. If, after performing this calculation, the receiver finds that the value does not match, it discards the datagram because the contents have changed during transit. If the value matches, the header is deemed good and the receiver processes the datagram.

- **Length**—Contains the length of OSPF datagram in bytes. This value specifies how much data follows.

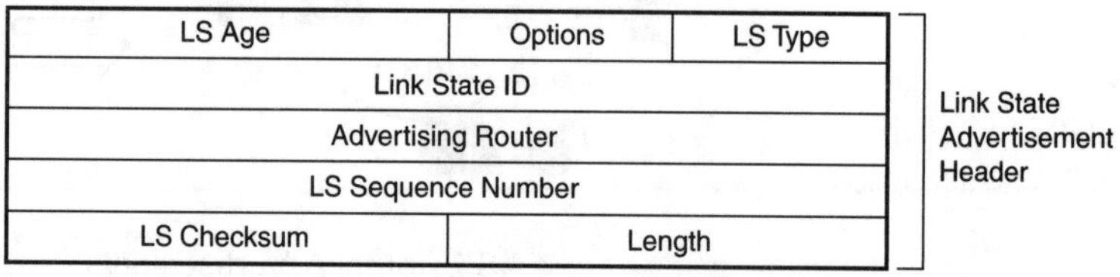

FIGURE 6.7

This figure shows the format of an OSPF link state advertisement header and fields.

TABLE 6.2 Link State IDs

Value	Description
1	Slave router ID
2	DR
3	IP address of the destination network being advertised
4	ASBR router ID
5	IP address of the destination network being advertised

OSPF Router States

As discussed earlier in this chapter, routers must first form an adjacency (they must become neighbors) before they can exchange route information. OSPF routers go through the following states from beginning to end:

- Down

- Init

- Exstart

- Exchange

- Loading

- Full

You can easily remember the first and the last states. *Down* means OSPF is either not enabled on this router or the interface has been reset. In other words, this router cannot currently participate, or is not currently participating, in route information exchange. The *full* state is where the route table has converged and the router can actively route datagrams. Routers must pass through all other states to get to the full state.

Init

Initially, a router identifies itself to all its neighbors when you enable OSPF on an interface. It does this by generating a multicast hello datagram (to the destination 224.0.0.5) announcing itself and its parameters to all other routers. At this point no adjacency between neighbors exists. Figure 6.8 shows an example of the init state.

Init State - No DR

FIGURE 6.8
Routers exchange hello messages to establish and maintain neighbor relationships with other routers on the same segment.

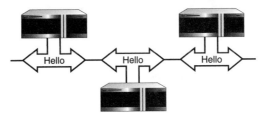

- Routers send "Hello" messages to establish adjacencies with neighbor routers.

In the init state, no DR or BDR router exists because the DR and BDR election process has not taken place yet. The router passes through this state when an administrator initially enables OSPF or resets an interface. In this state routers transmit hello messages announcing their presence to all other routers on the network. All routers send this advertisement to all OSPF routers on the same segment. Routers attached to the same subnet receive this hello message, learning of their new neighbor and incorporating them into their Adjacency database.

Two-Way

After the router receives the response hellos from the other local routers, adjacencies begin to form. Each router learns who its neighbors are, adding them to their local Adjacency database. Adjacencies only form if the following hello fields match:

- Area ID

- Hello and dead timers

- Authentication

- Stub ID

This list displays only a portion of the hello parameters. We will discuss all hello parameters in more detail later in this chapter. Figure 6.9 shows the parameters within the hello messages that must match.

OSPF "Hello" Announcements

FIGURE 6.9
The OSPF area ID, hello, and dead interval timers, stub area flag, and password (if set) must match for neighbors to become adjacent.

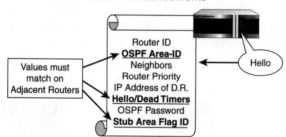

Note: If an authentication password is assigned, this too must match!

Routers use OSPF hello messages to build and maintain the Adjacency database. After routers have formed adjacencies with neighbor routers, they continue to send these hello messages every 10 seconds to maintain the relationship. If a hello message has not been received from a neighbor router within four 10-second intervals, that router is considered dead and removed from the Adjacency database. For routers to form an adjacency with other routers, certain parameters must match: area ID, hello and dead timer values, stub flag, and authentication password (if defined). If any of these values do not match, neighbor routers will not form an adjacency, and thus cannot exchange route information. At this point all routers on the local segment know their neighbors and have established a bi-directional relationship (see Figure 6.10).

FIGURE 6.10

In the two-way state, routers on the same network have achieved a bi-directional relationship.

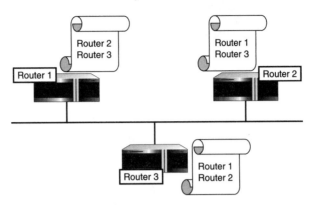

Two-Way State - No DR

• Each router adds all other routers to their Database.

This state assumes that routers have received and exchanged the initial hello messages and incorporated them into their adjacency tables.

Exstart

After the init and two-way states finish, all routers on the segment have enough information to elect a DR (Designated Router) and BDR (Backup Designated Router). The exstart state requires that all routers form a master/slave relationship with the DR and BDR on the segment for the purpose of exchanging route update information. After the election the DR and BDR (master and backup master respectively) become the focal point for all route updates. All other routers are slaves to the DR and BDR. The DR and BDR receive route updates from all slaves on the segment. DR and BDR responsibilities will be discussed later in this chapter.

Each broadcast network (LAN) must elect one DR and one BDR per segment. This election process involves all routers on the attached segment. Routers use two parameters taken from the previously exchanged hello messages to elect the DR and BDR:

- Priority ID (considered first)
- (And/or) Router ID (considered second)

The routers consider the priority ID first and the router ID second. The routers elect the router with the highest priority ID as the DR and the router with second highest priority ID as the BDR. If all routers have the same priority ID, the router with the highest router ID becomes the DR and the router second highest becomes the BDR. You can modify both of these parameters to manipulate the DR and BDR selection.

The DR and BDR, once elected, become the focal point of the segment. The DR and BDR have the following responsibilities:

- Collecting all route advertisements from the local routers

- Building the Link State database

- Disseminating this information to all other routers on the same segment (DR only, BDR in standby)

All other routers become slaves to the DR and BDR (masters), changing their adjacency relationship with all other routers to make the DR and BDR the recipient of all router advertisements.

Both the DR and BDR belong to the multicast group 224.0.0.6, to which all routers address their route advertisements. Once a DR and BDR exist, they both receive and process the local type 1 router advertisements from all other routers on the segment. However, only the DR has the responsibility for distributing this information to the local routers, addressing them to the destination multicast group 224.0.0.5. The BDR remains in standby mode until the DR cannot disseminate this information (becomes unavailable). At this time the BDR becomes the DR. If the DR fails, the BDR takes over; if the DR returns, it does not supersede the current router performing the DR role.

Electing a DR for each segment reduces the number of adjacencies necessary throughout the internetwork, limiting the processing of OSPF multicast traffic done by all routers. You can think of this state exstart in this way: Before an OSPF router can start exchanging route information, it needs to identify the local DR and form a master/slave relationship (see Figure 6.11).

ExStart State

FIGURE 6.11

In the exstart state all routers form a master/ slave relationship with the DR and BDR.

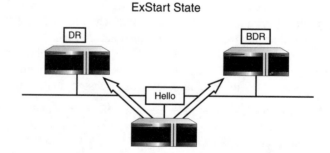

- All Routers send LSAs to the DR and BDR using multicast 224.0.0.6.

Think of the exstart state as the state routers must pass through prior to *starting* their route information *exchange*. In this state all routers on the segment form a master/slave relationship (adjacency) with the routers functioning as the DR and BDR. The DR and the BDR belong to the multicast group address 224.0.0.6—the address all slave routers use to transmit their hello messages to form the adjacency with the DR and BDR.

Exchange

As the name implies, all slave routers exchange route information with the DR and BDR during this stage, sending their updates to both the DR and BDR and receiving the synchronized full copy of the Link State database from the DR only. At this state, the routers build a topology map (Link State database) describing all routers and networks within an area (see Figure 6.12).

Exchange State

FIGURE 6.12
The exchange state allows routers to exchange their route information with the DR and BDR. The DR transmits the synchronized database to all routers using 224.0.0.5.

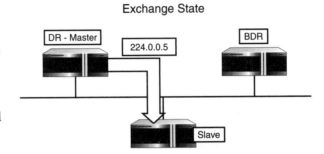

In this state all slave routers transmit their route information to the DR/BDR address 224.0.0.6. Both the DR and BDR assimilate the database changes. However, only the DR manages the synchronization and dissemination of this information. The DR (master) transmits learned route information to all slave routers on the segment on multicast address 224.0.0.5.

If any of the previous states fail (init, two-way, or exstart), OSPF routers the adjacency and/or master/slave process will not be formed. If OSPF routers do no enter the exchange state, the topology map of the OSPF area will not get built and routing can not occur. The first time a router enters the exchange state, it has an empty Link State database (map); therefore, it must receive route information for the entire OSPF area to build it. After that, routers send only updates with topology changes. However, OSPF routers send all their route information every 30 minutes just to make sure that all OSPF routers have the current topology.

Loading

The router only enters this state when it receives conflicting information during the exchange state with the DR. If the information received differs from the currently held topology map, a router may enter the loading state sending an LSR (Link State Request) for more specific information to complete the map. If it finds no discrepancies, it skips this state.

Full

A router reaches the full state after it passes through all the other states. In this final state the router builds the route table from the topology map (Link State database). The router derives and installs the best routes to destinations in the forwarding database (route table) by running the SPF algorithm on all routes identified within the Link State database.

Note

Note that routers only transition through all of the previously mentioned states when an administrator first enables OSPF and they have not actively participated in OSPF.

After a router has reached the full state, it only transitions through one of the following three states:

- Exchange
- Loading
- Full

OSPF routers cycle through each of the previously mentioned states each time a change occurs in an area. When a new link comes online or an existing link fails, the OSPF router detecting the change generates a triggered update (entering the exchange state) and floods this update throughout the area. DRs on each segment receive, process, and disseminate this information to all routers within the area. If a router received route information that conflicts with previously received information, it enters the loading state. In the loading state, the router requests more information from the local DR. After it receives the necessary information from the DR, it runs the SPF algorithm against the Link State database, convergence occurs, and routing begins (the router enters the full state).

OSPF Router Types

OSPF defines different roles that routers assume based on their placement within the AS (see Figure 6.13). Remember, an AS functions as a group of routers exchanging information via a common routing protocol (in this case, OSPF). A router may assume multiple roles at the same time. OSPF has four router types:

- Internal
- Backbone
- ABR (Area Border Router)
- ASBR (Autonomous System Boundary Router)

Figure 6.13 shows the different OSPF router types.

Backbone routers have one or more interfaces connecting to Area 0. Internal routers have all interfaces within a single area. ABRs connect areas, typically subareas to Area 0. ASBRs run OSPF and some other routing protocol and advertise route information learned from the other protocol through the OSPF network. OSPF can exist as a combination of router types, such as an internal backbone—a router with all of its interfaces contained within Area 0.

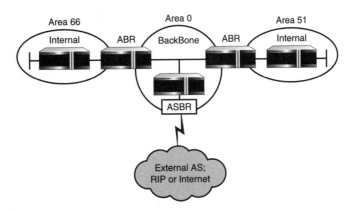

FIGURE 6.13

A router's placement within an OSPF network determines its type.

Internal Router

An internal router has all of its attached interfaces contained within a single OSPF area. This type of router does not run any other routing protocol.

Backbone Routers

A backbone router has at least one interface connected to Area 0. A router that has all interfaces within Area 0 functions as an internal backbone router.

ABR (Area Border Router)

An ABR router sits on the border of two OSPF areas. These routers connect to multiple areas, typically a subarea to Area 0. ABRs connecting to Area 0 also function as backbone routers. ABRs maintain multiple Link State databases, one for each area they connect to.

ASBR (Autonomous System Boundary Router)

An ASBR router sits on the boundary of two Autonomous Systems that run OSPF and some other routing protocol, such as RIP (any routing protocol besides OSPF). You can configure ASBRs to advertise non-OSPF routes into the OSPF AS, disseminating this external route information to all other areas within the AS.

Operation Over Various Data Link Architectures

As mentioned earlier OSPF functions over various network types. However, functionality differs based on the type of network it runs over. OSPF supports broadcast-based architectures as well as point-to-point and non-broadcast networks.

Broadcast-Based Networks

The broadcast-based LAN networks (Ethernet, Token-Ring, and FDDI) support broadcast and multicast traffic, allowing for the dynamic discovery of neighbors, election of DR and BDR, and route information exchanges (see Figure 6.14).

Neighbor Relationships on
Broadcast Multi-Access Networks:

FIGURE 6.14
Each broadcast multi-access network has one DR and one BDR. Because these types of networks support broadcast and multicast traffic by default, neighbor relationships and DR/BDR happen automatically.

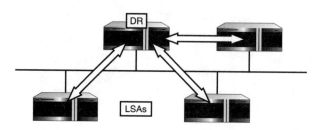

Point-to-Point

A point-to-point or dedicated leased-line connection consists of two routers connected at each end of the link. In this environment, you need to manually configure routers with the IP address of its neighbor. This facilitates the capability to form an adjacency across the link and exchanging route information. Because only two routers exist, there's no need to have a DR or BDR controlling the creation and synchronization of the LS Database (see Figure 6.15).

NBMA (Non-Broadcast Multi-Access)

NBMA networks consist of two or more routers communicating over a non-broadcast network, such as X.25 or Frame Relay. Because NBMA does not support broadcasts, you need to manually configure each router with the IP address of all other neighbor routers for adjacencies to form. By manually configuring the routers with this information, they can elect a DR and BDR and exchange route information without the use of broadcasts.

Just consider whether the underlying architecture supports broadcasts or not. If it does not, you need to manually configure neighbor information. If it does, everything having to do with neighbor discovery, DR/BDR election, and route information exchange happens automatically (see Figure 6.16).

Neighbor Relationships on
Point to Point Serial Connections:

FIGURE 6.15

Point-to-point WAN links
do not have a DR or BDR
because a dedicated leased-
lined connection has only
two hosts (routers) at each
end of the link. This eliminates the need to manage
the route information
synchronization. Routers
need the specific configuration of the other router's
IP address for them to
form adjacencies with one
another and to exchange
route information.

No DR or BDR election is required since
there are only two devices on the link.

Neighbor Relationships
Non-Broadcast Multi-Access Networks

FIGURE 6.16

NBMA networks do not
support broadcast.
Routers connected to the
links require configuration
of the IP address of all
other routers to facilitate
adjacencies, DR/BDR
elections, and route
information exchange.

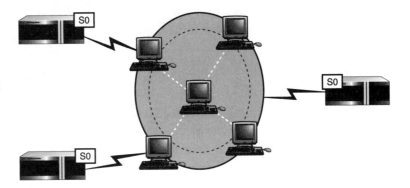

Multiple Areas

You can implement OSPF in a single area for a small to medium size internetwork; however, most medium to large OSPF internetworks typically subdivide the AS into smaller, more manageable subareas.

A single area implementation has one big disadvantage: As the number of networks and routers grow, so does the size of the Link State database. When the Link State database grows, it requires routers within a single area to keep track of changes to any router or network state change within that area. Storing and maintaining a large database requires a lot of memory and CPU time for all routers involved. Whenever a link within the area becomes unavailable or available, all routers within the area must recalculate the SPF algorithm for all routes within the database.

When you hierarchically divide an OSPF AS into multiple areas, you can effectively reduce the amount of route update traffic and SPF calculations routers have to deal with. Each subarea within the AS isolates updates to only those routers in that area, reducing the overall size of the Link State database. Routers only maintain a Link State databases for areas to which they directly connect. This isolates intra-area route update traffic to the area where it originated. State changes affecting routes in one area do not require routers in other areas to recalculate. Because routers do not have to recalculate their route tables when the status of a route in another area changes, this also dramatically reduces the number of SPF calculations a router performs.

You can break up your AS any way you like, but typically design follows geography, with each location representing a subarea. When you use multiple area design, a special area referred to as the Area 0 or backbone area must exist as a major transit area for all inter-area traffic (see Figure 6.17). Just like all roads lead to Rome, all roads must lead to and through Area 0.

FIGURE 6.17

When multiple areas exist in an OSPF implementation, the entire OSPF routing domain is referred to as the OSPF AS. All multiple subareas must connect to the main backbone transit area, known as Area 0.

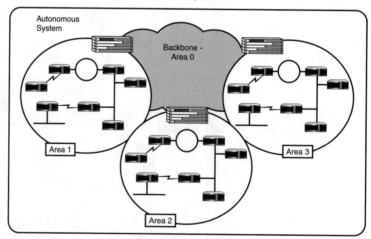

AS with Multiple Areas

Routers within an area may only exchange information with routers in their same area. In this example, three subareas exist: 1, 2, and 3, all physically connected to Area 0 through ABR routers. ABR routers summarize and advertise routes into the core, which in turn advertises the other area's route information into their own areas.

Area Types

Within a multiple area environment each Area type defines the type of LSA (Link State Advertisements) that it will accept and which router types will generate these LSAs. OSPF has three main area types:

- Backbone (Area 0)

- Standard

- Two Stub Areas (Standard Stub and NSSA—Not So Stubby Area)

Note

Virtual links are notOSPF areas. Rather, virtual links provide a logical link between two areas through another (referred to as the transit area).

Backbone—Area 0

You can consider the backbone as the glue for all other areas. In addition to all intra-area advertisements that propagate within its own area, all inter-area summary (sent by ABR's) and External AS routes (sent by ASBR's) traverse this area en route to subareas. This area can accept all OSPF Link State Advertisements; therefore, it accepts all LSA types 1 through 5, except type 7.

Standard Area

Standard areas function as subareas of Area 0. This area accepts intra-area type 1 and 2 LSAs and inter-area summarized routes, type 3 and 4 from other subareas sent by the ABR connecting this area to the backbone. In addition, this area accepts External AS routes advertised by an ASBR connected to this area (Type 5). You can have standard areas physically connected to Area 0 through multiple gateways, providing redundant paths to and through the core.

Two Stub Areas

A *stub* has only one way in and one way out, a single connection to Area 0. You typically do not need to have OSPF updates sent across this link, especially if you have a slow WAN link or dial-up connection. Most often in this situation, you would use a default route to identify the path to networks outside of a stub area. Configuring a default or static route eliminates update traffic on the link, conserving precious bandwidth. RFC 1583 defines two types of stub areas:

- Standard stub area

- NSSA (Not So Stubby Area)

Cisco Systems has added its own proprietary stub area known as *Totally Stubby*, which we do not discuss in this book. Stub areas have the following general restrictions:

- Area 0 and ASBRs cannot be part of a stub area

- An administrator must configure routers connected to or within a stub or NSSA network as stub routers.

Standard Stub Area

Although stubs cut down on the OSPF advertisements sent into the area by implementing a default router, the standard stub area accepts intra- and inter-area routes, which is type 1, 2, 3, and 4. This area does not accept any external route advertisements (Type 5 or 7) by ASBRs.

NSSA (Not So Stubby Area)

NSSA areas restrict LSAs accepted to intra-area (type 1 and 2) because without intra-area advertisements there would be no point to running a routing protocol if it cannot at least learn routes within its own area. This area does not accept external route advertisements (type 5) by ASBRs. However, the "not so stubby name" indicates that it allows something else into this area. In fact, this area allows external routes to be carried through this area en route to area 0 as a LSA type 7 generated by an ASBR. Type 7 external route advertisements are converted to type 5 (see Figure 6.18) by the ABR connecting the NSSA stub area to the core (area 0).

Note

ABRs convert type 7 external route advertisements to type 5 prior to advertising them into the core.

NSSA - Not So Stubby Area

FIGURE 6.18
NSSAs carry external routes through its areas into area 0.

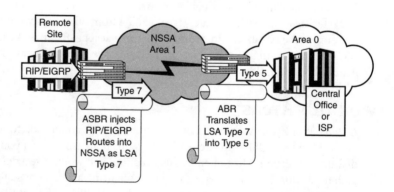

Using Figure 6.18 as an example, the NSSA (Area 1) directly connects to Area 0 via an ABR and to another non-OSPF routing domain (Autonomous System) via an ASBR. The ASBR connected to the non-OSPF routing domain runs the RIP, EIGRP, and OSPF protocols. The non-OSPF route information needs to be redistributed into the OSPF network at the ASBR. This causes the router to generate a type 7 LSA into the NSSA. After these external LSAs get to the ABR connecting the NSSA to area 0, these advertisements convert to regular external type 5 LSAs and propagate throughout the rest of the OSPF Autonomous Systems areas.

Virtual Links

Virtual links provide a logical path to Area 0 through a subarea. They connect either a new subarea to the backbone when a physical connection is impossible or when multiple area 0's exist but are physically separate, for example, when two companies with existing OSPF implementations have merged.

In either case, virtual links utilize a standard area as a transit path connecting the subarea to Area 0 or two backbones together (see Figures 6.19 and 6.20). You must manually configure virtual links configured on border routers. Configuration varies depending on vendor implementations and is beyond the scope of this book.

Virtual Link - Example 1

FIGURE 6.19
Virtual links are logical paths through subareas, connecting another area-to-area 0. In this figure, a new OSPF area was added, but no way existed to connect it to the core. Area 3, used as the transit area, provides a virtual path to the core.

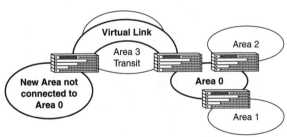

Virtual links create a logical path to Area 0.

Virtual Link - Example 2

FIGURE 6.20
In this figure, two departments with existing OSPF multiple area implementations have merged. Both OSPF area 0s need a link through a virtual path via a transit area, in this case, area 51.

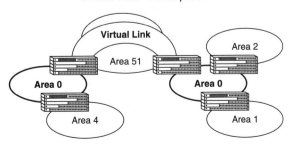

Standard OSPF fields

All five OSPF packet types (see Table 6.3) have the same common fields within the 24-octet OSPF header (see Figure 6.21). One of these five packet types performs protocol operations. We will discuss the various packet types and look at their headers later in this chapter. A standard OSPF header has the following seven fields:

FIGURE 6.21
All five OSPF packet types use the same standard header.

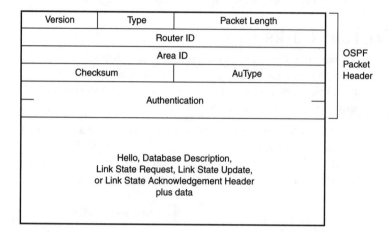

- **Version Number**—Identifies the OSPF version number. Currently, OSPF uses version 2.

- **Packet Type**—Identifies the OSPF packet type. Table 6.3 lists the five different packet types and their protocol function.

- **Packet Length**—Identifies the length in bytes of the OSPF datagram, including its header and contents.

- **Router ID**—Contains a unique value that identifies the router that originally sent the OSPF packet. OSPF uses this value for DR and BDR selection. An administrator can manually configure the router ID or it can happen dynamically.

- **Area ID**—Identifies the area of that OSPF datagram came from. Area 0 always has an area ID of 0.0.0.0. This value varies for subareas, and you can optionally configure the value to follow the subnet number of the subarea.

- **Checksum**—Verifies that the contents of the OSPF packet remain intact during transit. The checksum field excludes the authentication type field.

- **Authentication**—OSPF routers optionally support simple password authentication. When configured to do so, routers will only form adjacencies with routers sharing the same authentication password. Together these two fields validate the packet. The authentication type field contains 16 bits and authentication field contains 32 bits.

TABLE 6.3   OSPF Packet Types

Type	Name	Description
1	Hello	Establishes and maintains adjacencies
2	Database Description	Summarizes database content
3	Link State Request	Request for specific route information or complete update (database download)
4	Link State Update	Route information sent in response to a request (database update)
5	Link StateAcknowledgement	Acknowledges receipt of route information

Message Specific Headers

Every OSPF header contains an additional header with specific routing information about one of the five packet types found after the common fields in an OSPF header:

- Hello packet (Type 1)

- Database description (Type 2)

- Link State request (Type 3)

- Link State update (Type 4)

- Link State acknowledgement packet (Type 5)

We discuss these packets and their headers in the following sections.

Hello Packet

Hello datagrams are OSPF type 1 packets. Hello packets establish and maintain adjacencies. Figure 6.22 shows the basic format of a hello packet. Figure 6.23 shows a hello packet as seen through a Sniffer. We describe the hello packet fields in detail after both figures.

Using Figure 6.23 as an example, router 150.3.233.250 uniquely identifies itself with its router ID, which is used for BDR and DR selection. Remember the highest priority or router ID becomes the DR, the next highest, BDR. The area ID specifies the OSPF area from which this advertisement originated. If you implement authentication, which is optional, only gateways sharing the same password may form adjacencies.

Note that the header lists the subnet mask for this gateway (255.255.255.0) along with the options it supports. A value of 1 in the options capability section of the header indicates that it supports that particular option. In this case, this router has the "External Routing Capability" bit set, as seen in the header. This indicates that this gateway supports non-OSPF advertisements and either an ASBR or a router within an AREA that supports external routes passing through it exists.

In addition, this router identifies the IP address of the DR as 150.3.233.249 and announces itself as BDR. Lastly, this router lists the neighbors it knows of, in this case one, 1.0.0.5.

FIGURE 6.22
OSPF hello packet fields include network mask, hello interval, options, routing priority, dead interval, designated router, backup designated router, and neighbor.

Version	Type = 1	Packet Length	
Router ID			
Area ID			
Checksum		AuType	
Authentication			
Network Mask			
HelloInterval		Options	Rtr Pri
DeadInterval			
Designated Router			
Backup Designated Router			
Neighbor			

OSPF Packet Header

• • •

FIGURE 6.23
Router 150.3.233.250 multicasts (group address 224.0.0.5) an OSPF hello (type 1) message, announcing itself to its neighbors. Only OSPF routers with matching area IDs, authentication passwords, stub configurations, and hello and dead intervals will process this information and form an adjacency.

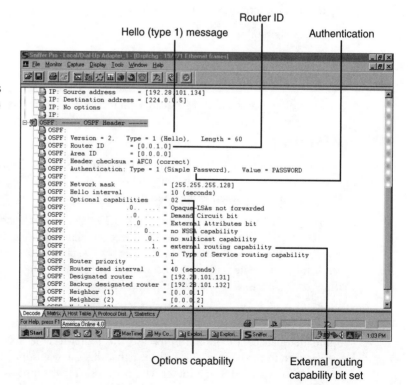

Router ID

Hello (type 1) message

Authentication

Options capability

External routing capability bit set

Network Mask

This field identifies the local interface subnet mask.

Options

The options field specifies the OSPF capabilities this router supports. All routers might not support options. If they do not support the options, the router either rejects or ignores the options. The following two options are defined:

- T bit
- E bit

Table 6.4 describes the two options. Vendors might implement other option bits in the future.

TABLE 6.4 Hello Packet Option Bits

Option Bit	Function
T bit	Used to indicate that this OSPF router can support ToS/QoS routing.
	ToS-capable routers indicate the level of ToS by setting this bit to a value greater than zero. A T bit set to zero indicates that this router does not have the capability to perform ToS routing.
	Routers enabled for ToS build multiple shortest path trees with themselves as the root, one for ToS-enabled routes avoiding non-ToS routers, and one for non-ToS routes.
E bit	Routers with this bit set can process external non-OSPF route information.
	Stub area routers do not support external route updates and therefore will not set or recognize the use of this bit.
	ASBR routers always have the E bit enabled.

Hello Interval

The hello interval controls how often the router transmits hello datagrams. This value varies depending on the Data Link layer topology OSPF is running over. On a broadcast network routers send hellos out every 10 seconds. On a non-broadcast network routers sends hellos out every 30 seconds by default.

Router Priority ID

OSPF routers use the router priority ID exclusively for electing a DR and BDR for each segment. The router that has the highest priority ID becomes the DR. The DR controls the collection, synchronization, and dissemination of route information for the segment.

The router that has the next highest priority ID becomes the BDR. The BDR only collects and builds the Link State Database. It remains in standby mode until the DR fails. If this occurs, it automatically promotes itself to DR for the segment and the OSPF router then elect a new BDR.

The default value for this parameter depends of vendor implementations.

If all routers have the same router priority value (an administrator has not configured the default value higher on any gateway), the router ID determines the DR and BDR for the segment.

Dead Interval

The dead interval is used to detect a failed neighbor. By default, a router considers a neighbor dead when it does not hear from a neighbor router (no hellos are received) within four hello intervals.

The dead interval has a value four times (in seconds) the hello packet value. This value varies depending on the Data Link layer topology OSPF is running over. On a broadcast network, routers send hellos out every 10 seconds, which makes the dead interval 40 seconds. On a non-broadcast network, routers send hellos out every 30 seconds by default, which makes the dead interval 120 seconds.

Designated Router

This field lists the IP address of the DR if known by this router. If the router does not know the IP address of the DR, this value appears as 0.0.0.0.

Backup Designated Router

This field lists the IP address of the BDR if known by this router. If the router does not know the IP address of the BDR, this value appears as 0.0.0.0.

Neighbor

The neighbor field lists the router IDs of all neighbor routers this router has learned about through local hello packets.

OSPF Database Description Packet

Data description packets (type 2) convey data needed to initialize the topographical databases of adjacent devices. Figure 6.24 shows the format of a database description packet.

Options

The options field describes the OSPF capabilities supported by this router. Although this field exists in other OSPF packet types, the bits mean different things depending on the packet type in use. The database description packet only uses the last three bits within this field (see Table 6.5).

FIGURE 6.24
OSPF database description packet fields include interface MTU, options, sequence number and a link state advertisement header.

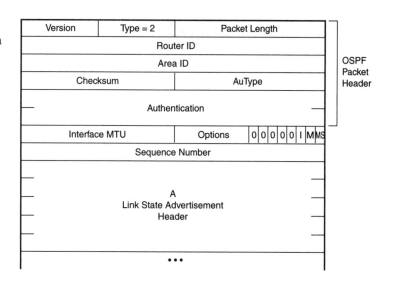

TABLE 6.5 Database Description Packet Options

Option Bit	Function
I (Init)	When set, the I bit, or Init bit, indicates that this is the first OSPF database description packet transmitted.
M (More)	When set, the M, or More bit, indicates that more database description packets should follow.
	If M bit has a value of zero, it indicates the last packet.
MS (Master/Slave)	The MS or Master/Slave bit identifies whether the transmitting router is a master (DR) or slave (all other routers).
	• MS=1 (router is master)
	• MS=0 (router is slave)

Sequence Number

The sender sequences all database description packets and the receiver acknowledges each packet. This initial value of the sequence number is uniquely chosen when the first DD packet is sent (Init bit = 1); thereafter it is sequentially incremented.

Link State Advertisement Header

A router can include one or more link state advertisements within a database description packet. We described the specific fields within the LSA header earlier in this section.

Link State Request Packets

OSPF link state request packets (type 3) get current route information or database download from a specific neighbor router. Figure 6.35 shows the format of a link state request packet. We describe each field after Figure 6.25.

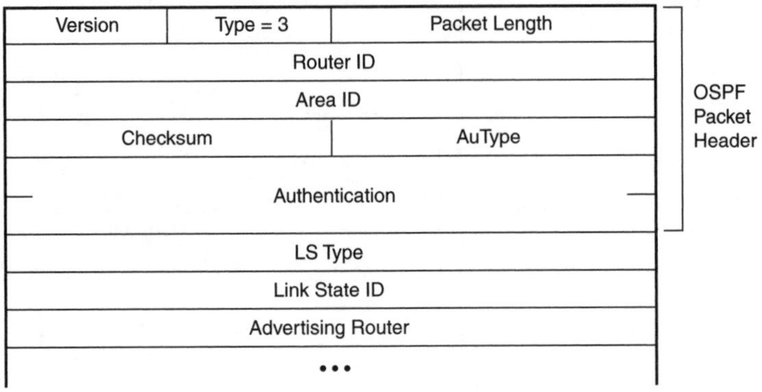

FIGURE 6.25
OSPF link state request packet fields include Link State type, Link State ID, and advertising router.

Version	Type = 3	Packet Length	
Router ID			
Area ID			OSPF
Checksum		AuType	Packet
Authentication			Header
LS Type			
Link State ID			
Advertising Router			
•••			

Link State Type

The Link State type field identifies the Link State advertisement. The next field, Link State ID, further describes the Link State advertisement.

Link State ID

The link state ID field assigns the advertisement a unique identification used by other routers.

Advertising Router

The advertising router field identifies the router that originally sent the link state advertisement.

Link State Update Packets

OSPF Link State update packets (type 4) route information sent in response to a request (database update). These packets contain information about the condition of various links within an internetwork. A single link state update packet can include several link state advertisements (described earlier in this section). Figure 6.26 shows the format of a link state update packet. We describe the various fields after the figure.

Number of Advertisements

The number of advertisements field identifies the number of Link State advertisements included in this update packet.

FIGURE 6.26
OSPF link state update packet fields include number of advertisements and link state advertisements.

Version
Type = 4
Packet Length
Router ID
Area ID
Checksum
AuType
Authentication
Advertisements
Link State Advertisements
OSPF Packet Header

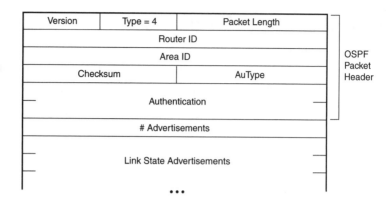

Link State Advertisements

The Link State advertisement field makes up the bulk of the Link State update packet. This field contains a list of Link State advertisements. Each Link State advertisement has a common header followed by one of six Link State advertisements. For a complete list of advertisements and description of fields, please refer to the OSPF operation section in this chapter.

Link State Acknowledgement Packet

The Link State acknowledgement packet (type 5) simply acknowledges the receipt of route information. This packet has a similar format to the database description packet and includes a list of link state advertisement headers. Figure 6.27 shows the format of a link state acknowledgement packet.

FIGURE 6.27
OSPF link state advertisement packet simply verifies the database information that it received.

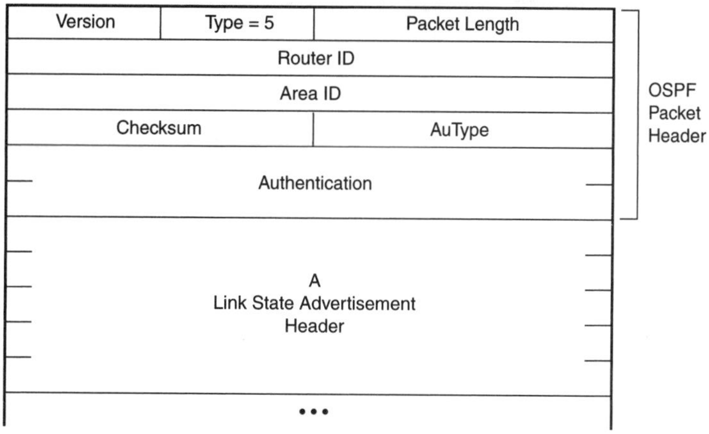

Version
Type = 5
Packet Length
Router ID
Area ID
Checksum
AuType
Authentication
A Link State Advertisement Header
OSPF Packet Header

Sample OSPF Configurations

Two examples of OSPF configuration are shown below. Both examples are taken from a Cisco router. The first example shows the configuration of a router in a single OSPF Area. The first line enables the OSPF route process indicating an arbitrary process ID of 10. This value is not the area ID. The second line activates OSPF for all directly connected networks and subnets (through locally attached interfaces), configuring them as part of the area ID, 51. Because this router only belongs to a single OSPF area, it is considered an internal router.

```
#router ospf 10
        network 0.0.0.0 255.255.255.255 area 51
```

The configuration of multiple OSPF areas is almost identical to that of a single area. In the next example, you can see that the OSPF route process has been started. The second line activates OSPF for the directly connected network 199.10.6.0, configuring it as part of the area ID, 51. The third line enables OSPF on all other interfaces of this router placing them in area 0. Because this router only belongs to multiple OSPF area, it is considered an ABR.

```
#router ospf 10
    network 199.10.6.0 0.0.0.255 area 51
    network 0.0.0.0 255.255.255.255 area 0
```

Now lets take a look at the output of two route tables. The first route table is taken from a single area router (see Figure 6.28). The second example (see Figure 6.29) shows a route table taken from a router within a multiple area environment.

FIGURE 6.28

Two OSPF intra-area routes have been learned and placed in the route table.

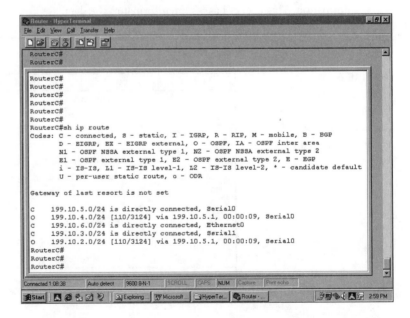

In Figure 6.29, the route table shows two routes with O in the leftmost column. This route code indicates that the routes are OSPF intra-area routes learned through type 1 or type 2 route updates.

FIGURE 6.29
Two OSPF intra-area routes have been learned and placed in the route table.

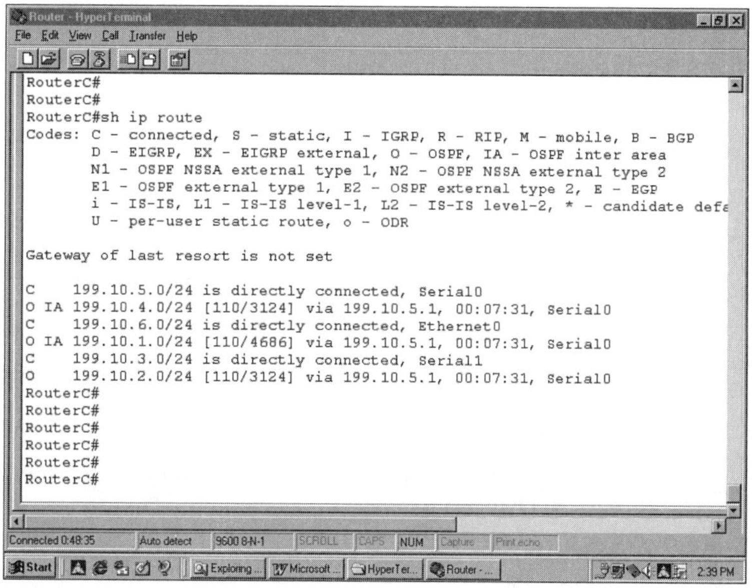
Router - HyperTerminal
File Edit View Call Transfer Help
RouterC#
RouterC#
RouterC#sh ip route
Codes: C - connected, S - static, I - IGRP, R - RIP, M - mobile, B - BGP
D - EIGRP, EX - EIGRP external, O - OSPF, IA - OSPF inter area
N1 - OSPF NSSA external type 1, N2 - OSPF NSSA external type 2
E1 - OSPF external type 1, E2 - OSPF external type 2, E - EGP
i - IS-IS, L1 - IS-IS level-1, L2 - IS-IS level-2, * - candidate defa
U - per-user static route, o - ODR
Gateway of last resort is not set
C 199.10.5.0/24 is directly connected, Serial0
O IA 199.10.4.0/24 [110/3124] via 199.10.5.1, 00:07:31, Serial0
C 199.10.6.0/24 is directly connected, Ethernet0
O IA 199.10.1.0/24 [110/4686] via 199.10.5.1, 00:07:31, Serial0
C 199.10.3.0/24 is directly connected, Serial1
O 199.10.2.0/24 [110/3124] via 199.10.5.1, 00:07:31, Serial0
RouterC#
RouterC#
RouterC#
RouterC#
RouterC#
RouterC#
Connected 0:48:35
Auto detect
9600 8-N-1
SCROLL
CAPS
NUM
Capture
Print echo
Start
2:39 PM

In Figure 6.29, the route table shows two intra-area routes indicated with an O and two inter-area routes O IA in the leftmost column. The O IA route code indicates that the routes are OSPF intra-area routes learned through either type 3 or type 4 route updates.

Summary

The OSPF (Open Shortest Path First) routing protocol (RFC 1583) uses a Link State routing algorithm, which allows it to make more intelligent path selection than Distance Vector routing protocols. When determining the best path to a destination, OSPF may consider any or all of the following metrics: bandwidth, delay, reliability, and load; however, OSPF uses bandwidth as its default metric.

All OSPF routers, networks, and subnets are logically grouped into areas. OSPF networks may consist of a single area or multiple areas organized hierarchically. The entire OSPF internetwork (whether a single or multiple area) is referred to as one routing domain, called an autonomous system (AS).

All OSPF routers build and maintain three databases for their particular AS. These databases include adjacency (neighbor table), link state (topology map), and forwarding (routing table). The neighbor table keeps track of OSPF routers connected to a common network segment, or "neighbor" routers. The topology map keeps tracks of all networks, subnets and destinations within an area. A route table stores the best paths to OSPF networks, subnets, and destinations.

OSPF can support various Data Link layer architectures. How adjacencies and database exchanges take place depend on the architecture OSPF runs over. OSPF routers maintain their databases by using Link State Advertisements. OSPF uses three different types of LSAs: intra-area, inter-area, and external. Each advertisement describes the type of Link State advertisement and where its propagation occurs.

Within a multiple area environment each area type defines the type of LSA that it will accept and which router types will generate these LSAs. OSPF has three main area types: backbone (Area 0), standard, and two stub areas (Standard Stub and NSSA—Not So Stubby Area).

Chapter Quiz

1. OSPF is considered what kind of routing protocol, Distance Vector or Link State?

2. Name the default metric OSPF uses to determine the best path to a destination.

3. Name the three databases all OSPF routers maintain and build and describe their purposes.

4. Name the seven OSPF router states. Briefly describe each state.

5. What is the OSPF multicast address used only by the Designated router to communicate with all OSPF routers?

6. Name the two Link State advertisements used for intra-area advertisements and brief description.

7. What type of OSPF router connects multiple OSPF areas?

8. What type of router connects an OSPF AS (routing domain) and any other routing domain (a different routing protocol)?

9. Name the area that serves as a transit area for all OSPF traffic.

10. What is a stub area?

CHAPTER 7

BORDER GATEWAY PROTOCOL (BGP)

> **You will learn about the following in this chapter:**
> - BGP operation
> - Autonomous System types
> - BGP attributes
> - Confederations
> - Route reflection

What Is the Border Gateway Protocol?

One of the most popular (and arguably the most important) routing protocols in use today is Border Gateway Protocol (BGP). BGP is a very robust protocol that has become the backbone of the Internet. The main purpose of BGP is to advertise a network's presence (and structures) to other BGP routers on the Internet (more specifically the routers of an ISP). BGP provides a common hierarchical routing structure linking disparate sites throughout the Internet together regardless of the underlying structure and routing protocols implemented within.

The Internet is a giant mesh of unrelated systems, architectures, and protocols; a situation that can be likened to a large party where every attendee (router) is from a different country (company), speaking different languages (routing protocols), though some of them are bilingual. During the party the phone rings. A waiter writes out a message, puts the intended recipient's name on the front of it and passes it to someone (router) in the crowd (hoping it will reach its destination).

If not one person (router) in the crowd can speak the same language as anyone else, the message will not get very far. Most likely the note will be discarded by any person it is handed to.

The message would have a more successful chance of delivery if everyone spoke the same language, such as RIP. In this case a bilingual interpreter (router running perhaps RIP and BGP) is necessary to decipher the message. A message given to any one attendee could easily find its way through the crowd of partygoers to its intended destination. The interpreter (BGP router), being able to read the message, could easily discern for whom the message was meant. Even if the person currently holding the message did not recognize the recipient's name, he could give it to someone whom might know the recipient.

BGP has become the link that breaks the language barrier that might have existed between the dissimilar systems of the Internet. The Border Gateway Protocol allows systems and networks to recognize (and be recognized by) unrelated systems. Systems running BGP can advertise their routes and structures to other systems, regardless of the differences in internal architecture of the networks involved.

> **Note**
>
> The protocol commonly known as BGP is actually BGP version 4 (which is be the subject of this chapter). The fourth incarnation of the Border Gateway Protocol is very different from all previous versions. However, BGP4 has become the most popular form of BGP after being adopted by Internet Service Providers and has simply become known and referred to as BGP.

Most routing protocols route data within a given networking environment. Protocols such as RIP are used to route data between internal networks and systems. This enables users on a network to exchange data with other users in the same area. But what happens when you want to extend your informational exchanges beyond the borders of your local network?

BGP routes data between networks (known as ASs or Autonomous Systems). That is, each network can be viewed as a complete, independent entity or Autonomous System. Each system (logically) has no inherent knowledge of any other system in the world. (Which makes sense, because for every network in the world to automatically know the topology of every network in the world would require some very hefty technology. Technology that really does not exist as of yet.) Because no system knows the topology (or for that matter the existence of) any other system, exchanging data between systems can be very difficult.

BGP (BGP4) as a protocol allows systems with no knowledge of one another to communicate freely. However, this definition can be a little misleading.

Although BGP is best known for its capability to route between dissimilar ASs, it is actually comprised of two separate protocols. The EBGP, or External Border Gateway Protocol, is used to route data between Autonomous Systems (what most people think of when they envision a BGP system), and the IBGP, or Internal Border Gateway Protocol, is used to route data within a particular AS.

Distance Vector Protocols

The Border Gateway Protocol is an example of a distance-vector protocol. Distance-vector protocols operate by determining the quickest path between systems (vectors). Commonly know as Next-hop routing, distance-vector protocols may take into account the number of hops (or jumps between routers). Figure 7.1 illustrates a common network with multiple router hops.

FIGURE 7.1

Distance vector routing
protocols use distance
(hops) to determine the
best route between
source and destination.
In this example two work-
stations are separated by
five subnets (five hops),
connected through
routers.

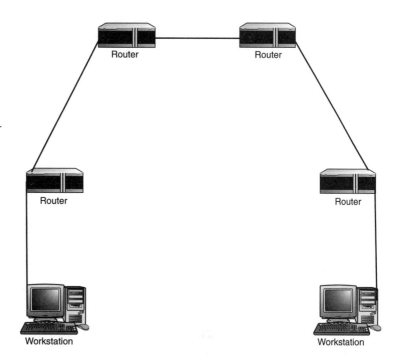

Note

Routing protocols can be divided into two main categories, link state or distance-vector. These categories describe the algorithm the protocol uses to calculate routes between systems.

All routing protocols (distance-vector or otherwise) rely on an algorithm to make the needed calculations, upon which all network routing decisions are based. The routing algorithm provides the formula that is applied to the metrics supplied by the router's routing table. (The metrics used by BGP are discussed later in the chapter. .

Note

A metric is a value (usually administrator-assigned and usually arbitrary) that is used to indicate anything from the cost associated with a link to the amount of delay experienced when transmitting data.

In the case of distance-vector protocols, most use the Bellman-Ford algorithm (or a modified version of it). The Bellman-Ford algorithm works by calculating the routing metrics associated with each hop on a network looking for the lowest values. Figure 7.2 illustrates how the Bellman-Ford algorithm reacts to the network.

FIGURE 7.2

Routing metrics can be configured by administrators to affect the way datagrams are forwarded. Metrics are cumulative for the path end to end, with the lowest value being the best route.

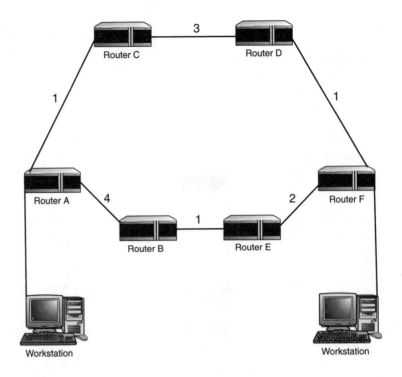

The metrics shown in Figure 7.2 are completely arbitrary and do not represent any particular factor (such as cost); we'll call this factor "weight" for our example. Using the Bellman-Ford algorithm, what path would the data take from system A to system F?

The weight of the path A-C-D-F is 5 ([A, C=1] + [C, D=3] + [D, F=1] = 5), this makes it the path of the lowest value.

For BGP routing, the hops could be internal routers (within a particular AS), that is, any router that is wholly contained within a particular network environment. The routing of IBGP or the Interior Gateway Protocol would cover these interior routers.

The routing hops could also represent a large grid of routers such as those found on the Internet. These routers are known as exterior routers connecting Autonomous Systems and route using EBGP or the Exterior Border Gateway Protocol.

For BGP every network or related group is know as an AS or Autonomous System. The next section discusses what makes up an AS and how BGP deals with them.

Autonomous Systems

Autonomous Systems are the heart of BGP networks. The AS is the main routing unit of the BGP protocol. BGP is an Inter-AS routing protocol, providing routes through and across the Internet. AS' are operated and managed independently by private organizations and ISPs. However, each AS coordinates the routing of information between and through these AS' by implementing BGP.

Note

An Autonomous System can be a single network or a group of related networks (such as a WAN).

To understand Autonomous Systems, first let's look at how they are physically formed; then you can see how BGP differentiates between systems. An AS is a related group of systems (because we are dealing with a routing protocol we will be speaking in terms of routers, however there are obviously end systems involved). That is, just like a local or wide area network, an AS is an environment. Figure 7.3 illustrates a typical AS.

FIGURE 7.3
An Autonomous System is a collection of subnets, routers and routing protocols.

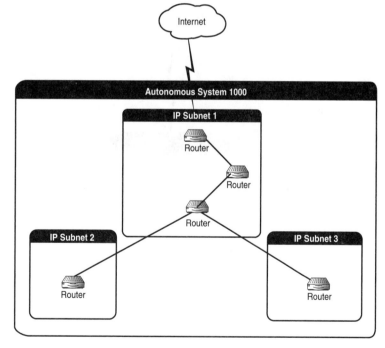

The network shown in Figure 7.3 is a fairly small LAN divided in a couple of subnets. These subnets are in different geographical areas and communicate back to the main office. The only outside access from the network stems from the main subnet.

Because the small, external subnets do not have a separate connection to the Internet (they gain their connection through the central office) they are considered part of the same AS. All three subnetworks pictured in Figure 7.3 form one Autonomous System (AS 1000).

> **Note**
>
> The term *POP* or *Point of Presence* describes a connection or access point to the Internet. ISPs typically have one or more points of presence. ISPs provide Internet access to downstream clients through their POP. Often the term POP is used when referring to the ISP site.

Autonomous Systems can be even more basic then the one illustrated in Figure 7.3. A small network such as a POP or Point of Presence may have no more that one or two heavy-duty routers. Figure 7.4 shows a small one-router network as an AS.

FIGURE 7.4

A single Autonomous System with one router.

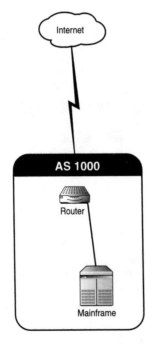

The network in Figure 7.4, albeit small, is still a valid Autonomous System. The one router connecting the servers of the POP to the central office would qualify the POP as an AS.

What makes an AS? Routers alone do not turn a network into an Autonomous System. If that were the case almost every LAN, WAN, MAN, and SOHO (small office home office) in the country would be an AS, which is simply not true. Therefore there are a couple of designators in determining if a network is an Autonomous System.

The first requirement is a connection to the Internet. For most companies this means a link to an ISP. Given that BGP enables effective communication between systems, there must be a carrier in place to connect them. This step is pretty logical and elementary, but it ties into the next requirement.

The second requirement is an ASN or Autonomous System number must be assigned. A network's Autonomous System number is its identity on the Internet (among other BGP systems).

Note

Every routing protocol has a standard base unit to work within. For example PNNI (explained in Chapter 9) uses Domains and IS-IS (discussed in Chapter 8) uses Peer-Groups. Essentially these units or groups are all the same. Therefore, do not let the changes in terminology catch you off guard. The different conglomerations of machines that protocols work within are fancy terms for the same network environments.

Each protocol may treat the network, AS, PG, or domain differently, however the unit itself remains the same.

Autonomous System Numbers

An Autonomous System number, like an IP address, must be assigned to you from a governing body (assuming you need to communicate to the outside world using EBGP). In most cases your ISP assigns you an ASN as a subset of its own. The ASN can range from 1 to 65,535.

Note

In the United States, the governing body in charge of registering and releasing Autonomous System numbers is ARIN (the American Registry for Internet Numbers). A list of the assigned Autonomous System numbers and the entities that own them can be found at //rs.arin.net/netinfo/asn.txt.

Obviously, being that Autonomous System numbers only range from 1 to 65,535, there is a finite number of ASNs that can be assigned. Therefore, a smaller range of addresses has been set aside from private use.

Note

The use and assignment of Autonomous System numbers is closely related to that of IP addresses. Both are assigned by governing bodies, both have public and private ranges, and (unfortunately) both are finite.

There are two main categories of ASNs, public and private. Public Autonomous System numbers range from 1 to 64,511. These numbers are assigned to entities requiring their network be advertised to the Internet. Most often ISPs and other large, global companies are assigned these numbers.

Private ASNs range from 64,512 to 65,535. Like their IP address (private IP addresses were discussed in Chapter 2) counterparts these numbers cannot be advertised to the Internet and are not routable. Rather these numbers are used for IBGP routing within a larger BGP network. The numbers in the private ASN range can be used freely by anyone.

To qualify for a public Autonomous System number, a network needs to supply proof of multihoming. Multihomed networks are networks with multiple external connections to one or more remote networks (usually ISPs). Typically these connections are used to load balance traffic and provide fault tolerance. In other words, there are three classifications of Autonomous Systems; of these three a network needs to be multihomed to obtain a public ASN. The three classes of Autonomous Systems are as follows:

- Stub

- Multihomed

- Transit

A stub AS is a network with only one connection to the Internet. Figure 7.5 shows a stub network attached to an ISP.

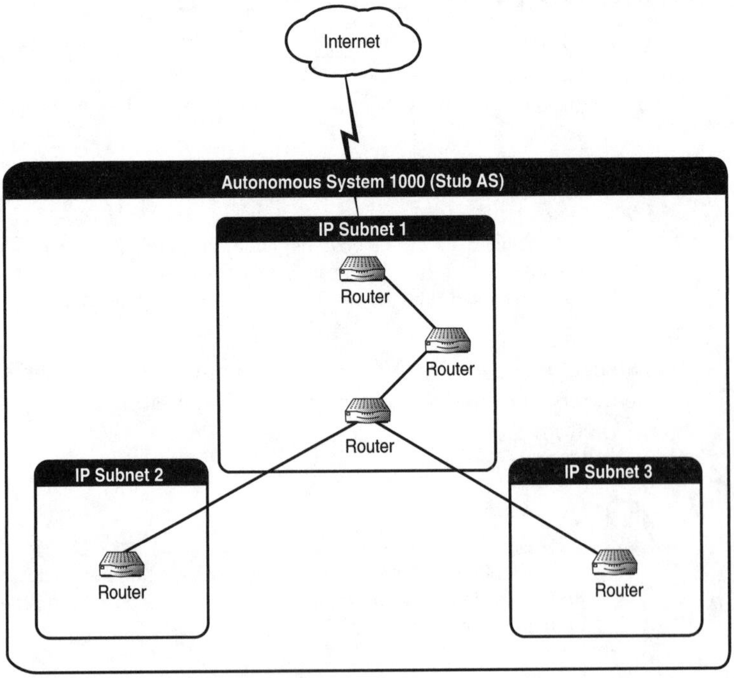

FIGURE 7.5
A stub AS has a single link connecting it to another AS, with only one way in and out.

Stub Autonomous Systems are usually treated as extensions of a larger AS. That is, because there is only one path to and from the stub AS, no further policies are required. It is also not logical to host a massive list of BGP routes on a Gateway with only one path to choose from.

Most Autonomous Systems often only qualify as stubs. However, a larger network may have stub sites that are attached to it but are considered the same Autonomous System. These stub Autonomous Systems do not require private ASNs.

Multihomed systems are networks with multiple links to external Autonomous Systems. The multihomed AS would accept routed information from all of the systems linked to it, but it only routes internal data. Figure 7.6 illustrates a multihomed Autonomous System.

FIGURE 7.6

Multihomed AS 1000 has connections to two other AS', 2000 and 3000.

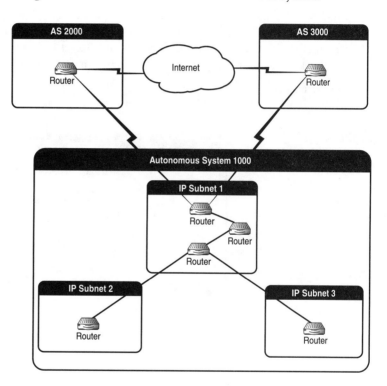

In Figure 7.6 the Autonomous System 1000 is multihomed because it connects to both AS 2000 and AS 3000. However, because a multihomed AS only routes internal data, AS 2000 would not be able to send information to AS 3000 through AS 1000. AS 1000 only accepts data bound for its internal network and route data from this network.

The third type of Autonomous System is a transit AS . Transit Autonomous Systems are multi-homed systems that accept and route information from other external Autonomous Systems. If the multihomed AS in Figure 7.6 were a transit AS then AS 2000 would be able to send data to AS 3000 via AS 1000.

Autonomous System Numbers and IP Addresses

The link between Autonomous Systems and IP addresses goes deeper than just regulations on how the two are utilized. IP plays a big part in the operation of BGP and the formation of Autonomous Systems.

An ASN is directly linked to the IP addresses (IP and IP addressing was discussed in Chapter 2) of the Autonomous System to which it belongs. In other words, an ASN needs to be associated with the IP address segments of the network to which it is attached. This ensures the proper traffic gets routed to the proper Autonomous System.

For example, Figure 7.7 illustrates a network that will soon be an Autonomous System. In this figure, all of the IP segments are labeled with their appropriate addresses.

FIGURE 7.7

A example of a segmented IP network.

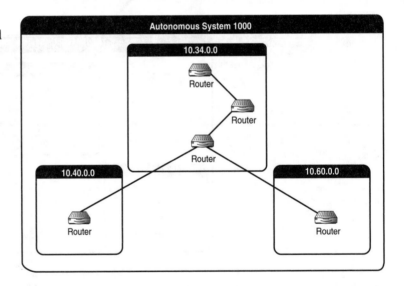

Only IP addresses specifically assigned to the ASN are routed from the gateway. Having the proper IP address configured for the correct ASN ensures that any external Autonomous Systems route the correct data to your border gateways. If you leave out a subnet or change IP addressing schemes without modifying your ASN, your network will not correctly receive data bound for it.

BGP Speakers, Border Gateways, and Peers

Now that we've discussed what Autonomous Systems are, we can dive into how they work. The remainder of this section identifies and discusses BGP terms that describe a router's role within an Autonomous System. Obviously without routers there would be no need for BGP, but how you refer to a router within an AS is based on the role it has assumed. The three roles are the BGP speaker, the border gateway, and the BGP peer.

BGP Speakers

All of the routers within an AS (that are configured for BGP) are known as BGP speakers. These BGP speakers need to be configured by an administrator with the ASN of the Autonomous System they belong to. If the AS is comprised of more than one IP subnet, all of the IP networks need to be associated with the ASN.

If a BGP speaker in an AS has an IP address that is not associated with the ASN, the speaker is not able to participate in the AS. Consequently any other systems or BGP speakers that are behind the non-participatory speaker do not receive data from the rest of the AS. Figure 7.8 illustrates an AS with one speaker that has not associated its IP subnets with the AS and not a participatory speaker within the AS.

FIGURE 7.8
An AS that is not fully
functional.

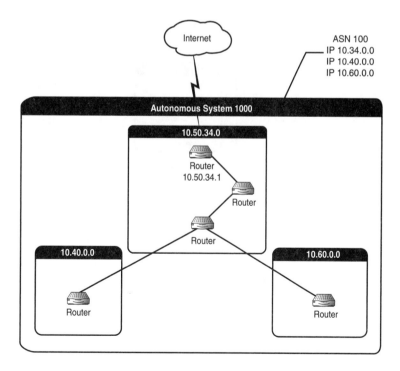

The two BGP speakers (and the end systems linked to them) located behind speaker 10.50.34.1 would not be able to participate in the AS. Even though the IP subnets that they belong to are located within the AS , no data would pass through speaker 10.50.34.1. .

Border Gateways

BGP speakers that connect two or more Autonomous Systems are known as border gateways. Figure 7.9 illustrates an Autonomous System with a border gateway. .

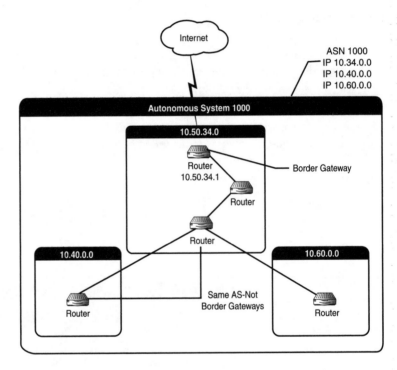

FIGURE 7.9
An Autonomous System with a border gateway. Border gateways connect Autonomous Systems together.

Autonomous Systems do not necessarily need a border gateway. A border gateway is only needed if the AS will be using EBGP to connect and communicate with other Autonomous Systems on the Internet. Conversely, any one Autonomous System can have multiple border gateways.

If an Autonomous System interfaces with more than one external AS through more than one BGP speaker, the AS will have multiple border gateways.

The job of the border gateway is to advertise routes within its Autonomous System (and any other routes that it has knowledge of) to any external BGP speakers with which this gateway communicates. This may seem like a pretty broad job description, but it will make more sense after you look at "Exterior Border Gateway Routing," later in this chapter. .

BGP Peers

Like all other routing protocols, BGP works by sharing .routing information among the network's participants. That is, every BGP speaker in an environment needs to exchange routing information (topographical and metric) with other BGP speakers to successfully route network data.

This exchange of routing information takes place during BGP peering sessions. When a BGP router is ready to exchange routing data with another BGP speaker it opens a BGP peering session with one or more BGP speakers. The two BGP speakers involved in the peering session are now BGP peers.

Note

Because BGP uses TCP as its native protocol, all peering session connections are established and run on TCP port 179.

For BGP to function correctly BGP speakers must be BGP peers with all other speakers in their Autonomous System. That is, they need to form a logical *routing mesh*. Depending on the amount of BGP speakers in your AS, this mesh can get rather large and hard to control or keep track of. In addition, each BGP session requires a logical TCP connection to be established guaranteeing reliable delivery of route information.

The BGP peers do not need to be directly connected to each other; however, they do need to communicate. A standard path of communication must exist between the two BGP speakers for them to initiate a peering session.

Note

BGP can establish a peering session between two routers that are not directly connected. This is known as *EBGP multihop peering*. Using the external peering capabilities of EBGP, a BGP speaker can initiate a peering session with speakers that are multiple router hops away.

However, the most common (and least complicated) form of peering is between two directly connected speakers.

Upon initiating a peering session, BGP speakers exchange their entire routing tables. This can make the process rather lengthy. Depending on the number of advertised routes on any given router, the initial update exchange can be very intensive. BGP routers can hold hundreds to thousands of advertised routes. During the first update for a new BGP speaker, each one of these routes would need to be transferred.

However, all future updates between existing BGP peers consist of only changes made to the routing table. Therefore the longer a router is functioning in the Autonomous System, the less intensive the table exchanges are.

After a BGP speaker has its routing configuration it is ready to begin sending and receiving data. Depending on the needs of the network, the speaker uses one of two protocols, IBGP or EBGP.

Exterior Border Gateway Routing

This section covers the EBGP or Exterior Border Gateway Protocol. EBGP is used to establish communication between BGP speakers in different Autonomous Systems. Situations where EBGP is used include communication between an ISP and a POP or a large enterprise and multiple communications vendors. Functionally there are few differences between EBGP and its counterpart IBGP; however, the differences are profound enough to warrant separate discussions (IBGP will be covered in the next section).

BGP routers learn about their surroundings from other BGP routers. That is, during peering sessions BGP routers tell each other about the routes they know. These routes are the backbone of BGP operation, especially for speakers in different Autonomous Systems. The key to the (sometimes) smooth and quick operation of the Internet is BGP's capability to communicate and exchange routes with speakers in dissimilar networks.

For any BGP speaker outside of your AS to be able to successfully route data to you, it needs to be aware of your location and what address you represent. However, a route can mean more than "Here are the addresses of the networks within my AS." Often times a BPG speaker advertises routes it knows to other Autonomous Systems (that is, paths to Autonomous Systems other than its own).

A BGP route simply states "I know how to get information bound for XXX.XXX.XXX.XXX from here to there." The routes specify an IP network address and (if the network is not within the sending devices AS) a *next hop* router address. The next hop router address is the address of the Border Gateway that must be used to reach the destination. This information allows BGP speakers to advertise routes they are not directly connected to, enabling data from different Autonomous Systems to reach virtually anyone.

When a BGP speaker has information about a route that needs to be sent (such as an update) to other BGP speakers (internal or external), it advertises the route. Advertising (as one may expect) is a way for one speaker to offer routes or routing updates to other speakers. Other BGP speakers then receive these routes as routing updates.

The most common form of BGP route advertisement is *BGP route redistribution*. Let's take a look at how BGP route redistribution works. Figure 7.10 illustrates four Autonomous Systems connected through EBGP.

FIGURE 7.10

Four Autonomous Systems (1000, 2000, 3000 and 4000) connected through EBGP. The routers connecting these AS' together are considered border gateways.

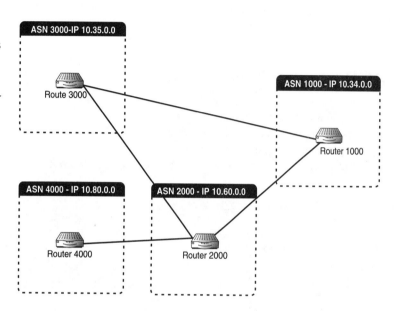

Router 2000 advertises (to Autonomous Systems 3000 and 4000) that it knows to route all traffic for IP network 10.34.0.0 to AS 1000 and all traffic for IP network 10.60.0.0 goes to AS 2000 (itself). It also advertises (to Router 1000) that it can route all traffic for IP networks 10.80.0.0 and 10.35.0.0 to Autonomous Systems 3000 and 4000 respectively. Router 2000 then redistributes the knowledge of these routes to Router 1000, Router 3000, and Router 4000.

Now, if Router 3000 receives any data for the IP network 10.34.0.0 it knows that by forwarding the data to Router 2000 the information will get to the intended recipient (AS 1000).

This form of route advertisement helps BGP speakers learn about each other and the networks they represent. Routes advertised by BGP speakers can be one of two kinds, dynamic or static.

A dynamic BGP route is one that the speaker learns about through BGP updates with other routers. In our example (see Figure 7.10), route information that Router 3000 and Router 4000 learn through their updates with Router 2000 (concerning the networks within AS 1000 and AS 2000) are considered dynamic routes.).

Note

The act of redistributing a dynamically learned route is known as *BGP dynamic route redistribution* (as opposed to BGP static route redistribution).

Conversely, an administrator can program a route into a BGP speaker. These routes are known as static routes. Using our previous example, you could say that Router 2000 knows about the networks within AS 1000 through a statically defined route. When Router 2000 redistributes that information to Router 3000 and Router 4000 it will be considered a BGP static router redistribution.

BGP Route Maps

BGP route maps are used to filter the redistribution of BGP routes from AS to AS. Imagine the number of BGP routes that are exchanged between routers throughout the Internet every day. If every BGP speaker redistributed every path it learned about, the traffic alone would bring the Internet to a halt. Route maps give an administrator a way to determine what learned BGP routes they want their speaker to redistribute to the Internet.

Note

Route maps only work at the update level. That is, a route map does not filter any routes coming into the router. Any route maps that may be in place affect only routes being sent.

A route map can consist of a list of criteria that, if met, permits or denies the advertisement or reset a particular metric (referred to within the BGP specification as path attributes) of the route. For example, using the networks from Figure 7.10 as our guide, an administrator could create a route map on Router 2000 that states:

"Do not redistribute any routes learned from AS 2000." (The actual technical language of the route map varies based on the brand of router being used.)

With this route map in place, Router 1000 would still receive updates from Router 2000. However it would run the route map against it and determine that it should not redistribute that route to Router 3000 or Router 4000. However, let's say that AS 3000 was also connected to AS 1000 (see Figure 7.11). .

After all of the BGP updates have been processed, Router 3000 in Figure 7.11 has two possible routes from which to select for sending data to AS 1000. It could send the data through Router 2000 or send it directly to Router 1000.

When faced with a choice like this the routing algorithm would decide which route to use based on the lowest cost or metric (path attribute) value. Path attributes are discussed later in this section.

FIGURE 7.11

Four interconnected
Autonomous Systems
using route maps for
redistribution.

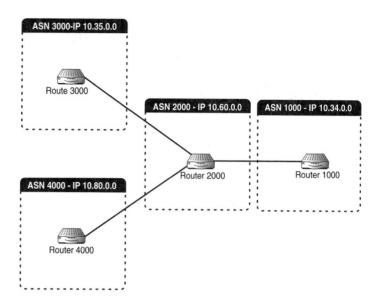

Note

Remember, metrics are (usually) administrator assigned values that represent the desirability of sending data over a particular path (as opposed to a different path to the same destination). The path that has the lowest total metric value or cost is the one that is chosen to send data over. The most common use of the route map feature is to change the BGP route attribute Local Preference (discussed later in this section).

The administrator of AS 2000, knowing that Router 2000 was one of the possible paths to AS 1000, could create a route map that would ensure the direct route (Router 3000 to Router 1000) would be used before the indirect route (Router 3000 to Router 2000 to Router 1000). Assuming that the route updates from Router 1000 are sent out with a default metric of 4, the route map on Router 2000 could say

"Redistribute any routes learned from Router 1000 with a metric of 10."

Then after Router 3000 has received all of its BGP updates it would have two choices for sending data to AS 1000. The data could either be sent directly through Router 1000 with a cost of 4 or through Router 2000 with a cost of 10. Ninety-nine times out of 100 the routing algorithm goes with the direct route (least cost path).

Conversely, if your site has the biggest and best in technology, and you want your BGP border gateway to be the preferred route to another AS, you can configure an artificially lower metric value for one of the paths. By implementing a route map that changes the metric for one or more routes through another Autonomous System to a lower value, you almost ensure your site's preference to use that path when forwarding data to that AS.

Implementing such a route map may be valuable during an acquisition of a company. If one company purchases another and wants the larger site to be the preferred route to the small one (before actual network changes can be made), they can implement a route map.

BGP Route Flapping and Flap Dampening

If a BGP speaker fails to connect to any of the routers in its BGP table (through a peering session), this route is said to be flapping. That is, if Router A learns about Router B (illustrated in Figure 7.12) through a dynamic BGP route redistribution and cannot open a peering session to it, the route to Router B is flapping.

FIGURE 7.12
Router A is unable to establish a peer relationship with router B due to a flapping route.

Router A

Router B

The cause of a route flap could be anything from a T1 line becoming temporarily dislodged (causing the line to transition from operational to non-operational) to an entire network going belly-up. Either way, route flaps can be a processor-clogging hassle. If one route were to flap and every BGP speaker connected to that route continued to redistribute it around the Internet, a lot of information would overwhelm the routers going nowhere.

Therefore a failsafe was put into place known as flap dampening. Flap dampening works by black listing any route that flaps for a certain amount of time (usually two BGP updates). When a route is dampened, it is removed from its peers' BGP route tables. Then any further updates would not include the route. The consequence of this is the erasing of the route from all BGP routers throughout the Internet. By removing a route that constantly flaps you reduce the need for all routers to perform route recalculations.

Note

Many times routes that are down temporarily must wait a certain amount of time (after coming live again) before they can be re-advertised, resulting in a longer down time then necessary. This is one of the down sides of flap dampening.

It is always best to check with your provider if you suddenly loose connectivity. Many times a problem on the provider's side (a cable coming loose) can cause the routes to your site to be dampened, which makes your site invisible for up to a few hours.

BGP Headers

Before we can discuss the particular metrics that BGP routers use to make route decisions, you need to understand how the BGP protocol header is formed—that is, the header of the message that carries information from router to router.

There are four different BGP headers that can be attached to a BGP message. Each header contains information specific to the type of message being delivered. However, a common header precedes each of the four message headers. The BGP common header introduces the message and indicates to other systems that it is intended for BGP routers. .

The BGP Common Header

The BGP common header, also known as the BGP protocol header, is found on all packets sent from a BGP router. The common header designates the packet as being BGP and indicates what type of information is contained within. Figure 7.13 illustrates the fields of the BGP common header.

FIGURE 7.13

All BGP messages share a common header.

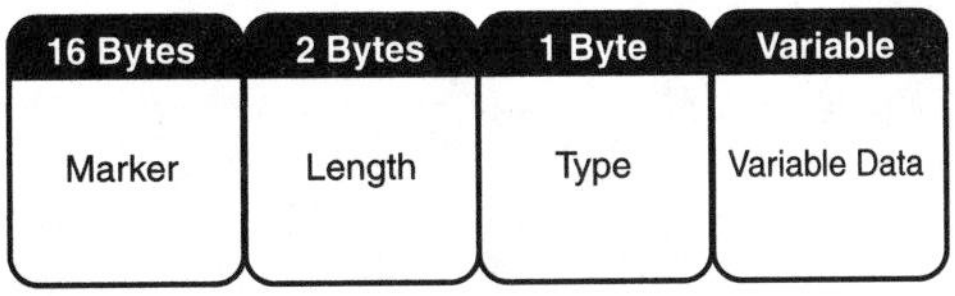

16 Bytes	2 Bytes	1 Byte	Variable
Marker	Length	Type	Variable Data

The four fields of the BGP common header are the header marker, length, type, and variable data. The 16-byte header marker field indicates the message is a BGP message. A receiving BGP router uses an internal calculation to predict what the marker field should be. If the router receives a packet and the maker field is different from the field it predicted, the router knows that the packet is being sent out-of-sequence and should be discarded.

The 2-byte length field is the total length (in bytes) of the BGP packet (not the length of the header).

This 1-byte type field indicates whether the message that follows is open, update, notify, or keepalive.

The variable data field is the message itself. A message-specific header precedes the data in the variable data field. This field can vary in size depending on the type of message.

The BGP Open Message Header

BGPopen messages are sent by routers to request that a BGP session be established with its peer. The receiving router confirms the connection establishment by returning a keepalive. After the routers establish a session using TCP, they exchange update messages containing route information. Figure 7.14 illustrates the fields of an open message header.

FIGURE 7.14

A BGP open message header.

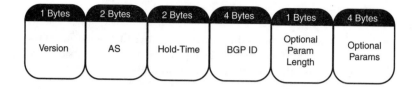

The 1-byte version field indicates which version of BGP the sender is using. Indicating versions of BGP helps the routers determine whether they are using compatible protocols.

This 2-byte indicator field is the Autonomous System number of the router sending the message.

The sending router uses the 2-byte hold-time field to determine if the recipient is online. If the router that sent the open message does not receive a reply within the time indicated by the hold-time field, the recipient is assumed to be offline.

The 4-byte BGP identifier refers directly to the sender of the message. The BGP identifier usually consists of the sending router's MAC address and their ASN.

The remaining two fields are optional. The first is the optional parameter length field. This 1-byte field contains the length of the optional parameter field. If the optional parameters are not set, this field is set to 0.

The optional parameters field contains any parameters that the sending router wants to pass on to the recipient. Currently (in BGP 4) there is only one optional parameter that can be sent in an open message. The authentication information parameter is used in cases where the packet must be authenticated before use.

The BGP Update Message Header

An update message is distributed between BGP routers to amend the routing table information. A 5-field header precedes these messages within the variable data portion of the common BGP header. Figure 7.15 illustrates the fields of the update message header.

FIGURE 7.15

A BGP update message header.

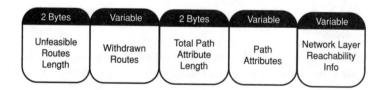

The first two fields in the update message header concern any paths that should be removed from the recipient's routing tables. These paths are known as withdrawn routes. The first field of the header is the unfeasible route length. This 2-byte value indicates the length of the withdrawn route's field. If there are no withdrawn routes, the unfeasible route length is set to 0.

The withdrawn routers are the IP prefixes of any routes that should be deleted from the routing table. The withdrawn route's field is a variable length field that contains this information.

The third field in the update message header is the 2-byte total path attribute length field. The field that immediately follows is the path attribute field. The path attribute field contains the metrics used by BGP to assign values to particular paths (explained later in this section).

The final field in the update message header is the network layer reachability information. This variable length field contains the IP prefixes of the paths that are to be added to the routing table.

The BGP Notification Message and Keepalive Message

A BGP notification message is a message exchanged between BGP routers when an error occurs. That is, when one router experiences a problem it sends a 3-field notification message, and then disconnects any open sessions. The three fields are comprised of an error code, and error subcode, and the error data.

A keepalive message is sent in one of two instances:

- To confirm a BGP open request sent by a peer

- To maintain open yet idle BGP sessions, for instance, when a hold-time is about to expire.

The keepalive message is comprised of one field that lets the recipient know not to expire any hold-timers.

BGP Metrics and Attributes

BGP, like most routing protocols, relies on the use of metrics to aid in the route decision process. We have already discussed how the use of route maps can allow an administrator to change a metric to a higher or lower value (depending on the desirability of a particular route). In BGP these metrics are know as attributes and are very important in deciding how data is routed. Here are some of the most important attributes used by BGP routers when making their path selection: AS-Path/AS-Set, Next-Hop, Origin and Local Preference.

AS-Path/AS-Set

The AS-Path is an attribute that is attached to a BGP route update. The AS-Path indicates a cumulative account of the Autonomous Systems a BGP update passed through before reaching its destination. To illustrate this, let's follow an AS-Path through a BGP network in Figure 7.16.

FIGURE 7.16
The advertised network 10.34.0.0 follows an AS-Path from Router A through B, C, and finally to Router D.

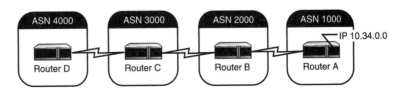

Router A advertises the path "10.34.0.0 belongs to ASN 1000." When router B processes the update, the AS-Path that the update came from is added (as a prefix) to the update. Therefore the update now says "AS 1000 says that 10.34.0.0 belongs to ASN 1000."

Next, router B advertises the same route to router C. After router C processes the update the path would read "ASN 2000 says that ASN 1000 says that 10.34.0.0 belongs to ASN 1000." Finally when the update reaches router D the AS-Path to network 10.34.0.0 would include ASN 3000-ASN 2000-ASN 1000. As each router receives the updates it processes the information contained within and includes the learned routes in their local route tables.

	Note

A complete AS path is known as an AS-Set.

Now when router D has a message for IP network 10.34.0.0, it just needs to look at the AS-Set in its route table. The AS-Set gives the router the complete AS-Path to the destination. In our example, router D would forward any data for 10.34.0.0 to the first AS-Path (ASN 3000). Router C would forward that data to (what it sees as the first AS-Path) ASN 2000, and so on until the information reaches ASN 1000.

Next Hop

The next hop attribute functions similarly to the AS-Path; however, it specifies the IP address of the router interface used to reach a particular AS. To use our previous example, Router C only advertised to Router D the AS-Path for data going to 10.34.0.0 is through ASN 3000. This information doesn't do Router D any good if it doesn't understand how to get to ASN 3000.

The next hop attribute is used by router D to identify the IP address of the physical router interface that router D can use to access router C (ASN 3000).

Origin

The origin attribute indicates where a particular update came from, or better yet, how it came from there. BGP routes data (somewhat) differently based on whether the path is internal (IBGP) or external (EBGP). Therefore BGP needs a way to determine (quickly) what the origin of a route is.

The origin can be one of three values:

- IGP
- EGP
- Incomplete

Note

Do not confuse IGP and EGP with IBGP and EBGP. Whereas IBGP and EBGP are specific protocols within BGP, IGP and EGP are designators that stand for Internal Gateway Protocol and External Gateway Protocol. These designators are used to determine how a route was learned and placed into the BGP route table. The designators do not necessarily represent IBGP or EBGP learned routes. In fact, often times you find other protocols being used to aid in the transportation of BGP data. Protocols such as IGRP and EIGRP (Interior Gateway Routing Protocol and Enhanced Interior Gateway Routing Protocol) can be used to route IBGP data.

Therefore the BGP origin is specifying (generally) which type of protocol the route was forwarded on.

An origin or IGP indicates that the route was learned from an internal routing protocol such as RIP, OSPF, or IBGP. Therefore the BGP speaker can assume that any path with an origin of IGP is within its own AS.

An origin of EGP indicates that the route was learned through an external update. This would cause the BGP speaker to use EBGP to reach any route with an origin of EGP.

An origin of incomplete means that the route was obtained through a process other then internal or external learning. In most case an incomplete origin represents a route that was obtained through route redistribution.

Local Preference

The local preference path attribute is a metric used to determine the desirability of one path over another when there are two paths to a particular destination. When a router is presented with two (seemingly equal) paths to the same destination, it compares the local preference attribute of the paths to determine which to use.

The higher a path's local preference is, the more likely it is to be used. If no local preference is defined, the default value is 100. To ensure a particular path is used the local preference of the preferred path should be modified to a higher value.

Interior Border Gateway Routing

As previously mentioned, BGP operates by opening a peering session between two routers through a specific logical IP address (identifying a physical interface) and TCP port. That is, BGP peering sessions are always established between two routers on TCP port 179.

In EBGP, this process poses a problem: If the specified physical interface is unavailable, the peering session cannot be established. IBGP fixes this problem by using a loopback address. One of the major differences between EBGP and IBGP is that IBGP uses a loopback address.

A loopback address is an IP address that represents a logical internal interface (not tied to any physical interface) within a router, which can be accessed through any active physical router port. Because the loopback address is not tied to a specific interface and can be accessed through any active interface, it ensures that a BGP neighbor still gains connectivity regardless of the availability of the physical ports.

Loopback addresses are only found in IBGP because of the reachability of the routers. More often than not, routers connected through EBGP are only connected on one physical port whereas routers connected by IBGP normally share an entire networking environment.

BGP Confederations

To better understand some of the ways IBGP Autonomous Systems can be configured we need to discuss BGP Confederations. As previously mentioned, all BGP speakers in an AS need to be fully meshed to communicate successfully. That is, every BGP speaker (running IBGP) in a specific AS needs to have a physical connection to every other IBGP speaker. Figure 7.17 illustrates a large, fully meshed AS.

FIGURE 7.17
In a fully meshed Autonomous System all routers must be physically connected to one another.

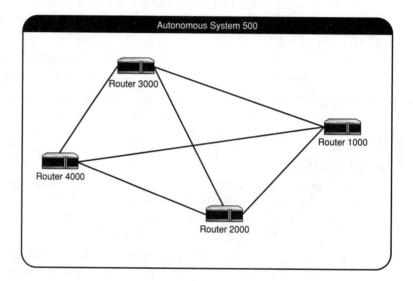

It is quite obvious from the example that as the number of IBGP speakers increases, the number of physical connections increases exponentially. Utilizing, tracking, and administering such a number of connections can be trying, even for the most seasoned of network professionals.

One method for reducing the number of physical router connections without limiting the number of IBGP speakers is to configure multiple BGP confederations. A BGP confederation is a subgroup within an AS. That is, one larger AS can be divided into multiple smaller ASs while retaining the same ASN, yet reducing the number of physical connections between speakers.

The function of BGP confederations can be compared to that of IP subnets. Where IP subnets break down the physical size of IP networks while retaining their identity as a larger entity, confederations create smaller sub-ASs that retain all of the outward characteristics of the original, larger AS.

To divide an AS into several confederations you need to do a bit of planning. That is, map on paper where your confederation borders are. This helps you visualize how you should configure the speakers within the confederations. After you have decided where to divide the AS into confederations, you need to assign confederation identifiers to the new AS subgroups.

Note

A confederation identifier is a number assigned to a confederation that distinguishes it from other confederations within the same AS. Confederation identifiers act as, and follow the same conventions as, Autonomous System numbers.

Keep in mind, a confederation is a small AS. In other words, IBGP peers within a confederation do need to be fully meshed. However, the IBGP peers within a confederation do not need to be fully meshed with the IBGP peers of another confederation (even if they are within the same AS). This lack of meshing between confederations creates a more manageable environment.

Therefore, once the confederation identifiers have been assigned, the inter-confederation physical links can be broken down. You should now have completely self-contained confederation with an AS. However, how do the confederations communicate with each other?

To enable intra-confederation communication, thus creating a fully functional Autonomous System, you need to define IBGP confederation peers. Confederation peers are routers that communicate from confederation to confederation. They act as BGP speakers for the individual confederations. Defining confederation peers can be confusing because of one small aspect of the process. Confederation peers speak EBGP to each other.

Because confederations each have their own confederation identifier, EBGP speakers are needed to enable communication between two or more confederations. However, because these EBGP speakers are contained within an IBGP environment, they follow all of the rules of IBGP speakers. Therefore confederation peers share routes like IBGP peers and not EBGP speakers (even though they are technically running EBGP).

Once the confederation peers are defined, connecting all of the confederations within your AS by a single physical link, you should have a fully functional group of confederations that appear as one large AS to the outside world. Figure 7.18 illustrates an AS divided into multiple confederations.

FIGURE 7.18

A group of confederations.

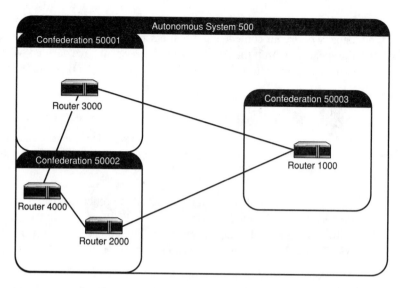

BGP Synchronization

Now that we have discussed the formations of confederations within IBGP routing environments, we can tackle the subject of BGP synchronization. I touched upon the subject of EBGP updates earlier in this chapter. However, there is a larger part if the topic that deals with IBGP. This is known as BGP synchronization.

Within a BGP environment you may have more than one protocol being run through your routers. That is, all routers not running BGP should be running another routing protocol to facilitate the delivery of packages. Keep in mind, BGP is a Border Gateway Routing Protocol; your environment needs an IGP (Interior Gateway Protocol) to route data through the rest of your internal network.

Your routers may be running OSPF, RIP, IS-IS, or any other IGP on the remaining portions of the network that are not serviced by BGP. The IGP that your remaining routers are running communicate with and supply table information to the local BGP speakers. This information is used by the BGP speakers to update each other as to the current condition of the network.

However, running two or more routing protocols simultaneously can pose a big problem. Each protocol is going to run its own routing updates. The problem is that if one router is running both IGRP and BGP, both of which receive routing table updates from different sources, which protocol's updates take precedence?

BGP synchronization helps the router determine what updates to include in its routing table (and then pass on to other BGP routers). Through BGP synchronization a BGP router can hold its BGP updates until all routers have reported receiving updates from the IGP.

For example, the network in Figure 7.19 shows two Autonomous Systems. Each AS is running both BGP and OSPF. Notice that some routers are running both protocols while others are running only OSPF.

FIGURE 7.19

An AS running two routing protocols, BGP and OSPF. OSPF provides intra-AS routing, while BGP provides Inter-AS routing.

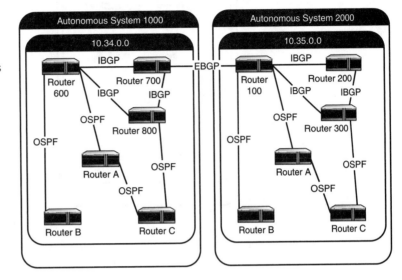

Before the BGP can begin its routing updates, it needs to wait for each router to receive an OSPF update. This ensures that each router is receiving the most accurate information.

One topic that ties in closely with BGP synchronization is BGP route reflection. I briefly discussed route maps earlier in this chapter; now we can touch on a more complex issue, BGP route reflection.

BGP Route Reflection

As previously mentioned, within an Autonomous System all IBGP peers must be fully meshed. One of the reasons for this is that an IBGP peer cannot distribute routes learned from one IBGP peer to another.

IBGP peers only propagate updates that relate directly to their own routes. This allows IBGP routers to send out updates that the routers know about firsthand, reducing the number of incorrect or outdated routes. However, the obvious problem is that every IBGP peer must be physically linked to every other IBGP peer. The solution to this problem is BGP route reflectors, which allow partial mesh configurations to exist.

IBGP peers can be configured as BGP reflectors. IBGP peers that are route reflectors can distribute, or reflect, routes learned from one BGP peer to another BGP peer. In other words, a BGP router can send an update to another BGP router without being physically meshed to that router. Figure 7.20 illustrates route reflection.

FIGURE 7.20
Route reflection is necessary in a partially meshed AS. Routes are reflected between peers connected by a BGP reflector.

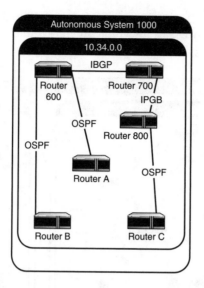

In Figure 7.20, router 700 can reflect routes from router 600 to router 800. Route reflectors are a great tool administrators can use to help reduce the number of physical links needed between IBGP peers. However, the use of route reflectors does require more router overhead than a standard BGP router.

Configuring BGP

Although this chapter should provide you with enough information to have an understanding of how BGP works, some things are better understood through example. Even though this book is not geared towards the use of a particular brand or manufacturer of router equipment, the following BGP configurations are derived from a Cisco router.

The examples in this section are from *Sams Teach Yourself Cisco Routers in 21 Days* by J.F. DiMarzio. I have included them because they clearly show how BGP is configured. These sample router configurations should help you visualize the intricacies of BGP.

The following simple command example shows a router being configured for BGP. The router is also being added to a confederation.

Note

Some Cisco-specific commands not directly related to BGP have been deleted for clarity.

```
router bgp 500
bgp confederation identifier 500
bgp confederation peers 65654 65655
neighbor 10.198.30.1 remote-as 65654
neighbor 10.198.30.1 weight 1000
neighbor 10.198.50.1 remote-as 65655
neighbor 10.198.50.1 weight 2000
```

Notice that the routers 10.198.30.1 and 10.198.50.1 that were both added are confederation peers and assigned weight metrics. While this is a simplistic example, it shows how routers relate to each other within a BGP environment. This process would need to be repeated on all BGP routers.

The following table excerpt from router 10.198.14.1 (configured in the previous example) shows BGP routing table with metrics.

```
BGP table version is 567123, local communication server ID is 10.198.40.1
Status codes: s suppressed, * valid, > best, i - internal Origin codes:
i - IGP, e - EGP, ? - incomplete

Network  Next Hop  Metric LocPrf Weight Path

*>i10.198.30.0 10.198.30.1 0  100  1000 65654 800 i
*>i10.198.50.0 10.198.50.1 0  100  2000 65655 900 i
```

The actual table data in this example begins at the first asterisk (*). The first line of table data shows that router 10.198.40.1 can reach network 10.198.30.0 through router 10.198.30.1. The weight for this link (as defined in the previous example) is 1000. This link is part of AS 65,654 which leads to AS 800. The second line relates to the second neighbor in the confederation, 10.198.50.1.

These two examples should have given you a good base of knowledge to begin working with and understanding BGP.

Summary

BGPv4 is a distance-vector based routing protocol. It is the primary routing protocol used throughout the Internet. BGP routes data between networks (known as ASs or Autonomous Systems). BGP, unlike other routing protocols, provides reliable guaranteed exchange of route information through the use of TCP sessions between peers utilizing TCP port 179. BGP routers within the same AS are said to be internal peers. BGP routers belonging to different ASs are external peers. IBGP is used to maintain route information within an AS, whereas EBGP is used to communicate route information between ASs. Autonomous systems are a collection of related networks. Each AS is assigned a unique number by a governing body or ISP (assuming you need to communicate to the outside world using EBGP). The AS number assigned is within the range 1 to 65,535.

There are four different BGP message types; open message, update, notification, and keepalive. Sessions are established with the exchange of the open message followed by a keepalive. Once open, updates are used to exchange routes. Notifications are sent when an error occurs.

Chapter Quiz

1. What is the current version of BGP, v3 or v4?

2. Name the TCP port used in BGP sessions.

3. Which two main BGP protocols facilitate the exchange of route information?

4. What parameter must be shared between peers within the same BGP routing domain?

5. What type of relationship do two routers from different ASs have?

6. IBGP supports partial mesh networks through what feature?

7. After TCP has established a transport layer session between peers, which BGP message is used to request the start of a peering relationship?

8. Which BGP message type is used to alert peers of an error?

9. What is a confederation?

10. What three types of ASs exist?

CHAPTER 8

IS-IS

You will learn about the following in this chapter:

- DecNet routing
- DecNet phase V
- IS-IS routing

- IS-IS addressing
- IS-IS areas and domains
- IS-IS messages

The History of IS-IS, Part I (DECnet)

The IS-IS (Intermediate system–to–Intermediate system) protocol is a link state routing protocol. IS-IS is crucial to anyone who needs to route IP, pure OSI, or a mixture of the two. However, before you can fully understand what IS-IS is and how it works, you need to understand where it came from and why it was developed.

The ISO developed IS-IS (based on DECnet Phase V) to work with the CLNP (Connectionless Network Protocol). However, because of the protocol's great flexibility it could work with OSI and DNA (proprietary network model developed by Digital Equipment Corporation) architectures, providing a type of protocol bridge between DECnet's proprietary DNA model and the widely accepted OSI. .

Note

ISO (International Standards Organization) is a group of countries working together to create standard platforms in everything from technology to cosmetics and documentation. These countries have there own affiliate organizations whose members are the voting parties of ISO. The United States' ISO affiliate is ANSI (American National Standards Institute). ISO and its OSI model were discussed in Chapter 1, "Overview of Industry Models-Standards and TCP-IP Protocols."

Some of the technological advances to have been accepted by ISO include the OSI model, Ethernet, and IS-IS.

IS-IS's flexibility made it a very popular routing protocol on DECnet Phase V networks; therefore you need to look at how DECnet works. Understanding DECnet helps you understand the need that IS-IS filled and how that later translated to the IP routing market. Although I discuss IS-IS in terms of routing IP, knowing the origins of DECnet phases IV and V and ISO CLNP gives you a good introduction to the terminology, the technology, and the flexibility of IS-IS.

In The Beginning: The Age of DECnet

Digital Equipment Corporation developed DECnet as a protocol suite i.n 1975. DECnet is the primary protocol for its popular VAX line of computers. Each release, or version, of DECnet is known as a phase (Phase I, Phase II, and so on).

Note
IS-IS was based on DECnet Phase V, although much of what made DECnet Phase V work was actually implemented in DECnet Phase IV.

Like all protocols, DECnet needed to follow a specific architecture to move information from one system to another. A protocol model (known as the DNA architecture) was developed to address how data would move from the user interface of one system, through the PC, over the transmission media, and into the destination system. Most protocols today adhere to the OSI model architecture. The problem is that the OSI model was not yet in existence when DECnet was initially released, making it impossible to use.

DECnet was (and still is) a proprietary system used to enable communication between DEC equipment. The first four phases of DECnet did not adhere to the OSI model; rather, they were based on the DNA (Digital Network Architecture). (Digital would later develop an OSI-compliant version of DECnet known as DECnet Phase V or DECnet OSI/DNA).

Note
All phases of DECnet are designed to be backward-compatible, which means that DECnet Phase III is backward-compatible with Phase II. When DEC began developing the DECnet Phase V (OSI-compliant), it realized that the protocol needed to be implemented in such a way to be backward-compatible with the DECnet DNA architecture. This would later become a very important feature of IS-IS.

DECnet Phase IV DNA was comprised of eight layers that correlated (more or less) to the seven layers of the OSI model. Figure 8.1 shows the eight layers of Phase IV DNA and how they relate to the OSI model.

If you are already familiar with the OSI model you will notice some small differences between Digital's DNA and ISO's OSI. The main difference resides in the upper layers of the two models. Many of DNA's upper layers span multiple OSI layers. The lower layers (those crucial for routing) are relatively the same, which would later help Digital make an easier transition from its DNA model to the OSI model.

FIGURE 8.1

The eight layers of the DECnet Phase IV DNA architecture.

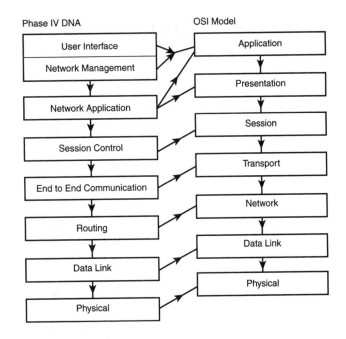

DECnet Areas and Nodes

Because of the differences in the upper and lower layers between the DNA and OSI architectures, DECnet addresses are structured differently then those from other protocols. DECnet addresses are comprised of two parts, an area and a node (a concept that would later be carried over to IS-IS). DECnet logical network addresses are 16 bits long and formulated as follows. Figure 8.2 illustrates a common DECnet address.

FIGURE 8.2

DECnet addresses have two main parts, area and node. These two pieces of information uniquely define a system.

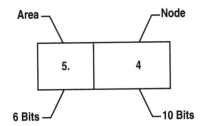

The first 6 bits of a DECnet logical network layer address are known as an *area*. An area can be any valid number between 1 and 63 (64 bytes and 0 bytes are invalid). The last 10 bits of the address are the *node*, addressed as the numbers 1 through 1,023 (with 1,024 bytes and 0 bytes being invalid). This creates a total pool of 64,449 possible nodes on a DECnet network. For example, if one DECnet network is comprised of three areas (5, 6, and 7) and each area has four nodes (1,2,3, and 4) the network would be addressed as shown in Figure 8.3. Figure 8.3 illustrates a DECnet network with multiple area and node addresses.

FIGURE 8.3

Note that this addressed DECnet network has three areas and four nodes.

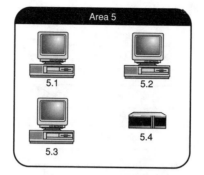

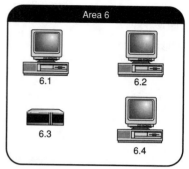

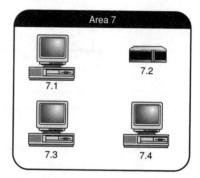

Note

The MAC address or burned-in address is (generally) a static number assigned by the IEEEm burned into network interface cards, such as Ethernet, by vendors to ensure uniqueness in large networks. It is possible (but unlikely) to manually change this number to fit the needs of certain networks.

Systems on a DECnet network have a MAC address dynamically assigned to them based on their area/node address. For example the MAC address for an end system with an area/node address of 4.2 would be AA-00-04-00-02-10. To arrive at this MAC address, DEC follows this convention:

1. The DECnet address needs to be converted to binary (remember the address format is 6 bits and 10 bits):

   `4.2 = 000100.0000000010`

2. The new binary area/node address needs to be divided into two, eight bit sections:

   `00010000   00000010`

Note

Remember that MAC addresses are 48 bits (essentially a series of eight-bit segments).

3. These sections are then flipped:

   `00000010  00010000`

4. The flipped binary sections are then converted to hexadecimal format:

   `02 10`

5. The new hexadecimal pairs are appended to the DEC Ethernet MAC vendor code AA-00-04. (A null pair of 00 is placed between the vendor code and the area/node to fill out the address.)

6. The end product is the MAC address AA-00-04-00-02-10.

   > DECnet (and later IS-IS) uses these dynamic MAC addresses to both route information and send update packets to other nodes. For anyone who has experience with IP addressing or routing, the DECnet address scheme may seem (at first) to be a little unconventional. However, understanding that DECnet provides the base on which IS-IS was formed is the key to understanding how IS-IS works.

DECnet Nodes

DECnet nodes can be defined as one of three entities:

- An end system (ES)
- A level 1 router (L1)
- A level 2 router (L2)

An end system is defined as anything that is not a router. The most common ES node is a user's PC; however, ESs can include printers, scanners, and other networked devices. The key to an ES is that end systems have only one addressable interface and can only communicate with level 1 routers. In a common network environment there should be more ESs than any other node types on the network.

Logically, a PC on a network cannot send data to any other PC without some assistance. Whether the data flows through a hub or router, another device is required to enable communication between more than two PCs. (The exception to this is when you only want to provide communication between two PCs. In that case you can connect the two devices with a crossover cable.) PCs do not provide any routing capabilities, making them ESs.

End systems can be considered the routed system on the network. The majority of data being routed around the network either starts at or terminates at an ES. Even though they perform no routing duties, the ESs are a very important part of the routing process in a DECnet environment.

The second category of node on a DECnet network is known as an L1 or level 1 router. A level 1 router is an intra-area router, which means it can only route within its own area. In routing terms, L1s have no knowledge of any network topology outside their own area. (This is a very important feature that was later ported to the IS-IS protocol. By not routing outside their own area, L1s dramatically cut down on the amount of network traffic in any given environment.)

When a router is routing between multiple networks, complex factors need to be taken into consideration. If a router has multiple interfaces for multiple networks it has to send multiple broadcast messages to complete certain tasks. For example, if a router has four network interfaces (A, B, C, and D) and receives a message for network C, the router generally sends a broadcast message to each interface. This broadcast message asks each interface what network it is on. After the router receives an answer from network C, it sends the message along. This process is necessary to build and maintain route information but results in an abundance of broadcast messages.

By dictating that L1s can only service one area, DECnet eliminates the overflow of broadcast messages. Broadcast messages are isolated to areas. That is, broadcasts in one area do not affect another area.

Referring to Figure 8.4, routers with area/node addresses 5.4 and 6.3 would be considered level 1 routers. Being a level 1 router, Router 5.4 can only route data around area 5 and 6.3 can only route data around area 6. Level 1 routers are limited to routing within the area in which they belong.

FIGURE 8.4

Two areas exist, Area 5 and 6. Each area contains one level 1 router. The level 1 routers are 5.4 and 6.3. Level 1 routers cannot route datagrams beyond there local area.

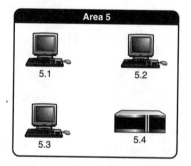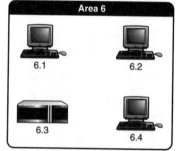

Another important feature of L1 routers is the way DECnet addresses them. Level 1 routers may have multiple interfaces; however, they can only have one area/node address. This means that every node interface, or port, on an L1 router generally has the same address. If L1 5.4 has four ports, and each is connected to a different ES, each port is addressed as 5.4. To illustrate this let's take a detailed look at area 5 in Figure 8.5.

Notice how each hub in area 5 is connected to a different interface on router 5.4. However, each interface is still addressed as 5.4.

Router 5.4 can only communicate to end systems 5.1, 5.2, and 5.3. If ES 5.2 wanted to send data to in another area that would require the services of level 2 routers.

Level 2 routers are routers that can communicate with other level 2 and level 1 routers in different areas. To transmit information between two different areas you need at least two L2s. Figure 8.6 illustrates the paths information can take when travelling from system to system across two areas.

FIGURE 8.5
Router 5.4 is a level 1
router with multiple con-
nections and only one
address.

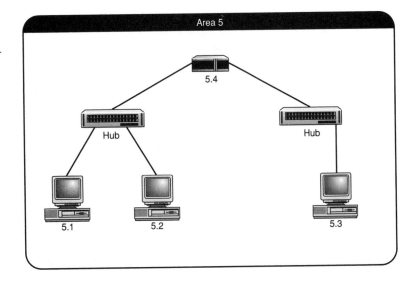

FIGURE 8.6
Level 2 routers provide
communication between
areas.

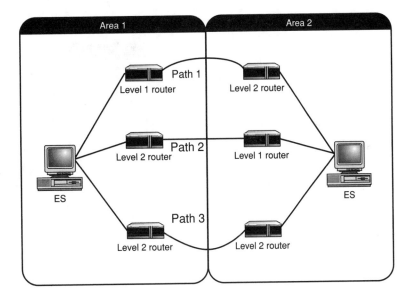

As shown in Figure 8.6 there are three possible paths that information can take when being
routed from ES to ES across areas:

- The first option is to send the data from the ES to a level 1 router in the same area. The
  level 1 router then routes the packets to a level 2 router in the target area. The level 2
  router can then pass the packets to the intended recipient.

- The second option is essentially option 1 in reverse. The data leaves the ES and is sent to
  an L2 in the ES's home area. The L2 then forwards the data to a level 1 router in the target area. Finally the data is sent along to the receiving ES.

- The final option is to have the data be transmitted from the ES to an L2 in the same area. The L2 then forwards the information to another L2 in the intended recipient's area. The recipient L2 then sends the data along to the final ES.

As you can see, level 2 routers can also interact with end systems (giving them the added capabilities of a level 1 router). Also, like level 1 routers, level 2 routers have only one address to share across all of its interfaces. Figure 8.7 illustrates a fully addressed, routable, DECnet network with three areas.

FIGURE 8.7

Routers 5.4, 6.5, and 7.2 provide routing between DECnet areas 5, 6, and 7.

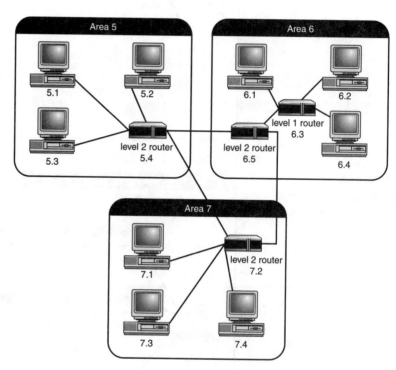

DECnet Routing Basics

The precursor to IS-IS was DECnet Phase IV's DRP (DECnet Routing Protocol). DRP worked by routing packets between systems in an orderly manner. At the heart of DRP is the Hello Message. Hello Messages are packets that are routinely sent from system to system to announce their presence and the status of attached links.

By passing around these Hello messages routers can learn the status of the links and routers around them. An ES sends a Hello Message to any L1 or L2 with which it interfaces. Figure 8.8 illustrates the life cycle of an intra-area Hello Message.

FIGURE 8.8

Hello messages are sent by end systems and routers to announce their presence. L1 and l2 routers transmit hellos periodically to maintain state information of attached links.

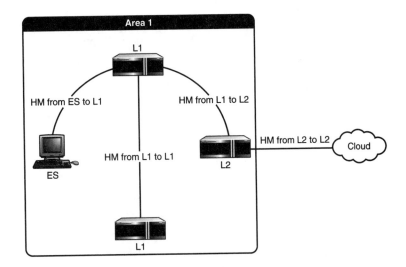

The ES sends hello messages to L1 routers announcing their presence. This hello message signals to the L1 that the ES is functioning on the network and able to receive packets. The L1 uses this information to build a picture of its home area. By assembling the Hello Messages from the ESs and the other L1s, any particular L1 can create an up-to-date picture of the network's topology.

Even though the L1 does not send a Hello Message directly back to an ES, the ES listens to the L1 to L1 messages to formulate its own picture of the current network topology.

Level 1 routers send Hello Messages to other L1s and L2s. These HMs serve the same purpose as those sent by ESs. The L1 alerts all other L1s and L2s in the same area as to its current state on the network.

Level 2 routers only send Hello Messages to other level 2 routers (remember L1s and ESs can only have knowledge of their own areas and because L2s have routing information for other areas, they cannot share Hello Messages with either).

When an ES has a packet to send to another ES there are steps it must follow. The first step is to check its local cache table to see if the destination address has recently been used and cached. If it finds the address, it addresses the datagram and sends it to the ES's local L1 router for delivery.

Most protocols (DECnet being no different) allow PCs to keep a routing cache. An ES always checks its own routing cache before releasing a packet onto the network. This routing cache contains a table relating a destination address with the address of the router that can get the packet there.

If the ES cannot find the router it needs in its cache, it adds the destination MAC address (see the formula in "DECnet Areas and Nodes" described earlier in this chapter) to the packet and forwards it to the closest L1 (or L2 as the case may be).

The receiving router examines the destination information and, using its routing table (formulated from various Hello Messages), forwards the packet on to its final target. If that target is in a different area, the L1 sends the packet to an L2 that can reach the foreign area. In some cases this process may involve more than one L2.

If a packet needs to be sent from an ES across multiple areas, it first reaches an L2 in its own area. Once the data reaches this L2 the router looks in its routing table for the location of the L2 attached to the target area. Because level two routers can share information across areas, the L2 in the home area should know the location of the L2 in the target area regardless of the number of areas between them. The data can then be forwarded along to its intended recipient.

DECnet Phase V

When DECnet Phase V came along, DEC decided to adopt the OSI model to base for its protocol. Remember, because all phases of DECnet are backward-compatible, DECnet Phase V needed to adhere to both the OSI and DNA standards.

Because the two architectures were very similar, DEC was able to successfully port DECnet to the OSI model. However, they now needed a routing protocol that could route in either OSI or DNA architectures and route the DECnet protocol (as well as IP). The solution was IS-IS. The Intermediate system–to–Intermediate system routing protocol, an OSI compliant routing protocol was adopted as the routing protocol of choice for DECnet Phase V networks.

The History of IS-IS, Part II (CLNP)

Just before the point in time where DECnet Phase V was being .developed, ISO was developing its CLNS (Connectionless Network Service) architecture with CLNP (Connectionless Network Protocol) to be the primary protocol within this architecture. CLNP is a pure OSI routed protocol that handles network layer addressing and allows for the connectionless transfer of data between two end systems. CLNP is quick, relatively small in size (using little network overhead), and is the OSI equivalent of the IP protocol.

Note

A connectionless protocol, as opposed to a connection-oriented one, does not require the acknowledgement of packet receipt. Because these protocols do not require an acknowledgement for every packet sent, they tend to be faster than their connection-oriented counterparts (however, they are also considered somewhat unreliable). IP is a connectionless protocol.

When DEC began developing DECnet Phase V OSI/DNA, it needed a fully OSI-compliant routed protocol to work on the third layer (network) of the OSI model. The protocol they were looking for was CLNP. However, there was one drawback to using CNLP in the backward-compatible, OSI- and DNA-based DECnet environment. As of this time there was no routing protocol flexible enough to handle the mixed architectures of OSI and DNA yet robust enough to work in a large connectionless environment.

Note

The third layer of both the OSI and DNA models are the layers used for routing network data. In the OSI model this is the Network layer, in DNA this is the Routing layer. Such similarities made the transition from DNA to OSI fairly easy for DECnet.

This is where the two histories of IS-IS collide. DEC needed a flexible routing protocol to route the new OSI-compliant DECnet Phase V. ISO had already developed the routed protocol used in the connectionless environment. So, DEC helped ISO develop IS-IS in the DECnet OSI (CNLP) environment.

IS-IS proves to be perfect for routing the OSI/DNA networks. ISO developed IS-IS as a quick, portable link state routing protocol for CLNP. As a routing protocol IS-IS filled the gap in the DECnet V environment.

Because CLNP was OSI-based and, by definition connectionless, with minimal adaptation, IS-IS would be able to also route IP (keep in mind IP is also a connectionless protocol).

In the past there was some discussion (every once and a while it still comes up) about making CLNP the default protocol of the Internet. Since then it has become clear that IP has a major stronghold on the Internet. Therefore, support for IP has been added to IS-IS, completing the protocol.

In the next section of this chapter I discuss link state protocols and how they function. IS-IS as an IP routing protocol works like many other Link State protocols. However, you will notice many of the characteristics of the DECnet Phase IV implementation still remain in one form or another in IS-IS (like areas, nodes, and the omnipresent Hello Message.)

IS-IS does not support IP by itself. When ISO started to tweak IS-IS to support IP many people were still using it to route purely OSI protocols. Therefore to distinguish between the two implementations of IS-IS, the newer version would be officially named Integrated IS-IS. Integrated IS-IS offers support for simultaneous multiple routed protocols, like CLNP and IP.

Let's look under the hood and see exactly how IS-IS (Integrated IS-IS) and other link state protocols work.

Link State Routing

Routing protocols are separated into categories based on the algorithms they use to route data. One common category of protocol is link state (Link State routing was discussed in Chapter 3, "IP Routing"). Almost every router on the market today can use one of the many link state protocols to move information around a network. Both IS-IS and Integrated IS-IS are considered link state routing protocols.

Routers running link state protocols identify neighbors and update each other through the exchange of LSAs or Link State Advertisements. LSAs (Link State Advertisements) are exchanged by routers to advertise the status (state) of every other router (link) in the environment. These exchanges have advantages and disadvantages; however, before I discuss them, let's define what sets IS-IS and other link state protocols apart from other routing protocols.

Note

Keep in mind, a routing protocol is the protocol used by routers and other connectivity devices to carry routed protocols across the network media. Routed protocols (such as IP and IPX) are used to encapsulate data for transmission to other devices.

All link state protocols are bound by a number of common characteristics. The main characteristic that binds all link state protocols together is the fact that they all work on a "shortest path first" basis. In other words, the main goal of any link state protocol is to find the shortest route between two end systems. For example, in Figure 8.9 there is a network with multiple paths between two locations running a Link State protocol (such as OSPF). In this scenario, the OSPF routing algorithm may choose path A as the shortest path between ES1 and ES2.

The term *shortest path* does not necessarily refer to the distance between two points. The shortest path can be the port with the most bandwidth, the cable that has the least amount of interference, the cheapest port to operate (as opposed to a leased line), or a combination of all of these factors.

For example, a company has four offices buildings (A, B, C and D) across a large city. These buildings are connected by cables (100Mbps Ethernet segments) from office A to B to C then D (for example, building A is cabled to building B, which is connected to building C and so on). However, there is also an ISDN line directly connecting building A to building D. So data being routed from building A to building D has two paths to choose from: either travel directly to building D via the ISDN line or be routed through building B and through building C to get to building D.

FIGURE 8.9

Link State protocols choose the shortest path when multiple routes between source and destination exist.

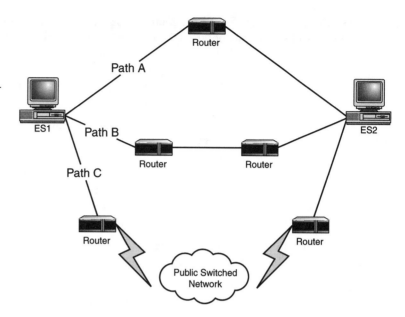

Obviously the ISDN line is the shortest (physical) path, but it may not be the best path. It would most likely be terribly expensive to continually send routed data across the ISDN line; therefore IS-IS would likely choose the Ethernet route, which contains more segments, but offers higher transfer rates. Figure 8.10 illustrates what link state protocols may take into consideration when choosing a shortest path.

FIGURE 8.10

The shortest physical path from A to D is through the ISDN link, but this path is not chosen because the collective bandwidth capacity across the path through networks B and C are greater, making this the best path.

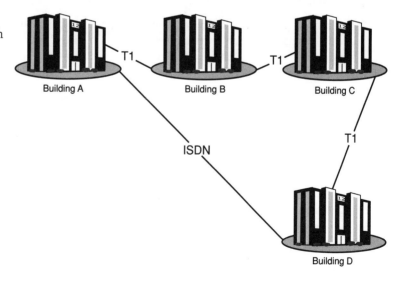

As you can see in Figure 8.10, the router chose the shortest path first (that which has the highest bandwidth capacity), not the shortest physical path. Link State routing protocols are called shortest path first, not shortest path only. If the actual shortest path from one system to another is not available, the protocol opens the next shortest path (and so on). By opening the shortest path between systems, link state protocols reduce the amount of time required to move information from one PC to another.

Referring back to the previous example, the ISDN line connecting building A with building D would not sit around unused just because it is not the shortest path. If the shortest path became unavailable or the amount of traffic across that path begins to back up (causing delays and network latency), the speed of the ISDN line would outweigh the cost. The ISDN line would then become the shortest path (until the traffic on the first shortest path once again becomes available or less congested). Then the bulk of the routed traffic would switch back to the Ethernet segments.

This form of load balancing (see refer to Chapter 3) makes most link state protocols very attractive to administrators with multiple routes between destinations.

Less expensive (yet reliable) lines can be assigned a lower cost (forcing IS-IS to consider the line as a better route over another comparable path) while more expensive leased lines can be given a slightly higher cost. These higher cost leased lines can then be used by IS-IS when the less expensive lines become congested. This keeps data flowing in a smooth and economical manner.

When designers are choosing routing protocols for their networks, several factors are considered. However, especially in larger networks, speed and monetary expenses are almost always at the top of the list. The obvious advantage to having a fast routing protocol is getting information from point A to point B in the shortest possible time.

Fast routing protocols also have other advantages. By moving data onto and off of the network as quick as possible, many network congestion-related problems (such as traffic jams and bandwidth over usage) can be avoided. This makes for a clean, virtually error-free routing environment. Every network manager can appreciate not having to worry about the routers and the routing protocols.

Although link state protocols such as IS-IS do offer an opportunity to route data quickly from point A (or Intermediate system) to point B, link state protocols do have disadvantages. Link state protocols go through a process known as flooding, which is triggered by an event such as a link becoming available or a failure in an existing link. During flooding a router sends a large amount of LSAs (Link State Advertisements) across the network. The neighboring routers receive these advertisements, update their own tables, and send the updates to their neighboring routers. Figure 8.11 shows an example of an LSA.

This flooding is the necessary process a link state router goes through to build an accurate picture of the environment around them (The routers use the information contained within the LSA to create a dynamic table. The router then runs its routing algorithms against this table to calculate the shortest path for every packet.) The amount of time an LSA flood lasts depends on the number of updates, or changes, in the routing environment, and the convergence time.

FIGURE 8.11

Level 1 router L1.1 sends a LSA to L1.2, including the link cost (three) and the status of attached hosts.

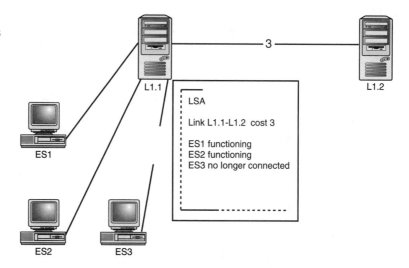

Note

In routing, convergence is the amount of time it takes for routers to agree on a particular set of changes. In other words, it is the time the routers need to sync up with each other (resulting in all routers working from the same picture of the environment).

Flooding, however, can cause traffic havoc on some networks. The heartiest networking environments may not feel the effects of a large-scale convergence; however, most networks notice some network latency during a flood. The environments that are affected the most by a flood are larger networks that already have some bandwidth issues.

Larger networks with plenty of bandwidth, and smaller networks with fewer routers, may not have as much trouble during an LSA flood. These networks either have plenty of available bandwidth to handle both LSAs and normal daily traffic, or there are not enough routers to generate a mass amount of advertisements.

In a network of any size, having enough available bandwidth before you implement IS-IS is one of the keys to getting through an LSA flood with no noticeable latency. If you are working on an existing network and you are contemplating implementing IS-IS, make sure you have the bandwidth to deal with LSA floods. This one factor will save you many headaches down the road.

LSA floods affect networks in two ways: excessive traffic and increased overhead on routers to process them. Excessive traffic is caused by LSA flooding, which generates a large amount of traffic and normal network data may have trouble getting through. Keep in mind every router on the network needs to tell its neighboring routers (in the same area) what changes were made to its table. Then the routers that received the LSA information need to send out more LSAs telling everyone about the changes they just received from the first round of LSAs and so on until every router has the same picture of the network (that's a lot of packets).

The second drawback of LSA flooding is evident in the amount of memory and processing power needed by the router to process the updates. Depending on the number of LSAs on the network and the number of updates in each one, a router may devote the majority of its available memory and processor time to processing LSAs (in an attempt to converge as quickly as possible). LSA packets always have (processing) priority over a routed protocol packet. Those network packets that do make it through the traffic jam of LSAs may not get processed.

The reason why a link state router always processes an LSA over a routed protocol packet is simple: You want the environment to converge as quickly as possible. Therefore, the quicker an LSA can be processed and applied, the quicker a router can resume its normal daily function.

As far as routing protocol downsides go, this one really isn't that bad. Generally, link state protocols have one of the quickest convergence times of all routing protocol types. Therefore the network latency one would experience during a flood may not last very long. This can be very good news for administrators implementing IS-IS on a larger network with minimal bandwidth. The other benefit of flooding is that changes in a network's topology, such as a link becoming available or unavailable, is discovered quickly and communicated to all other routers fast. This allows routers to react to changes in the network, converge, and agree on the topology quickly. Convergence is key because without it, routers will not forward traffic.

Controlling Link State Floods

IS-IS does have a few built-in mechanisms for controlling the amount of LSAs sent out during a flood. The first control is a form of a split horizon. That is an IS-IS router can never send an LSA out on the same link it received it on. This keeps the same update information from looping infinitely between two routers. Figure 8.12 illustrates the use of split horizon.

FIGURE 8.12
IS-IS Router B sends an LSA to Router A, which Router A sends in the opposite direction to Router C.

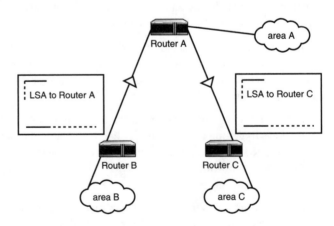

In Figure 8.12, notice router A received an update from router B on port 1. Router L1A used that information to update its routing table and sent its own LSA to router C on port 2. Router A (observing the split horizon rule) does not send this update information back out port 1 to router B. Because router B started the flood, and the only information in the update pertained to its own links, it doesn't need to receive router A's updated table information.

If you were to follow this scenario until the end of the update flood, you would see that router C would then block the path between router A and itself. Then any router receiving an update from router C would block their ports as well. By blocking (also known as killing or poisoning) the link between two routers after an update has been sent, IS-IS ensures that the minimum amount of LSAs are flooded onto the network during an update.

You may already be thinking of a hole in the split horizon rule. Figure 8.13 illustrates a router with multiple ports to receive the same update. How would the router handle this information?

FIGURE 8.13

Four routers (A, B, C and D) are connected together, all are observing the split horizon.

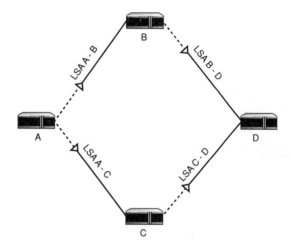

In the example illustrated in Figure 8.12, router A sends its update to routers B and C. Both of these routers are also connected to router D. So, what happens when router D receives two LSAs on two different ports for the same update? Obviously the router can only process one of the updates. But will it then send an LSA to the router that it didn't receive the update from first?

The short answer is router D processes the first update it receives, but does not send an update to either. To understand why, let's take a look inside an LSA packet and see what kind of information is included in an update. This gives you the answer you need.

Two fields within the LSA header control whether an IS-IS router can continue receiving updates if the updates are valid. These fields are remaining life and sequence.

The remaining life field is a time setting used by the router after the LSA is processed. When the router examines the LSA, a timer is started corresponding to the value indicated in the remaining life field. Then, until that timer expires, the router cannot process any LSAs pertaining to link(s) involved in the last LSA.

Using Figure 8.12 as an example, 8., router D receives an LSA from router B stating that the link between router A and router B is down. Router D processes the LSA, starts the remaining life timer, and updates its table. However, before router C receives the same update, it sends out its normal periodic LSA. This LSA (en route to router D) still states that the link between router A and router B is fine.

Because the remaining life timer has not yet expired, router D (recognizing the LSA pertains to an update that already occurred) ignores the update. Eventually router C gets the updated LSA and convergence can occur. Also, the remaining life timer restricts router D from sending any updates pertaining to the link between routers A and B until it expires. In this way, routers are not needlessly receiving conflicting information about a link's status, and they do not send out multiple LSAs for the same problem.

The second control field in an LSA packet is the sequence field. The receiving router, to identify the update contained within an LSA, uses the sequence field. A router does not process any LSA update that is out of sequence. By using the remaining life and sequence fields, IS-IS can control the sometimes-overwhelming LSA floods.

Another piece of good news for network administrators (who are adept at keeping network changes to a minimum) is they can control LSA flooding through configuration parameters. Good news usually comes with bad news, so here it is: You need to be extremely careful when changing default control values. The best advice is to keep the number of administrative network changes to a minimum. An improperly configured router may not be able to communicate with other routers. Changes you make on one router should also be made on all other routers that exchange information. That is, routers must agree on settings.

While administrative controls do s not eliminate floods all together, they can be used to minimize the frequency LSAs are sent. LSA floods are sent out periodically to detect non-administrative changes, and they are triggered after a change. By reducing the administrative changes the number of floods can be reduced. This may not be a very practical way to keep traffic down, but it is effective.

An administrator really has no control over the flooding of LSA updates; they are going to happen no matter what. However updates are triggered by an administrative change in the networking environment. This change could be the reassignment of a metric, a line being administratively reset or shut down, or anything that would change a possible path for data. Figure 8.14 shows an administrative change made to a router.

In Figure 8.14 the metric change to the cost value associated with the link connecting Router A to C will trigger an LSA update. This administrator (arbitrarily) assigned metric is the key calculation used by IS-IS's routing algorithm to figure out the shortest path between two systems.

IS-IS Metrics and Algorithms

The routing protocols installed on your router do not instinctively know the shortest route to every possible location on the network. Rather, they must consider certain elements of the environment. Then these elements must be acted upon to produce a definite result. Several factors help link state protocols decide which path is the shortest to a particular destination. These factors are known as metrics and algorithms.

FIGURE 8.14

An administrator has changed the metric to 4 on Router A. Router A's route table (stored in memory) indicates the metric cost to Router C is 5.

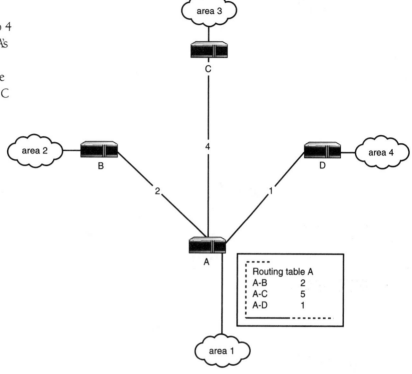

Metrics are the network variables used in deciding what path is shortest. For link state algorithms these metrics are values assigned by a network administrator. Many routing protocols use multiple metrics such as bandwidth, priority, monetary expense, transit delay, and other dynamic or statically assign factors. However, IS-IS simplifies the process by using only one, referred to as the Default metric. IS-IS' Default metric is an assigned value set by an administrator used to associate a cost value with a link. The lower the value the better the cost. Lower cost paths become preferred routes and are placed into the route table.

Optional Metrics
There are actually three other optional and one mandatory metric that can be defined be the administrator for a line. However, the current implementation of IS-IS only recognizes the mandatory metric of Default. The other metrics are
DELAY—The amount of delay on a particular line
EXPENSE—The value associated with operating a particular line
ERROR—The relative amount of errors associated with a particular line. Similar to the reliability metric recognized by OSPF.
DEFAULT—Arbitrary cost value assigned on a per link basis by an administrator.
Expressing values for these metrics does not affect the IS-IS algorithm in any way. Future versions of IS-IS may plan to make use of these values.

In an IS-IS environment the most important job of an administrator is to assign a cost (Default) metric to every link locally attached to every router. Figure 8.15illustrates an IS-IS network with all of the metrics assigned.

FIGURE 8.15

All routers have been configured with four metric values for each link; cost, delay, expense, and error.

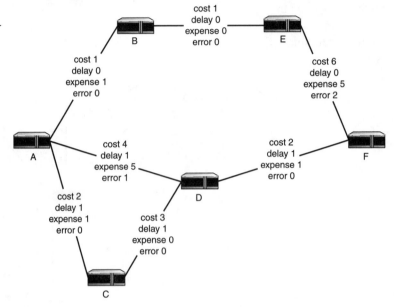

As far as an IS-IS administrator is concerned the Default metric cost is totally arbitrary. There is no formula or science to choosing a cost for a particular link. However, here are some guidelines to keep in mind when assigning a cost to a link:

- When IS-IS applies its algorithm to all of the metrics on the network, the *lowest* metrics form the shortest path.

- Reliable lines, such as those that are newer or not prone to interference (such as fiber) should always have a lower cost.

- Less expensive lines (such as those owned by the company installing the routers) should always be assigned a lower cost than leased lines such as ISDN.

- Higher bandwidth lines (like T3s) should be assigned a lower cost than a low bandwidth line.

- The assigned (Default) cost metrics, whatever you decide they should be, are going to govern what path will be chosen as the shortest path between to end points. Before you go off assigning metric to all of your links, be aware, there is a limit to the Default cost metric.

- A cost for a specific link cannot exceed 64. Therefore, any line assigned a cost of 65 will not be recognized as a valid path. However, there is no law against using duplicate values for different links. So, if you have a router with more then 64 ports, you may have to double up on costs.

Note

Links with the same metric values configured on physical interfaces of the same router weighs equally when run against the algorithm. In this case IS-IS distributes packets over either link, load balancing traffic.

The other limit placed on the cost metric applies to the total cost of a path (after being calculated by the routing algorithm). This is the cumulative total of all path costs to the destination. IS-IS does not route data over any path that has a total cost greater than 1024.

Note

If the numbers 64 and 1024 sound familiar, they are a direct correlation to the amount of memory used by IS-IS to store the routing information.

Therefore, some planning is required before establishing your IS-IS costs, especially on a larger network. Fully map out your routes and links before you begin implementing your IS-IS routers. Then assign all of your values on paper, add them up, and confirm that they are in line. Finally, you can implement your routers and let the algorithm take over.

IS-IS implements the Dijkstra algorithm, which was discussed in detail within Chapter 4, "RIP v1 and v2." The algorithm computes the shortest path, using the metric values assigned, to every other point throughout the network emanating from a single point.

IS-IS Addressing, Areas, and Domains

IS-IS, like every other routing protocol, addresses devices based on their location within an environment. IS-IS is no exception. IS-IS identifies devices by a two-part location identifier. These identifiers are the areas and domains to which a device can belong. To understand IS-IS addressing let's define the divisions of the IS-IS networks, the areas and the domains.

IS-IS routing networks are divided into two groups, areas and domains. By dividing IS-IS networks into areas and domains, administrators have greater control over the flow of data in an environment. This concept can be better visualized in terms of a state road map.

Let's use the state of Texas as an example. There are hundreds of thousands of roads and highways in Texas. Each road has a name assigned to it, and each highway has a number. Because there are multiple cities in the state, road names can be reused and recycled in every city, and county highway numbers can be reused per county.

The cities also serve as geographic markers within the counties (and the counties with the state). For example, if you are looking for a road in Dallas not only do you immediately know what part of the county you need to be in you also already know the general part of the state as well. Counties and cities help keep the problem of finding geographic locations from getting out of control.

Now, referring to the example, take away the cities and counties. Finding your way around the state becomes next to impossible. Not only does every city road and county highway need to be uniquely named, you may never find them after you're done. For example, if you are looking for a particular road, and there are no cities or counties to reference, you would have to comb the entire state looking for that one road. Even if you had a road map, not knowing the general area to start in would make the task very daunting.

Apply this logic to networking and you have the reason behind assigning areas and domains to IS-IS environments. IS-IS domains are the equivalent to the counties in a state, whereas IS-IS areas are the cities. These areas and domains aid the router in finding roads (links) that lead to ESs quickly, especially in large environments.

IS-IS Areas

An IS-IS area is a single subset of ESs and ISs. That is, a network of ESs (end systems) and ISs (intermediate systems) that all share the same area number or ID is considered one area. Figure 8.16 shows an IS-IS area with one level 1 router and five ESs.

FIGURE 8.16
This particular IS-IS area consists of one L1 router with five attached end systems.

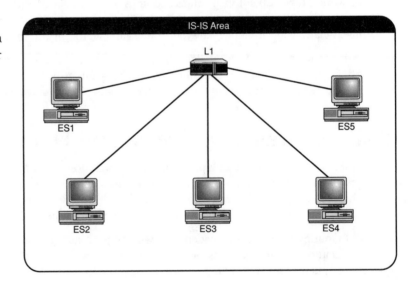

Note

The concept of IS-IS areas and domains is a direct reference back to the DECnet Phase IV architecture. All DECnet networks are also divided into areas.

If you are familiar with IP networks and IP subnetting, IS-IS areas and domains will not be that hard to follow. However, areas and domains do not correlate directly to their IP cousins. Rather it is more accurate to say that both IS-IS areas and domains together are equivalent to an IP subnet. IS-IS areas can be thought of as a sub-subnet.

Areas tend to be fairly small and self-contained. A network architect would not necessarily design an area in the same fashion he or she would design an IP subnet. IS-IS areas are not as general as IP subnets. An area is very localized.

Previously in this chapter we discussed routing within areas as being accomplished by L1s, or level 1 routers. Just as in DECnet Phase IV, L1s are used for intra-area data routing. L1s are the major interior routing device of IS-IS areas. However, keeping true to their DECnet counterparts, level 1 routers cannot route outside of their own local area. Therefore, a group of areas have greater routing requirements then the sum of their parts. (In other words, just by putting a bunch of areas in a room you are not guaranteeing that they will communicate with each other. In fact, they won't.) For this reason groups of areas are considered *domains* and have different requirements than the smaller, more localized areas.

A collection of related areas is known as a domain. In IS-IS terms, a domain is a group of areas bridged by a pair of level 2 routers. To fully qualify this definition, only level 2 routers can form a domain. One area with a level 1 router connected to a level 2 router (that also bridges another area) is not a considered domain. Figures 8.17 and 8.18 illustrate a correct and an incorrect IS-IS domain respectively.

FIGURE 8.17

A correctly formed IS-IS domain requires L2 routers connecting areas.

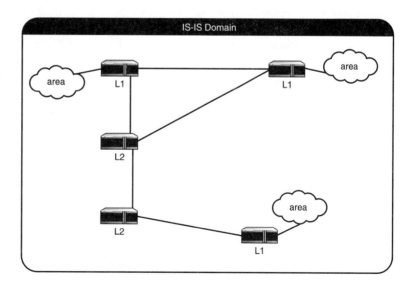

Notice the two L2s with a backbone running between them. The presence of this L2 pair (with areas on either side) forms the IS-IS domain. The following figure shows an invalid IS-IS domain.

FIGURE 8.18
This domain is incorrect because level 1 routers may not be used to connect areas.

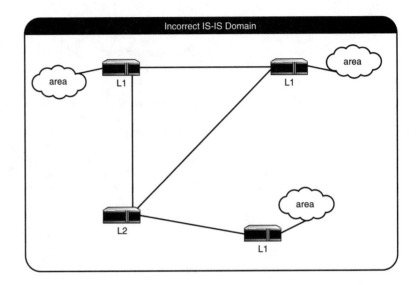

Having the correct area/domain layout (on paper) before you begin planning your IS-IS network can make all of the difference in the world. If you inadvertently end up with an area/domain configuration like the one shown in Figure 8.18 your environment will not route correctly.

However, as with every protocol, just having the correct physical layout is not enough. The protocol address must correspond to the physical topology. IS-IS's address scheme is a mixture of pure OSI routing address conventions and the DECnet Phase IV area/node MAC addresses.

IS-IS Addresses

IS-IS's address scheme is derived from that of OSI and DECnet Phase IV. This was not done by accident. Combining the two architectures was a necessary task for ensuring the interoperability of IS-IS and the DNA based DECnet. This allows the protocol to easily route data on multiple platforms, for multiple routed protocols. IS-IS addresses are also a key part of defining IS-IS areas and routing domains. Let's look inside an IS-IS routing packet to see how the addresses are defined.

Pure OSI protocols utilize an address known as an NSAP (network service access point). The NSAP defines an ES's location on a network, down to the area in which they are located. Because IS-IS is an OSI-compliant protocol, it too utilizes NSAP addresses. However, because IS-IS is not a pure OSI routing protocol, it interprets the address a little differently than other OSI protocols.

Note

The actual purpose of the NSAP is to address the specific point in the network layer (of the OSI model) on a specific device. Rather than arbitrarily assigning an address to a machine, OSI chooses to address the information entry point to the device.

The format for device addresses is pretty standard among network protocols, and an NSAP address is no exception. Like most protocol addresses, an NSAP is divided into two parts to provide a more precise form of device location. NSAPs are divided into an IDP and a DSP. The combination of these defines the location of the point of entry for the device's network layer.

The IDP (Initial Domain Part) is the portion of the address that refers to the domain to which a device belongs. The IDP itself also contains two parts, the AFI and the IDI. The AFI (Authority and Format Identifier specifies the authority assigning the address to the domain whereas the IDI (Initial Domain Identifier) specifies general information about the domain.

The second part of the NSAP, the DSP (Domain Specific Part) contains the literal address information. The DSP holds the address of the domain to which a particular device belongs. This holds true on all pure OSI protocols; however, IS-IS is not a pure OSI protocol. Let's discuss how IS-IS interprets the NSAP.

IS-IS divides the NSAP address into two main portions, the area address and the system ID. (A third part attached to the end of the NSAP is the address selector and is almost always set to 0). The area address, which incorporates the IDP of the NSAP, specifies the area (within a domain) to which the device belongs, whereas the system ID (much like a MAC address) addresses the actual device.

NSAP Area Address

The area address, comprised of the NSAP IDP, indicates the area to which a device belongs. All devices in a specific area will have the same area address. The administrator assigns this address, comprised of at least one hexadecimal octet of data, at design time.

In an environment with multiple areas, the area address becomes very important to the routing of data within the network. All ESs and L1s in one area will have the same area address, allowing for the correct identification of all systems in the area by extra-area devices.

NSAP System ID

The system ID identifies a system with an area. Just as the DECnet Phase IV systems use the area/node ID to modify the MAC address, IS-IS systems use a modified MAC address to create the system ID of the NSAP. The device-specific system ID will never be shared or duplicated on an IS-IS network. The system IS stands as a reliable marker for uniquely identifying and locating a system in an area.

In the next section I discuss the messages the IS-IS routes on a network. The final section puts the entire picture together and discuss how IS-IS accomplishes routing tasks.

IS-IS Messages

IS-IS routes data through the networking environment through the use of IS-IS packets. These packets encapsulate the data that IS-IS is routing around the network. However, not all packets are meant for shuttling data. Some packets are for the internal use of IS-IS devices. These packets help IS-IS determine the configuration and topology of devices connected to an IS-IS environment.

There are three types of packets used in the IS-IS environment:

- Hello messages

- Link state packets

- Sequence number packets.

This section discusses how IS-IS uses each of these packet types to help devices route data from system to system.

If you were to dissect a packet, any packet, you would be able to divide it into three major sections, consisting of headers, data, and a trailer referred to as the checksum. Figure 8.19 illustrates a typical IP packet.

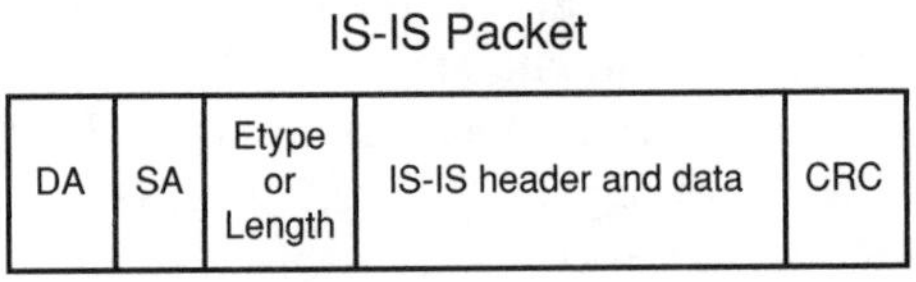

FIGURE 8.19

An IP packet contains three main components; headers, data, and a trailer.

IS-IS Packet

DA	SA	Etype or Length	IS-IS header and data	CRC

The header portion informs the device receiving the packet what kind of packet it is and identifies the protocols being carried within. The first header within the packet specifies the data link layer information, which might be an Ethernet address. Beyond the data link header are other headers specifying the network layer protocol, such as IP. If the packet is an IS-IS packet like a hello message, it would contain an IS-IS header with the data portion of the frame carrying information identifying this router to its neighbors. The final field, the checksum, is simply used to verify that the frame has not been damaged in transit.

Note

It is important to note that although IS-IS supports the routing of IP traffic it does not run on top of IP or utilize IP logical addresses for its delivery.

All IS-IS packets follow the same basic format. All IS-IS packet share a common 8-byte header. Depending on the IS packet type being sent, an extended IS header containing other fields may be present. Figure 8.20 illustrates a standard IS-IS packet.

FIGURE 8.20

All IS-IS packets share a common 8-byte header.

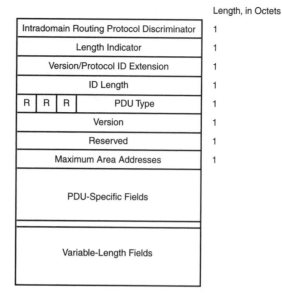

The common 8-byte header is the part of the packet that you want to look at here. The header, regardless of the IS-IS packet type (Hello Message, Link State Packet, or Sequence Number Packet), starts with the same eight fields. These fields supply the recipient with all the information it needs to process the packet correctly.

The eight common fields of an IS-IS header are as follows:

- **Protocol Discriminator**—Identifies the packet as being an IS-IS packet. The ISO assigned value for IS-IS is 0x83 hexadecimal.

- **Length Indicator**—Holds the value equal to the length of the IS-IS header.

- **Version/Protocol ID**—Specifies the version of IS-IS and will always be a value of 1.

- **ID length**—Specifies the length of the System ID portion of the recipients address.

- **Three Reserved fields**—The value within these fields are always zero as they are reserved for future use.

- **Packet Type**—Designates the packet as being either LSP, HM, or SNP. IS packet types are described later in this section. Table 8.1 shows the IS PDU (Protocol Data Unit) type values.

- **Version**—Re-states the version of IS-IS being used. This value will always be 1.

- **Reserved**—This field is reserved for future use.

- **Maximum Address Area**—Specifies the maximum number of area addresses allowed. Most implementations do not support more than three area addresses, in which case this value will be zero.

TABLE 8.1 Protocol Data Unit Type Values

Packet Type	PDU	Type Value
Hello (HM)	Level 1 LAN	15
	Level 2 LAN	16
	Point to Point	17
Link State Packet (LSP)	Level 1	18
	Level 2	20
Sequence Number Packets (SNP), partial or complete		
Complete SNP	Level 1	24
Complete SNP	Level 2	25
Partial SNP	Level 1	26
Partial SNP	Level 2	27

This packet format is the same for every IS-IS packet. The fields following the header, however, change depending on the packet type. The fields after the header are the actual data being sent from system to system.

The following section examine these fields contained for each of three types of IS-IS packets—hello messages, link state packets, and sequence number packets.

Hello Messages

HMs or hello messages are used by IS-IS devices to alert others as to their functional presence on the network. That is, to discover and form a neighbor relationship with other IS devices on the link, similar to OSPF. The hello message follows the standard common header, which is separated by six more reserved fields and always contains zeros. The specific fields contained within the hello message are as follows:

- **Circuit Type**—Indicates the type of router originating the PDU as either an L1 with a value of 01, L2 value 10, or L1/L2 value 11.

- **Source ID**—System ID of the device sending the message.

- **Hold Time**—Value used to determine how long to wait for a Hello Message from a neighbor before declaring it dead.

- **PDU Length**—Identifies the entire length in bytes of the PDU.

- **Priority**—Indicates priority value of the router. Similar to OSPF, the priority is used in the selection of a Designated Router on LANs (Broadcast Multi-Access Networks). L1 and L2 routers elect separate DRs. DR election is based on the router with the highest priority value. Unlike OSPF there is no BDR (Backup Designated Router). If the DR fails a new DR is elected. No DR is necessary on point-to-point links where only two devices exist.

- **LAN ID or Circuit ID**—specifies the LAN ID for broadcast multi-access networks, derived from the address of the L1 or L2 DR. On point-to-point links this field is changed to Circuit ID.

- **Variable Fields**—May include authentication information, addresses of IS neighbors and more.

Figure 8.21 illustrates a full hello message packet with header information.

FIGURE 8.21

IS-IS hello messages are sent periodically to establish and maintain neighbor relationships.

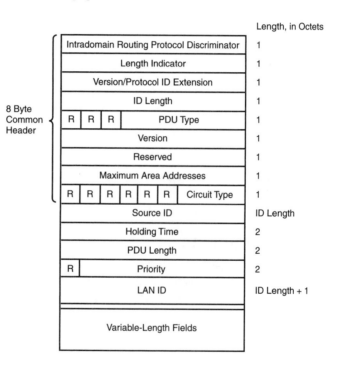

An IS sends out a hello message periodically to inform the other ISs on the network that they are in a state to receive information. The packet also lets the recipient IS know the administrator-assigned priority, the IS type, and the address of the IS sending the hello message. The hello message for IS is similar to the hello message in OSPF allowing IS devices to discover and establish neighbor adjacencies with other IS systems on the same segment.

When an IS receives a hello message, it replies with a hello message of its own. This confirms that both links are functioning and no changes have occurred in the networking environment. After the functionality of the link between the two devices has been confirmed, the two ISs add each other's information to their lists of neighboring ISs, forming an adjacency by adding all neighbors to their local adjacency database. IS-IS adjacencies are similar to OSPF. Routers must form adjacencies with local neighbor routers for the exchange of route information and successful forwarding of traffic. Two adjacency databases are built, one for L1 and one for L2 adjacencies.

Link State Packets

LSPs or Link State packets are the core of all Link State protocols. The LSP is the delivery device for all routing updates. Once neighbor ISs have successfully discovered and established adjacencies, it may begin exchanging route information.

Route information is flooded through LSPs. During a link state flood, all of the ISs on a network release LSPs to update the routing tables of the other routers in the environment. A result of the exchange of LSPs is the creation or update of the Link State Database or topology map of the network. Two separate databases are created, one for L1 routes and one for L2 routes. Therefore an LSP must contain all of the pertinent information a router would need to correctly move data from on IS to another. Without correct and timely information data released onto the network may never reach its intended recipient.

The fields within an IS-IS LSP are as follows:

- **PDU Length**—Specifies in bytes the size of the entire PDU.

- **Remaining Lifetime**—Specifies in seconds the amount of time the PDU has before expiration.

- **LSP ID**—Identifies the system ID of the originating router and the LSP number.

- **Sequence Number**—Set by the originating router. Used to track update messages.

- **Checksum**—Used to verify the header has not been damaged in transit.

- **P (Partition)**—Although present in L1 and L2 LSPs, this bit is only used in L2. If set this bit identifies routers that support partition repair. Most vendors do not support partition repair, therefore this value will almost always be zero.

- **ATT (Attachment)**—Identifies whether the originator of. the LSP is connected to one or multiple IS areas and which metrics are supported. There are four metrics supported: error, expense, delay, and default. The *error* metric relates to reliability of the link. The *expense* metric refers to monetary cost. The *delay* metric measures the roundtrip transmission delay through the link. The *default* metric is an arbitrary value that may be assigned by an administrator. All of these metrics may be used by routers when determining the best route between source and destination.

Note

Although four metrics are supported by IS-IS most vendor implementations only implement the Default metric. The lower the value the better the route. Routes with equal values will be considered equal cost paths and may be used for load balancing.

- **OL (Overload)**—Generally zero. Set by the originating router to indicating it has experienced a shortage of memory. Receiving routers recognize this router's hardship and discontinue sending traffic through this router until this bit is cleared.

- **IS Type**—Identifies the capabilities of the originating router as either an L1 or L2.

- **Variable Fields**—May include addresses of IS neighbors, protocols supported such as CLNP or IP only or both, authentication information, a list of internal and external network reachability information, and more.

Internal and external reachability information contained within the LSP conveys all the routes this router knows about to receivers. Reachability information includes the IP address and associated mask and metric being used for the route.

The LSP contains fields for routing table updates. When an IS receives an LSP, it compares the newly acquired information to either its local L1 or L2 Link State Database depending on the type of update sent.

Note

Keep in mind because L1s can only have knowledge of their local area, any foreign information that may be received is discarded.

After the LSPs are received and processed, the IS runs the Dijkstra algorithm against the new data contained within the database to calculate the new optimal paths and include them in its local route table. Figure 8.22 illustrates a link state packet.

FIGURE 8.22

Link State packets carry
route information.

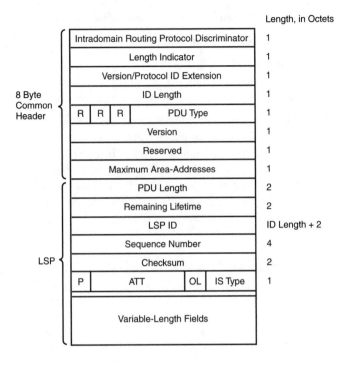

Sequence Number Packets

The purpose of the sequence number packet is to ensure that every IS being updated by LSPs is getting the correct information to maintain its Link State database. There are two types of SNPs: Complete and Partial. CSNPs (Complete SNP), when sent, include a complete listing of all LSP information contained within the Link State database. PSNPs (Partial SNP) contain a subset of LSPs. CSNPs are sent by DRs (Designated Routers) on broadcast multi-access networks to describe the entire contents of the Link State database. DRs (Designated routers were discussed in Chapter 6, "OSPF." PSNPs are used on a regular basis on broadcast and point-to-point links to request the retransmission of lost LSP information or request more up-to-date LSPs when a discrepancy exists in the database. Because L1 and L2 databases are maintained separately, CSNPs and PSNPs will be sent as either L1 or L2.

The fields within a CSNP and PSNP are as follows:

- **PDU Length**—Specifies in bytes the size of the entire PDU.

- **Source ID**—Specifies the System ID of the originator or Circuit ID if this a point-to-point connection.

- **Start LSP ID**—Only present in CSNPs. Used to designate the starting range of LSP information contained within the packet.

- **End LSP ID**—Only present in CSNPs. Used to designate the ending range of LSP information contained within the packet.

- **Variable Length Fields**—Includes LSP entries within the database, which repeat depending on the number of LSPs contained in the packet (see Table 8.2).

TABLE 8.2   Variable Length Fields

LSP Entry	Description
Remaining Life	Shows the remaining life of the LSP (during this time the IS cannot accept any other updates).
SP ID	System ID.
SP Sequence Number	Sequence number of update.
Checksum	Verifies that the LSP information was not damaged in transit.

These variable length fields tell the receiving IS whether they have the correct update and for how long that update is valid. Figure 8.23 illustrates a sequence number packet with its header information.

FIGURE 8.23

Sequence number packets contain one or more LSP entries. SNP packets are referred to as complete when they contain all LSP entries from the Link State database, whereas partial SNPs contain a subset of entries.

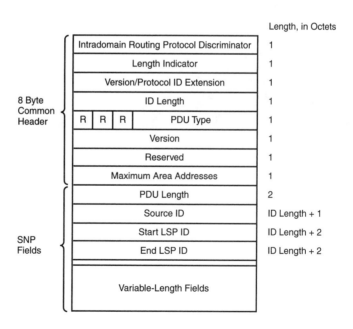

All of the packets I have discussed thus far are crucial to the successful operation on an IS-IS environment. In the final section of this chapter, I discuss how all these elements are combined to route data through an IS-IS network.

IS-IS Routing

Now that you know the history and the technology behind IS-IS, it's time to look into how it accomplishes its routing tasks. Routing in IS-IS is achieved through the successful and timely update of the topological information pertaining to the local IS-IS areas.

IS-IS within its own areas and domains elects one IS to be the master or designated IS. This IS is responsible for the actions of the environment.

Note

This concept, that of a *master node* to watch over the operations of a network, is not new. If you are familiar with the master browser in Microsoft networking or the active monitor in Token Ring, you've got the idea.

The first concept you need to learn is that of the designated IS, also referred to as *Designated Router*, similar to OSPF. IS-IS nodes elect a designated IS to be the initiator during network events.

Designated IS

The major job of the designated IS is to send out LSPs that include LAN-wide information. The designated IS generates (after collecting the link state updates for the network) an overall picture of the networking environment and send it to all other ISs on the LAN. This is done to control the number of redundant LSPs an IS may receive.

Note

A designated IS device is not necessary on point-to-point links because only two devices exist.

When an IS receives an LSP from the designated IS, all other LSP information contained within its local L1 or L2 Link State Database is compared to it for accuracy. This also ensures that convergence occurs quickly.

During an IS election (to determine the designated IS), the IS neighbors involved compare their priorities.

Note

The IS priority is one of the administrator-assigned values. A network administrator assigns each IS a priority (an arbitrary numeric value, 1 being the highest). This value can be changed and, like the Default cost metric, is determined solely by the administrator.

The priority field is also used in IS-IS hello messages to indicate the status of an IS. In the event an ISs priority changes an LSP flood and an election would take place to elect a new designated IS.

After all of the ISs have compared their priorities, the IS with the highest priority is determined to be the designated IS. In the event that more than one IS is found to have equal 'highest priorities,' they will then compare their MAC addresses. The IS holding the MAC address with the highest numerical value is then elected the designated IS. Upon completion of the election, the designated IS will then resume the job of collecting a distributing LSP on behalf of the LAN as a whole (known as a pseudo-node).

If one IS has interfaces that span multiple LANs, it will be involved in the elections on all of them. In other words, elections occur based on the LAN to which an IS is physically connected. If an IS is present on more than one LAN it may participate in more than one election. Therefore there is a chance that an IS can be a designated IS for more than one IS-IS networking environment. To prevent an IS from becoming the designated IS, the priority value for the IS must be set to zero. The priority value for designated election purposes may be set to any value between 0 and 127.

In any case, the designated IS treats the remaining ISs on its LAN as one entity, know as a pseudo-node.

Pseudo-Nodes

After a designated IS is chosen, the remaining ISs are grouped together and collectively treated as a single pseudo-node. The pseudo-node is seen and treated as one entity, when in reality it is a collection of ISs. IS-IS networks use these pseudo-nodes to receive information concerning the LAN as a whole.

The ISs in the pseudo-node accept LSPs from the designated IS. During an LSP flood each IS will send an LSP to each IS to which it is connected. (Obviously an IS can only send an update to a device to which it is directly connected.) This LSP (known as a non-pseudo-node LSP) contains all the information about an IS's directly connected links.

For example, Figure 8.24 illustrates an LSP flood with four ISs. During this flood router A would receive an LSP from router B stating that all of it links (router C) are functioning properly.

FIGURE 8.24

Four IS routers (A, B, C, and D) are participating in a link state flood.

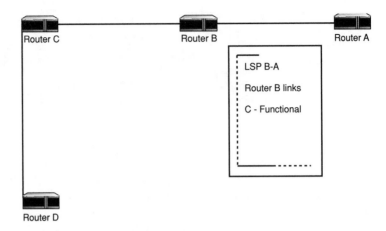

Therefore, in its routing table, router A would know that routers B and C were functioning properly. However, it would have no way of knowing the state of router D.

If every router were to send every other router the updates for the entire network, a never ending loop of updates would occur. Router A would be receiving updates about router D from routers B, C, and D. However, the concept of pseudo-nodes fixes this problem.

The job of the designated IS (similar to the Designated Router in OSPF) is to collect all of the update information and create a master table or picture of the network topology. The designated IS then sends one update to the pseudo-node. All of the ISs in the pseudo-node process this information against the updates from their neighbors. This process keeps all of the IS's updates and keeps the network free of update loops.

Every IS must be addressed differently to be unique. IS-IS has to make considerations for addressing a group of nodes as a pseudo-node. IS-IS accomplishes this through the use of multicast addressing.

There are four Ethernet addresses that can be used for multicasting by IS-IS. The addresses are separated by destination. In other words, the address used depends on the group of devices being contacted.

Table 8.3 shows the multicast addresses used by IS-IS and their intended destinations.

TABLE 8.3   Ethernet Multicast Addresses for IS-IS

Need TC here	
0180C2000014	Used to contact all L1s only
0180C2000015	Used to contact all L2s only
09002B000005	Used to contact all ISs. This is also the address used to contact the pseudo-node
09002B000004	Used to contact all ESs only

All of the nodes on an IS-IS network know to process packets sent to the multicast addresses. Therefore, the designated IS only needs to send one update to the pseudo-node multicast address to have it processed by every device.

Routing

Routing in an IS-IS environment is accomplished two different ways based on the IS router handling the datagram. Level 1 routers are limited to routing within local areas, whereas level 2 routers are not. Level 2 routers have greater routing responsibilities than level 1 routers. Level 2 routers are responsible for moving data throughout and between areas, domains, and LAN-wide environments, whereas level 1 routers are responsible only for local areas.

Let's look at the routing process from the perspective of an L1 router. The source ES sends the packet to be routed to the nearest (directly connected) L1. Because the ES cannot move the data itself, it needs to go to either an L1 or L2. The L1 now has some decisions to make based on the information in the header of that packet.

The L1 scans the header looking for the destination address of the packet. (The destination address holds two important pieces of information, the destination area and the destination system.) When the L1 finds the destination address it decodes the destination area.

Note
It is important to note that although IS-IS is capable of routing IP information, it does not utilize IP addresses to do this.

The L1 then compares the destination area of the packet to its own. (Remember that the L1 only has topographical knowledge of its own area. Therefore, if the destination area does not match its own, the L1 forwards the packet on to the next router.) After comparing the destination area to its own the L1 can come to two conclusions; either the packet should be routed within the local area or it should be forwarded to a neighboring router.

If the destination area is the local area, the router then re-scans the header for the destination system. Also part of the destination address, the destination system tells the L1 exactly which ES to forward the packet to. However, if the destination area matches the local area, but the destination system is unknown to the router, the packet is dropped.

If the destination area is not the L1's local area, the L1 examines its routing table to find the neighboring router that can reach the intended area. The packet is then routed to the L1 that governs the destination area. If the destination area cannot be found the packet is dropped.

The diagram shown in Figure 8.25 illustrates the process L1s follow when forwarding datagrams within an area.

FIGURE 8.25

L1 facilitates routing within local areas.

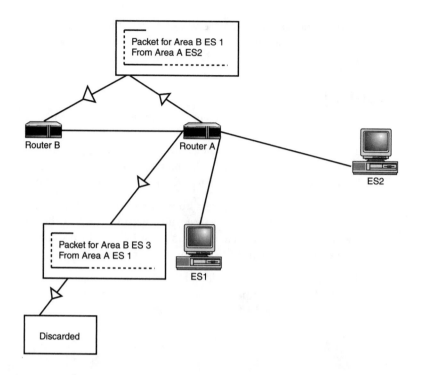

The process is a little easier to understand when you can see it diagrammed as in Figure 8.25. Even still, the routing procedure for L1s seems (and is) very straightforward. IS-IS is an efficient routing protocol that can move data pretty rapidly from one hop to another. There are relatively few routing decisions that need to be made, and the separation of duties between level 1 and level 2 routers make the process even easier by allowing the router to specialize on a specific area and not need to worry about the network as a whole.

The routing process for L2s is slightly different. When an L2 receives a packet, the first couple of steps in the routing process are similar to the L1 process. If the destination area is local to the L2 and destination ES is known, the datagram is forwarded. If the destination ES is unknown, the packet is dropped.

Because an L2 can have directly connected areas, the L2 determines the destination area and compares this to its own group of area L1s. If the destination area is one of the L2 level 1 neighbors, the packet is passed to the L1 on the destination area.

However, if the destination address does not match that on any of the L2's know areas, the L2 then looks at the prefix information.

Note

Areas that are not local to the L2 are appended to a prefix in the L2's routing table. This not only allows the L2 to differentiate between local and non-local areas, but it helps the L2 determine where to send packets that are not local.

These local and non-local areas are known as internal or external routes. Typically internal routes are intradomain. This means that only L1 and L2 routers within the domain will perform routing. External routing, or Inter-Domain, involves L2 only routers because routes can span multiple domains and any number of L2s may be required.

If the packet is destined for an internal route, the packet is forwarded to the appropriate L1. Figure 8.26 illustrates Internal Route routing.

FIGURE 8.26

Internal routing occurs within a domain.

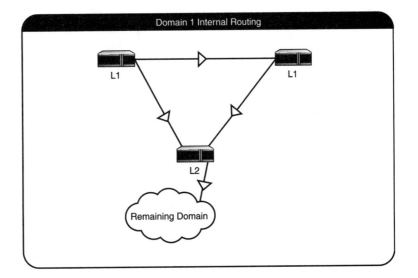

If the packet is destined for an external route, the L2 forwards the packet to its L2 neighbor. Figure 8.27 illustrates external route routing.

If the packet's destination area cannot be determined the packet is dropped.

FIGURE 8.27

External routes span
domains and involve
multiple L2 routers.

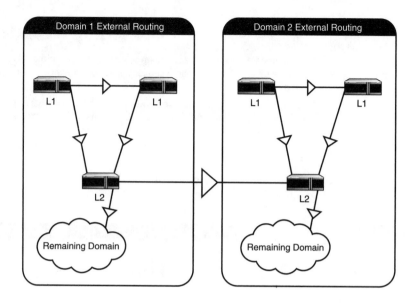

Summary

The IS-IS routing protocol was originally designed by ISO for its CLNS (Connection-Less Network Services) OSI-based environment using CLNP (Connection-Less Network Protocol) for network layer addressing and delivery of datagrams. It was adopted by Digital Equipment Corporation for use in its DECnet Phase V DNA architecture and has since been further enhanced to support the routing of IP datagrams. This added support resulted in the name change from IS-IS to Integrated IS-IS. Integrated IS-IS supports pure CLNP, pure IP, or integrated networks. However, even though IS-IS supports the routing of IP packets it does not utilize IP addresses to perform this function. IS-IS does not run on top of IP, rather it uses its own network layer protocol CLNP at the network layer of the OSI model.

IS-IS consists of one of three main entities, an end system or ES, a level 1 router or L1, and a level 2 router or L2.

An end system is defined as anything that is not a router. A level 1 router is an intra-area router. That means level 1 routers can only route within their own area. L1s have no knowledge of any network topology outside their own area. Level 2 routers are routers that can communicate with other level 2 and level 1 routers in different areas. Therefore to transmit information between two different areas you need at least two L2s.

Pure OSI protocols utilize an address known as an NSAP (network service access point). The NSAP defines an ES's location on a network, down to the area in which they are located. NSAPs are divided into an IDP and a DSP. The combination of these defines the location of the point of entry for the device's network layer.

Hello Messages are packets that are routinely sent from system to system as a form of updating each to the status of the others. An ES sends a Hello Message to an L1. This Hello Message signals to the L1 that the ES is functioning on the network and able to receive packets. Level 1 routers send Hello Messages to other L1s and L2s. Level 2 routers only send Hello Messages to other level 2 routers.

IS-IS routing networks are divided into two groups, areas and domains. An IS-IS area is a single subset of ESs and ISs. A collection of related areas is known as a domain.

IS-IS supports three other optional and one mandatory metric, Delay, Expense, Error, and Default. Most implementations only support the Default metric.

There are three types of packets used in the IS-IS environment, hello messages, link state packets, and sequence number packets. HM messages are used to discover and form neighbor relationships with other IS devices on the link, similar to OSPF. LSPs are the update messages used to exchange all routing updates. SNPs ensure that every IS being updated LSPs is getting the correct information to maintain its Link State database.

IS-IS is a Link State routing protocol and is very similar in function to OSPF in that it utilizes three separate databases; Adjacency, Link State, and Route. It also utilizes Dijkstra's algorithm creating a shortest path from a central point to determine the best route to all networks. Elects a designated router on broadcast multi-access networks.

Chapter Quiz

1. Name the network layer protocol used within ISO's CLNS architecture that handles logical source and destination addressing.

2. Name the three databases IS-IS devices maintain.

3. What two types of Sequence Number Packets exist and why?

4. What three entities exist in an IS-IS environment?

5. What criteria does an IS device use to elect a designated router?

6. What is the purpose of the OL bit?

7. What IS packet is used to build the adjacency database?

8. What is the name of the mandatory metric used by all IS-IS implementations?

9. The IS-IS routing protocol originally only supported the routing of which protocol?

10. Integrated IS-IS describes enhancements to the routing protocol, to allow support for what routed protocol?

CHAPTER 9

PNNI

You will learn about the following in this chapter:

- Overview of ATM (Asynchronous Transfer Mode)

- PNNI (Private Network to Network Interface) operation and functions

- UNI (User to Network Interface) and NNI (Network to Network Interface) signaling

PNNI (Private Network to Network Interface) and the ATM (Asynchronous Transfer Mode) Forum

PNNI, the Private Network to Network Interface (also known as Private Network to Node Interface) is defined within the ATM Forum af-pnni-0055.000 specification. PNNI is a protocol used to pass data between ATM switched networks. PNNI handles the routing of information to and from multiple ATM groups on a local or worldwide scale. ATM (Asynchronous Transfer Mode) is a cell-based switching technology typically used in WAN environments. We will discuss ATM in more detail later in the chapter.

The term PNNI itself actually represents a logical interface through which multiple ATM networks can connect and communicate with one another. However PNNI as a specification includes suggestions and regulations for the routing of data between large networks of ATM systems.

The ATM Forum created PNNI in 1996 as an efficient way to route information between ATM environments. When the ATM Forum set out to create the standards that would later become PNNI, it looked to pre-established technologies to base the specifications on. By first looking to existing technologies, the members of the ATM Forum could save themselves years of work trying to create something (that might not work) or developing a technology that may already have been developed.

Note

The ATM Forum (formed in 1991) is an alliance of corporations that work together towards a greater acceptance of ATM technology in business. The member companies of the ATM Forum set and accept standards and advances in ATM switching technology.

PNNI is actually divided into two main functions, the PNNI routing protocol and PNNI signaling protocol. The first function is fulfilled by the PNNI routing protocol. The purpose of the PNNI routing protocol is to move data from one ATM cluster or group to another. To route the very fast moving ATM cells efficiently, the ATM forum based the designs for the PNNI routing protocol on other link-state routing protocols.

The PNNI routing protocol is considered a Link State routing protocol. Through the use of hello and update packets, a node on the network can discover and update other nodes as to the state of its links. As a link state protocol PNNI systems must discover neighbors for the purpose of forming adjacencies, flood updates when topology changes occur to facilitate fast convergence, and elect a segment master (referred to as a Peer Group Leader) for the purpose of controlling updates for a group. In general, these link state protocols tend to route data in a quick and efficient way.

The second function of PNNI is signaling and control. PNNI includes two protocols, signaling and control, used to build, tear down, and maintain ATM end systems and ATM switches or switch to switch connections. This function is critical in ATM networks. Before PNNI can function in an ATM environment, it must facilitate and manage connections between two (or more than two) ATM systems. PNNI signaling is discussed later in this chapter.

Note

ATM end systems provide an entry point to an ATM network. This could be a router, traditional data switch, or even a PC with an ATM interface card connected to an ATM switch. End systems are discussed later in this chapter.

This chapter will introduce you to the technology behind PNNI and the two PNNI signaling protocols. However, before we can discuss how PNNI works, you need to understand basic ATM networking.

ATM Architecture

ATM was developed to enable the high-speed transfer of data, voice, and video over public data lines. ATM, unlike many networks that people are familiar with, operates as a cell switched environment. Although ATM can provide connectionless services, it is primarily implemented as a connection-oriented protocol creating logical virtual circuits between switches and end systems for the reliable transfer of data. ATM efficiently transfers data over public lines at rates ranging from 25Mbps up to gigabit speeds. Figure 9.1 illustrates a typical ATM architecture.

FIGURE 9.1

ATM is the primary protocol used in the Internet. ATM networks transfer data in cells through ATM switches.

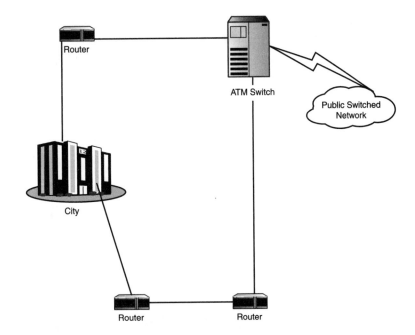

Unlike ATM, most of the technologies that are common on networks today are connectionless (IP being the most popular). The overall, inescapable problem with connectionless transfers of data is that there is no guarantee the data will reach its intended destination. ATM, being connection-oriented, builds session length circuits between end systems and ATM switches or switch to switch. After the session is completed (all of the data has been transferred between the two systems), ATM then tears down the circuit. This allows another session to use one or both of the ports for another connection. Figure 9.2 illustrates the process of building and tearing down ATM connections.

ATM is far from the only architecture to use connection-oriented transfers of data. In fact, IP's protocol relative, TCP, is a connection-oriented protocol. However, without a doubt, ATM is the best example of functional connection-oriented data transfer.

The key to ATM's quick transfer rates is in the underlying format of its data. ATM does not transfer variable length packets like most protocols. Most LAN and WAN architectures such as Ethernet (LAN) and Frame Relay (WAN) (see Chapter 1,) transfer packets that may vary in size depending on the data being transferred. Because of this the receiving device must scan the header of the packet to determine the size of the data before it can process the packet. With a variable length packet the amount of time needed to process each packet changes from packet to packet. The larger the packet is, the longer it takes to process.

ATM devices packages and transfers all information in a fixed length format known as a cell. ATM cells are always the same length, no matter how much data needs to be sent. Figure 9.3 illustrates an ATM cell.

FIGURE 9.2
Data is transferred over logical virtual circuits between ATM end systems and switches. These virtual circuits are set up prior to data being transferred, and then torn down upon completion.

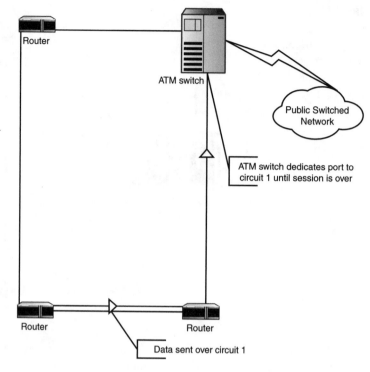

FIGURE 9.3
ATM cells are fixed in length. Each cell has a static 5 byte header with 48 bytes available for the payload.

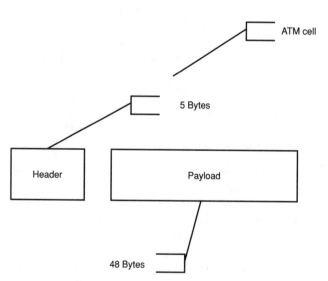

ATM cells, regardless of the amount of data being moved, are always 53 bytes long. As shown in Figure 9.3, ATM cells consist of a 5-byte header and a 48-byte data segment, referred to as a "payload."

Note

Even though ATM cells are fixed length (eliminating the need for a header length field), they still need a header. The header of an ATM cell specifies the source and destination of the payload.

The fixed length of ATM cells makes them perfect for carrying digital audio and video. Because cells are always 53 bytes with a constant header and data area, receiving ATM devices do not have to deal with random bursts of slow and fast processing (dependant on packet size); therefore, signals are received evenly and quickly. Any slowdown in the digitizing of the signal will most likely equal the sample rate of the video (or audio) and not be noticed.

Another factor in ATM's success is the fact that it is *asynchronous*. This means that ATM systems can both send and receive signals at the same time. A pair of switches communicating on the same circuit can send each other data at the same time, thus cutting the transfer (circuit up) time in half.

Again, ATM's asynchronous nature is due to its fixed cell format. Because the ATM cells are a fixed 53 bytes in length, each ATM switch knows exactly how long it is going to take to receive and buffer each cell. In between sending cells, the switch can open itself up to receive any cells arriving from the switch on the other end on the circuit.

Before you can further explore how ATM switching and signaling (and ultimately PNNI) work, you need to look at the layout of a typical ATM network. Because PNNI was not only created to work on ATM networks, but it was also based on an existing protocol UNI v3 (User to Network Interface), you need to better understand the architecture of ATM switched sites.

ATM Network Layout

There are two types of ATM networks, public and private. A public ATM network exists in the public cloud. That is, somewhat like the Internet, a public ATM network is a group of public access ATM networks usually managed by one or more public telecom firms. A private ATM network, on the other hand, exists completely within the domain of one enterprise.

Note

Public ATM network are comprised of ATM switches (known as public switches).

Of course, as with many things in life, the lines of definition are not always that clear. For example, you can have two private ATM networks connected by a public one. In this case each network is its own group and not viewed as one entity (the private networks are private and the public are public).

ATM networks are relatively simple in design, but not in technology. The devices in ATM networks are split into two categories (device classifications), ATM switches and ATM edge devices:

- The *ATM switch* is the device that connects to the mesh of the network. That is, the ATM switch is the device that moves data in the form of cells to and from the network. In the early days of ATM, the ATM switch would have been the final point of presence on a company's network.

- The *ATM end system* is any device on an ATM network that is not an ATM switch. ATM end systems provide non-ATM hosts with access to an ATM network. For example, PCs, routers, and data switches with ATM interfaces are considered end systems. Edge devices have no cell switching capability. They are end points in the ATM network that may send and receive cells on behalf of end systems. These devices interface directly with one or more ATM switches when transmitting and receiving cells over the ATM network.

ATM end systems perform cell packaging upon entry into the ATM network and unpackage the cells upon exit. End systems are generally routers or traditional data switches that have LAN connections on one side and an ATM interface providing access to the ATM network. After the LAN datagram is packaged as an ATM cell it is sent to the upstream ATM switch, where it is transferred switch to switch through the ATM network, until it reaches its destination.

Note

ATM end systems do not perform cell switching. They provide exit and entry points into the ATM network. Some end systems perform fragmentation and reassembly. For example, a router connected to an Ethernet segment and ATM network would need to break up the variable length Ethernet frames into 53 byte cells prior to transmission on the ATM network. This process would be reversed when data within an ATM cell needs to be sent out on the Ethernet network.

ATM switches only handle cells. They provide the cell switching infrastructure within the ATM network and do not perform fragmentation or reassembly.

When ATM was first developed, these two device classifications (switches and edge systems) made designing ATM environments fairly easy. The first uses for ATM were in public switched networks. In other words, the company's local network connected to an ATM switch. The information from this ATM switch was then carried over the public switching network (usually a public telephone company). The public switched network carried the data to the ATM switch at the destination network. Figure 9.4 illustrates an ATM public switched network.

In Figure 9.4 a corporate LAN is connected to the public switched ATM network. The PBX at the service provider is an ATM switch serving as the point of entry for the corporate network into the public switch network.

FIGURE 9.4
Private ATM networks can use the public switched telephone network to connect geographically separate corporate networks.

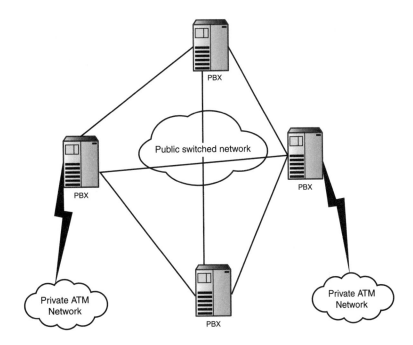

ATM Connections and Signaling Protocols

ATM network connections are referred to as either user-to-network or network-to-network depending on the type of connection being made. User-to-network connections provide an end system entry point into the public ATM network, whereas network-to-network connections are exclusively between ATM switches. As you can see in Figure 9.5 all connections on the corporate network are labeled UNI (or User to Network Interface). The ATM switched connections within the public switched network are considered NNI (Network to Network Interface).

Note

UNI (User to Network Interface) describes the ATM end system providing the entry or exit point of an ATM network. NNI connections are strictly refer to ATM switch to switch connections.

The initial implementations of ATM in public networks required a set of protocols to handle these connections. The two protocols developed are known as UNI (User to Network Interface) and NNI (Network to Network Interface). These protocols were created solely for the purpose of signaling to the public switches that another ATM switch or end system had data to transmit. Figure 9.5 illustrates where the two different protocols are used.

FIGURE 9.5

UNI connections are made between ATM end systems and ATM switches, whereas NNI connections are strictly between ATM switches.

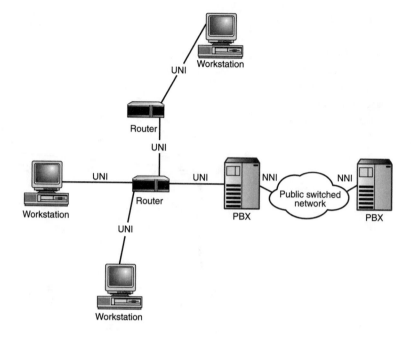

Figure 9.5 illustrates a typical connection between a private ATM network and a public switched network. Because there are two type of ATM networks (public and private), there are two types of UNI and NNIprotocols required to set up and maintain connections. UNI allows the local PBX (or end system) serving as an ATM switch on a private network to signal to an unknown public switch that it had data to send. UNI signaling is used to create a circuit between the private ATM switch and the public ATM switch. After the session between the two switches is completed, UNI tears down the circuit. The private version of the protocol (P-UNI) could be used to connect ATM end systems with private ATM switches.

The PNNI signaling protocol was based on another ATM Forum specification UNI (the user-to-network interface). The ATM Forum had developed the UNI signaling protocol to be a quick, adaptable signaling protocol between public and private networks. With a few minor revisions UNI was modified to become the PNNI Signaling protocol.

As ATM networks began to grow, a protocol needed to be developed to handle the intense communicational load of switch-to-switch signaling. NNI (and its private counterpart, PNNI) were developed just for this purpose. The NNI signaling protocol was modeled after UNI (see "The UNI Signaling Protocol" section in this chapter) to ensure proper communication standards were adhered to.

The UNI Signaling Protocol

UNI, or the User to Network Interface, is a signaling and control protocol that establishes and maintains communications between end systems and private switches or private switches and public switches. Signaling protocols send specially formatted messages to switches. The receiving switch then allows for an open line (or circuit) of communication between the devices.

UNI signaling controls two types of circuits in an ATM environment, point-to-point (see Figure 9.6) or point-to-multipoint (see Figure 9.7). Point-to-point connections are between any two ATM devices, such as edge to switch or switch to switch, whereas point-to-multipoint involves more than two. Point-to-multipoint connections are established when a single ATM device creates logical circuits to more than one ATM device at a time.

FIGURE 9.6

A point-to-point circuit involves two ATM devices.

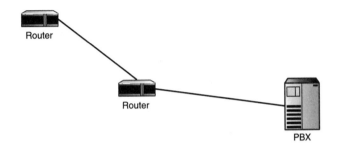

When UNI opens a point-to-point circuit, one ATM system contacts another and requests a session. Once the receiving system accepts the signal, a control circuit is open between the two. Acting much like a direct cable connection, a point-to-point circuit allows communication between two systems or points.

The major advantage to a point-to-point circuit is the use of asynchronous ports. A point-to-point ATM connection can establish bi-directional communication between systems. This is very desirable in a networking environment.

FIGURE 9.7

A point-to-multipoint circuit is established between multiple ATM systems.

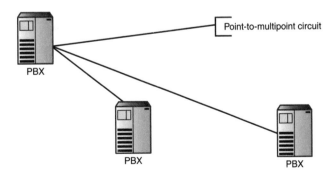

A point-to-multipoint connection is established when one system needs to open a circuit with multiple systems. One possible reason for opening a point-to-multipoint circuit would be for multicasting. The major disadvantage to ATM point-to-multipoint connections is they are not asynchronous.

A point-to-multipoint circuit will only allow communications in one direction (from the point to the multipoints). This is not an issue with the UNI protocol, rather the field within the ATM cell does not allow for the needed entries to open a point-to-multipoint asynchronous (known as multipoint-to-multipoint) circuit.

As previously mentioned ATM systems transfer all information within 53 byte cells. When point-to-point or point-to-multipoint circuits are created through UNI or NNI uses various fields within the cell to accomplish this. Let's look at the fields within a UNI ATM cell to see how a point-to-point circuit is established.

A standard ATM cell has a 5-byte header. This header contains the required information for any system to determine what kind of cell it is, who it is intended for, and who sent it. The header itself contains different fields depending on the type being sent(for example, a UNI cell header contains different fields than a NNI cell). Figure 9.8 illustrates the fields within a UNI cell header.

FIGURE 9.8

Each ATM cell consists of a 5 byte header containing UNI or NNI specific fields and payload.

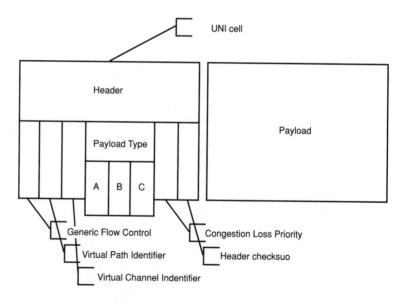

TABLE 9.1 The Fields Within the Header

Generic Flow Control (4 bits)	Generally unused
VPI or Virtual Path Identifier (8 bits)	This field in conjunction with the VCI value are used to uniquely identify the logical circuit that should be used to forward cells to their intended destination. (A cell may need to travel through multiple switches before reaching its destination.)
VCI Virtual Channel Identifier (16 bits)	This field in conjunction with the VPI value are used to uniquely identify the logical circuit that should be used to forward cells to their intended destination. Some VPI/VCI values (also known as pairs) are well-known and reserved for specific purposes such as VPI=0/VCI=18, which is used for PNNI route information exchange.
Payload Type (3 bits)	Identifies the contents of the cell.
Bit A	If this bit is on the payload contains data.
Bit B	Indicates congestion.
Bit C	Marker used it signal the last in a series of cells.
Congestion Loss Priority (1 bit)	This field is used by the switch to discard any cells that have taken too long to reach their destination.

Header Checksum—Used to calculate the size and verify integrity of the header.

As the cell is passed through the network (see Figure 9.9), each switch modifies the Virtual Path Identifier and the Virtual Channel Identifier (VPI/VCI pair) fields to aid in the successful routing of the cell. As each switch passes the cell along the path, the cell is marked as shown in Figure 9.9.

In Figure 9.9 an ATM-enabled end system sends a UNI cell to the local ATM switch across a logical circuit identified as VPI=Switch1. This switch then opens a logical virtual circuit with the next ATM switch en route to the destination with a VPI/VCI identification of switch2. In reality VPI/VCI pairs are numerical values that uniquely identify the circuit and path through the switch. We are using simple labels to make things easy. When the cell reaches its final destination, the last switch makes a decision to either accept or reject the circuit. If the switch accepts the cell, the path the cell took to reach its destination is turned into an end to end circuit. Figure 9.10 illustrates a UNI circuit.

FIGURE 9.9

A UNI cell is sent from a PC with an ATM interface through two ATM switches.

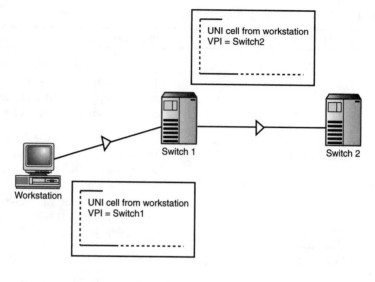

UNI cell from workstation
VPI = Switch2

Switch 1

Switch 2

Workstation

UNI cell from workstation
VPI = Switch1

FIGURE 9.10

A UNI circuit is set up end to end over the ATM when the destination switch accepts the connection.

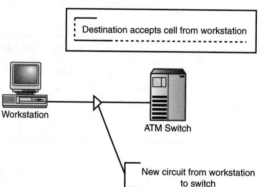

Destination accepts cell from workstation

Workstation

ATM Switch

New circuit from workstation
to switch

UNI is a good protocol for moving information around an ATM network. However, when the communication requirements dictate that a circuit be open between two private switches, a different protocol is needed. UNI does not have the routing or signaling capacity needed to fully handle the task of establishing and tearing down circuits, as well as advertising routing paths. When the members of the ATM forum set out to create a protocol to do just that, they started with UNI. By modeling the new Private network-to-network interface (PNNI) after UNI, they were ensured a good base to build the protocol on.

PNNI Hierarchy

Although PNNI networks may be implemented as a flat architecture (single routing domain), they generally, like the OSPF routing protocol, follow a hierarchical structure. That is, certain systems or groups of systems are granted precedence over others in the hierarchy to establish optimal paths. This section describes how the PNNI hierarchy works and how that fits the ATM architecture.

If PNNI did not accommodate a routing hierarchy, the entire ATM network would be treated as a single routing domain with all ATM systems belonging to this domain. That is, every group or cluster of systems would be equal to every other. Flat networks can hurt performance in a couple of ways.

The first way a flat environment can hurt network performance is by increasing the amount of memory and processing power needed by routers to make forwarding decisions. If every ATM system is considered to be part of one big routing domain, there is no way for a router or routing protocol to separate them into smaller groups. A router using an algorithm to calculate a routing path within the domain would need to build and maintain a complete topology database and compute the path to every system on the network. Keeping track of all routes throughout the flat network would take a very large amount of memory. Storing a complete topology map and calculating paths to every system for this type of network would require a lot of memory and even more processing power.

The second problem behind having a flat routing environment is giving up some speed. The more variables a router must consider when making a decision, the longer that decision takes. A router on a flat network must consider every system (because every system is the same) as a possible variable, which slows the routing decision. On a larger network, the processes of routing data could require the use of so many variables that network speed would be unbearably slow.

PNNI guards against problems associated with flat networks by implementing a hierarchical network scheme defined by levels. PNNI places all lower-level peer systems into a group. Those groups are then placed into larger upper level groups, creating an endless possibility to the size of the hierarchy that can encompass a network.

Physical connections between systems consist of bi-directional data paths each with potentially varying characteristics. These bi-directional paths allow data to flow in both directions. These paths are treated as two one-way flows each with a transmitting port identifier and node address. The lowest level group, also considered the base for everything else in the hierarchy, is known as a peer group.

PNNI Peer Groups

PNNI networks are divided into Peer Groups known as PGs. Every peer group has its own address on the network. This address (known as a PG number or group address) is unique peer group and shared by all of the members of the PG.

How the ATM end systems (or ES') are separated into peer groups depend on the address of the switch. That is, because a PG is designated by the common address of its members, and a member's address is derived from the switch it is attached to, the separation of the PGs relies on the addressing of the switches.

The purpose of a PNNI peer group is purely for routing. Within these peer groups, the ATM end systems and their switches pass data among themselves and the other members of the same PNNI peer group. This limits the amount of traffic that is passed from switch to switch. Being the lowest member of a hierarchy has its advantages.

For PNNI routing purposes, the members of a peer group can only have topographical knowledge of the end systems in their peer group. End systems for any given PG will never know the specific composition of any other PNNI peer group. Therefore, by creating a lowest level group like this, PNNI can control the amount of data that border nodes need to process.

Systems identify their peers within a group through the exchange of Hello messages. These hello messages serve the same purpose as OSPF hello messages, described within Chapter 5, to identify neighbors and to form and maintain adjacencies with these neighbors for the purpose of routing. For systems to form adjacencies they must share the same PG ID. The PG ID may be up to 13 bytes and is defined by an administrator.

Note

A border node is an ATM switch that connects peer groups. By routing data through a border node, information can be sent from one peer group to another.

PNNI NSAP Addressing

Most private ATM networks use the NSAP (Network Service Access Point) addressing format. (Other protocols, such as IS-IS, also utilize the NSAP address format, or a modified version of it.) The 20-byte NSAP address for ATM, defined within the E.164 specification, is comprised of some network specific fields and the device's MAC address or node address. Figure 9.11 illustrates the fields that make up an NSAP address.

FIGURE 9.11
ATM systems use NSAP
addresses to uniquely
identify the system
within an ATM network.

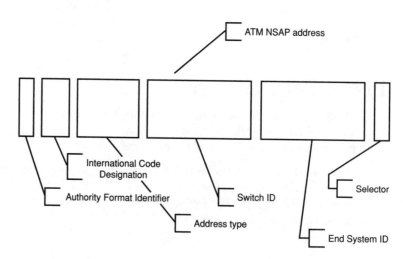

TABLE 9.2   The Fields of the NSAP Address in PNNI

Authority Format Identifier (1 byte)	Specifies the authority assigning the address.
International Code Designator (2 bytes)	This field is specific to the addressing authority (used for international uniqueness).
Address Type (4 bytes)	Signifies whether the address is ICD, NSAP, or DCC.
Switch ID (6 bytes)	Unique address of the switch.
End System Identifier (6 bytes)	The MAC address of the specific interface on the switch.
Selector (1 byte)	Unused by PNNI routing.

A typical ATM switch address may look like this (the example used supplies the AFI and ICD of Cisco Systems). Figure 9.12 illustrates a populated ATM switch address.

FIGURE 9.12
An ATM switch address consists of an AFI, ICD, address type, and switch ID followed by an ESI and selector field.

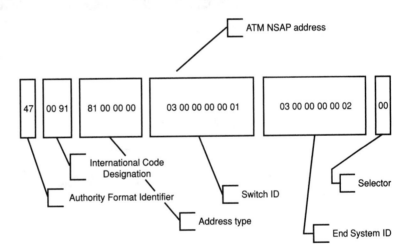

The first 13 bytes of the ATM address are referred to as the prefix address. In a peer group all of the systems share the prefix identifier. Because the first 13 bytes of the ATM address are going to be constant for every ES in the PG, these 13 bytes are the peer group number. (In essence the PG identifier will be all but the last seven bytes of the switch's ATM address.) The peer group id does not include the switch's unique interface (6 byte) ESI or (1 byte) selector byte. ATM switches with multiple interfaces will have more than one ESI. ESI addresses are derived from the ATM switch's interface MAC address. Each interface MAC address of an ATM switch is represented as a 6 byte end system ID that follows the prefix identifier (or peer group ID). This value is used to uniquely identify each of the interfaces on the ATM switch. All end systems attached to the switch use the same prefix, and then append the ESI of the specific interface they are attached to completing the address.

When a new ES is attached to the switch it adopts the switch's prefix identifier as its peer group ID) and appends the switches interface ESI.

For example, a switch with an end system attached to interface (030000000002) would use the following addressing scheme: 47.009181000000.030000000001.030000000002.00

A 13 byte prefix or peer group ID of 47.009181000000. 030000000001 with a 6 byte MAC address (or ESI) of 030000000002 will produce an end system ATM address of 47.009181000000.030000000001. 030000000002.00

Using the preceding logic, PNNI can dynamically create peer groups. Whenever an end system is connected to an ATM switch, it dynamically assigns the NSAP address and is adopted into the peer group. These peer groups are at the heart of the PNNI hierarchy model. The following example (Figure 9.13) shows three ATM peer groups.

FIGURE 9.13

Each ATM peer group is represented by a peer group number (A.1, B.1, and C.1).

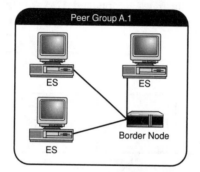
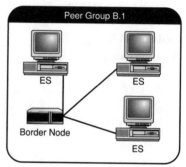
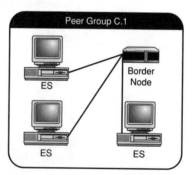

As illustrated in Figure 9.13, the new peer groups are identified by peer group numbers. Notice that the structure of the address appears different from the previous example. The reason is simple.

Because the first 13 bytes of the ATM address are the same for every node in the peer group, a letter can be used to represent them (in our example we use the letter A). The number after the dot (A.1) is the 13th byte of the ATM address (of the ATM switch). Referring back to the ATM address used in the previous example (47.009181000000.030000000**01**. 030000000002.00) the value 01 (or 1) would be added after the dot. This number is unique to the switch and completes the representation of the peer group number. The ESI (or MAC address of the ATM interface) of each node is attached to this peer group number to represent each individual end system uniquely within the group.

Before routing can begin between the new peer groups one more step needs to be taken. To complete the PNNI hierarchy an administrator must assign each peer group switch a PNNI peer group level. This level determines the peer group's standing in the PNNI hierarchy. The group with the lowest PNNI PG level number is considered the dominant group. The dominant peer group is given routing priority over other PGs. A PNNI PG level can be any numeric value from 0 to 104.

A peer group with a configured level of 104 is going to have a very low routing priority as compared to a PG with a level of 0. By employing levels, the peer groups can be continuously combined into larger and larger entities. For example, two peer groups A.1 and A.2 in Figure 9.14 can be combined and considered one larger group. The peer group with the lowest level ID, would become the peer group leader for the combined group and handles the routing decisions in this larger group.

FIGURE 9.14
PNNI Levels.

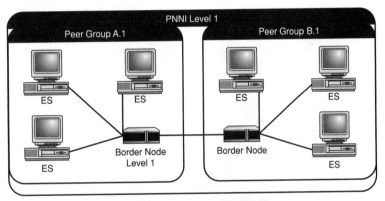

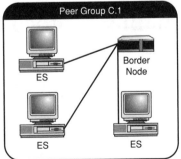

If an end system in peer group A.1 (see Figure 9.14) needs to send data to an end system in peer group A.2, it must follow a few steps to get there. The switch in A.1, not having direct knowledge of the end systems in A.2, determines that the cell is not meant for the local peer group. The switch then forwards the packet to the switch for peer group A.2 (routing protocols take over from here).

By continually combining the peer groups into larger entities, PNNI eliminates the problems of a flat routing network. Even though the members of a peer group only have knowledge of the topography of their peer group, the lower level switches have topographical knowledge of each peer group above them.

> **Note**
>
> The topology of a peer group refers to the location of the end systems in relation to the switch.

To keep the routing traffic between switches to a minimum, each peer group acts as a self-contained network. As these groups grow in size, the amount of memory needed to keep track of the topology and handle the routing requests grow as well. Therefore, a division mechanism was needed to allow the potential limit of the PNNI architecture to be circumvented.

> **Note**
>
> One of the keys to the success of the PNNI network structure is its ability to scale to networks of almost any size. The PNNI hierarchy model, with its use of peer group numbers and peer group levels, can be adapted to most any network.

By taking the logic of PNNI levels and expanding it to hundreds of switches, PNNI networks can be scaled to almost any size. Once the PNNI levels have been determined, the environment is ready for routing. The PNNI routing protocol handles the passing of data from switch to switch.

PNNI Signaling Protocol

As mentioned earlier in the chapter, PNNI is actually split into two functions, signaling and routing. The first function is circuit setup and teardown. The second is the routing of data. The PNNI routing process relies on the PNNI signaling protocol to set up, manage, and tear down logical control circuits between ATM systems.

Once the circuit is established, data may be sent from an end system to a switch. The PNNI routing protocol handles the actual moving of the data from switch to switch. Figure 9.15 illustrates a PNNI network. The notation in the figure shows what protocols work in certain areas of the ATM environment.

FIGURE 9.15

An ATM with logical UNI circuits connecting end systems to ATM switches and PNNI routing running between switches.

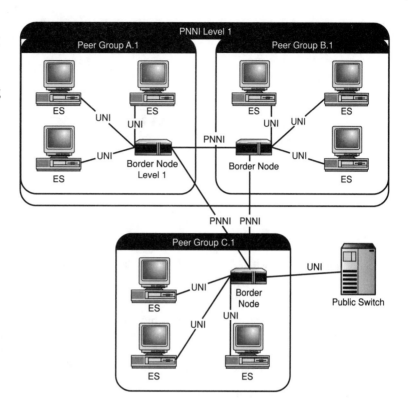

Following the flow of data (via protocols) on an ATM network can be rather confusing if you have never seen it before. Even though the signaling portion of PNNI may seem a little foreign, the routing part is pretty straightforward. PNNI routing will be discussed later in this chapter. First we will explore how PNNI circuits are built.

Circuit Setup, Management, and Teardown

PNNI routing cannot occur and data cannot be forwarded until logical circuits are set up. The ATM architecture is circuit-based. Circuits need to be established before data can be routed over them. The PNNI signaling protocol is the portion of PNNI required to establish and tear down connections between devices. The signaling protocol takes into account any metrics (including QoS) to request circuits be opened for routing purposes. After the signaling protocol has successfully built a circuit between two points, the PNNI routing protocol can take over.

When an end system on an ATM network needs to send data, the PNNI signaling protocol starts the process by contacting the closest, directly connected ATM switch and notifying them of the request. Figure 9.16 illustrates an ATM end system with a routing request.

FIGURE 9.16

An ATM end system send requests a circuit setup to a remote end system in peer group D. ATM switches along the path must build circuits with one another to facilitate the forwarding of data.

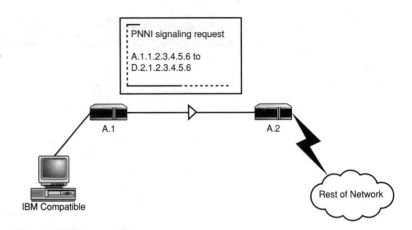

In Figure 9.16, switch A.1 uses a PNNI signaling protocol to contact switch A.2 on behalf of the end system. The signaling protocol notifies switch A.2 that the end system is requesting the switch to open a circuit to an end system in the remote peer group D.

Even though the end system knows which specific end systems it needs to contact in peer group D, it has no topographical knowledge of that group. In this case it would simply request the circuit to the border node of the peer group. Peer group D's border node would then route the cells to the correct end system.

Eventually the signaling request reaches the destination border node. Here, the switch can either accept or deny the circuit. If the circuit is accepted, the border node passes the cells to the destination end system and a circuit is established between the two systems. If the destination border node refuses the request, the data from the end system is discarded.

PNNI Routing Protocol

The PNNI routing protocol is based on the very successful link state category of protocols. Let's quickly review link state protocols before discussing the technology behind the PNNI routing protocol.

The concept behind link state protocols can be summed up very easily. Link state protocols are quick and efficient routing protocols that keep track of a system's link status. These protocols use triggered updates, which are flooded throughout an area to ensure every router has the latest information to correctly move data around the network.

Link state protocols use packets known as hello messages to identify and maintain neighbor relationships with its peers, and routing updates to notify other routing devices of changes in the network. These routing updates each contain a different view of the network's topology. When the updates are combined, each device has a complete picture of the network's current condition. (Or at least as complete as they are allowed to have. Remember each peer group will only have complete knowledge of the topology of their own group.)

Each hello message includes the identity and peer group ID of the neighbor. Successful or unsuccessful reception of neighbor hello messages are used to determine the current state of the sending device's links. These links represent the devices that are directly connected to the originating device. Because a device only knows the state of its own links, it needs to combine this data with the updates from other routers to understand the layout of the environment.

Link status information is then flooded within update messages to peers within the group. PNNI updates are sent as PTSPs (PNNI State Topology Packets), which consist of a series of PTSEs (PNNI State Topology Elements) describing individual link state information. From these updates the topology database is built, giving each peer within the group a complete map used to calculate routes to any given destination throughout the PNNI routing domain.

PNNI Packets

PNNI routers must exchange several types of packets to facilitate routing. The first type of packet exchanged is the hello. These packets are sent to establish and maintain neighbor relationships with other PNNI routers. Once neighbors are discovered PNNI routers can begin exchanging route information to build a local topology map and from this map comes the route table. There are five PNNI packet types used for different purposes (see Table 9.3).

TABLE 9.3   PNNI Packet Types and Their Descriptions

PNNI type	Packet description
1 Hello	Used to discover neighbors and maintain adjacencies. Also used for PNNI peer group leader election.
2 PTSP (PNNI State Topology Packet)	Contains route advertisements consisting of one or more PTSE entries.
3 PTSE (PNNI State Topology Element) Ack	Acknowledgement message used to confirm receipt of PTSP route updates.
4 Database Summary	Summarized PTSE route advertisements. Used to synchronize PNNI route databases upon system initialization. Database Summary packets include the PTSP header and one or more PTSEs describing route information. PTSP and PTSE headers and fields are discussed later.
5 PTSE Requests	Sent by systems to request retransmission of missing or more current PTSP information. All PNNI packets share a common 8-byte header. The common header is primarily used to distinguish the PNNI packet type being sent. Table 9.4 shows the fields within the common header.

TABLE 9.4   PNNI Common Header Fields and Descriptions

Field Name	Byte Size	Description
Packet type	2 bytes	This value will be one of the five above depending on the PNNI packet type. For example, type 1 would indicate a hello.
Packet length	2 bytes	This value specifies the length in bytes of the pnni packet.
Protocol version	1 byte	Identifies the PNNI version used by the originator.
Newest version supported	1 byte	Used for protocol version negotiation between systems.
Oldest version supported	1 byte	Used for protocol version negotiation between systems.
Reserved	1 byte	Unused

Hello Messages

Every switch on an ATM network advertises its presence and includes PTSE information, which describes the state of its local links and specific node parameters within hello messages sent to its nearest neighbors. Each system's PTSE information identifies the reachable links by this device. The process of exchanging hello messages continues as long as the link is operational and is used to detect failures and elect peer group leaders. Once hellos have been exchanged and adjacency has been formed, all neighbors now know the state of the links connected to each of its neighbors. Figure 9.17 illustrates the passing of a hello message on an ATM network.

In Figure 9.16, switch A.1 advertises to switches B.1 and A.2 the statuses of all end systems directly attached to it. In other words, switch A.1 tells A.2 and B.1 that the five end systems connected to it and the links connecting them are up and functional. Included with this hello message is all of the metrics needed to associate the particular systems with a path.

When switch A.2 receives the hello message from A.1 it will realize that (from the peer group ID) A.1 is in the same peer group. The two routers then form a link between them, establishing that they are within the same peer group.

Hello messages include the common 8-byte PNNI header shared by all packet types. Beyond the common header hello messages fields have the following fields. Table 9.5 shows the specific hello message fields and functions.

FIGURE 9.17
ATM hello messages.

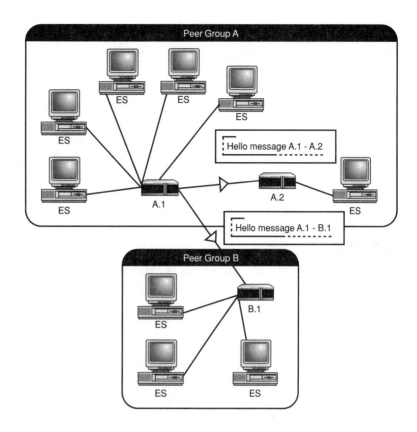

TABLE 9.5 Specific Hello Message Fields

Field Name	Byte Size	Description
Flags	2 bytes	Reserved, currently unused.
Node ID	22 bytes	Originators node identifier.
ATM ES address	20 bytes	ATM ESI source system.
Peer Group ID	14 bytes	Identifies the value of the originating system's peer group. Used to develop adjacencies. When two systems share the same PG ID they are considered peers within a common group.
Remote node ID	22 bytes	This value represents the remote neighbors node id learned through previous hello messages. This value will be zero if a hello message has not been received (no adjacency exists) from its neighbor. See Two Way (Inside or Outside) later in this chapter.

TABLE 9.5   Continued

Field Name	Byte Size	Description
Port ID	4 bytes	This value identifies the sending system's local port ID.
Remote port ID	4 bytes	This value identifies the receiving port ID of this system's neighbor. This value will be zero if a hello message has not been received (no adjacency exists) from its neighbor. See Two Way (Inside or Outside) later in this chapter.
Hello interval	2 bytes	Specifies the time interval between hello transmissions.
Reserved	2 bytes	Reserved, currently unused.

PNNI Hello States

State changes may occur as a result of a link becoming available or unavailable. Systems pass through the following hello state changes prior to exchanging PNNI route updates:

- **Down**—In this state there is no PNNI routing active. Could indicate a problem with the link.

- **Attempt**—One of two situations may exist resulting in this state: 1) No hellos have been received by this end system or 2) Hello messages received have parameters that are inconsistent with this system's parameters and therefore are rejected. Systems in this state continue to send hellos periodically in an attempt to move on to the next state.

- **One-Way (Inside or Outside)**—The one-way state is achieved when a hello has been successfully received by a neighbor system. If the peer IDs match, the two neighbors are considered to be in the same peer group and the one-way state inside is complete. If the peer IDs do not match, the two neighbors are considered to be in different peer groups and the one-way state outside is complete.

- **Two-Way (Inside or Outside)**—The two-way state is achieved when a response hello has been successfully received by neighbors on both side of the link. At this point neighbor systems are considered adjacent and learn remote node and port IDs of its neighbors.

After the two-way state completes a functional bi-directional circuit exists between the neighbors completing the hello process. Systems are now able to exchange PTSE information (or route information).

PSTP and PSTE Messages

PTSPs are formed by combining the PTSE information received from all neighbors into one or more PTSP messages. These messages are then distributed to every other switch in the ATM environment regardless of peer group through the process of flooding. .

The process of sending PTSP messages is know as a link state flooding. During this process every system involved floods the network with PTSP messages, advertising the PTSE entries contained within its local database. Flooding occurs upon initialization when a system's link state database is empty or triggered whenever a change in the topology has been detected. Systems coming online trigger flooding of PTSPs by sending a PTSE request. These messages are collected, processed, and disseminated by group PGLs (when multiple group levels exist) or by all of the switches on the network when only one level exists (flat network). PGLs are discussed later in this section. Link state floods have a tendency to be very bandwidth- and processor-intensive.

Note

PTSP messages or link state floods are initiated by a change in the ATM environment. These changes can be the destruction of restoration of a link, the change of a routing metric, or other administrative environmental change. Some changes however, like those that pertain to QoS metrics, might not be great enough to kick off a link state flood. QoS as it relates to ATM is discussed later in this chapter.

Because every switch sends out the advertisements, the PTSP message floods are going to be worse on larger networks than they will be on smaller ones. However, no matter how many switches are on the network, one precaution will make a lot of difference in how the switches handle the floods.

An ATM switch always processes a PTSP message before processing a cell for routing. Therefore, the more memory (and larger processor, if possible) will aid the switch in processing the messages quickly. By processing the messages as quick as possible, the switches can return to normal operation. This process (obtaining the latest network routing information quickly) is known as convergence.

Convergence occurs when every switch is operating with the same picture of the network. That is, every switch has processed the PTSP messages and agreed that the contents (PTSEs) of those messages describe the current network topology.

The process of flooding is facilitated by PGLs (Peer Group Leaders). PGLs are elected after hello message exchange. Within the hello message specific node parameters are sent identifying each system's leadership eligibility (PGL priority) value. This process is similar to OSPF in that the device with the highest priority becomes the group leader (or in the case of OSPF the DR for the subnet). And just like the DR in OSPF the PGL is responsible for synchronizing and disseminating PNNI route information.

However, the PGL's responsibility is not limited to directly connected neighbors, but applies to the peer group as a whole. In addition to collecting and disseminating this information within its own group, it is also responsible for aggregating local more specific PTSE information and presenting this as a summarized route to its parent group within a PTSP packet.

PTSP packets containing summarized information flow from lower levels to upper levels within the hierarchy. PTSEs originating from a parent group are flooded down through the hierarchy into and within each of the child groups. PGLs within each group disseminate this information within the group.

Each group has one PGL at every level within the hierarchy except the highest level. There is no need for a PGL within the top-most level because there are no parent levels above.

Unlike OSPF, there is no backup PGL. If the PGL fails, the system with the next highest PGL assumes this role. If a new system comes online with a higher priority, it takes over the role from the current PGL.

In short, PGLs control the distribution of PTSEs within and between peer groups. Receiving PNNI routing systems process the PTSE information in the PTSP messages building a topology database. The topology database serves as a map which allows PNNI routing systems to formulate an overall picture of the network. Each PTSE within the PTSP message is inspected and compared by the PNNI system to previously received reachability information.

If a PTSE received by the PNNI routing system is found to contain more current information than a previously received PTSE this new PTSE is included within the local system's database and flooded to all neighbors. All PTSEs (contained within PTSPs or Database Summary packets) must be acknowledged by receiving hosts with a PTSE ACK packet.

PTSP packets include multiple PTSEs with the headers and fields as described in Table 9.6. Remember the PTSP, like all other PNNI packets, includes the 8-byte common header (left out here to avoid redundancy). The first two PTSP fields are static, only appearing once within the PTSP header to identify the advertising system.

TABLE 9.6   PTSE Headers

Field Name	Byte Size	Description
Originating Node ID	22 bytes	Specifies the ES ATM address of the originator
Originating Node Peer Group ID	14 byte	Specifies the PG ID of the originating system
Type	2 bytes	Identifies the PTSE protocol value. This will always be 64 (PTSE).
Length	2 bytes	Identifies the length of the PTSE header.
PTSE Type	2 bytes	Identifies the PTSE advertisement type; Internal, External, and so on. Internal PTSEs contain information pertaining to routes within a PNNI routing domain. External PTSEs contain route information learned from some external routing domain.
Reserved	2 bytes	Currently reserved, not in use.

TABLE 9.6   Continued

Field Name	Byte Size	Description
Identifier	4 bytes	Set by originating system to identify the PTSE entry uniquely. PTSEs are the entries that comprise the local link state database. ID numbers are given to distinguish them.
Sequence Number	4 bytes	Set by the originating system. Used to match the corresponding PTSE acknowledgement. Also used to i dentify more current versions of PTSE information. Higher sequence numbers indicate more recent information and supercede lower sequence numbered entries of the same PTSE.
Checksum	2 bytes	Calculated by the originating system prior to transmission. Recalculated by receiver to verify the integrity of the PTSE entry.
Remaining Lifetime	2 bytes	Measured in seconds, this field is used to determine whether a PTSE entry is valid. When the PTSE lifetime expires an entry is no longer considered valid.

PNNI Routing Metrics

Deciding which path is the shortest is the job of the link. state routing algorithm. The routing algorithm is a formula used by the PNNI device to calculate the metrics found in its topology map to produce the best path to a destination. Once a path is selected, a virtual connection is established end to end lasting for the duration of the call.

PNNI devices are configured with different metrics to indicate a link's likelihood for being chosen as the shortest path. Therefore, to understand the algorithm used on PNNI networks, you need to know what variables or metrics routers used to calculate the paths.

The metrics that can be used by PNNI routing systems on a PNNI network to describe a device are

- Administrative Weight (AW)—An administrator-assigned cost. The metric is purely arbitrary.

- Available Cell Rate (AvCR)—The bandwidth of a line.

- Maximum Cell Transfer Delay (MaxCTD)—The experienced delay in transmitting cells over a particular link.

- Cell Loss Ratio (CLR)—The number of cells typically lost over a particular link.

- Cell Delay Variation (CDV)—A combined metric representing the link's CLR minus the average CLR for the environment.

- Maximum Cell Rate (MaxCR)—The maximum cell capacity of the line.

Each of the metrics can be assigned, either dynamically or statically by an administrator. The values are used by PNNI's routing algorithm to calculate the overall value or usefulness of a particular link in reaching the cell's ultimate destination.

Path selection to a destination in PNNI is determined by the source (referred to as source routing). This is a departure from traditional hop-by-hop routing, which allows path selection to occur independently at each device along the path.

PNNI's source routing begins with a call setup request by the originating system. Included within this request is a DTL (Designated Transit List) detailing the desired path (identifying systems and links within its group and group IDs of other peer groups) this system intends to use to reach its destination. Metrics are included within the initial call setup. If the combination of the metrics proves that the current link is the ideal link for routing, the cells are forwarded across the line.

If a particular system along the path cannot support the requested service level due to resource constraints or restrictions, the setup request is denied and a crankback occurs. *Crankbacks* allow alternative paths to be selected when the requested path is unavailable or unsuitable. Crankback messages are generated by the rejecting system and sent back to the originator of the DTL.

Source routing does not guarantee the path requested by the source will be used. The DTL is more like a request for a preferred path. At each system along the path a routing algorithm must be applied resulting in the next transit path selection.

Routing algorithms vary widely and are not standardized; each request must be inspected and processed by each system separately based on service level and bandwidth capacity available. If the resources are available to complete the call across the preferred path, the link is used and the call request is forwarded to the next system named in the DTL request. If not, a crankback is sent describing the problem, thereby clearing the call all the way back to the originating system. With this new information the originator builds a new DTL request and makes another attempt. Crankbacks are discussed later in this chapter.

All of the metrics listed, with the exception of Administrative Weight, are considered QoS metrics. QoS or Quality of Service routing is a standard set forth in RFC 2386 and is discussed in Chapter 10, "Type of Service and Quality of Service Routing."

PNNI and QoS

PNNI adheres to the QoS specifications for ATM. That means ATM, like every QoS-compliant architecture, supports the same metrics for providing a consistent level of routing service to the end systems. Although many protocols have been adapted or enhanced to meet QoS standards, PNNI was designed to handle QoS natively. Therefore, no extra hardware or software to implement the metrics is required for QoS ATM routing.

Note

QoS involves the identification and classification of traffic. Traffic classification is based on the type of traffic (data, voice, or video) being sent over a connection. Traffic is identified and mapped to a particular service class allowing it to be queued and forwarded based on an application or administratively set level of service.

Metrics such as maxCR (Maximum Cell Rate) and CLR (Cell Loss Rate) are used to ensure a cell is going to be forwarded over a link that can handle it. The QoS metrics maximum cell transfer delay, cell loss ratio, cell delay variation, and maximum cell rate, and the administrative weight metric are all statically defined. That is, they rarely change without the administrator's intervention. The maximum cell transfer delay measures the delay involved in the transmission of cells over a particular link. Cell loss ratio keeps track of the number of cells lost during transmission over a particular link. Cell delay variation represents the link's cell loss rate minus its average loss for the environment. Maximum cell rate measures cells in units per second transferred across a connection and administrative weight is a arbitrary value that may be manually assigned.

The QoS metric of available cell rate is a dynamic metric that can fluctuate, depending on the current link traffic. However, because this metric is dynamic, a change in this cost generally does not cause a link state update. A change in the available cell rate needs to surpass a preset threshold to trigger a network-wide update.

When a cell needs to be routed on a PNNI network, the PNNI signaling protocol (discussed earlier in this chapter)requests a minimum (QoS) value that the circuit needs to successfully route the cells.

Note

Depending on the switch being used in the ATM environment, a different QoS algorithm may be used to help determine the available paths. PNNI allows for two different QoS algorithms that can be used. The two algorithms are Simple GCAC (Generic Call Admission Control) and Complex GCAC.

The Simple GCAC weighs only the available cell rate metric when making a decision. Complex GCAC uses available cell rate and two new metrics: cell rate margin and variance factor.

The PNNI signaling protocol uses QoS values when setting up logical circuits. Each PNNI signaling setup message includes a set of QoS requests listing the desired application or administratively service level. QoS requests are passed from switch to switch. When a switch receives the QoS requirements, it first finds the links that can meet those metrics. The remaining links are exempt for consideration. The request is then passed down the optimal link to the next switch.

Note

If no links are found that meet the QoS requirements of the signaling request, the request is denied. The information from the source end system is then discarded.

For example, the PNNI signaling protocol might request the use of a circuit having a certain bandwidth capacity. In this case only links that fall within the requested QoS bandwidth metric can be considered by the algorithm as a possible path. Figure 9.18 illustrates a QoS circuit request.

FIGURE 9.18

QoS metrics are included within PNNI signaling protocol setup requests.

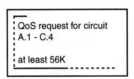

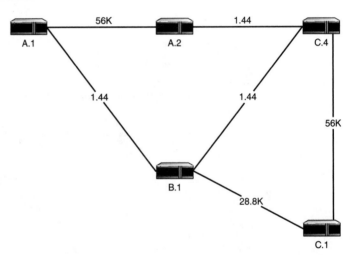

In Figure 9.18, data is attempting to be routed from A.1 to C.4. The signaling protocol (covered in "PNNI Signaling Protocol") requests that a link with at least 56K of constant bandwidth be opened to route the cells. This request automatically leaves the link between B1 and C1 out of consideration for carrying the cells.

PNNI determines what paths are used for routing data by weighing each link's metrics against a routing algorithm. This algorithm examines the cost associated with every link and determines which is the best to use.

The algorithm of choice for many link state protocols is Dijkstra's algorithm. PNNI is no exception. PNNI can utilize the Dijkstra algorithm very well (see Chapter 9 for a complete description of Dijkstra's algorithm). Once the considerations for QoS have been made, the algorithm can then choose the shortest path for the data.

Dijkstra's algorithm uses the metrics assigned to each link to determine the shortest path between all possible points on a network simultaneously. That is, Dijkstra's algorithm dynamically calculates the costs of every link on the network at the same time. This makes the algorithm a very quick and reliable way to determine paths.

Combining native QoS and shortest path routing is one of the attributes that make PNNI an attractive protocol, especially for the ATM environment.

Figure 9.19 illustrates an ATM network with all of the metrics populated. Let's look at the path the signaling protocol would take from end system A.1.X.X.X.X.X.X to end system D.1.X.X.X.X.X.X.

FIGURE 9.19

An ATM end system is requesting a connection to a remote system through the ATM network. The request states that only paths with a minimum QoS bandwidth level of 56kbps be used.

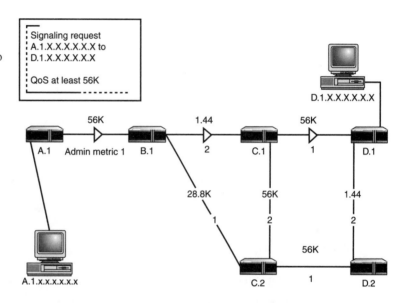

In Figure 9.19, the signaling protocol would send the request from the source end system to switch A.1. The QoS requirements state that only paths with at least 56K of bandwidth be used. When A.1 receives the signaling request it evaluates all available links to determine which have a minimum 56K bandwidth capacity. In this case there is only one link, and it does have 56K. The signaling request is then forwarded from A.1 to B.1.

At B.1 the switch has two choices; the cells can be sent over the B.1–C.1 link or the B.1–C.2 link. Because the B.1–C.2 link does not meet the QoS requirements, the link is not considered for the path and the request is then forwarded to C.1.

When C.1 gets the request, it has two choices. The links C.1 to C.2 and C.1 to D.1 both meet the QoS requirements for the circuit. The switch then turns to its routing algorithm, which determines that the shortest path is the link C.1 to D.1. The signaling request is then forwarded to D.1 over this path.

D1 receives the request, determining that the end system D.1.X.X.X.X.X.X is within its local peer group. At this point, ATM switch D.1 can then either accept the circuit request by forwarding it to end system D.1.X.X.X.X.X.X or it can reject the request. If D.1 accepts the request, a circuit is established between the two end systems. Figure 9.20 illustrates this completed circuit.

FIGURE 9.20

A completed ATM circuit has been built end to end using the path A.1 to B.1 to C.1 to D.1.

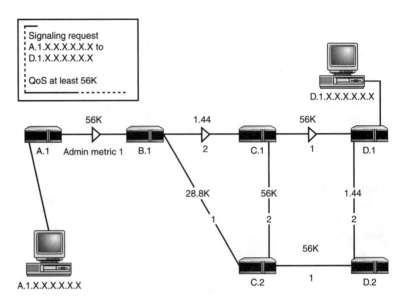

If the signaling request is rejected by D.1, the switches C.1, B.1, and A.1 are notified with a return message. This message cancels the circuit's requests on the switches and discards any cells (pertaining to the circuit) that the switch may have processed.

When the end system A.1.X.X.X.X.X.X completes its session with D.1.X.X.X.X.X.X the PNNI signaling protocol tears down the circuit, leaving the links clear for routing. Upon session tear down ATM systems release resources used by the session making them available to other sessions.

Because some of the QoS metrics are dynamically assigned, there is a chance that they might change during a transmission. PNNI has a built-in mechanism to deal with such an event. PNNI can implement its crankback mechanism if QoS metrics change unfavorably during a transmission.

PNNI Crankback

During the lifespan of a circuit, the QoS metrics, such as available cell rate, may change. If a QoS metric changes detrimentally to the circuit (for example, the circuit requires a delay of 10ms and the delay jumps to 200ms), the PNNI protocol performs an action known as a crankback.

During a crankback the protocol rolls back the circuit to the last ATM switch that still meets the QoS requirements. Figure 9.21 shows a circuit during a crankback operation being rolled back.

FIGURE 9.21

D.1 rejects the circuit request sent by C.1 due to a lack of resources. D.1 issues a crankback letting C.1 know that this link does not support a minimum of 56Kbps.

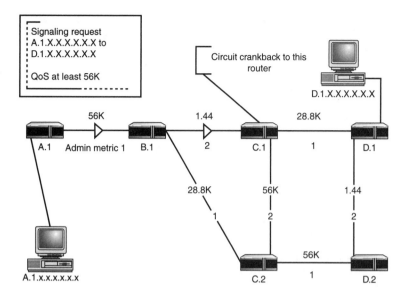

In Figure 9.21, the link between C.1 and D.1 does not support the minimum QoS bandwidth request of 56Kbps. When the signaling request from C.1 is sent to D.1 to open a logical circuit this request is rejected because it does not meet the minimum requirements. The circuit is then rebuilt from the last good switch link (or C.1). While rebuilding the circuit, the QoS requirements are re-evaluated. Using the example in Figure 9.21, the rebuilt circuit would look like the circuit in Figure 9.22.

FIGURE 9.22

A rebuilt circuit after a crankback is built from C.1 through D.2, and then D.1.

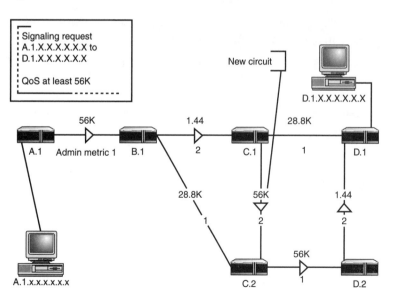

Crankbacks allow the originating system to choose an alternative path through the network when a previously chosen path does not meet its QoS criteria.

Sample PNNI Data

To get a better understanding of how PNNI works, and to help you understand PNNI operation, let's look at a sample PNNI display taken from a Cisco ATM switch. This PNNI interface parameter display clearly shows the information that PNNI requires for seamless operation:

```
PNNI node 1 is enabled and running
Node name: Switch
System address 47.00918100000000400B0A3081.00400B0A3081.00
Node ID 56:160:47.00918100000000400B0A3081.00400B0A3081.00
Peer group ID 56:47.0091.8100.0000.0000.0000.0000
Level 56, Priority 0, No. of interfaces 4,
No. of neighbors 2
Node Allows Transit Calls
Hello interval 15 sec, inactivity factor 5,
Hello hold-down 10 tenths of sec
Ack-delay 10 tenths of sec, retransmit interval 5 sec,
Resource poll interval 5 sec
PTSE refresh interval 1800 sec, lifetime factor 200 percent,
Min PTSE interval 10 tenths of sec
Auto summarization: on, Supported PNNI versions: newest 1, oldest 1
Default administrative weight mode: uniform
Max admin weight percentage: -1 Next resource poll in 3 seconds
Max PTSEs requested per PTSE request packet: 32
Redistributing static routes: Yes
```

The first part of this display shows the system ID, the network ID, and the peer group ID. As you can see by the addresses, this particular switch is the primary for the peer group.

Next you are shown the number of physical interfaces and neighbors related to the switch. This information is helpful in diagnosing any problems with connectivity or lost packets. Because this information is gathered directly from the switch's tables, it should be very accurate. Therefore, any missing neighbors (or inaccurate physical interface counts) should be investigated.

Moving down the display you come across the hello interval and the hello hold-down timers. These settings dictate the rate at which PNNI switches within a peer group communicate with each other. Also related to inter-switch communication is the *ack-delay* and the resource poll interval.

The *acknowledgment delay* indicates the rate that the switch replies to messages, whereas the resource poll interval tells the switch when to determine if its resources are present and functional.

The last line (Redistributing static routes: Yes) in the output is important for administrators to note. This particular switch is set to redistribute static routes. In other words, any paths to other ATM switches and PGs that have been hard-coded into this switch (as opposed to those learned from other switches) will be passed along to neighboring switches.

This setting is an important one to check. In certain circumstances you may not want your switch to advertise routes that have not been learned through PNNI (redistribute), such as static routes. For example, if a switch has access (through a static route) to a PG that its neighbors do not, you would not want the neighboring switches to learn that path.

By being able to now visualize how PNNI switches store and represent the data that drives the ATM protocols you should have gained a better understanding of their operations.

Summary

PNNI (Private Network to Network Interface) is a protocol used to pass data between ATM switched networks. The PNNI specification handles the routing of information to and from multiple ATM groups on a local or worldwide scale; however, the term PNNI represents a logical interface through which multiple ATM network can connect and communicate with one another.

PNNI has two main functions, the PNNI routing protocol and the PNNI signaling protocols. The routing protocol moves data from one ATM cluster or group to another. The signaling protocols build, tear down, and maintain ATM end systems and ATM switches or switch-to-switch connections.

PNNI networks generally follow a hierarchical structure with certain systems or groups of systems having precedence over others to establish optimal paths. If PNNI did not accommodate a routing hierarchy, it would treat the entire ATM network as a single routing domain with all ATM systems belonging to this domain. PNNI places all lower-level peer systems into a group. Those groups are then placed into larger upper level groups, creating an endless possibility to the size of the hierarchy that can encompass a network.

Most private ATM networks use the NSAP (Network Service Access Point) addressing format. The 20-byte NSAP address for ATM (E.164 specification) is comprised of some network specific fields and the device's MAC address or node address.

Chapter Quiz

1. Name the 5 PNNI packet types and what are their functions?

2. Identify the two main functional PNNI protocols.

3. What is the term used to describe a collection of related neighbors within a PNNI hierarchy?

4. What type of PNNI packet is used to establish and maintain neighbor adjacencies?

5. What is the name and size in bytes of the transfer unit used to switch data in an ATM environment?

6. What is the term used to describe the role a system plays within a peer group responsible for synchronizing and disseminating update information?

7. What is UNI and what is its function?

8. What is a DTL and what is it used for?

9. Describe the two-way hello state.

10. What is the PNNI crankback feature?

CHAPTER 10

TYPE OF SERVICE AND QUALITY OF SERVICE ROUTING

You will learn about the following in this chapter:

- IP ToS (Type of Service)
- ICMP ToS and QoS (Quality of Service) Messages
- QoS protocols and architectures

*B*eyond Best Effort Delivery

Since its inception IP has been the foundation for all upper-layer protocols and applications within the TCP/IP protocol suite, providing best effort delivery of datagrams. Best effort delivery stems from IP's unreliable, connectionless datagram delivery service. As a connectionless protocol IP does not guarantee that datagrams will successfully reach their destination. Nor does it guarantee that these datagrams will be received in the same order as they were sent.

IP relies on upper layers like TCP to provide reliability. The Internet Protocol's primary function is the logical network layer addressing of hosts and delivery of information in the form of datagrams or packets between end systems. IP simply addresses datagrams and sends them out hoping they reach their destination. Until recently this method of best effort delivery of datagrams had been sufficient for most applications. Historically, communication between end systems has been either *unicast* (one to one) including only two devices, or *broadcast* (one to everyone on a local segment). If a datagram were lost while in transit upper-layer protocols would eventually detect this and retransmit the datagram. Applications like FTP or Telnet could tolerate the loss and subsequent retransmissions, while other less tolerant applications might drop their connections, forcing the session to be re-established. Generally speaking, applications tolerated packet loss and retranmission whether they liked it or not because IP's best effort delivery was the only game in town.

However, as applications and services evolve they have become more intelligent, requiring more resources such as bandwidth and more consistent delivery. Applications are increasingly intolerant of slow response times, dropped connections, and lost information.

User applications, such as voice and video conferencing, are becoming more prevalent. These applications do not typically operate through unicast communication, instead sending *multicasts*, where a single host communicates with a group of hosts. Applications such as this require a consist stream of datagrams to maintain the quality of audio and visual data stream between end systems. IP multicasts and multicast routing are discussed in detail in Chapter 11, "IP Multicast Routing."

With the popularity of the Internet, resource demands from users and applications are pushing the boundaries of best effort delivery to its limit.

This does not mean that IP's best effort delivery is or should be replaced. IP continues to be the mainstay for most end system communication. What is does mean is that existing mechanisms within IP must be exploited to facilitate more selective delivery based on the needs of different applications and services. To do this, some way of identifying and characterizing traffic is needed. This need has given way to ToS and QoS routing.

ToS and QoS routing have one basic goal—to provide user- and application-level traffic with better than best effort delivery. Recall that older routing protocols determine path selection (when multiple paths exist to a destination) based on limited information. Generally, these protocols choose the path with the proverbial shortest (which may be hops) distance as the best route. Paths that may appear to be the shortest distance to a destination may not be the optimal path in reality, perhaps costing more in terms of delay, congestion, lower throughput, and so on.

In this chapter we will discuss how ToS and QoS may be used to facilitate the routing of datagrams, taking application needs into consideration.

IP ToS

IP ToS (Type of Service) was a first attempt within the IP community to address the delivery of datagrams based on a level of service requested. IP's ToS capabilities have been present since the inception of IP, though relatively unused until recently.

IP ToS provides for slightly more intelligent path selection than best effort delivery. To make use of the IP ToS bits contained within the IP header, upper layer services, such as applications, set bits indicating the type of service it is requesting for the delivery of its datagrams. Setting ToS bits within the IP header does not guarantee datagrams will receive the service level requested, but serves as a hint to routers capable of delivering such service.

For datagrams to receive the level of service requested, all routers and routing protocols along the entire path end-to-end must support and understand them. Even if routers that are running routing protocols that do not recognize these bits, they do not drop the received datagrams.

Instead, they forward these datagrams using standard best effort delivery without regard for the level of service requested. This follows the traditional hop-by-hop paradigm, where each system handling datagrams along the path treats each datagram and next hop path selection independently.

If routers and their routing protocols do understand these bits, they fulfill the wishes of the originator by forwarding datagrams along paths that support the service level requested.

IP ToS Header and Fields

Within the IPv4 header the ToS 1-byte header (8 bits) is broken up into three main parts: the precedence (3 bits), ToS (4 bits), and a 1-bit reserved field (see Figure 10.1). The reserved field is currently unused and will always be zero. Precedence bits are used to prioritize datagrams. ToS bits (which bears the same name as the header) are used to influence datagram forwarding based on criteria such as bandwidth, delay, and more. Collectively, the precedence and ToS bits constitute what is referred to as the ToS header. Applications (that are ToS-aware) and administrators can use any of these bits to achieve better than best effort delivery. We will discuss the Precedence and ToS bits describing their uses and functions in terms of routing next.

FIGURE 10.1

The IP ToS header and fields are included within all IP datagrams.

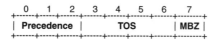

```
   0     1     2     3     4     5     6     7
+-----+-----+-----+-----+-----+-----+-----+-----+
|   Precedence   |         TOS         |  MBZ  |
+-----+-----+-----+-----+-----+-----+-----+-----+
```

Note

RFC 1349 describes the specific uses and functions of these bits within the IP ToS header.

Precedence

The three-bit Precedence field within the IP ToS header may be set manually by an administrator or dynamically by applications (that are ToS-aware). Once set the precedence bits are acted upon by routers and routing protocols. The general idea is to prioritize datagram delivery based on a perceived level of importance. ToS-aware applications set the importance level of each IP datagram by setting the bit associated with the level being requested within the IP ToS header, Precedence field. If an application is not ToS-aware (it has not been programmed for ToS support) manual intervention is necessary. In this case an administrator manually configures routers with information to identify traffic related to this application, setting the desired ToS level.

Until recently most applications have been unaware of ToS and therefore did not use the precedence bits (leaving the bit values undefined or zeros). The DoD (Department of Defense) Intelligence Agency was the first to require the implementation of the precedence bits to facilitate the identification and forwarding of traffic based on security levels. Applications running within governmental network implementations are required to support the setting of precedence bits for multilevel security functions.

Precedence bits 0 through 2 are present in the IP ToS header. The value of these bits determines the priority a datagram is given when forwarded by routers. Table 10.1 describes the various precedence bits set.

TABLE 10.1   Bits 0-2 = Precedence

Bit Position	Description
000	Routine information
001	Priority information
010	Immediate delivery
011	Flash
100	Flash override
101	Critical information
110	Internetwork control
111	Network control

The next three bits within the ToS field are the most commonly used for influencing traffic patterns.

ToS

Over the years the 4-bit ToS field, within the ToS header has continually been in transition. For instance, the original ToS field defined within RFC 791 specified a 3-bit set (bits 3–5), with bits 6 and 7 considered reserved and unusable.

Since then the ToS field was redefined within RFC 1122 as a 5-bit field including bits 3 through 7, overriding any preexisting reserved bits. Once again, it has been revised within RFC 1349 (the most current ToS RFC) as a 4-bit field (bits 3–6), leaving the eighth bit as unusable.

Even though there are four ToS bits within the ToS field, potentially providing up to 2^4 (or 16) service levels, this is not the case. This is because RFC 1349 has predefined six levels of service, each represented by a single value, wasting 10 additional possible levels. The first and default ToS level is zero or 0000 (normal service). Normal service equates to IP's best effort delivery.

TABLE 10.2   RFC 1349—ToS (Four Bits 3–6)

0000 or zero	(Default ToS) or Normal Service—When all ToS bits are zero datagrams are routed as if no ToS was requested, that is normal datagram best effort delivery is used.
1000	Low Delay—Delay is based on the end-to-end propagation delay of data transmitted over a link. Best for applications requiring user interaction, such as Telnet
0100	High Throughput—Routers will attempt to select paths with higher bandwidth capacity to forward datagrams. Best for applications performing large data transfers, such as FTP.0010 High Reliability—Routers will attempt to forward datagrams along paths that have proven over time to be more reliable in terms of loss of datagrams. Best for critical applications and services, such as routing protocols.
0001	Minimize Cost—Routers will attempt to forward datagrams along lower-cost paths, such as high-speed LAN links or low-cost dial-up links as opposed to high-cost dedicated leased lines. Best implemented where link service monetary costs are an issue.
1111	maximize security—Routers will attempt to forward datagrams along paths perceived to be more secure than others, based on preconfigured security information. Best for security-sensitive applications.

Note

RFC 1700 describes recommended ToS values for popular applications and services.

Note

Keep in mind that ToS bits in no way guarantee that the delivery service will be adhered to by routers. ToS-enabled devices simply take ToS bits set by a user or application into consideration during path selection. However the ultimate path chosen is based on routing protocol, links, and link characteristics available at the time forwarding is to be performed.

Not all routing protocols understand these bits. The following routing protocols understand ToS:

- OSPF
- EIGRP
- IGRP
- BGP
- IS-IS
- PNNI

The following protocols do not understand ToS:

- RIP v1

- RIP v2

Routers and routing protocols forward datagrams as independent entities making routing decisions based on (among other things) the level of service requested by a user or application. This all assumes that there are routes within the route table to support this delivery.

As you well know routers may learn and install routes in the route table from many sources—static, dynamic, and so on. ToS-enabled routers maintain separate route entries within their tables for each ToS value supported when multiple paths exist to a destination. Whatever method used, the router consults its route table when a datagram arrives for forwarding. As datagrams arrive, the specified destination address is compared to the existing routes looking for a route with a matching ToS value.

Note
Although a routing protocol might have the capability to understand and be capable of acting upon these bits, it still requires configuration. If an administrator has not configured the routing protocol to support ToS, the router simply ignores this information and forwards the datagram using the default ToS level. Typically routers then generate an ICMP message back to the source indicating the error.

Let's look at an example of how ToS works. When an application requests datagrams to be sent via a low-delay path, it sets the ToS bits within the ToS field to 1000 (refer to Table 10.2). Routers along the path (configured to support ToS) attempt to send datagrams across links offering faster transmissions, such as 100Mbps Ethernet versus slower WAN links. Remember, delay is measured by the round trip propagation delay across the link. Therefore, a link with a lower delay would be the preferred path. Routers not capable of forwarding datagrams with the requested ToS level will use best effort delivery (or the default ToS 0000). In addition an ICMP message may be sent to the source indicating this. ICMP messages were discussed in Chapter 2.

High throughput translates to high capacity links, which have the capability to carry larger amounts of data in a short time frame. This is useful for applications that perform large file transfers. To request high throughput the ToS bits must be set to 0100 (refer to Table 10.2).

If reliability is the objective, such as the case in an application performing critical processes or requiring security, an application may request a more reliable transmission path by setting the ToS bits 0010. This may be a transaction-based processing application, which requires access to a company's fault-tolerant backbone.

Caution

It is very important to understand that by setting these bits, you change the way routers route traffic. Without a thorough understanding of the types of protocols, applications, traffic flows, and protocol timers within your network, this manipulation could have catastrophic results. With that in mind, it is imperative that you baseline your network thoroughly before attempting to implement them. When properly used, they can dramatically increase the performance of your network and network applications.

ICMP ToS Messages

You might recall from our discussion in Chapter 2 that ICMP messages are sent by routers to alert hosts of problems with the delivery of datagrams, ICMP does not guarantee a solution to these problems.

In this chapter we will only focus on message type 3, Destination Unreachable, and message type 5, Redirect, because these are the only messages that are relevant to ToS. Our discussion will begin with type 3 then move on to type 5.

Destination Unreachable Messages

Destination Unreachable (type 3 ICMP messages), are sent by routers to alert a source host of delivery problems encountered while trying to reach the destination. Several code values within the ICMP header are used to further describe the function of the ICMP message being sent. Each code type describes a different delivery problem encountered. Although many different types of destination unreachable messages may be sent by routers only four of them are relevant to ToS:

Note

Routers append a copy of the offending IP header within the ICMP header that caused the error. By including a copy of the offending IP header, the source may be able to use this information to correct the problem that resulted in this ICMP message being sent.

- **11 = Network Unreachable for ToS ****—This message occurs when a router receives an IP datagram that it cannot deliver or forward to a particular network because the ToS requested is not available.

- **12 = Host Unreachable for ToS ****—This message occurs when a router receives an IP datagram that it cannot deliver or forward to a particular host because the ToS requested is not available.

- **14 = Host Precedence Violation** **—This message occurs when a router receives an IP datagram that it cannot deliver or forward to a particular host because the precedence level requested does not match and is not accepted or is invalid. This could be a source host attempting to access a high security host without the necessary security clearance values.

- **15 = Precedence Cutoff in Effect** **—This message occurs when a configured minimum precedence value exists. Datagrams received by routers with lower precedence levels violate this minimum.

Note
It is important to remember that routers continue to forward datagrams even though the requested ToS level may be unavailable. The default ToS value is used in this case.

Redirect Message

A router sends a redirect (type 5) error to the sender of an. IP datagram when the sender should have sent the datagram to a different router or directly to an end host (if the end host is local). The message assists the sending host to direct a misdirected datagram to a gateway or host. This alert does not guarantee proper delivery; the sending host has to correct the problem if possible.

Routers generate redirect messages to inform source hosts of misguided datagrams. Note that a router receiving a misdirected frame does not trash the offending datagram if it can forward it. The router forwards the frame, sends an alert message to the source, and hopes the source host will properly direct future frames to the designated host or router indicated in the message. Figure 10.2 shows an example of a ICMP redirect message.

Four redirect error codes can occur. Only those indicated by ** are relevant to routing of ToS traffic:

- 0 = Redirect for Network

- 1 = Redirect for Host

- 2 = Redirect for Type-of-Service and Network **

- 3 = Redirect for Type-of-Service and Host **

Type 2 and 3 redirects are sent when datagrams received cannot be forwarded to the destination host or network using the requested type of service. This does not necessarily mean that a route to that host or network is not available and the datagram is not discarded. If another route exists to the destination, it may be used to forward the traffic. Generally speaking, datagrams arriving with ToS values that are not recognized or do not have matching ToS routes are forwarded using the default ToS value 0000 (no ToS) best effort delivery. .

FIGURE 10.2

In this example, a gateway (36.53.0.1) alerts host (36.53.0.174) that it should be sending future datagrams to the following gateway Internet address (36.53.2.2). This alert message also includes a copy of the offending IP header for the source host's inspection.

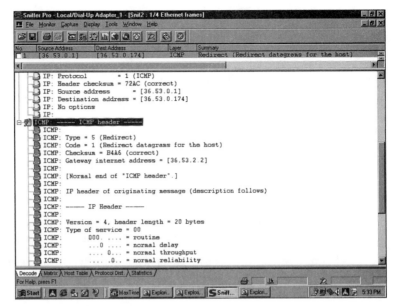

Quality of Service (QoS)

QoS is a hot topic in the Internet community today. But, you might ask, what is it? QoS represents the next generation service level datagram forwarding architecture, all but replacing ToS in the industry. QoS in and of itself is not a thing, but represents the conceptual implementation of several industry protocols and mechanisms that allow intelligent deterministic delivery of data between end systems across Internet.

There are currently three major QoS protocols: IntServ's RSVP (Integrated Service's ReSerVation Protocol), DiffServ (Differential Services), and MPLS (Multi-Protocol Label Switching). These protocols can be categorized as either priority- or reservation-based.

Priority-based QoS protocols perform traffic identification (referred to as classification) providing access to available bandwidth based on priority. For example, real-time applications negatively impacted by lost datagrams or delays in delivery could be given a much higher priority than a standard FTP data transfer. An example of this type of QoS is DiffServ.

Reservation-based QoS protocols allow applications to initiate a request to reserve resources (for example, bandwidth) along the path to a destination. An example of this type of QoS is RSVP.

Throughout the Internet many types of applications exist, each with varying levels of tolerance or intolerance to conditions like congestion, packet loss, and delay (also referred to as jitter). A wide variety of applications are vying for a finite amount of resources, while expecting the highest level of service available. With more hosts and applications being added on a daily basis, providing the highest level of possible service to all applications without exhausting these resources is a daunting task to say the least. QoS is an attempt at addressing this issue.

For QoS protocols to do their magic they must first be able to identify and characterize traffic. This can be done on a per-flow or per-aggregate basis. Per-flow is a one-way conversation from one application to another, identified through five components within a packet: source and destination address, transport protocol (TCP or UDP), and source and destination ports. These five components clearly identify the sending and receiving hosts as well as the applications running within the hosts.

The other method of identification is per-aggregate. This method considers two or more flows with common components when characterizing traffic.

Selecting a specific mechanism will depend on the type of applications, policies, and network topology implemented. Private implementations vary widely. Imagine for instance two end hosts communicating through a connection across the Internet. This virtual connection is entirely dependent on the resources of multiple unknown networks along the path, making support for true QoS end to end even more complex. If one of the unknown networks along the path does not support QoS, best effort delivery will be used to deliver datagrams across that network. In addition, each network along the path may be implementing a different type of QoS. For example, one end-to-end connection could, upon entry into the Internet (at an ISP), begin with RSVP, and then switch to MPLS at the next network, and then back to RSVP prior to exiting as an example. There are no specific mandates requiring a homogenous implementation end to end.

QoS protocols and architectures are typically mixed and matched to provide end to end solutions. An example of this might be to have RSVP implemented at edge networks with a mixture of DiffServ and MPLS used in the Core (see Figure 10.3).

In Figure 10.3 multiple QoS protocols are being implemented within separate networks. These networks may be part of single organization, each representing a geographic area or independent Autonomous Systems serving as transit areas through the Internet. The networks on the bottom left and right are both running the RSVP protocol, while the network in the middle is running a mixture of MPLS and DiffServ.

We will discuss the four main protocols in more detail in this chapter.

Since IP's inception over 20 years ago, the most prevalent datagram queuing and transmission mechanism has been and still is FIFO (first in first out). With FIFO, datagrams are placed in the output queue of the interface that a router intends to use to reach the destination in the order they were received. Datagrams are then transmitted out this interface in the same order they were queued. This method of queuing and transmission is fine when network resources, such as bandwidth, are sufficient. However, as network resources become congested due to a high volume of traffic exceeding the links capacity, packets must be dropped.

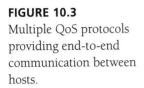

FIGURE 10.3

Multiple QoS protocols providing end-to-end communication between hosts.

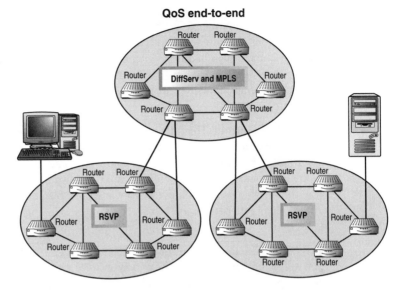

When packets are dropped applications must detect this loss and recover by retransmitting the datagrams involved. When traffic flows are not managed properly, packets may take too long to arrive at their destination or not at all, causing applications to time out and fail. Although QoS-related protocols and architectures are designed to address these specific issues they are not the "silver bullet" solution for networks that are chronically overloaded. By identifying and classifying traffic types, finite network resources can be apportioned properly, offering better delivery to datagrams than the traditional best effort. Several QoS protocols may be used to accomplish this. The first QoS protocol we will discuss is IntServ's RSVP, before moving on to DiffServ and MPLS.

IntServ (Integrated Services) and RSVP

The RSVP (ReSerVation Protocol), as the name implies, is reservation based. RSVP is the major component within an industry model known as IntServ (Integrated Services), which extends IP's standard best effort delivery to include services supporting real-time applications and bandwidth management controls supporting link sharing. To support reservation-based QoS the IntServ model defines four components:

- **Classification**—Classification involves identification of data flows. As datagrams are received by a router, they are identified and mapped to specific predefined class types or QoS. Once datagrams have been classified, they are mapped to a corresponding output queue. Classification is usually based on a combination of five things: source and IP address, protocol ID, and source and destination TCP or UDP ports.

- **Scheduling**—The scheduling process manages interface output queues and controls datagram transmissions based on classification. Datagram scheduling schemes may be priority-based (high priority datagrams are always transmitted first) or round robin (priority and threshold values). The goal of scheduling is to order datagrams, such that delay and packet loss are minimized for those applications requiring a higher level of service, without compromising the delivery of lower-level service datagrams. By managing traffic through queues the scheduling process determines which datagrams are transmitted and when. The scheduler must also be able to identify when a queue is overloaded, dropping packets from traffic flows that are less likely to be negatively impacted by delayed datagrams (not time sensitive).

- **Admission control**—The IntServ model requires routers or forwarding devices to accept or reject resource requests based on the availability of resources. Admission control occurs at every forwarding device along the path end to end and is subject to local policy restrictions, such as user authentication. Rejecting a request for a particular service level does not mean a packet will not be forwarded. Implementations may instead select a path with a lower service level than requested, generating an error message back to the source.

- **RSVP**—RSVP is the mechanism that facilitates resource reservations between end systems. It is a signaling protocol used by end systems and routers to set up, maintain, and tear down RSVP circuits. There are seven RSVP messages used to create, manage, and tear down sessions: Path Setup, Resv Setup, Path Tear, Resv Tear, Path Error, Resv Error and Resv Confirm (see table 10.3).

TABLE 10.3 The seven RSVP messages used to create, manage, and tear down sessions.

Path setup or Path message	Sent by originator(s) to identify a resource path to a destination system
Resv setup or Resv message	Sent by receiver(s) in the reverse direction of the path setup to reserve resources end to end.
Path tear	Sent by originator(s) to tear down a session
Resv tear	Sent by receiver(s) to tear down a session
Path error	Sent by routers to originator notifying of path error.
Resv error	Sent by routers to receiver notifying of resource reservation error.
Resv confirm	Sent by end system or router in response to confirmation request previously included within Resv message. This message will not be sent if no request for confirmation was included within Resv message.

RSVP allows network elements, such as applications or routers, to reserve resources between communicating end systems. Resource reservations are considered receiver-centric rather then sender-centric. The receiver determines the resources reserved based on its applications needs.

The reason RSVP was designed as receiver-centric instead of sender centric is to accommodate multicast (from one to many) conversations. A single host sends a datagram to multiple unknown hosts belonging to the same multicast group. Because these hosts are unknown and group membership to the multicast group will vary as hosts leave or join the group it is necessary to place the responsibility for resource reservation on the receiver.

You may be thinking, how does the receiving host known when to reserve resources if it is not the initiator of the conversation? The answer is, it does not. It is obvious that before a conversation between any two hosts may commence, one side must get the ball rolling so to speak. Figure 10.4 shows the RSVP path and resv messages.

Mapping a Multicast Address to MAC Address

FIGURE 10.4
RSVP path messages are forwarded from sender to receiver. Resv messages flow in the opposite direction.

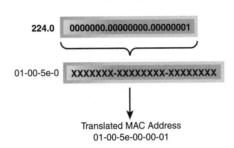

In Figure 10.4, the sending or source system's application issues a path request, which is forwarded by routers along the entire path, basically testing each link along the path end to end for quality of service. The receiving end system responds by sending a reservation, reversing the path taken by the source hosts path request.

Path setup involves an RSVP Path message. Included within this message are the specific resources requested, such as minimum and maximum bandwidth requirements as well as delay. This message is forwarded hop by hop along the path end to end. At each point routers may accept or reject (referred to as Admission Control) the path message based on their capability to deliver the level of service.

If the router is able to accommodate and facilitate the connection, the router passes the message to the next hop router while making note of the IP address of the router it just received the message from. When an RSVP path message transits a non-RSVP enabled network, only the IP addresses of the inbound (or ingress) and outbound (or egress) RSVP routers are added to the Path message. This continues until the message reaches the ultimate destination.

The next step involves the receiving host. This host transmits a RESV message along the same path the path message was received except in the reverse direction. This RESV message states what resources (required by the end system) it would like routers to reserve along the path end to end. Once again each router along the path inspects the request, installs the route and passes it along. Once the message reaches the original sending host, the path is established between these hosts as a virtual circuit, used throughout the conversation and torn down upon completion.

The IntServ RSVP protocol implementation is probably the most robust QoS protocol in use today. However, providing end to end QoS requires more resources and overhead than other technologies.

DiffServ (Differential Services)

DiffServ provides a simple method of identifying and classifying (marking datagrams by setting bits within the IP header) flows and then prioritizing them for transmission. Typically datagrams are marked upon entry into a network by the ingress router (or conditioner). Although the sending host may perform this function as well, it is uncommon. Marked traffic is unmarked upon exit by an egress router.

> **Note**
>
> Ingress and egress are terms used within industry to describe routers that are serving as entry (ingress) and exit (egress) points or network boundaries. For example, take a network, implementing the RSVP protocol, which connects to multiple networks using different QoS protocols. Routers connecting the network Running RSVP to other networks (not running RSVP) would serve as ingress and egress points through the RSVP network. Whether a router is referred to as ingress or egress depends on the direction the communication is flowing (in or out of this router).

To support DiffServ the IP precedence and ToS fields within the IPv4 header had to be changed. This change is defined in rfc 2474, renaming the first six bits within the ToS header to the Differential Services (also referred to as the DS Code Point) field. Compare Figure 10.1 to Figure 10.5, which shows the reassignment of the IPv4 precedence and ToS fields.

FIGURE 10.5

The ToS header has been renamed the Differential Services (DS) field. Precedence bits within this header are now referred to as *class selector codepoints*.

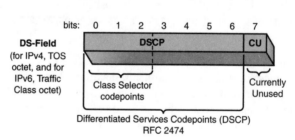

In the first three bits, originally precedence values have been preserved for backward-compatibility, but are now referred to as Class Selector Codepoints. The codepoint values are used by DiffServ-enabled hosts and routers to identify different service levels. When set, the DSCPs (or DiffServ Codepoints) are mapped to PHBs (Per Hop Behaviors) by forwarding devices along the path between source and destination. PHBs dictate how each packet will be handled, that is, the type of service level applied when the datagram is forwarded.

There are three categories of code points: mandatory, recommended, or vendor-specific. The marking and unmarking of datagrams as they enter or leave a DiffServ environment not only provides backward-compatibility with IPv4 (precedence field only) implementations that do not support DiffServ, but also allow packets to traverse networks using different QoS methods, such as IntServ (RSVP). This means coordination between ISPs and organizations must exist to properly configure border routers enabling QoS end to end.

DiffServ, like any QoS protocol, requires scheduling and queuing mechanisms to facilitate the ordering and transmission of datagrams. Many queuing and scheduling *mechanisms* exist, such as priority, round robin, and so on. For example, priority queuing orders datagrams for transmission within an output queue based on arbitrary priorities assigned to types of traffic. For instance, Telnet datagrams may be given a higher priority than FTP datagrams, causing them to be transmitted first, even if they were queued last. The round robin method of queuing generally involves thresholds (set by an administrator) that when exceeded causes the router to move on to the next queue. Vendors are free to implement their own strategies based on their needs. Scheduling and queuing methods vary among vendors and will not be discussed within this book.

The most important component, which all others depend on, is the clear classification of traffic based on its tolerance to delay and packet loss. The end result is that applications with a lower tolerance for delay or packet loss be given preferential treatment. DiffServ defines four levels of delay: high, medium, low, and no sensitivity. Generally speaking connectionless applications (transferring non–time-sensitive information) can support high to medium levels of delay. If occasionally datagrams are lost during transmission, this generally does not result in a failed session. Connection-oriented applications are less forgiving, typically only tolerating low delay. Even less tolerant are applications that are extremely time-sensitive, such as video conferencing.

Packet loss typically occurs when congestion is experienced. Forwarding devices employ packet drop procedures during this period. When no indication exists, the router simply drops packets at random until the situation subsides. DiffServ allows routers to determine which packets to drop based on the relative drop preference level specified within the DSCP.

MPLS (Multi-Protocol Label Switching)

MPLS is a label-switching and bandwidth management architecture. Traffic flows are identified and categorized, then assigned a label by ingress routers. Bandwidth is allocated based on these labels. These labels are mapped to queue and scheduling mechanisms that control datagram forwarding throughout the MPLS environment. End systems and their applications are not involved in the MPLS process at all.

In addition, MPLS, unlike some of the other QoS implementations, is protocol and datalink independent. Routers (referred to as LSRs, Label Switching Routers) are the key elements within the technology. Labels are added upon entry to an MPLS network and removed upon exit. This simplistic approach is what makes MPLS so attractive.

Local policies configured assist ingress routers in the labeling process. Once datagrams are assigned labels they are passed on to the next hop router. Each router along the path to a destination uses the existing label as a reference pointer that it compares to a local table to determine the next hop router and label to use. Label switching requires less overhead and processing time, thereby increasing overall performance. .

Labels and their assignment are configured and controlled by network administrators and are beyond the scope of this book.

Note

The best laid QoS plans do not always result in success. If a networks infrastructure is already exceeding capacity and congestion is an issue, then no traffic queuing in this world can help it. You may even make the situation worse.

Summary

IP ToS (Type of Service) was the first attempt at delivering datagrams based on a level of service requested. ToS, although relatively unused until recently, provides for slightly more intelligent path selection than best effort delivery through the use of the IP ToS bits contained within the IP header. Upper-layer services, such as applications, set these bits indicating the type of service it is requesting for the delivery of its datagrams.

The three-bit precedence field can be used to prioritize datagram delivery based on a perceived level of importance.

QoS or Quality of Service is an industry buzzword that encompasses multiple protocols and architectures, which provide better than best effort delivery of datagrams across the Internet. There are currently three major QoS protocols: RSVP (ReSerVation Protocol), DiffServ (Differential Services) and MPLS (Multi-Protocol label Switching). These protocols can be categorized as either priority or reservation based.

RSVP is the major protocol within the IS Integrated Services (also known as IntServ) model. RSVP is reservation-based, allowing applications or ingress routers to reserve resources end to end prior to communication.

DiffServ and MPLS are priority-based. DiffServ uses the IP Differential Service field bits to classify and prioritizes traffic within output queues. MPLS is a label switching architecture. Traffic is identified and assigned a label. Labels provide indicators to routers as to how to forward the traffic.

Chapter Quiz

1. Name the three main parts of the IP ToS field within the IP header.

2. What is the significance of the Precedence bits within the IP header?

3. Name the three main ICMP message types.

4. Name the seven RSVP messages.

5. What is the significance of Admission Control?

6. Name the four major components of the IntServ model.

7. Name the three major QoS protocols.

8. Name the two ICMP message types relevant to ToS.

9. Name the QoS protocol that labels and prioritizes traffic flows.

10. Which QoS implementation is considered receiver-centric and relies on resource reservations?

11. What is the purpose of the scheduling service within QoS?

IP MULTICAST ROUTING

What Is an IP Multicast?

IP multicasts are datagrams sourced from a single host to a group of hosts. Hosts can belong to one or more logical groups for the purpose of receiving communication directed at members of the specific group. Multicasts are designed to reduce the amount of traffic congestion plaguing our networks by narrowing the focus of communication to specific hosts belonging to groups. Communication between systems can be sent using one of three methods, unicast, broadcast or multicast.

Unicast Datagrams

Unicast datagrams are examples of point-to-point communication between only two systems. Unicast transmission involves only one receiver and one sender (also referred to as directed datagrams). These datagrams are specifically addressed by the sending host, identifying the recipient's unique IP address. This type of communication is the most common and efficient way of communicating with a single host. This method does not involve other hosts not specifically addressed within the datagram (see Figure 11.1).

Unicast Communication

FIGURE 11.1
Unicast communication
occurs between two
systems.

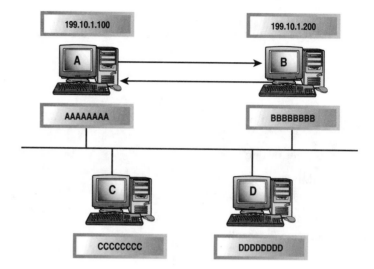

In Figure 11.1, Host A wants to communicate with Host B. Host A packages a datagram with its logical IP address as the source and Host B's IP address as the destination transmitting the datagram out on the wire. All hosts connected to the same physical wire will detect the signal, buffer the datagram at the data link layer, and check the destination MAC address to see if the address specified (unique 6 byte address BBBBBBBB) is theirs (the MAC address matches). Upon finding that the address does not match, these hosts simply flush their local buffers, trashing the frame and take no further action. Host B is the only host that has this address and therefore continues to process the frame, sending it to the upper layers for further processing. This process occurs each time a datagram is transmitted.

Broadcast Datagrams

Broadcasts are datagrams addressed to destination "everyone." All systems recognize, buffer, and process datagrams addressed to this destination even if they have no idea what to do with its contents (see Figure 11.2).

In Figure 11.2, Host 199.10.1.100 (MAC address AAAAAAAA) wants to send a message to everyone on its local subnet. This host addresses the datagram with the appropriate logical network layer broadcast address (199.10.1.255) for this subnet and data link layer broadcast address (FFFFFFFF). A full discussion of IP addressing was discussed in Chapter 2, "IP and IP Addressing." Broadcasts allow a host to send a single datagram with a well-known destination MAC address (represented in binary as all ones, or hexadecimal as all FFFFFFFFs) recognized by everyone.

Broadcast Communication

FIGURE 11.2
Broadcasts are sent by
one host addressed to
everyone on the same
network or subnet.

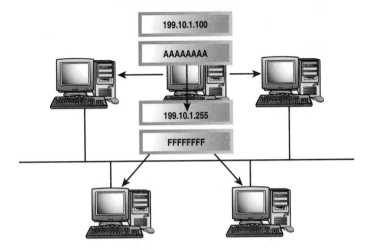

The fact that a datagram is addressed as broadcast means that all systems must recognize, buffer, and at least make an attempt to process its contents. Upon reception the broadcast datagram is passed up layer by layer within the system to determine whether this system needs to continue to process this datagram. If the determination is made by an upper layer that the purpose of this broadcast is unknown or of no use to this host, it ceases processing and discards the datagram without taking any further action. If the datagram contents are pertinent to some process running within the host, it fully processes the contents and, if necessary, sends a response. Because broadcast datagrams are addressed to everyone, all hosts must upon reception stop what they are doing and at least attempt to process them, which adds to each system's overhead. If systems continue to receive large amounts of useless broadcasts, they are continually interrupted, using precious resources that could be best used elsewhere. When networks are congested this additional broadcast traffic and processing overhead can cause serious performance degradation.

Now, you might wonder why you would even use or need broadcasts. Broadcasts are a necessary evil in networking. Consider a world without broadcasts; a host wanting to send the same message to every host on the same network would have to individually address datagrams to each host. This would cause an extreme amount of traffic to be added to the network and is not practical.

Many network applications and protocols function through the use of broadcast messages. For example, routing protocols like RIP (see Chapter 5) and IGRP (see Chapter 6) broadcast their entire route tables on a regular basis. Other broadcast-related protocols, like name (NetBIOS) and address (ARP, RARP, BootP, and DHCP) resolution protocols operate through the use of broadcasts, adding overhead to networks. We discussed ARP, RARP, BootP, and DHCP in Chapter 2.

For example, the NetBIOS (Network Basic Input Output System) provides name registration and resolution to network layer addresses for end systems. As a broadcast-based protocol, it provides a simple, dynamic way for NetBIOS hosts to locate and access resources on remote hosts.

NetBIOS end systems are identified by user-friendly names. When you want to access a host, you can refer to the name instead of a numerical address. If you use a host name rather than an address, the name must be resolved to the end systems address. NetBIOS performs broadcast-based name-to-address resolution, resolving the name to a logical network layer address of the destination system.

After a name has been resolved to a logical network layer address, this address must be resolved to a data link layer address (MAC). This process is performed through the use of ARP. The source end system broadcasts a local ARP to resolve the network layer address of the end system to a data link address. After the data link address is determined, data may be transferred between end systems.

The NetBIOS Protocol

The NetBIOS protocol has been the cornerstone of all Microsoft operating system products until the release of Windows 2000. NetBIOS clients advertise their presence to neighbors by broadcasting their NetBIOS name on the network. NetBIOS-enabled systems locate resources on remote systems by broadcasting NetBIOS queries asking, "Does anyone recognize the name 'HeathersPC'". If a host exists with that name it will respond by resolving this name to its network layer address and communication can begin. Although this book is not about Microsoft, it is the de facto operating system of choice throughout the world and therefore is extremely important in this discussion because routers are expected to forward datagrams for systems using these protocols.

NetBIOS was not designed to be routed between subnets. It was originally ported over NetBEUI (Network Basic Extended User Interface), which is a non-routable layer 2 transport service (not to be confused with true transport layer protocols, such as TCP or UDP).

When NetBIOS and NetBEUI were introduced, routers and routing protocols did not exist. Networks were connected together through layer 2 devices such as bridges. Bridges and switches do not block broadcasts, therefore NetBIOS registration and resolution flowed freely to all devices throughout this flat network.

Over the years as the number of hosts, users, and application resource demands increased this broadcast method of locating resources began to overwhelm network resources. New services were added to address these issues, such as WINs (Windows Internet Name Servers), which allow devices to send a unicast datagram to a central server instead of broadcasting their presence to all hosts. This server would maintain a registration table and assist devices in locating remote hosts. With the introduction of routers into the mix (which block all broadcast traffic) it was necessary to add these servers strategically throughout the network and configure clients to use these servers to facilitate communication beyond local segments, but minimize broadcast propagation between networks.

As you can see broadcasts are very useful, but need to be managed. Broadcasts in and of themselves are not the problem. The problem is the quantity and frequency of these broadcasts. When too many broadcasts are sent in a short time frame, they can overwhelm network devices.

Routers can be used to control broadcasts. Because routers do not forward broadcasts, they can effectively isolate this type of traffic to local segments, keeping it from being propagated to other segments unnecessarily.

Note

Routers can be configured to forward broadcasts, although this practice is not recommended and defeats one of the main purposes of implementing a router.

The Daily Use of Broadcasts

You may not be aware that you have already been using broadcasts in your daily lives. Think of your TV set sitting in your home. Television technology is based on Broadband signaling, which allows multiple channels to be carried within a single physical medium (the copper cable) distinguishing each channel through the use of varied frequency and modulation techniques. Frequency and modulation techniques are used to manipulate electrical signals to represent data in terms of ones and zeros. For the purposes of this book how this is performed is not important. What is important is that these signals are broadcast to your TV, which is in essence a receiver by a transmitter located at your local cable company. Broadcast communication is one way, with one system acting as a transmitter and all others acting as receivers. Now, just because the signal technically is broadcast to everyone everywhere does not mean you will get every channel on earth. There are distance limitations dictating how far a signal can reach and local cable companies employ scrambling devices, which basically filter frequencies (relating to pay channels like HBO and so on) until you pay for them.

Multicast Datagrams

Multicasting is essentially a broadcast to a set of hosts belonging to a particular group. The development of multicasting was prompted by the need to minimize the impact caused by systems processing unnecessary datagrams and to reduce network traffic loads caused by unnecessary broadcasts. Multicasting technology has been around for some time, but has been implemented in a limited manner until recently.

Multicasts have several benefits. First, they target a subset of hosts (receivers) rather than every host like broadcasts do. Multicasts allow only those hosts that need the datagram to receive and process it. The other benefit of multicasts is the capability to dynamically discover applications and services running in remote hosts spread throughout the world. These applications and services may be as simple as a game like Doom or may be mission critical audio and video-cast meetings between corporate users within the same geographic location or spread across the world. Doom was one of the first Internet games introduced where a player upon initialization of the game can dynamically locate one or more opponents (Doom players) through the use of IP multicasting. The dynamic discovery of services can be extended to all kinds of applications, such as DNS, DHCP, video conferencing, and so on.

How a device becomes a member of a group and the routing protocols that make IP multicasting possible will come later. For simplicity sake we will assume for now that it has happened magically. In Figure 11.3 four hosts on a local network belong to the same multicast group. One of the hosts transmits a message addressing it to the specific group address 224.0.0.x (x represents the multicast group identifier). Multicast group addresses will be discussed in further detail later on in this chapter.

Multicast Communication

FIGURE 11.3
Host 199.10.1.100 sends
a message to hosts
belonging to the same
multicast group.

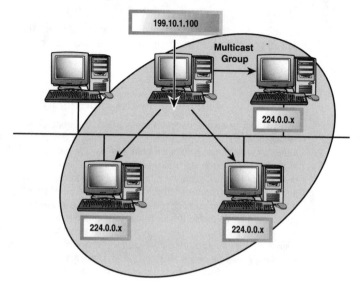

Only hosts belonging to the same group will fully process the datagram. All other hosts, after determining they are not a member of the group, will simply discard the datagram. IP multicasting is a hot topic within company networks and throughout the Internet and although it has been around for many years, is still under development. Multicasts can be thought of as a broadcast from a single source to a group (consisting of one or more members). In terms of the direction of communication between source and destination, the sending system does not know where or even if any other group members exist.

Class D Addresses

If you recall from our discussion in Chapter 2 about IP addressing and class types, there are five class-based addressing pools. Three of these pools—Class A, B, and C—may be used to assign registered addresses to individuals and corporations. The last two, Classes D and E, are reserved by ARIN for special purposes; Class D addresses for IP multicasting and Class E for experimental purposes. These address classes cannot be assigned to individuals or organizations. All Class D addresses start with a 4-bit value of 1110 within the first byte of the 32-bit IP address. The Class D value within the first byte range is 224 to 239 for a total address space of 224.0.0.1 through 239.255.255.255. ARIN has reserved the Class E address for future use. The first byte value range falls between 240 and 247. Common Class D multicast addresses used by routing protocols and the groups they represent are listed in Table 11.1. A complete list of Multicast addresses are available in Appendix C, "IP and Multicast Protocol Addresses."

TABLE 11.1   Common Class D—Multicast Addresses and Group Descriptions

Multicast Group Description	IP Multicast Address
All IGMP systems on this subnet	224.0.0.1
All routers on this subnet	224.0.0.2
DVMRP Routers	224.0.0.4
OSPF—All routers	224.0.0.5
OSPF—Designated router	224.0.0.6
RIP version 2—All routers	224.0.0.9
IGRP—All routers	224.0.0.10
PIM—All routers	224.0.0.13
RSVP	224.0.0.14
IS-IS—All level 1 routers	224.0.0.19
IS-IS—All level 2 routers	224.0.0.20
IGMP	224.0.0.22

ARIN has reserved the address range 224.0.0.1 through 224.0.0.255 for routing, group member reports, and data link layer discovery protocols. Addresses beyond this range are either reserved for future uses or privately used within organizations and are not publicly routable through the Internet. We will discuss how routers and routing protocols forward multicast traffic later in this chapter.

Multicast to MAC Address Translation

IP multicast addresses, like regular IP addresses, must be resolved to a data link layer MAC address. Multicast addresses (32 bit IP addresses) must be translated into valid MAC addresses prior to transmission by the source host. MAC addresses are 48 bits or 6 bytes in length. The translation from logical IP multicast to MAC address is illustrated in Figure 11.4.

Obviously with only 32 bits, a multicast address cannot be mapped bit for bit to a 48-bit MAC address. Forty-eight bit multicast MAC addresses always start with the first 25 bits the same, leaving 23 bits used for IP multicast translation. As you can see in Figure 3.4, only the last 23 bits of the multicast address are mapped directly to the MAC address. The first 3 bytes (or 24 bits) of the MAC address will always be 01-00-5E hexadecimal (or 00000001-00000000-01011110 in binary) with the 25th bit (the high order bit) within the fourth byte being a 0. The last 23 bits of the multicast address are copied to the end of the MAC address completing the translation. In this case the last 23 bits in hexadecimal are 00:00:01.

FIGURE 11.4
The last 23 bits of IP multicast address 224.0.0.1 has been mapped to a data link MAC address.

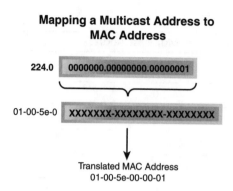

Mapping a Multicast Address to MAC Address

224.0   0000000.00000000.00000001

01-00-5e-0   XXXXXXX-XXXXXXXX-XXXXXXXX

Translated MAC Address
01-00-5e-00-00-01

Note

The IANA controls MAC address allocation and has reserved the following MAC addresses for IP multicasting; 01-00-5E-00-00-00 through 01-00-5E-7F-FF-FF hexadecimal.

IGMP (Internet Group Management Protocol)

Now we will discuss how systems become members of multicast groups. First the system must be running some type of process or service that requires IP multicasting capability. The application or service requiring the use of multicasts must join the appropriate group or groups. Systems with multiple processes requiring multicasting will become a member of multiple groups. For each group a process would like to become a member of a separate join message for that group must be sent. After the application or service has joined a group it then listens to all datagrams addressed to that multicast group.

When systems belonging to the same group reside on the same subnet there is no routing involved. However, when systems are remote, multicast-enabled routers must exist to facilitate the forwarding of these datagrams. We will discuss the different multicast routing protocols later in this chapter. Right now our focus is on how a process with a host joins, listens, and removes itself from a multicast group.

To dynamically facilitate these critical steps a protocol was developed, IGMP (Internet Group Management Protocol), also referred to as the Internet Group Multicast Protocol. IGMP version 2 is defined within RFC 2236. There are actually three IGMP versions; 1, 2 and 3. The most common standard in use today is version 2.

Version 1, although still in use, is virtually obsolete. Versions 2 and 3 are very similar with one notable difference. Version 3 supports selected source multicasting, which means that multicasts can be filtered based on the sender's address. This allows Version 3 hosts to deny the reception of messages from hosts not matching the filter requirements. This enhancement is certainly a plus when a company needs to achieve secure multicast communication across the Internet.

Note

This chapter will focus on IGMP version 2 because version 3 is still in the development stage. This chapter will only discuss version 1 only when compatibility issues need to be addressed.

IGMP employs four message types between IGMP-enabled clients and routers. Each of these messages shares a common header (see Figure 11.5) and is carried within an IP datagram using the registered protocol value of 2 representing IGMP. IGMP version 1 messages are limited to 8 bytes in length. To allow version 1 datagrams to coexist with other versions, version 2 and 3 enabled devices will ignore anything beyond this range when receiving version 1 messages.

IGMP Messages

FIGURE 11.5
All IGMP messages share a common header.

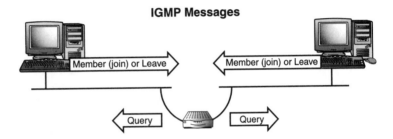

Type

The first field within the IGMP header identifies the type of IGMP message being sent. The hexadecimal value (or type code) contained in this field specifically identifies the message as a member query (0x11), version 1 member report (0x12), version 2 member report (0x16), or member leave (0x17). Table 11.2 describes the different types codes contained in the type field.

TABLE 11.2   IGMP Code Types

Code Type	Message	Sent by	Description
0x11	IGMP Member Query (see Figure 11.6)	Routers	Sent by routers to discover multicast group members on local segments.
0x12	IGMP version 1 Member Report (see Figure 11.7)	IGMP version 1 enabled hosts	Sent unsolicited by IGMP version 1 hosts to 224.0.0.1 (all local systems) to join a multicast group. Also sent in response to a router query to maintain an existing membership.
0x16	IGMP version 2 Member Report (see Figure 11.7)	IGMP version 2 enabled hosts	Sent unsolicited by IGMP version 2 hosts to 224.0.0.1 (all local systems) to join a multicast group. Also sent in response to a router query to maintain an existing membership.

TABLE 11.2 Continued

Code Type	Message	Sent by	Description
0x17	IGMP Leave Message	IGMP version 2 enabled hosts	Only supported by version 2-enabled devices. Sent by hosts to 224.0.0.2 (all local routers), indicating this host no longer wishes to belong to the multicast group.

There are two types of IGMP member query messages, general and specific. Both member queries are supported by IGMP versions 1, 2 and 3. Routers send these types of messages to learn of multicast group members.

The general query message is used to discover which multicast groups have active members. The general message assists a router in discovering groups and members on local subnets. The specific query message is sent by IGMP-enabled routers to discover whether a specific multicast group has active members. The specific query message assists a router in discovering a specific multicast group and its members attached to local subnets.

FIGURE 11.6
IGMP query messages are sent by routers through local interfaces to discover multicast group members.

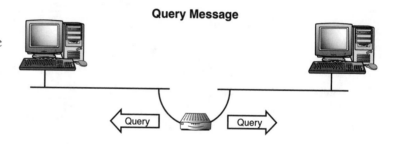

Query Message

FIGURE 11.7
Member reports are sent by host processes to either join a group or maintain membership in a group it had previously joined.

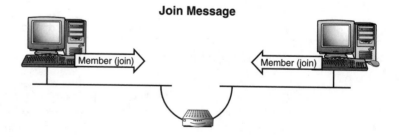

Join Message

Note

IGMP member reports are commonly referred to as *join messages*. Systems send these messages to announce their intent to join a multicast group. Routers keep track of which interfaces and subnets have active groups. Leave messages are only generated by version two IGMP systems. When the last active member connected to a subnet leaves the group routers prune (de-activate) the forwarding of multicasts for that group over that interface.

Join Message

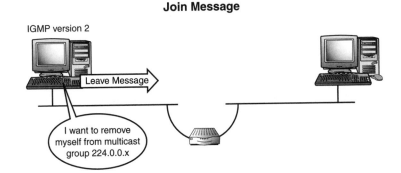

FIGURE 11.8
Leave messages are only sent by IGMP version 2 hosts. This message is sent when a host wants to remove itself from a multicast group.

Note

IGMP version 1 devices do not support the leave message type and therefore do not use it. When they no longer wish to belong to a group version 1, devices withdraw their membership by silently leaving the group, without sending a message indicating this.

As new applications for IGMP evolve within the industry, new message types will be employed beyond the basic four. Currently, any other message type not listed here will be ignored and discarded.

Maximum Response Time

Set by routers within query messages only. This time value is measured by 1/10th second increments. The purpose of this timer is to specify the maximum amount of time value the receiver may use to transmit its member report. This value is used by hosts to generate a random transmit timer using a value between zero and the maximum response time indicated within the query. This random transmission timer is calculated by all systems independently, causing them to generate member reports at varied intervals, instead of responding all at once to a query. This decreases network congestion caused by query messages.

Checksum

Used to verify the contents of the IGMP header have not been damaged while in transit. This value is calculated by the sender and added to the IGMP header. Receivers will recalculate this value, discarding datagrams when the checksum does not match.

Group Address

In general query messages this value will always be zero. In specific queries this value will contain the specific multicast group address being queried. Member or leave messages will contain the specific multicast group address.

Note
Multicast datagrams are carried within IP packets. The TTL value within the IP header can be used to limit the distance a multicast will travel. This may be necessary when multicast traffic is only necessary within an organization or geographic location. A TTL value of 1 would limit the distance to a single segment (the datagram would not be forwarded by a router). A TTL value of zero would cause a datagram to be discarded. If you recall our discussion in Chapter 2, routers decrement this value as they forward datagrams. When a router receives a TTL value set to 1 it reduces it to zero, which results in the datagram being discarded. Any value greater than 1 can be used to limit the number of hops or networks to which the multicast is forwarded. The following TTL settings have been defined by MBone (Multicast Backbone), an Internet multicast testing group; site = 15, region = 63, and world = 127.

IP Multicast Operation

IP multicasting involves at least one or more hosts, running applications that require multicast capabilities. For the Internet Protocol to support multicasting, extensions had to be added to the protocol. These extensions are defined with RFC 1112 and allow IP to support the reception and transmission of multicast datagrams and the IGMP protocol.

The IGMP protocol is a dynamic protocol that allows host to join or leave groups from anywhere at any time. Group membership is not limited by location. Hosts can be located anywhere within a network or across the Internet. Multiple group memberships may be necessary when multiple processes running within a host require it.

Let's start simple by learning how multicasting works on a LAN, where no routers are involved with forwarding multicast traffic. When a user on a LAN starts a process that requires multicasting, the process initiates the transmission of an IGMP membership report out on the local LAN, identifying this host as a member of the multicast group. This message is sent addressed to the destination group's address announcing this host's membership. The multicast group address is left in a listening state within the host. The listening state is necessary so the host may receive datagrams from other hosts sending multicasts to this address. There may or may not be another host on the same network participating in the same group, nonetheless an IGMP report (which is the Join message) must be sent.

Note

MBone, an Internet multicast testing group, was established in 1992 (consisting of forty subnets in four countries). The main goal of MBone was and still is to successfully deploy multicast applications and services across the Internet. Currently MBone has grown to include more than 3,000 subnets in more than 25 countries. MBone basically consists of a collection of networks and multicast-enabled routers (referred to as multicast islands) connected by IP tunnels.

IP tunnels are used to encapsulate datagrams within IP in order to carry multicast datagrams through an IP network. An IP tunnel consists of two routers (not necessarily on the same physical segment) that serve as entry and exit points of the tunnel. Traffic sent to the entry router of the IP tunnel performs encapsulation, whereas the exit router de-encapsulates datagrams. An example of its use is to logically connect multicast islands together encapsulating this traffic within a unicast IP datagram allowing multicast traffic to be carried through a non-multicast–enabled network or networks.

If group members are separated by one or more routers, such as across the Internet, things get much more complicated. To facilitate communication between remote group members, the following must occur. First all host processes (wherever they are) must send IGMP member reports to their local router to announce their intention to join or leave a multicast group. Routers store group information in local cache tables, keeping track of only the existing groups it has heard reports from and the interfaces these reports were received on, not the specific hosts belonging to those groups. It is not important to a router to know who is part of a group, just that there is at least one active member of a group attached to a local interface. If routers had to keep track of all group members this would be a waste of resources. As host processes join and leave groups randomly, the constant updating of this information could overwhelm a router. As long as there is one active member located on a local subnet, the router knows it must forward multicast traffic for that interface (in or out depending on which way the datagram is going).

Routers can determine what groups are out each local interface by periodically transmitting an IGMP general or specific query. We discussed the various IGMP message types earlier in this chapter. You may recall that general queries are sent to identify all groups that exist out each interface, whereas the specific queries are used to identify membership of a particular group. Because host processes may join or leave at will these queries are necessary.

When a router sends a query (either general or specific), it sends the query to the default "all hosts" multicast address 224.0.0.1. All hosts must respond with a member report stating the groups they are members of (have joined). When the router sends this message, it sets the maximum response timer, providing hosts with a timer value used to generate a random member report. This random interval prevents all hosts from responding at the same time, overwhelming the router with member reports. Even though the query is sent to all hosts and they are expected to respond, in actuality, only one from each multicast group responds when multiple members of the same group exist on the same subnet.

Note

Query messages are sent by routers to learn of multicast members on local segments. Report messages are sent by host processes to either join multicast groups or maintain an existing group membership.

This is a due to the random transmit timer operation. Remember that hosts set their timer as a random variable used to determine when to transmit their member report. However, if prior to their transmission a multicast member report is seen from another host belonging to the same group, this host does not transmit its member report. This is because routers do not care who is in the group, just that the group exists (there is one active member). This reduces the overall traffic generated by IGMP on the subnet.

When more than one router is attached to the same segment, one of them (typically the one with the lowest IP address) assumes the role of querier, keeping track of the active multicast groups for that segment. Queriers periodically, for lack of a better word, query their local subnets to see if active members are present for previously joined multicast groups. If after repeated attempts these queries go unanswered, the router assumes there are no active members on the local segment and clears this group from its table. Any multicast datagrams received by this router through other interfaces will not be forwarded out this interface; in essence this path is pruned back from the multicast forwarding tree for this group. We will discuss the concept of multicast forwarding trees later in this chapter.

Pruning also occurs when an IGMP version 2 leave message is sent by a host alerting the local router that it no longer wishes to be an active member of a multicast group. This message includes the specific group address being left. As mentioned earlier, version 1 IGMP-enabled devices do not support leave messages and do therefore not send them upon removing themselves from a group, this lack of notification leaves routers believing the multicast group still has active members for a period of time. Eventually they will figure this out after sending queries and receiving no response. However, this could take some time and meanwhile the router is still forwarding multicasts to this segment needlessly. Because version 2 IGMP devices send leave messages the pruning of these segments occur in more timely manner, reducing the overall traffic load caused by the unnecessary forwarding of multicasts.

Multicast Routing

By now you know the basic requirements of hosts and routers to participate in multicasting. Now let's focus our discussion on how multicasts are forwarded by routers between source and destination (multicast group members). In the beginning of this chapter we discussed unicast, broadcast, and multicast transmission, describing unicast as point-to-point, broadcast as one-to-many and multicast as one-to-a-group. Routers and routing protocols naturally forward unicast datagrams, but do not forward broadcasts and multicasts. So how do routers actually manage to forward these datagrams between remote hosts across the Internet? Well, that is where multicast routing comes into play.

Note

For multicast transmission to reach hosts and processes separate by one or more routers, all routers, firewalls, and intermediate devices along the path between them must support IP multicasting. Not all devices support IP multicasting. If this is the case IP tunneling may be necessary.

Multicast routing consists of protocols and algorithms that operate in tandem with regular IGP and EGP routing protocols discussed throughout this book to achieve multicast routing. Multicast routing protocols rely on underlying routing protocols and their tables to perform path selection and achieve multicast forwarding between members. You can think of multicast routing as logically running on top of the regular routing structure (multicast routing on top of regular routing). Some multicast routing protocols are routing protocol–dependent, that is, they only run on top of a particular routing protocol, such as MOSPF, which only works with OSPF. Others are routing protocol–independent and will work with any routing protocol. An example of this is PIM, which stands for Protocol Independent Multicast. Each routing protocol has its advantages and disadvantages.

Dense Versus Sparse Mode Multicasting

With the advent of MBone, islands of multicast networks sprouted up throughout the Internet community providing multicast paths across the world. These islands, linked by IP tunnels through non-multicast networks, provide the communication paths necessary to support multicast applications and services. The routing protocols that move multicasts through these islands and tunnels follow one of two general approaches (dense or sparse) based on the distribution of multicast members. When many multicast members exist on subnets and bandwidth is not a problem the dense approach is best. Dense mode relies on multicasting routing protocols that flood multicast datagrams. Sparse mode is best implemented when active multicast members are not centrally located and bandwidth is limited. Sparse mode multicast routing protocols assume that members are distributed and bandwidth is not plentiful and therefore try to avoid wasting resources by building a multicast delivery tree, adding and pruning branches (subnets) as members join or leave multicast groups. The following multicast routing protocols are considered to follow the dense mode approach; DVMRP, MOSPF, and PIM-DM. Sparse mode protocols are CBT and PIM-SM. We will discuss each of these protocols later in this chapter.

Dense Mode

Dense mode protocols operate on the assumption that group members are not distributed and bandwidth is abundant. Based on this assumption, dense mode multicast protocols use a technique referred to as flooding. Although this method is the simplest, fastest method of getting multicast messages where they need to go, it is inefficient. Flooding occurs when a router receives a multicast group's datagram for the first time. Routers flood these datagrams out all interfaces, except the one it was received on. Flooding guarantees that all routers receive the multicast (see Figure 11.9).

If this is not the first time it has seen this multicast it simply discards the datagram. This eliminates loops within the topology. However, for a router to know that this is the first time it has seen a datagram from a multicast group, all multicast-enabled routers must maintain a local tables of all recently seen datagrams. Maintaining this type of table is extremely resource-intensive.

FIGURE 11.9
Dense mode routing protocols flood multicast datagrams to all multicast-enabled subnets.

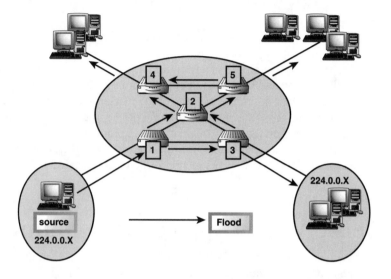

In Figure 11.9 a source host belonging to multicast group 224.0.0.X has sent a multicast datagram for the first time to its local router for forwarding. This router floods it out all other ports except the one it was received on making sure that all other routers receive the datagram. All other multicast-enabled routers do the same. Only hosts connected to routers 1 and 3 are members of the multicast group. However, because the message has been flooded, all routers and hosts receive it unnecessarily. Flooding is fast, but wastes bandwidth.

Note
Dense mode protocols are source-driven, that is, flooding is initiated when a member of a group transmits a multicast datagram. The flooding of this datagram starts from the source and radiates out in all directions (from source to recipients). Protocols that support dense mode multicast routing are DVMRP, MOSPF, and PIM-DM.

DVMRP

DVMRP or Distance Vector Multicast Routing Protocol defined within RFC 1075 was the first multicast routing protocol developed. It served as the basis for MBone's multicast routing implementations and is still the most widely used multicast routing protocol today. As a distance vector routing multicast protocol DVMRP relies on distance vector routing protocols such as RIP v1 and RIP v2.

DVMRP follows the dense mode method of multicasting with a slight variation. Flooding multicasts to all routers and subnets is performed, however as non-member subnets are discovered these branches are pruned. This technique is referred to as *broadcast and prune*. Pruning is a result of the learned groups from IGMP messages. Routers that do not have active multicast members for the flooded group message send a prune message to their upstream neighbor notifying it that this branch (subnet) and all downstream (branches) subnets from this router should be pruned (see Figure 11.10).

FIGURE 11.10
DVMRP floods and prunes multicast datagrams. Routers send prune messages to upstream routers when no active members exist on downstream subnets.

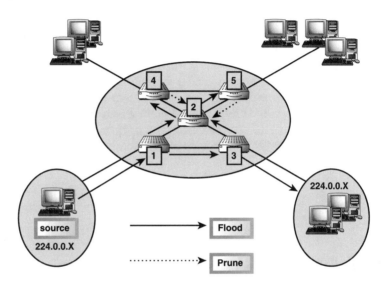

In this example, DVMRP routers 4 and 5, after receiving the initial flood message, send a prune message to their upstream neighbor (router 2). Prune messages are used to notify upstream routers that there are no active members of group 224.0.0.x attached to downstream subnets and there is no need to send multicasts for this group in this direction.

You should note that membership to multicast groups vary as members (wherever they are) randomly may join and leave groups at will. This means that branches previously pruned must be activated and added to multicast trees when members join. Routers keep track of membership through IGMP join and leave messages, notifying their upstream neighbor when a member has become active on an attached or downstream subnet. By building a tree structure from source to active group members, bandwidth resources are more efficiently used.

Note

DVMRP only floods, constructs trees, and forwards multicasts across networks implementing routing protocols that support DVMRP. This means that DVMRP flooding and trees are limited to the routing domain of the regular routing protocol, such as RIP. Border routers running multiple routing protocols, such as RIP and OSPF, would have two tree structures, one for DVMRP and one for MOSPF. MOSPF is discussed later in this chapter.

DVMRP routers must maintain member state information within their multicast route tables to keep track of groups seen and the active or inactive interfaces for those groups.

MOSPF

As the name implies Multicast OSPF is designed to work with the OSPF routing protocol to achieve multicast forwarding through OSPF areas. OSPF routing was discussed in Chapter 6, "OSPF." As you may recall OSPF is a hierarchical routing protocol, which breaks up its routing domain into multiple areas to reduce route update traffic and route table recalculations due to changes in other areas. All OSPF routers maintain a complete topology map of their area using this information to calculate the shortest path tree to all networks and subnets throughout the area. The identification of all networks and subnets and changes to them are propagated by flooded Link State Advertisements throughout the OSPF area. From this a topology map known as the Link State Database is built, providing a detailed picture of the entire area. This database is used by MOSPF to build shortest path trees from source to multicast group members. For every source-to-group multicast pair a separate tree must be built. Tree information must be stored locally by each router within a table.

Note

MOSPF is described within RFC 1584.

PIM-DM

Protocol Independent Multicast-Dense Mode may run on top of any regular routing protocol and therefore offers a more flexible solution to multicasting across diverse networks. PIM-DM is much like DVMRP in that routers initially (upon reception of the first multicast datagram) flood them out all ports except the one it was received on. PIM-DM then prunes links that do not have multicast members. However, the main difference between PIM-DM and DVMRP is that PIM-DM is not protocol-dependent and therefore does not require a specific routing protocol to facilitate its propagation of multicast floods and prunes.

Sparse Mode

Sparse mode operates on the assumption that multicast members are distributed geographically speaking. This does not imply that there are few members, but that these members are spread out in many different locations and bandwidth is a concern. Based on these assumption distribution trees are constructed through the network linking the source to all group members. Trees are rooted at the source system, with branches leading to receivers. There are two main sparse mode multicast protocols, CBT (Core Based Trees) and PIM-SM.

Note

Unlike dense mode, sparse mode multicast protocols are recipient-driven. Routers only participate in the construction of distribution trees when local or downstream hosts have actively joined a multicast group.

CBT

CBT uses a single shared tree to deliver multicast messages between members of multicast groups. This is a departure from the shortest path trees discussed in dense mode, where separate trees are constructed for every source-to-group communication. Everyone in the same multicast group uses the same tree regardless of where they are located or who transmits the multicast. With a single tree routers do not have to store and maintain multicast state information for every source-to-group tree built. This dramatically reduces the overhead involved with building and maintaining multicast tree information. One router within the shared tree serves as the role of "core" router. All other routers must send join messages to the core router or any router downstream of the core that is part of the tree to become a participant in the shared tree. Although shared trees are simple and easy to create (requiring less resources on routers to maintain state information for multiple trees) they cause all multicast traffic to pass through the core. This can seriously affect performance if there is heavy multicast traffic. In addition, a single shared tree does not take into consideration the shortest path between source and destination and therefore might also adversely effect communication, causing delays and even failures.

PIM-SM

PIM-SM routers construct shared multicast trees through a central point (router) of reference in the network, referred to as the *rendezvous point* or *RP*. The RP serves as the hub of all multicast forwarding. The term rendezvous implies a meeting place, and as such this meeting is between any sender and receiver(s). Unlike CBT, PIM-SM is not limited to a single shared tree. Any receiver may request the construction of a shared tree or separate shortest path tree.

Note

PIM-SM like PIM-DM is protocol-independent and can run on top of any routing protocol.

Summary

IP multicasts are datagrams sourced from a single host to a group of hosts. Hosts can belong to one or more logical groups for the purpose of receiving communication directed at members of the specific group. Only hosts belonging to the same group will fully process the datagram.

The IGMP protocol is used by end hosts and routers to facilitate the dynamic identification of multicast members and groups. There are three IGMP versions; 1, 2 and 3. The most common standard in use today is version 2.

IP multicasting involves at least one or more hosts, running applications that require multicast capabilities. For IP to support multicasting, extensions (RFC 1112) had to be added to the protocol. These extensions allow IP to support the reception and transmission of multicast datagrams and the IGMP protocol.

Multicast routing consists of protocols and algorithms that operate in tandem with regular IGP and EGP routing protocols. Multicast routing protocols rely on underlying routing protocols and their tables to perform path selection and achieve multicast forwarding between members. Multicast routing protocols can be either routing protocol–dependent or independent.

For multicast datagrams to be forwarded across routed networks, multicast routing protocols are required. These protocols fall into one of two categories, dense or sparse mode. Dense mode protocols flood multicasts assuming that there are members everywhere throughout the network and there is an abundant amount of bandwidth. DVMRP, MOSPF, and PIM-DM are dense mode multicast protocols. Sparse mode protocols assume that members are distributed and bandwidth is not plentiful. CBT and PIM-SM are examples of sparse mode multicast protocols.

Chapter Quiz

1. What Class D multicast IP address is recognized by all IGMP enabled ?

2. What protocol is used by hosts and routers to dynamically join and leave multicast groups?

3. What type of IGMP message do end systems send when they want to become members of a multicast group?

4. What is the purpose of MBone?

5. Which method of multicast routing assumes many members exist on subnets and bandwidth is not a problem?

6. Which method of multicast routing assumes members are distributed or decentralized and bandwidth is limited?

7. Which of the following multicast routing protocols are considered dense mode?

8. Which of the following multicast routing protocols are considered sparse mode?

9. Which of the following protocols implements a single shared multicast tree?

10. Which of the following protocols implements a rendezvous point?

APPENDIX A

RFCS

The following list of RFCs (Request For Comments) are organized by chapter and the topics discussed within. This list does not represent all RFCs in print. You may obtain a complete list of RFCs through the following:

- Text copy—Call the network Information Center at (800) 235-3155

- FTP download—The Internet (NIC) Network Information Center provides an FTP download of RFC 527. Access to this file requires a username and password. Use the name guest and anonymous as the password. The filename is rfc537.txt.

- E-mail—You may request any rfc be e-mailed to you by sending a request to service@nic.ddn.mil. Include the RFC and number requested in your subject line; also include the RFC and number within the body.

- Web—You may also simply browse the Web to search and retrieve this information on your own. There are many sites that host RFC documents throughout the Internet. You can simply type the keyword RFC or enter RFC followed by the RFC number you want ('RFC527'), which will narrow the search.

Chapter 1: Overview of Industry Model, Standards, and TCP/IP Protocols

RFC 196	Revision of the Mail Box Protocol
RFC 333	Proposed experiment with a Message Switching Protocol
RFC 458	Mail Retrieval via FTP
RFC 475	FTP and Network Mail System
RFC 498	On Mail Service to CCN
RFC 524	Thoughts on the Mail Protocol Proposed in RFC 524
RFC 539	Thoughts on the Mail Protocol Proposed in RFC 524
RFC 555	Responses to Critiques of the Proposed Mail Protocol
RFC 559	Standardized Network Mail Headers

RFC 574   Announcement of a Mail Facility at UCSB

RFC 577   Mail Priority

RFC 644   On the Problem of Signature Authentication for Network Mail

RFC 680   Message Transmission Protocol

RFC 706   On the Junk Mail Problem

RFC 718   Address Specification Syntax for Network Mail

RFC 724   Proposed Official Standard for the Format of ARPA Network Text Messages

RFC 726   Standard for the Format of ARPA Network Text Messages

RFC 743   MARS—A Message Archiving and Retrieval Service

RFC 751   Survey of FTP Mail and MLFL

RFC 752   Universal Host Table

RFC 756   NIC Name Server—A Datagram-based Information Utility

RFC 771   Mail Transition Plan

RFC 784   Mail Transfer Protocol: ISI TOPS20 Implementation

RFC 788   Simple Mail Transfer Protocol (SMTP)

RFC 799   Internet Name Domains

RFC 806   Proposed Federal Information Processing Standard: Specification for Message Format for Computer-based Message Systems

RFC 811   Hostname Server

RFC 818   Domain Naming Convention for Internet User Applications

RFC 821   Simple Mail Transfer Protocol (SMTP)

RFC 830   Distributed system for Internet Name Service

RFC 841   Specification for Message Format for the Computer-based Message System

RFC 854   Telnet Protocol Specification, 1983

RFC 881   Domain Names Plan and Schedule

RFC 884   Proposed Standard for Message Header Munging

RFC 897   Domain Name System Implementation Schedule—Revised

RFC 906   Bootstrap Loading Using TFTP

RFC 915   Network Mail Path Service

RFC 918   Post Office Protocol: POP Version 2

RFC 920   Domain Requirements

RFC 934   Proposed Standard for Message Encapsulation

RFC 937   Post Office Protocol: POP Version 2

RFC 953   Hostname Server

RFC 959   File Transfer Protocol, 1985

RFC 973   Domain System Changes and Observations

RFC 974   Mail Routing and the Domain System

RFC 984   PCMAIL: A Distributed Mail System for Personal Computers

RFC 987   Addendum to RFC 987: (Mapping between X.400 and RFC-822)

RFC 993   PCMAIL: A Distributed Mail System for Personal Computers

RFC 1001   Protocol Standard for a NetBIOS Service on a TCP/UDP Transport: Concepts and Methods. NetBIOS working Group. Defense Advanced Research Projects Agency, Internet Activities Board, end-to-end Services task force. Mar-01-1987. (Status: STANDARD)

RFC 1002   Protocol Standard for a NetBIOS Service on a TCP/UDP Transport: Detailed Specifications. NetBIOS working group. Defense Advanced Research Projects Agency, Internet Activities Board, end-to-end services task force. Mar-01-1987. (Status: STANDARD)

RFC 1009   Requirements for Internet Gateways. R. T. Braden, J. Postel. Jun-01-1987. (Status: HISTORIC)

RFC 1013   X-Windows System Protocol, 1987

RFC 1014   XDR: External Data Representation Standard. Sun Microsystems, Inc. Jun-01-1987. (Status: UNKNOWN)

RFC 1026   Addendum to RFC 987: (Mapping between X.400 and RFC-822). S. E. Kille. Sep-01-1987.

RFC 1031   MILNET Name Domain Transition. W. D. Lazear. Nov-01-1987. (Status: UNKNOWN)

RFC 1032   Domain Administrators Guide. M. K. Stahl. Nov-01-1987. (Status: UNKNOWN)

RFC 1033   Domain Administrators Operations Guide. M. Lottor. Nov-01-1987. (Status: UNKNOWN)

RFC 1035   Domain Names—Implementation and Specification, 1987

RFC 1047   Duplicate Messages and SMTP. C. Partridge. Feb-01-1998.

RFC 1049   Content-type Header Field for Internet Messages. M. A. Sirbu. Mar-01-1988.

RFC 1056   PCMAIL: A Distributed Mail System for Personal Computers. M. L. Lambert. Jun-01-1988.

RFC 1057   RPC: Remote Procedure Call Protocol Specification, 1998

RFC 1064   Interactive Mail Access Protocol: Version 2. M. R. Crispin. Jul-01-1988.

RFC 1067   Simple Network Management Protocol (SNMP). J. D. Case, M. Fedor, M. L. Schoffstall, J. Davin. Aug-01-1988. (Status: UNKNOWN)

RFC 1081   Post Office Protocol: Version 3. M. T. Rose. Nov-01-1988.

RFC 1082   Post Office Protocol: Version 3. Extended Service Offerings. M. T. Rose. Nov-01-1988.

RFC 1089   SNMP over Ethernet. M. L. Schoffstall, C. Davin, M. Fedor, J. D. Case. Feb-01-1989. (Status: UNKNOWN)

RFC 1090   SMTP on X.25. R. Ullmann. Feb-01-1989.

RFC 1091   Telnet Terminal-Type Option, 1989

RFC 1092   NFS: Network File System Protocol Specification. Sun Microsystems, Inc. Mar-01-1989. (Status: INFORMATIONAL)

RFC 1095   Common Management Information Services and Protocol over TCP/IP(CMOT). U. S. Warrier, L. Besaw. Apr-01-1989.

RFC 1098   Simple Network Management Protocol (SNMP). J. D. Case, M. Fedor, M. L. Schoffstall, C. Davin. Apr-01-1989. (Status: UNKNOWN)

RFC 1101   DNS Encoding of Network Names and Other Types. P. V. Mockapetris. Apr-01-1989. (Status: UNKNOWN)

RFC 1113   Privacy Enhancement for Internet Electronic Mail: Part I—Message Encipherment and Authentication Procedures J. Linn. Aug-01-1989

RFC 1114   Privacy Enhancement for Internet Electronic Mail: Part II—Certificate-based Key Management. S. T. Kent, J. Linn. Aug-01-1989.

RFC 1115   Privacy Enhancement for Internet Electronic Mail: Part III—Algorithms, Modes, and, Identifiers. J. Linn. Aug-01-1989.

RFC 1148   Mapping between X.400 (1988)/ISO 10021 and RFC 822. S. E. Kille

RFC 1153   Digest Message Format. F. J. Wancho. Apr-01-1990.

RFC 1161   SNMP over OSI. M. T. Rose. Jun-01-1990. (Status: EXPERIMENTAL)

RFC 1168   Intermail and Commercial Mail Relay Services. A. Westine, A. L. DeSchon, J. Postel, C. E. Ward. Jul-01-1990.

RFC 1176   Interactive Mail Access Protocol: Version 2. M. R. Crispin. Aug-01-1990.

RFC 1180   TCP/IP Tutorial. T. J. Socolofsky, C. J. Kale. Jan-01-1991.

RFC 1183   New DNS RR Definitions. C. F. Everhart, L. A. Mamakos, R. Ullmann, P. V. Mockapetris, Oct-01-1990. (Status: EXPERIMENTAL)

RFC 1184   Telnet Linemode Option, 1990

RFC 1187 Bulk Table Retrieval for the SNMP. M. T. Rose, K. McCloghrie, J. R. Davin. Oct-01-1990. (Status: EXPERIMENTAL)

RFC 1195 Use of OSI IS-IS for Fouting in TCP/IP and Dual Environments. R. W. Callon. Dec-01-1990. (Status: PROPOSED STANDARD)

RFC 1203 Interactive Mail Access Protocol: Version 3. J. Rice. Feb-01-1991.

RFC 1204 Message Posting Protocol (MPP). S. Yeh, D. Lee. Feb-01-1991.

RFC 1211 Problems with Maintenance of Large Mailing Lists. A. Westine, J. Postel. Mar-01-1991.

RFC 1212 Concise MIB Definitions. M. T. Rose, K. McCloghrie. Mar-01-1991. (Status: STANDARD)

RFC 1215 Convention for Defining Traps to Use with the SNMP. M. T. Rose. Mar-01-1991. (Status: INFORMATIONAL)

RFC 1225 Post Office Protocol: Version 3. M. T. Rose. May-01-1991.

RFC 1227 SNMP MUX Protocol and MIB. M. T. Rose. May-01-1991. (Status: HISTORIC)

RFC 1228 SNMP-DPI: Simple Network Management Protocol Distributed Program Interface Version 2.0. G. Carpenter, B. Wijnen. May-01-1991. (Status: EXPERIMENTAL)

RFC 1229 Extensions to the Generic-Interface MIB. K. McCloghrie. May-01-1991. (Status: PROPOSED STANDARD)

RFC 1239 Reassignment of Experimental MIBs to Standard MIBs. J. K. Reynolds. Jun-01-1991. (Status: PROPOSED STANDARD)

RFC 1270 SNMP Communication Services. F. Kastenholz. Oct-01-1991. (Status: INFORMATIONAL)

RFC 1283 SNMP over OSI. M. Rose. December 1991. (Status: EXPERIMENTAL)

RFC 1298 SNMP over IPX. R. Wormley, S. Bostock. February 1992. (Status: INFORMATIONAL)

RFC 1303 A Convention for Describing SNMP-based Agents. K. McCloghrie, M. Rose. February 1992. (Status: INFORMATIONAL)

RFC 1327 Mapping between X.400(1988)/ISO 10021 and RFC 822. S. Hardcatle-Kile. May 1992. (Status: PROPOSED STANDARD)

RFC 1339 Remote Mail Checking Protocol. S. Dorner, P. Resnick. June 1992. (Status: EXPERIMENTAL)

RFC 1341 Multipurpose Internet Mail Extensions (MIME)Part One: Format of Internet Message Bodies. N. Borenstein, N. Freed. June 1992. (Status: PROPOSED STANDARD)

RFC 1342 MIME (Multipurpose Internet Mail Extensions) Part Three: K. Moore. June 1992. (Status: INFORMATIONAL)

RFC 1343 A User Agent Configuration Mechanism for Multimedia Mail Format Information. N. Borenstein. June 1992. (Status: INFORMATIONAL)

RFC 1344 Implications of MIME for Internet Gateways. N. Borenstein. June 1992. (Status: INFORMATIONAL)

RFC 1348 DNS NSAP Resource Records. B. Manning. July 1992. (Status: EXPERIMENTAL)

RFC 1351 SNMP Administrative Model. J. Davin, J. Galvin, K. McCloghrie. July 1992. (Status: PROPOSED STANDARD)

RFC 1352 SNMP Security Protocols. J. Galvin, K. McClghrie, J. Davin. July 1992. (Status: PROPOSED STANDARD)

RFC 1353 Definitions of Managed Objects for Administration of SNMP Parties. K. McCloghrie, J. Davin, J. Galvin. July 1992. (Status: PROPOSED STANDARD)

RFC 1357A Format for E-mailing Bibliographic Records. D. Cohen. July 1992.(Status: INFORMATIONAL)

RFC 1369 Implementation Notes and Experience for the Internet Ethernet MIB. F. Kastenholz. October 1992. (Status: PROPOSED STANDARD)

RFC 1386 The US Domain. A. Cooper, J. Postel. December 1992. (Status: INFORMATIONAL)

RFC 1394 Relationship of Telex Answerback Codes to Internet Domains. P. Robinson. January 1993. (Status: INFORMATIONAL)

RFC 1405 Mapping between X.400 (1984/1988) and Mail-11 (DECnet mail). C. Allocchio. January 1993.(Status: EXPERIMENTAL)

RFC 1418 SNMP over OSI. M. Rose. March 1993. (Status: PROPOSED STANDARD)

RFC 1425 SMTP Service Extensions. J. Klensin, WG Chair, N. Freed, Editor, M. Rose, E. Stefferud & D. Crocker. February 1993. (Status: PROPOSED STANDARD)

RFC 1443 Textual Conventions for Version 2 of the Simple Network Management Protocol (SMIv2). J. Case, K. McCloghrie, M. Rose, & S. Waldbusser. April 1993. (Status: PROPOSED STANDARD)

RFC 1444 Conformance Statements for Version 2 of the Simple Network Management Protocol (SMIv2). J. Case, K. McCloghrie, M. Rose, & S. Waldbusser. April 1993. (Status: PROPOSED STANDARD)

RFC 1448 Protocol Operations for Version 2 of the Simple Network Management Protocol(SNMPv2). J. Case, K. McCloghrie, M. Rose, & S. Waldbusser. April 1993. (Status: PROPOSED STANDARD) DARD)

RFC 1452 Coexistence Between Version 1 and Version 2 of the Internet-standard Network Management Framework. J. Case, K. McCloghrie, M. Rose, & S. Waldbusser. April 1993. (Status: PROPOSED STANDARD)

RFC 1460 Post Office Protocol—Version 3. M. Rose. June 1993.

RFC 1464 Using the Domain Name System to Store Arbitrary String Attributes. R. Rosenbaum. May 1993. (Status: EXPERIMENTAL)

RFC 1477   The US Domain. A. Cooper & J. Postel. June 1993. (Status: INFORMATIONAL)

RFC 1494   Equivalences Between 1988 X.400 and RFC-822 Message Bodies. H. Alvestrand & S. Thompson. August 1993. (Status: PROPOSED STANDARD)

RFC 1495   Mapping Between X.400 and RFC-822 Message Bodies. H. Alvestrand, S. Kille, R. Miles, M. Rose & S. Thompson. August 1993. (Status: PROPOSED STANDARD)

RFC 1502   X.400 Use of Extended Character Sets. H. Alvestrand. August 1993. (Status: PROPOSED STANDARD)

RFC 1503   Algorithms for Automating Administration in SNMPv2 Managers. K. McCloghrie & M. Rose. August 1993. (Status: INFORMATIONAL)

RFC 1505   Encoding Header Message Field for Internet Messages. A. Costanzo, D. Robinson & R. Ullmann. August 1993. (Status: EXPERIMENTAL)

RFC 1519   Multipurpose Internet Mail Extensions (MIME) Part One: Mechanisms for Specifying and Describing the Format of Internet Message Bodies. N. Borenstein & N. Freed. September 1993. (Status: DRAFT STANDARD)

RFC 1522   MIME (Multipurpose Internet Mail Extensions) Part Two: Message Header Extensions for Non-ASCII Text. K. Moore. September 1993. (Status: DRAFT STANDARD)

RFC 1523   The Text/Enriched MIME Content-type. N. Borenstein. September 1993. (Status: INFORMATIONAL)

RFC 1535   A Security Problem and Proposed Correction with Widely Deployed DNS Software. E. Gavron. October 1993. (Status: INFORMATIONAL)

RFC 1544   The Content-MD5 Header Field. M. Rose. November 1993. (Status: PROPOSED STANDARD)

RFC 1556   Handling of Bi-directional Texts in MIME. H. Nussbacher & Y. Bourvine. December 1993. (Status: INFORMATIONAL)

RFC 1563   The Text/Enriched MIME Content-Type. N. Borenstein. January 1994. (Status: INFORMATIONAL)

RFC 1590   Media Type Registration Procedure. J. Postel. March 1994. (Status: INFORMATIONAL)

RFC 1591   Domain Name System Structure and Delegation. J. Postel. March 1994. (Status: INFORMATIONAL)

RFC 1615   Migrating Form X.400(84)to X.400(88). J. Houttuin & J. Craigie. May 1994. (Status: INFORMATIONAL)

RFC 1637   DNSAP Resource Records. B. Manning & R. Colella. June 1994. (Status: EXPERIMENTAL)

RFC 1641   Using Unicode with MIME. D. Goldsmith & M. Davis. July 1994. (Status: EXPERIMENTAL)

RFC 1642   UTF-7 A Mail-Safe Transformation Format of Unicode. D. Goldsmith & M. Davis. July 1994. (Status: EXPERIMENTAL)

RFC 1648   Postmaster Convention for X.400 Operations. A. Cargille. July 1994. (Status: PROPOSED STANDARD)

RFC 1651   SMTP Service Extensions. Klensin, N. Freed, M. Rose, E. Stefferud & D. Crocker. July 1994. (Status: DRAFT STANDARD)

RFC 1685   Writing X.400 O/R Names. H. Alvestrand. August 1994. (Status: INFORMATIONAL)

RFC 1706   DNS NSAP Resource Records. B. Manning & R. Colella. October 1994. (Status: INFORMATIONAL)

RFC 1711   Classifications in E-mail Routing. J. Houttuin. October 1994. (Status: INFORMATIONAL)

RFC 1712   DNS Encoding of Graphical Location. C. Farrell, M. Schulze, S. Pleitner & D. Baldoni. November 1994.

RFC 1725   Post Office Protocol—Version 3. J. Meyers & M. Rose. November 1994. (Status: DRAFT STANDARD)

RFC 1730   Internet Message Access Protocol—Version 4. M. Crispin. December 1994. (Status: PROPOSED STANDARD)

RFC 1740   MIME Encapsulation of Macintosh Files—MacMIME. P. Falstrom, D. Crocker & E. Fair. December 1994. (Status: PROPOSED STANDARD)

RFC 1767   MIME Encapsulation of EDI Objects. D. Crocker. March 1995. (Status: PROPOSED STANDARD)

RFC 1782   TFTP Option Extension. G. Malkin & A. Harkin. March 1995.

RFC 1785   TFTP Option Negotiation Analysis. G. Malkin & A. Harkin. March 1995. (Status: INFORMATIONAL)

RFC 1793   DNS Support for Load Balancing. T. Brisco. April 1995. (Status: INFORMATIONAL)

RFC 1806   Communicating Presentation Information in Internet Messages: The Content-Disposition Header. R. Troost, s. Dorner. June 1995.

RFC 1813   NFS Version 3 Protocol Specification. B. Callaghan, B. Pawlowski & P. Staubach. June 1995. (Status: INFORMATIONAL)

RFC 1820   Multimedia E-mail (MIME) User Agent Checklist. E. Huizer. August 1995. (Status: INFORMATIONAL)

RFC 1830   SMTP Service Extensions for Transmission of Large and Binary MIME Messages. G. Vaudreuil. August 1995. (Status: EXPERIMENTAL)

RFC 1838   Use of an X.500/LDAP Directory to Support Mapping Between X.400 and RFC 822 Addresses. S. Kille. August 1995. (Status: EXPERIMENTAL)

RFC 1844 Multimedia E-mail (MIME) User Agent Checklist. E. Huizer. August 1995. (Status: INFORMATIONAL)

RFC 1854   SMTP Service Extension for Command Pipelining. N. Freed. October 1995. (Status: PROPOSED STANDARD)

RFC 1856   The Opstat Client-Server Model for Statistical Retrieval. H. Clark. October 1995. (Status: INFORMATIONAL)

RFC 1864   The Content-MD5 Header Field. J. Myers & M. Rose. October 1995. RFC 1869 SMTP Service Extensions. J. Klensin, N. Freed, M. Rose, E. Stefferud & D. Crocker. November 1995. (Status: STANDARD)

RFC 1872   The MIME Multipart/Related Content-Type. E. Levinson. December 1995. (Status: EXPERIMENTAL)

RFC 1876   A Means for Expressing Location Information in the Domain Name System. C. Davis, P. Vixie, T. Goodwin & I. Dickinson. January 1996. (Status: EXPERIMENTAL)

RFC 1891   SMTP Service Extension for Delivery Status Notifications. K. Moore. January 1996. (Status: PROPOSED STANDARD)

RFC 1901   Introduction for Community-based SNMPv2. SNMPv2 Working Group, J. Case, K. McCloghrie, M. Rose, & S. Waldbusser. January 1996.(Status: EXPERIMENTAL)

RFC 1908   Coexistence Between Version 1 and Version 2 of the Internet-Standard Network Management Framework. SNMPv2 Working Group, J. Case, K. McCloghrie, M. Rose, & S. Waldbusser. January 1996. (Status: DRAFT STANDARD)

RFC 1912   Common DNS Operational and Configuration Errors. D. Barr. February 1996. (Status: INFORMATIONAL)

RFC 1945   Hypertext Transfer Protocol—HTTP/1.0. T. Berners-Lee, r. Fielding & H. Frystuk. May 1996. (Status: INFORMATIONAL)

RFC 1957   Some Observations on Implementations of the Post Office Protocol (POP3). R. Nelson. June 1996. (Status: INFORMATIONAL)

RFC 1982   Serial Number Arithmatic. R. Elz & R. Bush. August 1996. (Status: PROPOSED STANDARD)

RFC 1985   SMTP Service Extension for Remote Message Queue Starting. J. De Winter. August 1996. (Status: PROPOSED STANDARD)

RFC 1995   Incremental Zone Transfer in DNS. M. Ohta. August 1996. (Status: PROPOSED STANDARD)

RFC 2015   MIME Security with Pretty Good Privacy (PGP). M. Elkins. October 1996. (Status: PROPOSED STANDARD)

RFC 2033   Local Mail Transfer Protocol. J. Myers. October 1996. (Status: INFORMATIONAL)

RFC 2039   Applicability for Standards Track MIBs to Management of World Wide Web Servers. C. Kalbfleisch. November 1996. (Status: INFORMATIONAL)

RFC 2045   Multipurpose Internet Mail Extensions (MIME) Part One: Format of Internet Message Bodies. N. Freed & N. Borenstein. November 1996. (Status: DRAFT STANDARD)

RFC 2052   A DNS RR for Specifying the Location of Services (DNS SRV). A. Gulbrandensen, P. Vixie. October 1996. (Status: EXPERIMENTAL)

RFC 2054   WebNFS Client Specification. B. Callaghan. October 1996. (Status: INFORMATIONAL)

RFC 2060   Internet Message Access Protocol—Version 4rev1. M. Crispin. December 1996. (Status: PROPOSED STANDARD)

RFC 2065   Domain Name System Security Extensions. D. Eastlake, 3rd, C. Kaufman. January 1997. (Status: PROPOSED STANDARD)

RFC 2068   Hypertext Transfer Protocol—HTTP/1.1 R. Fielding, J. Gettys, J. Mogul, H. Frystyk, T. Berners-Lee. January 1997. (Status: PROPOSED STANDARD)

RFC 2069   HTTP Authentication: Basic and Digest Access Authentication. J. Franks, P. Hallam-Baker, J. Hostetler, P. Leach, A. Luotonen, E. Sink, L. Stewart. January 1997. (Status: PROPOSED STANDARD)

RFC 2076   Common Internet Message Headers. J. Palme. February 1997. (Status: INFORMATIONAL)

RFC 2090   TFTP Multicast Option. A. Emberson. February 1997. (Status: EXPERIMENTAL)

RFC 2107   Ascend Tunnel Management Protocol—ATMP. K. Hamzeh. February 1997. (Status: INFORMATIONAL)

RFC 2109   HTTP State Management Mechanism. D. Kristol, L. Montulli. February 1997. (Status: PROPOSED STANDARD)

RFC 2110   MIME Encapsulation of Aggregate Documents, such as HTML (MHTML). J. Palme, A. Hopmann. March 1997. (Status: PROPOSED STANDARD)

RFC 2112   The MIME Multipart/Related Content-Type. E. Levinson. February 1997. (Status: PROPOSED STANDARD)

RFC 2136   Dynamic Updates in the Domain Name System (DNS Update). P. Vixie, Ed., S. Thomson, Y. Rekhter, J. Bound. April 1997. (Status: PROPOSED STANDARD)

RFC 2142   Mailbox Names for Common Services, Roles, and Functions. D. Crocker. May 1997. (Status: PROPOSED STANDARD)

RFC 2145   Use and Interpretation of HTTP Version Numbers. J. C. Mogul, R. Fielding, J. Gettys, H. Frystuk. May 1997. (Status: INFORMATIONAL)

RFC 2152   UTF-7 A Mail-Safe Transformation Format of Unicode. D. Goldsmith, M. Davis. May 1997. (Status: INFORMATIONAL)

RFC 2156   MIXER (Mime Internet X.400 Enhanced Relay): Mapping Between X.400 and RFC 822/MIME. S. Kille. January 1998. (Status: PROPOSED STANDARDS)

RFC 2160   Carrying PostScript in X.400 and MIME. H. Alvestrand. January 1998. (Status: PROPOSED STANDARD)

RFC 2169   A Trivial Convention for using HTTP in URN Resolution. R. Daniel. June 1997. (Status: EXPERIMENTAL)

RFC 2177   IMAP4 IDLE command. B. Leiba. June 1997. (Status: PROPOSED STANDARD)

RFC 2180 IMAP4 Multi-Accessed Mailbox Practice. M. Gahrns. July 1997. (Status: INFORMATIONAL)

RFC 2181   Clarification of DNS Specification. R. Elz, R. Bush. July 1997. (Status: PROPOSED STANDARD)

RFC 2184   MIME Parameter Value and Encoded Word Extensions: Character Sets, Languages, and Continuations. N. Freed, K. Moore. August 1997. (Status: PROPOSED STANDARD)

RFC 2192   IMAP URL Scheme. C. Newman. September 1997. (Status: PROPOSED STANDARD)

RFC 2195   IMAP/POP Authorize Extension for Simple Challenge/Response. J. Klensin, R. Catoe, P. Krumviede. September 1997. (Status: PROPOSED STANDARD)

RFC 2197   SMTP Service Extension for Command Pipelining. N. Freed. September 1997. (Status: DRAFT STANDARD)

RFC 2220   The Application/MARC Content-Type. R. Guenther. October 1997. (Status: INFORMATIONAL)

RFC 2227   Simple Hit-Metering and Usage-Limiting for HTTP. J. Mogul, P. Leach. October 1997. (Status: PROPOSED STANDARD)

RFC 2230 Key Exchange Delegation Record for the DNS. R. Atkinson. October 1997. (Status: INFORMATIONAL)

RFC 2231   MIME Parameter Value and Encoded Word Extensions: Character Sets, Languages, and Continuations. N. Freed, K. Moore. November 1997. (Status: PROPOSED STANDARD)

RFC 2240   A Legal Basis for Domain Name Allocation. O. Vaughan. November 1997. (Status: INFORMATIONAL)

RFC 2257   Agent Extensibility (AgentX) Protocol Version 1. M. Daniele, B. Wijnen, D. Francisco. January 1998. (Status: PROPOSED STANDARD)

RFC 2261   An Architecture for Describing SNMP Management Frameworks. D. Harrington, R. Presuhn, B. Wijnen. January 1998. (Status: PROPOSED STANDARD)

RFC 2262   Message Processing and Dispatching for the Simple Network Management Protocol (SNMP). J. Case, D. Harrington, R. Presuhn, B. Wijnen. January 1998. (Status: PROPOSED STANDARD)

RFC 2263   SNMP Applications. D. Levi, P. Meyer, B. Stewart. January 1998. (Status: PROPOSED STANDARD)

RFC 2264   User-based Security Model (USM) for Version 3 of the Simple Network Management Protocol (SNMPv3). U. Blumenthal, B. Wijnen, January 1998. (Status: PROPOSED STANDARD)

RFC 2271 An Architecture for Describing SNMP Management Frameworks. D. Harrington, R. Preesuhn, B. Wijnen. January 1998. (Status: PROPOSED STANDARD)

RFC 2272 Message Processing and Dispatching for the Simple Network Management Protocol (SNMP). J. Case, D. Harrington, R. Preesuhn, B. Wijnen. January 1998. (Status: PROPOSED STANDARD)

RFC 2273 SNMPv3 Applications. D. Levi, P. Meyer, B. Stewart. January 1998. (Status: PROPOSED STANDARD)

RFC 2274 User-Based Security Model (USM) for Version 3 of the Simple Network Management Protocol (SNMPv3). U. Blumenthal, B. Wijnen. January 1998. (Status: PROPOSED STANDARD)

RFC 2275 View-Based Access Control Model (VACM) for the Simple Network Management Protocol(SNMP). B. Wijnen, R. Presuhn, K. McCloghrie. January 1998. (Status: PROPOSED STANDARD)

RFC 2295 Transparent Content Negotiation in HTTP. K. Holtman, A. Mutz. March 1998. (Status: EXPERIMENTAL)

RFC 2298 An Extensible Message Format for Message Disposition Notifications. R. Fajman. March 1998. (Status: PROPOSED STANDARD)

RFC 2302 Tag Image File Format (TIFF)—Image/Tiff MIME Subtype Registration. G. Parsons, J. Rafferty, S. Zilles. March 1998. (Status: PROPOSED STANDARD)

RFC 2308 Negative Caching of DNS Queries (DNS NCACHE). M. Andrews. March 1998. (Status: PROPOSED STANDARD)

RFC 2311 S/MIME Version 2 Message Specification. S. Dusse, P. Hoffman, B. Ramsdell, L. Lundblade, L. Repka. March 1998. (Status: INFORMATIONAL)

RFC 2317 Classless IN-ADDR.ARPA Delegation. H. Eidnes, G. de Groot, P. Vixie. March 1998. (Status: BEST CURRENT PRACTICE)

RFC 2318 The Text/css Media Type. H. Lie, B. Bos, C. Lilley. March 1998. (Status: INFORMATIONAL)

RFC 2342 IMAP4 Namespace. M. Gahrns, C. Newman. May 1998. (Status: PROPOSED STANDARD)

RFC 2347 TFTP Option Extension. G. Malkin, A. Harkin. May 1998. (Status: DRAFT STANDARD)

RFC 2348 Advancement of MIB Specifications on the IETF Standards Track. M. O'Dell, H. Alvestrand, B. Wijens, S. Bradner. October 1998. (Status: BEST CURRENT PRACTICE)

RFC 2359 IMAP4 UIDPLUS Extension. J. Myers. June 1998. (Status: PROPOSED STANDARD)

RFC 2384 POP URL Scheme. R. Gellens. August 1998. (Status: PROPOSED STANDARD)

RFC 2387 The MIME Multipart/Related Content-Type. E. Levinson. August 1998. (Status: PROPOSED STANDARD)

RFC 2424 Content Duration MIME Header Definition. G. Vaudreuil, G. Parsons. September 1998. (Status: PROPOSED STANDARD)

RFC 2425 A MIME Content—Type for Directory Information. T. Howes, M. Smith, F. Dawson. September 1998. (Status: PROPOSED STANDARD)

RFC 2426 vCard MIME Directory Profile. F. Dawson, T. Howes. September 1998. (Status: PROPOSED STANDARD)

RFC 2442 The Batch SMTP Media Type. N. Freed, D. Newman, H. Belissen, M. Hoy. November 1998. (Status: INFORMATIONAL)

RFC 2449 POP3 Extension Mechanism. R. Gellens, C. Newman, L. Lundblade. November 1998. (Status: PROPOSED STANDARD)

RFC 2476 Message Submission. R. Gellens, H. Klensin. December 1998. (Status: PROPOSED STANDARD)

RFC 2480 Gateways and MIME Security Multiparts. N. Freed. January 1999. (Status: PROPOSED STANDARD)

RFC 2487 SMTP Service Extension for Secure SMTP over TLS. P. Hoffman. January 1999. (Status: PROPOSED STANDARD)

RFC 2493 Textual Conventions for MIB Modules Using Performance History Based on 15 Minute Intervals. K. Tesink, Ed. January 1999. (Status: PROPOSED STANDARD)

RFC 2503 MIME Types for Use with the ISO ILL Protocol. R. Moulton, M. Needleman. February 1999. (Status: INFORMATIONAL)

RFC 2505 Anti-Spam Recommendations for SMTP MTAs. G. Lindberg. February 1999. (Status: BEST CURRENT PRACTICES)

RFC 2517 Building Directories from DNS: Experiences from WWWSeeker. R. Moats, R. Huber. February 1999. (Status: INFORMATIONAL)

RFC 2518 HTTP Extensions for Distributed Authoring-WEBDAV. Y. Goland, E. Whitehead, A. Faizi, S. Carter, D. Jensen. February 1999. (Status: PROPOSED STANDARD)

RFC 2524 Neda's Efficient Mail Submission and Delivery (EMSD) Protocol Specification Version 1.3. M. Banan. February 1999. (Status: INFORMATIONAL)

RFC 2535 Domain Name System Security Extensions. D. Eastlake. March 1999. (Status: PROPOSED STANDARD)

RFC 2539 Storage of Diffie-Hellman Keys in the Domain Name System (DNS). D. Eastlake. March 1999. (Status: PROPOSED STANDARD)

RFC 2554 SMTP Service Extension for Authentication. J. Meyers. March 1999. (Status: PROPOSED STANDARD)

RFC 2557   MIME Encapsulation of Aggregate Documents, such as HTML (MHTML). J. Palme, A. Hopmann, N. Shelness. March 1999. (Status: PROPOSED STANDARD)

RFC 2570   Introduction to Version 3 of the Internet-standard Network Management Framework. J. Case, R. Mundy, D. Partain, B. Stewart. April 1999. (Status: INFORMATIONAL)

RFC 2578   Structure of Management Information Version 2 (SMIv2). K. McCloghrie, D. Perkins, J. Schoenwaelder. April 1999. (Status: STANDARD)

RFC 2586   The Audio/L16 MIME

RFC 2593   Script MIB Extensibility Protocol Version 1.0

RFC 2595   Using TLS with IMAP, POP3, and ACAP

RFC 2606   Reserved Top Level DNS Names

RFC 2623   NFS Version 2 and Version 3 Security Issues and the NFS Protocol's Use of RPCSEC_GSS and Kerberos V5

RFC 2632   S/MIME Version 3 Certificate Handling

RFC 2645   On-Demand Mail Relay (ODMR) SMTP with Ddynamic IP Addresses

RFC 2646   The Text/Plain Format Parameter

RFC 2660   The Secure HyperText Transfer Protocol

RFC 2671   Extension Mechanisms for DNS (EDNSO)

RFC 2683   IMAP4 Implementation Recommendations

RFC 21095 IMAP/POP Authorize Extension for Simple Challenge/Response. J. Klensin, R. Catoe, P. Krumviede. January 1997. (Status: PROPOSED STANDARD)

Chapter 2: IP and IP Addressing

RFC 777   Internet Control Message Protocol

RFC 781   Specification of the Internet Protocol (IP) Timestamp Option

RFC 791   Internet Protocol

RFC 792   Internet Control Message Protocol

RFC 815   IP Datagram Reassembly Algorithms

RFC 826   Ethernet Address Resolution Protocol: Or Converting Network Protocol Addresses to 48.bit Ethernet Address for Transmission on Ethernet Hardware

RFC 903   Reverse Address Resolution Protocol

RFC 925   Multi-LAN Address Resolution

RFC 1011   Official Internet Protocols. J. K. Reynolds, J. Postel. Jun-01-1987. (Status: INFORMATIONAL)

RFC 1016   Something a Host Could Do with Source Quench. The Source Quench Introduced Delay (SquID). W. Prue, J. Postel. Jul-01-1987. (Status: UNKNOWN)

RFC 1018   Some Comments on SquID. A. M. McKenzie. Aug-01-1987. (Status: UNKNOWN)

RFC 1025   TCP and IP Bake Off. J. Postel. Sep-01-1987. (Status: UNKNOWN)

RFC 1027   Using ARP to Implement Transparent Subnet Gateways. S. Carl-Mitchell, J. S. Quarterman. Oct-01-1987. (Status: HISTORIC)

RFC 1029   More Fault Tolerant Approach to Address Resolution for a Multi-LAN System of Ethernets. G. Parr. May-01-1988. (Status: UNKNOWN)

RFC 1055   Nonstandard for Transmission of IP Datagrams over Serial Lines: SLIP. J. L. Romkey. Jun-01-1988. (Status: STANDARD)

RFC 1063   Path MTU Discovery Options. J. C. Mogul, C. A. Kent, C. Partridge, K. McCloghrie. Jul-01-1988.(Status: UNKNOWN)

RFC 1071   Computing the Internet Checksum. R. T. Braden, D. A. Borman, C. Partridge. Sep-01-1988.(Status: UNKNOWN)

RFC 1077   Critical Issues in High Bandwidth Networking. B. M. Leiner. Nov-01-1988. (Status: UNKNOWN)

RFC 1107   Plan for Internet Directory Services. K. R. Sollins. Jul-01-1989. (Status: INFORMATIONAL)

RFC 1112   Host Extensions for IP Multicasting. S. E. Deering. Aug-01-1989. (Status: STANDARD)

RFC 1141   Computation of the Internet Checksum via Incremental Update. T. Mallory, A. Kullberg. Jan-01-1990. (Status: INFORMATIONAL)

RFC 1188   Proposed Standard for the Transmission of IP Datagrams over FDDI Networks. D. Katz. Oct-01-1990.(Status: DRAFT STANDARD)

RFC 1191   Path MTU Discovery. J. C. Mogul, S. E. Deering. Nov-01-1990. (Status: DRAFT STANDARD)

RFC 1208   Glossary of Networking Terms. O. J. Jacobsen, D. C. Lynch. Mar-01-1991. (Status: INFORMATIONAL)

RFC 1219   On the Assignment of Subnet Numbers. P. F. Tsuchiya. Apr-01-1991. (Status: INFORMATIONAL)

RFC 1256   ICMP Router Discovery Messages. S. Deering. Sep-01-1991. (Status: PROPOSED STANDARD)

RFC 1293   Inverse Address Resolution Protocol. T. Bradley, C. Brown. January 1992. (Status: PROPOSED STANDARD)

RFC 1329   Thoughts on Address Resolution for Dual MAC FDDI Networks. P. Kuehn. May 1992. (Status: INFORMATIONAL)

RFC 1413   Identification Protocol. M. St. Johns. January 1993. (Status: PROPOSED STANDARD)

RFC 1433   Directed ARP. J. Garrett, J. Hagen & J. Wong. March 1993. (Status: EXPERIMENTAL)

RFC 1624   Computation of the Internet Checksum via Incremental Update. A. Rijsinghani, Editor. May 1994. (Status: INFORMATIONAL)

RFC 1788   ICMP Domain Name Messages. W. Simpson. April 1995. (Status: EXPERIMENTAL)

RFC 1868   ARP Extension-UNARP. G. Malkin. November 1995. (Status: EXPERIMENTAL)

RFC 1931   Dynamic RARP Extensions for Automatic Network Address Acquisition. D. Brownell. April 1996. (Status: PROPOSED STANDARD)

RFC 2002   IP Mobility Support. C. Perkins. October 1996. (Status: PROPOSED STANDARD)

RFC 2005   Applicability Statement for IP Mobility Support. J. Solomon. October 1996. (Status: PROPOSED STANDARD)

RFC 2041   Mobile Network Tracing. B. Noble, G. Nguyen, M. Satyanarayanan, R. Katz. December 1996. (Status: INFORMATIONAL)

RFC 2290   Mobile-IPv4 Configuration Option for PPP IPCP. J. Solomon, S. Glass. February 1998. (Status: PROPOSED STANDARD)

RFC 2390   Inverse Address Resolution Protocol. T. Bradley, C. Brown, A. Malis. August 1998. (Status: PROPOSED STANDARD)

RFC 2477   Criteria for Evaluating Roaming Protocols. B. Aboba, G. Zorn. December 1998. (Status: INFORMATIONAL)

RFC 2486   The Network Access Identifier. B. Aboba, M. Beadles. January 1999. (Status: PROPOSED STANDARD)

RFC 2501   Mobile Ad Hoc Networking (MANET): Routing Protocol Performance Issues and Evaluation Considerations. S. Corson, J. Macker. January 1999. (Status: INFORMATIONAL)

Chapter 3: IP Routing

RFC 777   Internet Control Message Protocol

RFC 781   Specification of the Internet Protocol (IP) timestamp option

RFC 791   Internet Protocol

RFC 792   Internet Control Message Protocol

RFC 815   IP Datagram Reassembly Algorithms

RFC 917   Toward an Internet Standard Scheme for Subnetting

RFC 932   Toward an Internet Standard Scheme for Subnetting

RFC 936   Toward an Internet Standard Scheme for Subnetting

RFC 940   Toward an Internet Standard Scheme for Subnetting

RFC 950   Internet Standard Subnetting Procedure

RFC 1011   Official Internet Protocols. J. K. Reynolds, J. Postel. Jun-01-1987. (Status: INFORMATIONAL)

RFC 1016   Something a Host Could Do with Source Quench. The Source Quench Introduced Delay (SquID). W. Prue, J. Postel. Jul-01-1987. (Status: UNKNOWN)

RFC 1018   Some Comments on SquID. A. M. McKenzie. Aug-01-1987. (Status: UNKNOWN)

RFC 1025   TCP and IP bake off. J. Postel. Sep-01-1987. (Status: UNKNOWN)

RFC 1027   Using ARP to Implement Transparent Subnet Gateways. S. Carl-Mitchell, J. S. Quarterman. Oct-01-1987. (Status: HISTORIC)

RFC 1029   More Fault Tolerant Approach to Address Resolution for a Multi-LAN system of Ethernets. G. Parr. May-01-1988. (Status: UNKNOWN)

RFC 1051   Standard for the Transmission of IP Datagrams and ARP Packets over ARCNET Networks. P. A. Prindville. Mar-01-1988. (Status: UNKNOWN)

RFC 1055   Nonstandard for Transmission of IP Datagrams over Serial Lines: SLIP. J. L. Romkey. Jun-01-1988. (Status: STANDARD)

RFC 1063   Path MTU Discovery Options. J. C. Mogul, C. A. Kent, C. Partridge, K. McCloghrie. Jul-01-1988. (Status: UNKNOWN)

RFC 1071   Computing the Internet Checksum. R. T. Braden, D. A. Borman, C. Partridge. Sep-01-1988. (Status: UNKNOWN)

RFC 1077   Critical Issues in High Bandwidth Networking. B. M. Leiner. Nov-01-1988. (Status: UNKNOWN)

RFC 1112   Host Extensions for IP Multicasting. S. E. Deering. Aug-01-1989. (Status: STANDARD)

RFC 1141   Computation of the Internet Checksum via Incremental Update. T. Mallory, A. Kullberg. Jan-01-1990. (Status: INFORMATIONAL)

RFC 1042   Standard for Transmission of IP Datagrams over IEEE 802 Networks. J. Postel, J. K. Reynolds. Feb-01-1988. (Status: STANDARD)

RFC 1136   Administrative Domains and Routing Domains: A Model for Routing in the Internet. S. Hares, D. Katz. Dec-01-1989. (Status: INFORMATIONAL)

RFC 1188   Proposed Standard for the Transmission of IP Datagrams over FDDI Networks. D. Katz. Oct-01-1990. (Status: DRAFT STANDARD)

RFC 1191   Path MTU Discovery. J. C. Mogul, S. E. Deering. Nov-01-1990. (Status: DRAFT STANDARD)

RFC 1208   Glossary of Networking Terms. O. J. Jacobsen, D. C. Lynch. Mar-01-1991. (Status: INFORMATIONAL)

RFC 1219   On the assignment of subnet numbers. P. F. Tsuchiaya. Apr-01-1991. (Status: INFORMATIONAL)

RFC 1234   Tunneling IPX Traffic Through IP Networks. D. Provan. Jun-01-1991. (Status: PROPOSED STANDARD)

RFC 1256   ICMP Router Discovery Messages. S. Deering. Sep-01-1991. (Status: PROPOSED STANDARD)

RFC 1335   A Two-Tier Address Structure for the Internet: A Solution to the Problem of Address Space Exhaustion. Z. Wang, J. Crowcroft. May 1992. (Status: INFORMATIONAL)

RFC 1347   TCP and UDP with Bigger Addresses (TUBA), a Simple Proposal for Internet Addressing and Routing. R. Callon. June 1992. (Status: INFORMATIONAL)

RFC 1365   An IP Address Extension Proposal. K. Siyan. September 1992. (Status: INFORMATIONAL)

RFC 1366   Guidelines for Management of IP Address Space. E. Gerich. October 1992. (Status: INFORMATIONAL)

RFC 1375   Suggestion for New Classes of IP Addresses. P. Robinson. October 1992. (Status: INFORMATIONAL)

RFC 1385   EIP: The Extended Internet Protocol. Z. Wang. November 1992. (Status: INFORMATIONAL)

RFC 1413   Identification Protocol. M. St. Johns. January 1993. (Status: PROPOSED STANDARD)

RFC 1433   Directed ARP. J. Garrett, J. Hagen & J. Wong. March 1993. (Status: EXPERIMENTAL)

RFC 1454   Comparison of Proposals for the Next Version of IP. T. Dixon. May 1993. (Status: INFORMATIONAL)

RFC 1466   Guidelines for Management of IP Address Space. E. Gerich. May 1993. (Status: INFORMATIONAL)

RFC 1475   TP/IX: The Next Internet. R. Ullmann. June 1993. (Status: EXPERIMENTAL)

RFC 1526   Assignment of System Identifiers for TUBA/CLNP Hosts. D. Piscitello. September 1993. (Status: INFORMATIONAL)

RFC 1550   IP: Next Generation (IPng) White Paper Solicitation. S. Bradner & A. Mankin. December 1993. (Status: INFORMATIONAL)

RFC 1597   Address Allocation for Private Internets. Y. Rekhter, B. Moskowitz, D. Karrenberg & G. de Groot. March 1994. (Status: INFORMATIONAL)

RFC 1624   Computation of the Internet Checksum via Incremental Update. A. Rijsinghani, Editor. May 1994. (Status: INFORMATIONAL)

RFC 1627   Network 10 Considered Harmful (Some Practices Shouldn't Be Codified). E. Lear, E. Fair, D. Crocker & T. Kessler. June 1994. (Status: INFORMATIONAL)

RFC 1705   Six Virtual Inches to the Left: The Problem with IPng. R. Carlson & D. Ficarella. October 1994. (Status: INFORMATIONAL)

RFC 1707   CATNIP: Common Architecture for the Internet. M. McGovern & R. Ullmann. October 1994. (Status: INFORMATIONAL)

RFC 1710   Simple Internet Protocol Plus White Paper. R. Hinden. October 1994. (Status: INFORMATIONAL)

RFC 1715   The H Ratio for Addresses per Host. C. Huitema. November 1994. (Status: INFORMATIONAL)

RFC 1719   A Direction for IPng. P. Gross. December 1994. (Status: INFORMATIONAL)

RFC 1726   Technical Criteria for Choosing IP the Next Generation (IPng). C. Partridge & F. Kasten hoz. December 1994. (Status: INFORMATIONAL)

RFC 1744   Observations on the Management of the Internet Address Space. G. Huston. December 1994. (Status: PROPOSED STANDARD)

RFC 1752   The Recommendation for the IP Next Generation Protocol. S. Bradner & A. Mankin. January 1995. (Status: PROPOSED STANDARD)

RFC 1753   IPng Technical Requirements Of the Nimrod Routing and Addressing Architecture. N. Chiappa. December 1994. (Status: INFORMATIONAL)

RFC 1788   ICMP Domain Name Messages. W. Simpson. April 1995. (Status: EXPERIMENTAL)

RFC 1797   Class A Subnet Experiment. Internet Assigned Numbers Authority (IANA). April 1995. (Status: EXPERIMENTAL)

RFC 1809   Using the Flow Label Field in IPv6. C. Partridge. June 1995. (Status: INFORMATIONAL)

RFC 1814   Unique Addresses are Good. E. Gerich. June 1995. (Status: INFORMATIONAL)

RFC 1878   Variable Length Subnet Table for IPv4. T. Pummill & B. Manning. December 1995. (Status: INFORMATIONAL)

RFC 1881   IPv6 Address Allocation Management. IAB&IESG. December 1995. (Status: INFORMATIONAL)

RFC 1883   Internet Protocol, Version 6 (IPv6) Specification. S. Deering & R. Hinden. December 1995. (Status: PROPOSED STANDARD)

RFC 1897   IPv6 Testing Address Allocation. R. Hinden, J. Postel. January 1997. (Status: EXPERIMENTAL)

RFC 1900 Renumbering Needs Work. B. Carpenter & Y. Rekhter. February 1996. (Status: INFORMATIONAL)

RFC 1916 Enterprise Renumbering: Experience and Information Solicitations. H. Berkowitz, P. Ferguson, W. Leland & P. Nesser. February 1996. (Status: INFORMATIONAL)

RFC 1918 Address Allocation for Private Internets. Y. Rekhter, B. Moskowitz, D. Karrenberg, G. J. de Groot & E. Lear. February 1996. (Status: BEST CURRENT PRACTICES

RFC 1933 Transition Mechanism for IPv6 Hosts and Routers. R. Gilligan & E. Nordmark. April 1996. (Status: PROPOSED STANDARD)

RFC 1955 New Scheme for Internet Routing and Addressing (ENCAPS) for IPNG. R. Hinden. June 1996. (Status: INFORMATIONAL)

RFC 1970 Neighbor Discovery for IP Version 6(IPv6). T. Narten, E. Nordmark, W. Simpson. August 1996. (Status: PROPOSED STANDARD)

RFC 1981 Path MTU Discovery for IP version 6. J. McCann, S. Deering & J. Mogul. August 1996. (Status: PROPOSED STANDARD)

RFC 2002 IP Mobility Support. C. Perkins. October 1996. (Status: PROPOSED STANDARD)

RFC 2005 Applicability Statement for IP Mobility Support. J. Solomon. October 1996. (Status: PROPOSED STANDARD)

RFC 2008 Implications of Various Address Allocation Policies for Internet Routing. Y. Rekhter, T. Li. October 1996. (Status: BEST CURRENT PRACTICES)

RFC 2019 Transmission of IPv6 Packets over FDDI Networks. M. Crawford. October 1996. (Status: PROPOSED STANDARD)

RFC 2023 IP Version 6 over PPP. D. Haskin, E. Allen. October 1996. (Status: PROPOSED STANDARD)

RFC 2036 Observations on the Use of Components of the Class A Address Space within the Internet. G. Huston. October 1996. (Status: INFORMATIONAL)

RFC 2041 Mobile Network Tracing. B. Noble, G. Nguyen, M. Satyanarayanan, R. Katz. December 1996. (Status: INFORMATIONAL)

RFC 2080 RIPng for IPv6. G. Malkin, R. Minnear. January 1997. (Status: PROPOSED STANDARD)

RFC 2081 RIPng Protocol Applicability Statement. G. Malkin. January 1997. (Status: INFORMATIONAL)

RFC 2101 IPv4 Address Behavior Today. B. Carpenter, J. Crowcroft, Y. Rekhter. February 1997. (Status: INFORMATIONAL)

RFC 2113 IP Router Alert Option. D. Katz. February 1997. (Status: PROPOSED STANDARD)

RFC 2133 Basic Socket Interface Extensions for IPv6. R. Gilligan, S. Thomson, J. Bound, W. Stevens. April 1997. (Status: INFORMATIONAL)

RFC 2147   TCP and UDP over IPv6 Jumbograms. D. Borman. May 1997. (Status: PROPOSED STANDARD)

RFC 2185   Routing Aspects of IPv6 Transition. R. Callon, D. Haskin. September 1997. (Status: INFORMATIONAL)

RFC 2194   Review of Roaming Implementations. B. Aboba, J. Lu, J. Ding. W. Wang. September 1997.(Status: INFORMATIONAL)

RFC 2290   Mobile-IPv4 Configuration Option for PPP IPCP. J. Solomon, S. Glass. February 1998. (Status: PROPOSED STANDARD)

RFC 2292   Advanced Sockets API for IPv6. W. Stevens, M. Thomas. February 1998. (Status: INFORMATIONAL)

RFC 2344   Reverse Tunneling for Mobile IP. G. Montenegro. May 1998. (Status: PROPOSED STANDARD)

RFC 2373   IP Version 6 Addressing Architecture. R. Hinden, S. Deering. July 1998. (Status: PROPOSED STANDARD)

RFC 2390   Load Sharing Using IP Network Address Translation (LSNAT). P. Srisuresh, D. Gan. August 1998. (Status: INFORMATIONAL)

RFC 2450   Proposed TLA and NLA Assignment Rule. R. Hinden. December 1998. (Status: INFORMATIONAL)

RFC 2452   IP Version 6 Management Information Base for the Transmission Control Protocol. M. Daniele. December 1998. (Status: PROPOSED STANDARD)

RFC 2454   IP Version 6 Management Information Base for the User Datagram Protocol. M. Daniele. December 1998. (Status: PROPOSED STANDARD)

RFC 2460   Internet Protocol, Version 6 (IPv6) Specification. S. Deering. R. Hinden. December 1998. (Status: DRAFT STANDARD)

RFC 2461   Neighbor Discovery for IP Version 6(IPv6). T. Narten, E. Nordmark, W. Simpson. December 1998. (Status: DRAFT STANDARD)

RFC 2462   IPv6 Stateless Address Autoconfiguration. S. Thomson, T. Narten. December 1998. (Status: DRAFT STANDARD)

RFC 2463   Internet Control Message Protocol (ICMPv6) for the Internet Protocol Version 6 (IPv6) Specification. A. Contra, S. Deering. Decemer 1998. (Status: DRAFT STANDARD)

RFC 2464   Transmission of IPv6 Packets over Ethernet Networks. M. Crawford. December 1998. (Status: PROPOSED STANDARD)

RFC 2465   Management Information Base for IP Version 6: Textual Conventions and General Group. D. Haskin, S. Onishi. December 1998. (Status: PROPOSED STANDARD)

RFC 2466   Management Information Base for IP Version 6: ICMPv6 Group. D. Haskin, S. Onishi. December 1998. (Status: PROPOSED STANDARD)

RFC 2467 Transmission of IPv6 Packets over FDDI Networks. M. Crawford. December 1998. (Status: PROPOSED STANDARD)

RFC 2470 Transmission of IPv6 Packets over Token Ring Networks. M. Crawford, T. Narten, S. Thomas. December 1998. (Status: PROPOSED STANDARD)

RFC 2471 IPv6 Testing Address Allocation. R. Hinden, R. Fink, J. Postel (deceased). December 1998. (Status: EXPERIMENTAL)

RFC 2472 IP Version 6 over PPP. D. Haskin, E. Allen. October 1996. (Status: PROPOSED STANDARD)

RFC 2473 Generic Packet Tunneling in IPv6 Specification. A. Contra, S. Deering. December 1998. (Status: PROPOSED STANDARD)

RFC 2477 Criteria for Evaluating Roaming Protocols. B. Aboba, G. Zorn. December 1998. (Status: INFORMATIONAL)

RFC 2486 The Network Access Identifier. B. Aboba, M. Beadles. January 1999. (Status: PROPOSED STANDARD)

RFC 2491 IPv6 over Non-Broadcast Multiple Access (NBMA) networks. G. Armitage. P. Schulter, M. Jork, G. Harter. January 1999. (Status: PROPOSED STANDARD)

RFC 2501 Mobile Ad Hoc Networking (MANET): Routing Protocol Performance Issues and Evaluation Considerations. S. Corson, J. Macker. January 1999. (Status: INFORMATIONAL)

RFC 2521 ICMP Security Failures Messages. P. Karn, W. Simpson. March 1999. (Status: EXPERIMENTAL)

RFC 2526 Reserved IPv6 Subnet Anycast Addresses. D. Johnson, S. Deering, March 1996. (Status: PROPOSED STANDARD)

RFC 2529 Transmission of IPv6 over IPv4 Domains without Explicit Tunnels. B. Carpenter, C. Jung. March 1999. (Status: PROPOSED STANDARD)

RFC 2545 Use of BGP-4 Multiprotocol Extensions for IPv6 Inter-Domain Routing. P. Marques, F. Dupont. March 1999. (Status: PROPOSED STANDARD)

RFC 2553 Basic Socket Interface Extensions for IPv6. R. Gilligan, S. Thomson, J. Bound, S. Stevens. March 1999. (Status: INFORMATIONAL)

RFC 2590 Transmission of IPv6 Packets over Frame Relay

RFC 2675 IPv6 Jumbograms

RFC 2710 Multicast Listener Discovery (MLD) for IPv6

Chapter 4: RIP v1 and v2

RFC 823   DARPA Internet Gateway

RFC 826   Ethernet Address Resolution Protocol: Or Converting Network Protocol Addresses to 48.bit Ethernet Address for Transmission on Ethernet Hardware

RFC 827   Exterior Gateway Protocol Formal Specification

RFC 875   Gateways, Architectures, and Heffalumps

RFC 888   Exterior Gateway Protocol Formal Specification

RFC 890   Exterior Gateway Protocol Formal Specification

RFC 903   Reverse Address Resolution Protocol

RFC 904   Exterior Gateway Protocol Formal Specification

RFC 925   Multi-LAN Address Resolution

RFC 985   Requirements for Internet Gateways—Draft

RFC 1027   Using ARP to Implement Transparent Subnet Gateways. S. Carl-Mitchell, J. S. Quarterman. Oct-01-1987. (Status: UNKNOWN)

RFC 1029   More Fault-Tolerant Approach to Address Resolution for a Multi-LAN System of Ethernets. G. Parr. May-01-1988. (Status: UNKNOWN)

RFC 1058   Routing Information Protocol. C. I. Hedrick. Jun-01-1988. (Status: HISTORIC)

RFC 1107   Plan for Internet Directory Services. K. R. Sollins. Jul-01-1989. (Status: INFORMATIONAL)

RFC 1112   Host Extensions for IP Multicasting. S. E. Deering. Aug-01-1989. (Status: STANDARD)

RFC 1136   Administrative Domains and Routing Domains: A Model for Routing in the Internet. S. Hares, D. Katz. Dec-01-1989. (Status: INFORMATIONAL)

RFC 1264   Internet Engineering Task Force Internet Routing Protocol Standardization Criteria. R. m. Hinden. Oct-01-1991. (Status: INFORMATIONAL)

RFC 1293   Inverse Address Resolution Protocol. T. Bradley, C. Brown. January 1992. (Status: PROPOSED STANDARD)

RFC 1322   A Unified Approach to Inter-Domain Routing. D. Estrin, Y. Rekhter, S. Hotz. May 1992. (Status: INFORMATIONAL)

RFC 1329   Thoughts on Address Resolution for Dual MAC FDDI Networks. P. Kuehn. May 1992. (Status: INFORMATIONAL)

RFC 1387   RIP Version 2 Protocol Analysis. G. Malkin. January 1993. (Status: INFORMATIONAL)

RFC 1388   RIP Version 2 Carrying Additional Information. G. Malkin. January 1993. (Status: PROPOSED STANDARD)

RFC 1389   RIP Version 2 MIB Extensions. G. Malkin, F. Baker. January 1993.(Status: PROPOSED STANDARD)

RFC 1433   Directed ARP. J. Garrett, J. Hagen & J. Wong. March 1993. (Status: EXPERIMENTAL)

RFC 1478   An Architecture for Inter-Domain Policy Routing. M. Steenstrup. July 1993. (Status: PROPOSED STANDARD)

RFC 1479   Inter-Domain Policy Routing Protocol Specification: Version 1. M. Steenstrup. July 1993. (Status: PROPOSED STANDARD)

RFC 1581   Protocol Analysis for Extensions to RIP to Support Demand Circuits. G. Meyer. February 1994.

RFC 1721   RIP Version 2 Protocol Applicability Statement. G. Malkin. November 1994. (Status: DRAFT STANDARD)

RFC 1723   RIP Version 2-Carrying Additional Information. G. Malkin. November 1994. (Status: DRAFT STANDARD)

RFC 1868   ARP Extension-UNARP. G. Malkin. November 1995. (Status: EXPERIMENTAL)

RFC 1923   RIPv1 Applicability Statement for Historic Status. J. Halpern & S. Bradner. March 1996. (Status: INFORMATIONAL)

RFC 1931   Dynamic RARP Extensions for Automatic Network Address Acquisition. D. Brownell. April 1996. (Status: PROPOSED STANDARD)

RFC 2082   RIP-2 MD5 Authentication. F. Baker, R. Atkinson. January 1997. (Status: PROPOSED STANDARD)

RFC 2091   Triggered Extensions to RIP to Support Demand Circuits. G. Meyer, S. Sherry. January 1997. (Status: PROPOSED STANDARD)

RFC 2092   Protocol Analysis for Triggered RIP. S. Sherry, G. Meyer. January 1997. (Status: INFORMATIONAL)

RFC 2390   Inverse Address Resolution Protocol. T. Bradley, C. Brown, A. Malis. August 1998. (Status: PROPOSED STANDARD)

RFC 2453   RIP Version 2. G. Malkin. November 1998. (Status: STANDARD)

RFC 2519   A Framework for Inter-Domain Route Aggregation. E. Chen, J. Stewart. February 1999. (Status: INFORMATIONAL)

Chapter 5: IGRP and EIGRP

RFC 823   DARPA Internet Gateway

RFC 827   Exterior Gateway Protocol Formal Specification

RFC 875   Gateways, Architectures, and Heffalumps

RFC 888   Exterior Gateway Protocol Formal Specification

RFC 890   Exterior Gateway Protocol Formal Specification

RFC 904   Exterior Gateway Protocol Formal Specification

RFC 911   EGP Gateway under Berkeley Unix 4.2

RFC 985   Requirements for Internet gateways—Ddraft

RFC 1104   Models of Policy-Based Routing. H. W. Braun. Jun-01-1989. (Status: UNKNOWN)

RFC 1125   Policy Requirements for Inter-Administrative Domain Routing. D. Estrin. Nov-01-1989. (Status: UNKNOWN)

RFC 1136   Administrative Domains and Routing Domains: A Model for Routing in the Internet. S. Hares, D. Katz. Dec-01-1989. (Status: INFORMATIONAL)

RFC 1222   Advancing the NSFNET Routing Architecture. H. W. Braun, Y. Rekhter. May-01-1991. (Status: INFORMATIONAL)

RFC 1254   Gateway Congestion Control Survey. A. Mankin, K. Ramakrishnan. Jul-01-1991. (Status: INFORMATIONAL)

RFC 1264   Internet Engineering Task Force Internet Routing Protocol Standardization Criteria. R. M. Hinden. Oct-01-1991. (Status: INFORMATIONAL)

RFC 1322   A Unified Approach to Inter-Domain Routing. D. Estrin, Y. Rekhter, S. Hotz. May 1992. (Status: INFORMATIONAL)

RFC 1477   IDPR as a Proposed Standard. M. Steenstrup. July 1993. (Status: EXPERIMENTAL)

RFC 1478   An Architecture for Inter-Domain Policy Routing. M. Steenstrup. July 1993. (Status: PROPOSED STANDARD)

RFC 1479   Inter-Domain Policy Routing Protocol Specification: Version 1. M. Steenstrup. July 1993. (Status: PROPOSED STANDARD)

RFC 1482   Aggregate Support in the NSFNET Policy-Based Routing Database. Mark Knopper & Steven J. Richardson. July 1993. (Status: INFORMATIONAL)

RFC 1517   Applicability Statement for the Implementation of Classless Inter-Domain Routing (CIDR). Internet Engineering Steering Group, R. Hinden. September 1993. (Status: PROPOSED STANDARD)

RFC 1519   Classless Inter-Domain Routing (CIDR): an Address Assignment and Aggregation Strategy. V. Fuller, T. Li, J. Yu, & K. Varadhan. September 1993. (Status: PROPOSED STANDARD)

RFC 1520   Exchanging Routing Information across Provider Boundries in the CIDR environment. Y. Rekhter & C. Topolcic. September 1993. (Status: INFORMATIONAL)

RFC 1701   Generic Routing Encapsulation (GRE). S. Hanks, T. Li, D. Farinacci, P. Traina. October 1994.(Status: INFORMATIONAL)

RFC 1702   Generic Routing Encapsulation over IPv4 networks. S. Hanks, T. Li, D. Farinacci, P. Traina. October 1994. (Status: INFORMATIONAL)

RFC 1786   Representation of the IP Routing Policies in a Routing Registry (ripe-81++). T. Bates, E. Gerich, L. Joncheray, J. M. Jouanigot, D. Karrenberg, M. Terpstra, & J. Yu. March 1995. (Status: INFORMATIONAL)

RFC 1787   Routing in a Multi-provider Internet. Y. Rekhter. April 1995. (Status: INFORMATIONAL)

RFC 1817   CIDR and Classful Routing. Y. Rekhter. August 1995. (Status: INFORMATIONAL)

RFC 2102   Multicast Support for Nimrod: Requirements and Solution Approaches. R. Ramanathan. February 1997. (Status: INFORMATIONAL)

RFC 2519   A Framework for Inter-Domain Route Aggregation. E. Chen, J. Stewart. February 1999. (Status: INFORMATIONAL)

Chapter 6: OSPF

RFC 827   Exterior Gateway Protocol Formal Specification

RFC 875   Gateways, Architectures, and Heffalumps

RFC 888   Exterior Gateway Protocol Formal Specification

RFC 890   Exterior Gateway Protocol Formal Specification

RFC 904   Exterior Gateway Protocol Formal Specification

RFC 911   EGP Gateway under Berkeley Unix 4.2

RFC 985   Requirements for Internet Gateways—Draft

RFC 1074   4NSFNET backbone SPF-Based Interior Gateway Protocol. J. Rekhter. Oct-01-1988. (Status: UNKNOWN)

RFC 1125   Policy Requirements for Inter-Administrative Domain Routing. D. Estrin. Nov-01-1989. (Status: UNKNOWN)

RFC 1131   OSPF Specification. J. Moy. Oct-01-1989. (Status: PROPOSED STANDARD)

RFC 1245   OSPF Protocol Analysis. J. Moy. Jul-01-1991. (Status: INFORMATIONAL)

RFC 1246   Experience with OSPF Protocol. J. Moy. Jul-01-1991. (Status: INFORMATIONAL)

RFC 1247   OSPF Version 2. J. Moy. Jul-01-1991. (Status: PROPOSED STANDARD)

RFC 1252 OSPF Version 2 Management Information Base. F. Baker, R. Coltun. Aug-01-1991. (Status: PROPOSED STANDARD)

RFC 1253 OSPF Version 2 Management Information Base. F. Baker, R. Coltun. Aug-01-1991. (Status: PROPOSED STANDARD)

RFC 1254 Gateway Congestion Control Survey. A. Mankin, K. Ramakrishnan. Jul-01-1991. (Status: INFORMATIONAL)

RFC 1264 Internet Engineering Task Force Internet Routing Protocol Standardization Criteria. R. M. Hinden. Oct-01-1991. (Status: INFORMATIONAL)

RFC 1322 A Unified Approach to Inter-Domain Routing. D. Estrin, Y. Rekhter, S. Hotz. May 1992. (Status: INFORMATIONAL)

RFC 1364 BGP OSPF Interaction. K. Varadhan. September 1992

RFC 1370 Application Statement for the OSPF. Internet Architecture Board, L. Chapin. October 1992. (Status: PROPOSED STANDARD)

RFC 1477 IDPR as a Proposed Standard. M. Steenstrup. July 1993. (Status: EXPERIMENTAL)

RFC 1478 An Architecture for Inter-Domain Policy Routing. M. Steenstrup. July 1993. (Status: PROPOSED STANDARD)

RFC 1479 Inter-Domain Policy Routing Protocol Specification: Version 1. M. Steenstrup. July 1993. (Status: PROPOSED STANDARD)

RFC 1582 OSPF Version 2. J. Moy. March 1994. (Status: DRAFT STANDARD)

RFC 1584 MOSPF: Analysis and Experience. J. Moy. March 1994. (Status: INFORMATIONAL)

RFC 1585 Guidelines for Running OSPF over Frame Relay Networks. OdeSouza & M. Rodrigues. March 1994. (Status: INFORMATIONAL)

RFC 1586 The OSPF NSSA Option. R. Coltun & V. Fuller. March 1994. (Status: PROPOSED STANDARD)

RFC 1765 OSPF Database Overflow. J. Moy. March 1995. (Status: EXPERIMENTAL)

RFC 1793 Extending OSPF to Support Demand Circuits. J. Moy. April 1995. (Status: EXPERIMENTAL)

RFC 1817 CIDR and Classful Routing. Y. Rekhter. August 1995. (Status: INFORMATIONAL)

RFC 1992 The Nimrod Routing Architecture. I. Casineyra, N. Chiappa, M. Steestrup. August 1996. (Status: INOFORMATIONAL)

RFC 2154 OSPF with Digital Signatures. S. Murphy, M. Badger, B. Wellington. June 1997. (Status: EXPERIMENTAL)

RFC 2178 OSPF Version 2. J. Moy. July 1997. (Status: DRAFT STANDARD)

RFC 2328 OSPF Version 2. J. Moy. April 1998. (Status: STANDARD)

RFC 2329   OSPF Standardization Report. J. Moy. April 1998. (Status: INFORMATIONAL)

RFC 2338   Virtual Router Redundancy Protocol. S. Knight, D. Weaver, D. Whipple, R. Hinden, D. Mitzel, P. Hunt, P. Higginson, M. Shand, A. Lindem. April 1998. (Status: PROPOSED STANDARD)

RFC 2370   The OSPF Opaque LSA Option. R. Coltun. July 1998. (Status: PROPOSED STANDARD)

RFC 2519   A Framework for Inter-Domain Route Aggregation. E. Chen, J. Stewart. February 1999. (Status: INFORMATIONAL)

Chapter 7: Border Gateway Protocol (BGP)

RFC 675   Transmission Control Protocol

RFC 700   Protocol Experiment

RFC 721   Out-of-Band Control Signals in a Host-to-Host Protocol

RFC 761   Transmission Control Protocol

RFC 791   Transmission Control Protocol

RFC 813   Window and Acknowledgement Strategy in TCP

RFC 823   DARPA Internet Gateway

RFC 827   Exterior Gateway Protocol Formal Specification

RFC 872   TCP-on-a-LAN

RFC 875   Gateways, Architectures, and Heffalumps

RFC 879   TCP Maximum Segment Size and Related Topics

RFC 889   Internet Delay Experiments

RFC 888   Exterior Gateway Protocol Formal Specification

RFC 890   Exterior Gateway Protocol Formal Specification

RFC 896   Congestion Control in IP/TCP Internetworks

RFC 904   Exterior Gateway Protocol Formal Specification

RFC 962   TCP-4 Prime

RFC 964   Some Problems with the Specifications of the Military Standard Transmission Control Protocol

RFC 975   Autonomous Confederations

RFC 985   Requirements for Internet Gateways—Draft

RFC 1006   ISO Transport Services on Top of TCP: Version 3. M. T. Rose, D. E. Cass. May-01-1987. (Status: STANDARD)

RFC 1072   TCP Extensions for Long-Delay Paths. V. Jacobson, R. T. Braden. Oct-01-1988. (Status: UNKNOWN)

RFC 1078   TCP Port Service Multiplexer (TCPMUX). M. Lottor. Nov-01-1988. (Status: UNKNOWN)

RFC 1092   EGP and Policy-Based Routing in the New NSFNET Backbone. J. Rekhter. Feb-01-1989. (Status: UNKNOWN)

RFC 1102   Policy Routing in Internet Protocols. D. D. Clark. May-01-1989. (Status: UNKNOWN)

RFC 1104   Models of Policy-Based Routing. H. W. Braun. Jun-01-1989. (Status: UNKNOWN)

RFC 1105   Border Gateway Protocol (BGP). K. Loughheed, Y. Rekhter. Jun-01-1989. (Status: EXPERIMENTAL)

RFC 1106   TCP Big Window and NAK Options. R. Fox. Jun-01-1989. (Status: UNKNOWN)

RFC 1110   Problem with the TCP Big Window Option. A. M. McKenzie. Aug-01-1989. (Status: UNKNOWN)

RFC 1125   Policy Requirements for Inter-Administrative Domain Routing. D. Estrin. Nov-01-1989. (Status: UNKNOWN)

RFC 1136   Administrative Domains and Routing Domains: A model for Routing in the Internet. S. Hares, D. Katz. Dec-01-1989. (Status: INFORMATIONAL)

RFC 1144   Compressing TCP/IP Headers for Low-Speed Serial Links. V. Jaconbson. Feb-01-1990. (Status: PROPOSED STANDARD)

RFC 1163   Border Gateway Protocol (BGP). K. Lougheed, Y. Rekhter. Jun-01-1990. (Status: HISTORIC)

RFC 1164   Application of the Border Gateway Protocol on the Internet. J. C. Honig, D. Katz, M. Mathis, Y. Rekhter, J. Y. Yu. Jun-01-1990. (Status: HISTORIC)

RFC 1185   TCP Extensions for High-Speed Paths. V. Jacobson, R. T. Braden, L. Zhang. Oct-01-1990. (Status: EXPERIMENTAL)

RFC 1254   Gateway Congestion Control Survey. A. Mankin, K. Ramakrishnan. Jul-01-1991. (Status: INFORMATIONAL)

RFC 1263   TCP Extensions Considered Harmful. S. O'Malley, L. L. Peterson. Oct-01-1991. (Status: INFORMATIONAL)

RFC 1264   Internet Engineering Task Force Internet Routing Protocol Standardization Criteria. R. M. Hinden. Oct-01-1991. (Status: INFORMATIONAL)

RFC 1265   BGP Protocol Analysis. Y. Rekhter. Oct-01-1991. (Status: INFORMATIONAL)

RFC 1266 Experience with the BGP Protocol. Y. Rekhter. Oct-01-1991. (Status: INFORMATIONAL)

RFC 1267 Border Gateway Protocol 3 (BGP-3). K. Lougheed, Y. Rekhter. Oct-01-1991. (Status: HISTORIC)

RFC 1268 Application of the Border Gateway Protocol in the Internet. Y. Rekhter, P. Gross. Oct-01-1991. (Status: HISTORIC)

RFC 1269 Definitions of Managed Objects for the Border Gateway Protocol: Version 3. S. Willis, J. W. Burruss. Oct-01-1991. (Status: PROPOSED STANDARD)

RFC 1322 A Unified Approach to Inter-Domain Routing. D. Estrin, Y. Rekhter, S. Hotz. May 1992. (Status: INFORMATIONAL)

RFC 1323 TCP Extensions for High Performance. V. Jacobson, R. Braden, D. Borman. May 1992. (Status: PROPOSED STANDARD)

RFC 1337 TIME-WAIT Assassination Hazards for TCP. R. Braden. May 1992. (Status: INFORMATIONAL)

RFC 1364 BGP OSPF Interaction. K. Varadhan. September 1992

RFC 1379 Extending TCP for Transactions—Concepts. R. Braden. November 1992. (Status: INFORMATIONAL)

RFC 1397 Default Route Advertisement in BGP2 and BGP3 Version of the Border Gateway Protocol. D. Haskin. January 1993. (Status: PROPOSED STANDARD)

RFC 1403 BGP OSPF Interaction. K. Varadhan. January 1993. (Status: INFORMATIONAL)

RFC 1478 An Architecture for Inter-Domain Policy Routing. M. Steenstrup. July 1993. (Status: PROPOSED STANDARD)

RFC 1479 Inter-Domain Policy Routing Protocol Specification: Version 1. M. Steenstrup. July 1993. (Status: PROPOSED STANDARD)

RFC 1482 Aggregate Support in the NSFNET Policy-Based Routing Database. Mark Knopper & Steven J. Richardson. July 1993. (Status: INOFRMATIONAL)

RFC 1504 Appletalk Update-Based Routing Protocol: Enhanced Appletalk Routing. A. Oppenheimer. August 1993. (Status: INFORMATIONAL)

RFC 1517 Applicability Statement for the Implementation of Classless Inter-Domain Routing (CIDR). Internet Engineering Steering Group, R. Hinden. September 1993. (Status: PROPOSED STANDARD)

RFC 1519 Classless Inter-Domain Routing (CIDR): an Address Assignment and Aggregation Strategy. V. Fuller, T. Li, J. Yu, & K. Varadhan. September 1993. (Status: PROPOSED STANDARD)

RFC 1520 Exchanging Routing Information across Provider Boundaries in the CIDR Environment. Y. Rekhter & C. Topolcic. September 1993. (Status: INFORMATIONAL)

RFC 1644 T/TCP—TCP Extensions for Transactions Functional Specifications. R. Braden. July 1994. (Status: EXPERIMENTAL)

RFC 1654 A Border Gateway Protocol 4 (BGP-4). Y. Rekhter & T. Li, Editors. July 1994. (Status: PROPOSED STANDARD)

RFC 1693 An Extension of TCP: Partial Order Service. T. Connolly, P. Amer & P. Conrad. November 1994. (Status: PROPOSED STANDARD)

RFC 1745 BGP4/IDRP for IP-OSPF Interaction. K. Varadhan, S. Hares, Y. Rekhter. December 1994. (Status: PROPOSED STANDARD)

RFC 1771 A Border Gateway Protocol 4 (BGP-4). Y. Rekhter & T. Li. March 1995. (Status: INFORMATIONAL)

RFC 1772 Application of the Border Gateway Protocol in the Internet. Y. Rekhter & P. Gross. March 1995e. (Status: DRAFT STANDARD)

RFC 1773 Application of the BGP-4 protocol. P. Traina. March 1995. (Status: INFORMATIONAL)

RFC 1774 BGP-4 Protocol Analysis. P. Traina, Editor. March 1995. (Status: INFORMATIONAL)

RFC 1786 Representation of the IP Routing Policies in a Routing Registry (ripe-81++). T. Bates, E. Gerich, L. Joncheray, J. M. Jouanigot, D. Karrenberg, M. Terpstra, & J. Yu. March 1995. (Status: INFORMATIONAL)

RFC 1787 Routing in a Multiprovider Internet. Y. Rekhter. April 1995. (Status: INFORMATIONAL)

RFC 1817 CIDR and Classful Routing. Y. Rekhter. August 1995. (Status: INFORMATIONAL)

RFC 1863 A BGP/IDRP Route Server Alternative to Full Mesh Routing. D. Haskin. October 1995. (Status: EXPERIMENTAL)

RFC 1930 Guidelines for Creation, Selection, and Registration of an Autonomous System

RFC 1965 Autonomous System Confederations for BGP. P. Traina. June 1996. (Status: EXPERIMENTAL)

RFC 1966 BGP Route Reflection: An Alternative to Full Mesh IBGP. T. Bates & R. Chandrasekeran. June 1996. (Status: EXPERIMENTAL)

RFC 1997 BGP Communities Attribute. R. Chandra, P. Traina, & T. Li. August 1996. (Status: PROPOSED STANDARD)

RFC 1998 An Application of the BGP Community Attribute in Multi-home Routing. E. Chen & T. Bates. August 1996. (Status: INFORMATIONAL)

RFC 2001 TCP Slow Start, Congestion Avoidance, Fast Retransmit, and Fast Recovery Algorithms. W. Stevens. January 1997. (Status: PROPOSED STANDARD)

RFC 2009 GPS-Based Addressing and Routing. T. Imielinski, J. Navas. November 1996. (Status: EXPERIMENTAL)

RFC 2018   TCP Selective Acknowledgement Options. M. Mathis, J. Mahdavi, S. Floyd, A. Romanow. October 1996. (Status: PROPOSED STANDARD)

RFC 2042   Registering New BGP Attribute Types

RFC 2140   TCP Control Block Interdependence. J. Touch. April 1997. (Status: INFORMATIONAL)

RFC 2283   Multiprotocol Extensions for BGPv4

RFC 2385   Protection of BGP Sessions via the TCP MD5 Signature Option. A. Heffernan. August 1998. (Status: PROPOSED STANDARD)

RFC 2398   Some Testing Tools for TCP Implementers. S. Parker, C. Schmechel. August 1998. (Status: INFORMATIONAL)

RFC 2414   Increasing TCP's Initial Window. M. Allman, S. Floyd, C. Partridg. September 1998. (Status: EXPERIMENTAL)

RFC 2415   Simulating Studies of Increased Initial TCP Window Size. K. Poduri, K. Nichols. September 1998. (Status: INFORMATIONAL)

RFC 2416   When TCP Starts Up With Four Packets into Only Three Buffers. T. Shepard, C. Partridge. September 1998. (Status: INFORMATIONAL)

RFC 2439   BGP Route Flap Damping. C. Villamiar, R. Chandra, R. Grovindan. November 1998. (Status: PROPOSED STANDARD)

RFC 2488   Enhancing TCP Over Satellite Channels using Standard Mechanisms. M. Allman, D. Glover, L. Sanchez. January 1999. (Status: BEST CURRENT PRACTICE) RFC

RFC 2519   A Framework for Inter-Domain Route Aggregation. E. Chen, J. Stewart. February 1999. (Status: INFORMATIONAL)

RFC 2525   Known TCP Implementation Problems. V. Paxson, M. Allman, S. Dawson, W. Fenner, J. Griner, I. Heavens, K. Lahey, H. Semke, B. Volz. March 1999. (Status: INFORMATIONAL)

RFC 2581   TCP Congestion Control. M. Allman, V. Paxson, W. Stevens. April 1999. (Status: PROPOSED STANDARD)

RFC 2582   The New Reno Modification to TCP'S Fast Recovery Algorithm. S. Floyd, T. Henderson. April 1999. (Status: EXPERIMENTAL)

Chapter 8: IS-IS

RFC 823   DARPA Internet Gateway

RFC 827   Exterior Gateway Protocol Formal Specification

RFC 875   Gateways, Architectures, and Heffalumps

RFC 888   Exterior Gateway Protocol Formal Specification

RFC 890   Exterior Gateway Protocol Formal Specification

RFC 904   Exterior Gateway Protocol Formal Specification

RFC 985   Requirements for Internet gateways—Draft

RFC 1102   Policy Routing in Internet Protocols. D. D. Clark. May-01-1989. (Status: UNKNOWN)

RFC 1104   Models of Policy-Based Routing. H. W. Braun. Jun-01-1989. (Status: UNKNOWN)

RFC 1125   Policy Requirements for Inter-Administrative Domain Routing. D. Estrin. Nov-01-1989. (Status: UNKNOWN)

RFC 1136   Administrative Domains and Routing Domains: A Model for Routing in the Internet. S. Hares, D. Katz. Dec-01-1989. (Status: INFORMATIONAL)

RFC 1142   OSI IS-IS Intradomain Routing Protocol. D. Oran. Feb-01-1990. (Status: INFORMATIONAL)

RFC 1195   Use of OSI IS-IS for Routing in TCP/IP and Dual Environments. R. W. Callon. Dec-01-1990. (Status: PROPOSED STANDARD)

RFC 1222   Advancing the NSFNET Routing Architecture. H. W. Braun, Y. Rekhter. May-01-1991. (Status: INFORMATIONAL)

RFC 1254   Gateway Congestion Control Survey. A. Mankin, K. Ramakrishnan. Jul-01-1991. (Status: INFORMATIONAL)

RFC 1264   Internet Engineering Task Force Internet Routing Protocol Standardization Criteria. R. M. Hinden. Oct-01-1991. (Status: INFORMATIONAL)

RFC 1322   A Unified Approach to Inter-Domain Routing. D. Estrin, Y. Rekhter, S. Hotz. May 1992. (Status: INFORMATIONAL)

RFC 1479   Inter-Domain Policy Routing Protocol Specification: Version 1. M. Steenstrup. July 1993. (Status: PROPOSED STANDARD)

RFC 1787   Routing in a Multi-provider Internet. Y. Rekhter. April 1995. (Status: INFORMATIONAL)

RFC 2519   A Framework for Inter-Domain Route Aggregation. E. Chen, J. Stewart. February 1999. (Status: INFORMATIONAL)

Chapter 9: PNNI

RFC 1932   IP Over ATM: A Framework Document

RFC 2022   UNI 3.0/3.1-Based ATM Networks. November 1996. [2] ATM Forum… 0065.000, September 1996. [3] ATM Forum, PNNI Augmented Routing (PAR) Version 1.0

RFC 2514   Network-Network Interface Specification, Version 1.0, af-pnni-0055.000, (March 1996)

RFC 2685   September 1999. [2] ATM-Forum, Private Network-Network Interface Specification Version 1.0. ATM Forum af-pnni-0055.000,

RFC 2843   Proxy-PARP. Droz, T. Przygienda, May 2000

RFC 2844   OSPF over ATM and Proxy-PAR. T. Przygienda, P. Droz, R. Haas, May 2000

RFC 3031   PNNI Version 1.0

Chapter 10: Type of Service and Quality of Service Routing

RFC 1046   Queuing Algorithms to Provide Type-of-Service for IP Links. W. Prue, J. Postel. Feb-01-1988. (Status: UNKNOWN)

RFC 1092   EGP and Policy-Based Routing in the New NSFNET Backbone. J. Rekhter. Feb-01-1989. (Status: UNKNOWN)

RFC 1102   Policy Routing in Internet Protocols. D. D. Clark. May-01-1989. (Status: UNKNOWN)

RFC 1104   Models of Policy-Based Routing. H. W. Braun. Jun-01-1989. (Status: UNKNOWN)

RFC 1122   Requirements for Internet Hosts—Communication layers

RFC 1125   Policy Requirements for Inter-Administrative Domain Routing. D. Estrin. Nov-01-1989. (Status: UNKNOWN)

RFC 1254   Gateway Congestion Control Survey. A. Mankin, K. Ramakrishnan. Jul-01-1991. (Status: INFORMATIONAL)

RFC 1349   Type of Service in the Internet Protocol Suite. July 1992

RFC 1478   An Architecture for Inter-Domain Policy Routing. M. Steenstrup. July 1993. (Status: PROPOSED STANDARD)

RFC 1479   Inter-Domain Policy Routing Protocol Specification: Version 1. M. Steenstrup. July 1993. (Status: PROPOSED STANDARD)

RFC 1482   Aggregate Support in the NSFNET Policy-Based Routing Database. Mark Knopper & Steven J. Richardson. July 1993. (Status: INFORMATIONAL)

RFC 1633   Integrated Services in the Internet Architecture: An Overview. June 1994

RFC 2205   Resource Reservation Protocol version 1—Functional Specification. September 1997

RFC 2208   RSVP: Resource Reservation Protocol version 1 Applicability Statement, September 1997

RFC 2210   The Use of RSVP with IETF Integrated Service. September 1997

RFC 2211   Specification of the Controlled-Load Network Element Service, September 1997

RFC 2212   Specification of Guaranteed Quality of Service, September 1997

RFC 2215   General Characterization Parameters for Integrated Service Network Elements, September 1997

RFC 2216   Network Element Service Specification Template, September 1997

RFC 2460   Internet Protocol, Version 6 specification, December 1998

RFC 2474   Definition of the Differentiated Services Field (DS Field) in the IPv4 and IPv6 Headers, December 1998

RFC 2475   An Architecture for Differentiated Services, December 1998

RFC 2490   RSVP Multicasting

RFC 2597   Assured forwarding PHB Group, June 1999

RFC 2598   An Expedited Forwarding PHB, June 1999

RFC 2622   Routing Policy Specification Language (RSPL)

RFC 2650   Using RPSL in Practice

RFC 2676   QoS Routing Mechanisms and OSPF Extensions

RFC 2996   Format of the RSVP DCLASS Object, November 2000

RFC 2998   A Framework for Integrated Services Operation over DiffServ Networks, November 2000

Chapter 11: IP Multicast Routing

RFC 1112   Host Extensions for IP Multicasting, August 1989

RFC 1054   Host Extensions for IP Multicasting, May 1998

RFC 1075   Distance Vector Multicast Routing Protocol. D. Waitzman, C. Partridge, S. E. Deering. Nov-01-1988. (Status: EXPERIMENTAL)

RFC 1301   Multicast Transport Protocol, February 1992

RFC 1458   Requirements for Multicast Protocols, May 1993

RFC 1469   IP Multicast over Token-Ring Local Area Networks, June 1993

RFC 1584   Multicast Extensions to OSPF. J. Moy. March 1994. (Status: PROPOSED STANDARD)

RFC 1582   MOSPF: Analysis and Experience. J. Moy. March 1994. (Status: INFORMATIONAL)

RFC 1949   Scalable Multicast Key Distribution, May 1996

RFC 1768   Host Group Extensions to OSPF, March 1994

RFC 2102   Multicast Support for Nimrod : Requirements and Solution Approaches. R. Ramanathan. February 1997. (Status: INFORMATIONAL)

RFC 2117 Protocol Independent Multicast-Sparse Mode (PIM- SM): Protocol Specification. D. Estrin, D. Farinacci, A. Helmy, D. Thaler, S. Deering, M. Handley, V. Jacobson, C. Liu, P. Sharma, L. Wei. June 1997. (Status: EXPERIMENTAL)

RFC 2189 Core Based Trees (CBT Version 2) Multicast Routing. A. Balardie. September 1997. (Status: EXPERIMENTAL)

RFC 2201 Core Based Trees (CBT) Multicast Routing Architecture. A. Ballardie. September 1997. (Status: EXPERIMENTAL)

RFC 2362 Protocol Independent Multicast-Sparse Mode (PIM- SM): Protocol Specification. D. Estrin, D. Farinacci, A. Helmy, D. Thaler, S. Deering, M. Handley, V. Jacobson, C. Liu, P. Sharma, L. Wei. June 1998. (Status: EXPERIMENTAL)

RFC 2365 Administratively Scoped IP Multicast, July 1998

RFC 2715 Interoperability Rules for Multicast Routing Protocols

APPENDIX B

ABBREVIATIONS AND ACRONYMS

A

ABR Area Border Router

ACK Acknowledgement

ANSI American National Standards Institute

API application program interface

ARP Address Resolution Protocol

ARPANET Advance Research Projects Agency network

AS Autonomous System

ASBR Autonomous System Border Router

ASCII American Standard Code for Information Interchange

ASN Autonomous System number

ASN.1 Abstract Syntax Notation One

ATM Asynchronous Transfer Mode

B

BDR backup designated router

BER Basic Encoding Rules

BGP Border Gateway Protocol

BIND Berkeley Internet Name Domain

BootP Bootstrap Protocol

BPF Berkeley Packet Filter

BRI Basic Rate Interface

BSD Berkeley Software Distribution

C

CBT core based tree

CCITT Consultative Committee for International Telegraphy and Telephony

CIDR classless interdomain routing

CIX Commercial Internet Exchange

CLNP Connectionless Network Protocol

CPU central processing unit

CRC cyclic redundancy check

CSMA/CD carrier sense multiple access collision detect

CSLIP compressed SLIP

CSMA carrier sense multiple access

CSNP complete sequence number packet

CSU channel service unit

D

DARPA Defense Advanced Research Projects Agency

DCE Distributed Computing Environment

DDN Defense Data Network

DDR Dial-on-Demand Routing

DECNet Digital Equipment Corporation Network

DEMUX Demultiplexer

DF don't fragment field, IP header

DHCP Dynamic Host Configuration Protocol

DiffServ Differential Services

DLC Data Link control

DLPI Data Link Provider Interface

DNA Digital Network Architecture

DNS Domain Name System

DoD Department of Defense (Reference Model)

DR designated router

DSAP Destination Service Access Point

DSU data service unit

DTP data transfer process

DTS Distributed Time Service

DUAL Diffusing Update Algorithm

DVMRP Distance-Vector Multicast Routing Protocol

E

EBGP external BGP (router)

EBONE European IP Backbone

ED end delimiter

EOL end of option list

EGP Exterior Gateway Protocol

EIGRP Enhanced Interior Gateway Routing Protocol

EMI electromagnetic interference

ES end system

F

FCS frame check sequence

FDDI Fiber Distributed Data Interface

FIFO first in, first out

FIN finish flag, TCP header

FQDN fully qualified domain name

FTP File Transfer Protocol

G-H

HA hardware address

HDLC high-level data link control

HEX hexadecimal

I

IAB Internet Architecture Board

IAC interpret as command

IANA Internet Assigned Number Authority

IBGP internal BGP (router)

ICMP Internet Control Message Protocol

IDRP Interdomain Routing Protocol

IEEE Institute of Electrical and Electronics Engineers

IESG Internet Engineering Steering Group

IETF Internet Engineering Task Force

IGMP Internet Group Management Protocol

IGP interior gateway protocol

IGRP Interior Gateway Routing Protocol

IntServ Integrated Services

IP Internet Protocol

IPNG Internet Protocol Next Generation

IPX Internetwork Packet Exchange

IRTF Internet Research Task Force

ISDN Integrated Services Digital Network

IS-IS Intermediate System to Intermediate System Protocol

ISN initial sequence number

ISO International Organization for Standardization

ISOC Internet Society

ISP Internet Service Provider

J-L

L1 Level one

L2 Level two

LAN local area network

LAPB Link Access Procedure, Balanced

LAPD Link Access Procedure on the D channel

LBX low bandwidth X

LCP link control protocol

LFN long fat network

LIFO last in, first out

LLC logical link control

LSA Link State advertisement

LSRR loose source and record route

M

MAC media access control

MBONE multicast backbone

MIB management information base

MILNET Military Network

MIME multipurpose Internet mail extensions

MOSPF multicast open shortest path first

MPLS Multi-Protocol Label Switching

M/S master/slave

MS message store

MSL maximum segment lifetime

MSAU Multi-Station Access Units

MSS maximum segment size

MTA maximum transfer agent

MTU maximum transfer unit

MUX Multiplexer

N

NAT Network Address Translation

NBMA non-broadcast multi-access

NCP Network Control Protocol

NDN non-delivery notification

NetBEUI Network Basic Extended User Interface

NetBIOS Network Basic Input Output System

NFS Network File System

NIC Network Interface Card

NIT network interface tap

NNI Network to Network Interface

NNTP Network News Transfer Protocol

NOP no operation

NSFNET National Science Foundation network

NSI NASA Science Internet

NSSA not so stubby area

NTP Network Time Protocol

NVT network virtual terminal

O

Opcode Operation Code

OSF Open Software Foundation

OSI Open Systems Interconnection (Reference Model)

OSPF Open Shortest Path First

P

PA protocol address

PDU protocol data unit

PGL Peer Group Leader

PHB per hop behavior

PI protocol interpreter

PIM protocol independent multicast

PIM-DM protocol independent dense mode

PIM-SM protocol independent sparse mode

PNNI Private Network-to-Network Interface

POP Point of Presence

PPP Point-to-Point Protocol

PRI Primary Rate Interface

PSH push flag, TCP header

PSNP partial sequence number packet

PTSE PNNI state topology element

PTSP PNNI state topology packet

Q

QoS Quality of Service

R

RARP Reverse Address Resolution Protocol

RFC Request for Comment

RFI radio frequency interference

RIP Routing Information Protocol

RP rendezvous point

RPC remote procedure call

RR resource record

RRQ read request

RST reset flag, TCP header

RSVP ReSerVation Protocol

RTO retransmission timeout

RTT round-trip time

S

SA source address

SACK Selective Acknowledgement

SAP service access point

SD start delimiter

SDLC Synchronous Data Link Control

SLIP Serial Line Internet Protocol

SMI structure of management information

SMTP Simple Mail Transfer Protocol

SNA System Network Architecture

SNAP SubNetwork Access Protocol

SNMP Simple Network Management Protocol

SNP sequence number packet

SOHO small office home office

SQE Signal Quality Error

SRB source route bridging

SRRT smooth round trip timer

SSAP source service access point

STP spanning tree protocol

SWS silly window syndrome

SYN synchronize sequence numbers flag, TCP header

T

TB transparent bridging

TCP Transmission Control Protocol

Telnet Telecommunication Network Protocol

TFTP Trivial File Transfer Protocol

TLI Transport Layer Interface

ToS Type-of-Service

TTL time-to-live

TUBA TCP and UDP with bigger addresses

U

UA user agent

UDP User Data Protocol

UI user interface

UNI User-to-Network Interface

URG urgent pointer flag, TCP header

UTC Coordinated Universal Time

UUCP Unix-to-Unix Copy

V

VC virtual circuit

VCI virtual circuit identifier

VLAN Virtual Local Area Network

VLSM Variable Length Subnet Mask

VPI virtual path identifier

W

WAN Wide Area Network

WINS Windows Internet Name service

WRQ write request

WWW World Wide Web

X-Z

XDR external data representation

XID transaction ID

APPENDIX C

IP AND MULTICAST PROTOCOL ADDRESSES

A ppendix C provides two tables: The first includes a complete list of registered Internet protocols, and the second identifies multicast addresses allocated by the IANA.

Registered Internet Protocol addresses are two byte values used to identify the protocol being carried within an IP datagram. This value can be found in the protocol type field within the IP header. A complete list of registered protocol addresses follows. This list includes the protocol type value, protocol name, and related RFC or industry reference.

TABLE C.1 Lists Registered IP Protocol Addresses

Assigned Internet Protocol Numbers			
Decimal	Keyword	Protocol	Reference
0	HOPOPT	IPv6 Hop-by-Hop Option	[RFC1883]
1	ICMP	Internet Control Message	[RFC792]
2	IGMP	Internet Group Management	[RFC1112]
3	GGP	Gateway-to-Gateway	[RFC823]
4	IP	IP in IP (encapsulation)	[RFC2003]
5	ST	Stream	[RFC1190,RFC1819]
6	TCP	Transmission Control	[RFC793]
7	CBT	CBT	[Ballardie]
8	EGP	Exterior Gateway Protocol	[RFC888,DLM1]
9	IGP	any private interior gateway (used by Cisco for their IGRP)	[IANA]
10	BBN-RCC-MON	BBN RCC Monitoring	[SGC]
11	NVP-II	Network Voice Protocol	[RFC741,SC3]
12	PUP	PUP	[PUP,XEROX]
13	ARGUS	ARGUS	[RWS4]

14	EMCON	EMCON	[BN7]
15	XNET	Cross Net Debugger	[IEN158,JFH2]
16	CHAOS	Chaos	[NC3]
17	UDP	User Datagram	[RFC768,JBP]
18	MUX	Multiplexing	[IEN90,JBP]
19	DCN-MEAS	DCN Measurement Subsystems	[DLM1]
20	HMP	Host Monitoring	[RFC869,RH6]
21	PRM	Packet Radio Measurement	[ZSU]
22	XNS-IDP	XEROX NS IDP	[ETHERNET,XEROX]
23	TRUNK-1	Trunk-1	[BWB6]
24	TRUNK-2	Trunk-2	[BWB6]
25	LEAF-1	Leaf-1	[BWB6]
26	LEAF-2	Leaf-2	[BWB6]
27	RDP	Reliable Data Protocol	[RFC908,RH6]
28	IRTP	Internet Reliable Transaction	[RFC938,TXM]
29	ISO-TP4	ISO Transport Protocol Class 4	[RFC905,RC77]
30	NETBLT	Bulk Data Transfer Protocol	[RFC969,DDC1]
31	MFE-NSP	MFE Network Services Protocol	[MFENET,BCH2]
32	MERIT-INP	MERIT Internodal Protocol	[HWB]
33	SEP	Sequential Exchange Protocol	[JC120]
34	3PC	Third Party Connect Protocol	[SAF3]
35	IDPR	Inter-Domain Policy Routing Protocol	[MXS1]
36	XTP	XTP	[GXC]
37	DDP	Datagram Delivery Protocol	[WXC]
38	IDPR-CMTP	IDPR Control Message Transport Proto	[MXS1]
39	TP++	TP++ Transport Protocol	[DXF]
40	IL	IL Transport Protocol	[Presotto]
41	IPv6	Ipv6	[Deering]

42	SDRP	Source Demand Routing Protocol	[DXE1]
43	IPv6-Route	Routing Header for IPv6	[Deering]
44	IPv6-Frag	Fragment Header for IPv6	[Deering]
45	IDRP	Inter-Domain Routing Protocol	[Sue Hares]
46	RSVP	Reservation Protocol	[Bob Braden]
47	GRE	General Routing Encapsulation	[Tony Li]
48	MHRP	Mobile Host Routing Protocol	[David Johnson]
49	BNA	BNA	[Gary Salamon]
50	ESP	Encap Security Payload for IPv6	[RFC1827]
51	AH	Authentication Header for IPv6	[RFC1826]
52	I-NLSP	Integrated Net Layer Security TUBA	[GLENN]
53	SWIPE	IP with Encryption	[J16]
54	NARP	NBMA Address Resolution Protocol	[RFC1735]
55	MOBILE	IP Mobility	[Perkins]
56	TLSP	Transport Layer Security Protocol (using Kryptonet key management)	[Oberg]
57	SKIP	SKIP	[Markson]
58	IPv6-ICMP	ICMP for IPv6	[RFC1883]
59	IPv6-NoNxt	No Next Header for IPv6	[RFC1883]
60	IPv6-Opts	Destination Options for IPv6	[RFC1883]
61		Any host internal protocol	[IANA]
62	CFTP	CFTP	[CFTP,HCF2]
63		Any local network	[IANA]
64	SAT-EXPAK	SATNET and Backroom EXPAK	[SHB]
65	KRYPTOLAN	Kryptolan	[PXL1]
66	RVD	MIT Remote Virtual Disk Protocol	[MBG]
67	IPPC	Internet Pluribus Packet Core	[SHB]
68		Any distributed file system	[IANA]
69	SAT-MON	SATNET Monitoring	[SHB]
70	VISA	VISA Protocol	[GXT1]

71	IPCV	Internet Packet Core Utility	[SHB]
72	CPNX	Computer Protocol Network Executive	[DXM2]
73	CPHB	Computer Protocol Heart Beat	[DXM2]
74	WSN	Wang Span Network	[VXD]
75	PVP	Packet Video Protocol	[SC3]
76	BR-SAT-MON Backroom	SATNET Monitoring	[SHB]
77	SUN-ND	SUN ND PROTOCOL-Temporary	[WM3]
78	WB-MON	WIDEBAND Monitoring	[SHB]
79	WB-EXPAK	WIDEBAND EXPAK	[SHB]
80	ISO-IP	ISO Internet Protocol	[MTR]
81	VMTP	VMTP	[DRC3]
82	SECURE-VMTP	SECURE-VMTP	[DRC3]
83	VINES	VINES	[BXH]
84	TTP	TTP	[JXS]
85	NSFNET-IGP	NSFNET-IGP	[HWB]
86	DGP	Dissimilar Gateway Protocol	[DGP,ML109]
87	TCF	TCF	[GAL5]
88	EIGRP	EIGRP	[CISCO,GXS]
89	OSPFIGP	OSPFIGP	[RFC1583,JTM4]
90	Sprite-RPC	Sprite RPC Protocol	[SPRITE,BXW]
91	LARP	Locus Address Resolution Protocol	[BXH]
92	MTP	Multicast Transport Protocol	[SXA]
93	AX.25	AX.25 Frames	[BK29]
94	IPIP	IP-within-IP Encapsulation Protocol	[JI6]
95	MICP	Mobile Internetworking Control Pro	[JI6]
96	SCC-SP	Semaphore Communications Sec. Pro.	[HXH]
97	ETHERIP	Ethernet-within-IP Encapsulation	[RDH1]

98	ENCAP	Encapsulation Header	[RFC1241, RXB3]
99		Any private encryption scheme	[IANA]
100	GMTP	GMTP	[RXB5]
101	IFMP	Ipsilon Flow Management Protocol	[Hinden]
102	PNNI	PNNI over IP	[Callon]
103	PIM	Protocol Independent Multicast	[Farinacci]
104	ARIS	ARIS	[Feldman]
105	SCPS	SCPS	[Durst]
106	QNX	QNX	[Hunter]
107	A/N	Active Networks	[Braden]
108	IPComp	IP Payload Compression Protocol	[RFC2393]
109	SNP	Sitara Networks Protocol	[Sridhar]
110	Compaq-Peer	Compaq Peer Protocol	[Volpe]
111	IPX-in-IP	IPX in IP	[Lee]
112	VRRP	Virtual Router Redundancy Protocol	[Hinden]
113	PGM	PGM Reliable Transport Protocol	[Speakman]
114		Any 0-hop protocol	[IANA]
115	L2TP	Layer Two Tunneling Protocol	[Aboba]
116	DDX	D-II Data Exchange (DDX)	[Worley]
117	IATP	Interactive Agent Transfer Protocol	[Murphy]
118	STP	Schedule Transfer Protocol	[JMP]
119	SRP	SpectraLink Radio Protocol	[Hamilton]
120	UTI	UTI	[Lothberg]
121	SMP	Simple Message Protocol	[Ekblad]
122	SM	SM	[Crowcroft]
123	PTP	Performance Transparency Protocol	[Welzl]
124		ISIS over IPv4	[Przygienda] .
125	FIRE		[Partridge]
126	CRTP	Combat Radio Transport Protocol	[Sautter]

127	CRUDP	Combat Radio User Datagram	[Sautter]
128	SSCOPMCE		[Waber]
129	IPLT		[Hollbach]
130	SPS	Secure Packet Shield	[McIntosh]
131	PIPE	Private IP Encapsulation within IP	[Petri]
132	SCTP	Stream Control Transmission Protocol	[Stewart]
133	FC	Fibre Channel	[Rajagopal]
134		RSVP-E2E-IGNORE	[RFC3175]
135-254		Unassigned	[IANA]
255		Reserved	[IANA]

Multicast-enabled hosts and routers are capable of sending and receiving multicast datagrams within the Class D range 224.0.0.1 through 239.255.255.255 (multicast addresses were discussed in Chapter 11, "IP Multicast Routing"). Some of the addresses within this range are used for multicast routing. Multicast addresses and multicast routing support communication between processes belonging to the same multicast group. Processes requiring multicast capabilities must join multicast groups through the use of IGMP member (join) reports. Table C.2 shows a complete list of multicast addresses and a description of the groups they represent.

TABLE C.2 Multicast Addresses and Group Descriptions

Multicast Address	Multicast Group	Reference
224.0.0.0	Base Address (Reserved)	[RFC1112,JBP]
224.0.0.1	All Systems on this Subnet	[RFC1112,JBP]
224.0.0.2	All Routers on this Subnet	[JBP]
224.0.0.3	Unassigned	[JBP]
224.0.0.4	DVMRP Routers	[RFC1075,JBP]
224.0.0.5	OSPFIGP OSPFIGP All Routers	[RFC2328,JXM1]
224.0.0.6	OSPFIGP OSPFIGP Designated Routers	[RFC2328,JXM1
224.0.0.7	ST Routers	[RFC1190,KS14]
224.0.0.8	ST Hosts	[RFC1190,KS14]
224.0.0.9	RIP2 Routers	[RFC1723,GSM11]
224.0.0.10	IGRP Routers	[Farinacci]

224.0.0.11	Mobile-Agents	[Bill Simpson]
224.0.0.12	DHCP Server/Relay Agent	[RFC1884]
224.0.0.13	All PIM Routers	[Farinacci]
224.0.0.14	RSVP-ENCAPSULATION	[Braden]
224.0.0.15	All-cbt-routers	[Ballardie]
224.0.0.16	Designated-sbm	[Baker]
224.0.0.17	All-sbms	[Baker]
224.0.0.18	VRRP	[Hinden]
224.0.0.19	IPAllL1ISs	[Przygienda]
224.0.0.20	IPAllL2ISs	[Przygienda]
224.0.0.21	IPAllIntermediate Systems	[Przygienda]
224.0.0.22	IGMP	[Deering]
224.0.0.23	GLOBECAST-ID	[Scannell]
224.0.0.24	Unassigned	[JBP]
224.0.0.25	router-to-switch	[Wu]
224.0.0.26	Unassigned	[JBP]
224.0.0.27	Al MPP Hello	[Martinicky]
224.0.0.28	ETC Control	[Polishinski]
224.0.0.29	GE-FANUC	[Wacey]
224.0.0.30	indigo-vhdp	[Caughie]
224.0.0.31	shinbroadband	[Kittivatcharapong]
224.0.0.32	digistar	[Kerkan]
224.0.0.33	ff-system-management	[Glanzer]
224.0.0.34	pt2-discover	[Kammerlander]
224.0.0.35	DXCLUSTER	[Koopman]
224.0.0.36	DTCP Announcement	[Cipiere]
224.0.0.37–224.0.0.250	Unassigned	[JBP]
224.0.0.251	mDNS	[Cheshire]
224.0.0.252–224.0.0.255	Unassigned	[JBP]
224.0.1.0	VMTP Managers Group	[RFC1045,DRC3]

224.0.1.1	NTP Network Time Protocol	[RFC1119,DLM1]
224.0.1.2	SGI-Dogfight	[AXC]
224.0.1.3	Rwhod	[SXD]
224.0.1.4	VNP	[DRC3]
224.0.1.5	Artificial Horizons - Aviator	[BXF]
224.0.1.6	NSS - Name Service Server	[BXS2]
224.0.1.7	AUDIONEWS - Audio News Multicast	[MXF2]
224.0.1.8	SUN NIS+ Information Service	[CXM3]
224.0.1.9	MTP Multicast Transport Protocol	[SXA]
224.0.1.10	IETF-1-LOW-AUDIO	[SC3]
224.0.1.11	IETF-1-AUDIO	[SC3]
224.0.1.12	IETF-1-VIDEO	[SC3]
224.0.1.13	IETF-2-LOW-AUDIO	[SC3]
224.0.1.14	IETF-2-AUDIO	[SC3]
224.0.1.15	IETF-2-VIDEO	[SC3]
224.0.1.16	MUSIC-SERVICE	[Guido van Rossum]
224.0.1.17	SEANET-TELEMETRY	[Andrew Maffei]
224.0.1.18	SEANET-IMAGE	[Andrew Maffei]
224.0.1.19	MLOADD	[Braden]
224.0.1.20	any private experiment	[JBP]
224.0.1.21	DVMRP on MOSPF	[John Moy]
224.0.1.22	SVRLOC	[Veizades]
224.0.1.23	XINGTV	[Gordon]
224.0.1.24	microsoft-ds	
224.0.1.25	nbc-pro	
224.0.1.26	nbc-pfn	
224.0.1.27	lmsc-calren-1	[Uang]
224.0.1.28	lmsc-calren-2	[Uang]
224.0.1.29	lmsc-calren-3	[Uang]
224.0.1.30	lmsc-calren-4	[Uang]

224.0.1.31	ampr-info	[Janssen]
224.0.1.32	mtrace	[Casner]
224.0.1.33	RSVP-encap-1	[Braden]
224.0.1.34	RSVP-encap-2	[Braden]
224.0.1.35	SVRLOC-DA	[Veizades]
224.0.1.36	rln-server	[Kean]
224.0.1.37	proshare-mc	[Lewis]
224.0.1.38	dantz	[Zulch]
224.0.1.39	cisco-rp-announce	[Farinacci]
224.0.1.40	cisco-rp-discovery	[Farinacci]
224.0.1.41	gatekeeper	[Toga]
224.0.1.42	iberiagames	[Marocho]
224.0.1.43	nwn-discovery	[Zwemmer]
224.0.1.44	nwn-adaptor	[Zwemmer]
224.0.1.45	isma-1	[Dunne]
224.0.1.46	isma-2	[Dunne]
224.0.1.47	telerate	[Peng]
224.0.1.48	ciena	[Rodbell]
224.0.1.49	dcap-servers	[RFC2114]
224.0.1.50	dcap-clients	[RFC2114]
224.0.1.51	mcntp-directory	[Rupp]
224.0.1.52	mbone-vcr-directory	[Holfelder]
224.0.1.53	heartbeat	[Mamakos]
224.0.1.54	sun-mc-grp	[DeMoney]
224.0.1.55	extended-sys	[Poole]
224.0.1.56	pdrncs	[Wissenbach]
224.0.1.57	tns-adv-multi	[Albin]
224.0.1.58	vcals-dmu	[Shindoh]
224.0.1.59	zuba	[Jackson]
224.0.1.60	hp-device-disc	[Albright]

224.0.1.61	tms-production	[Gilani]
224.0.1.62	sunscalar	[Gibson]
224.0.1.63	mmtp-poll	[Costales]
224.0.1.64	compaq-peer	[Volpe]
224.0.1.65	iapp	[Meier]
224.0.1.66	multihasc-com	[Brockbank]
224.0.1.67	serv-discovery	[Honton]
224.0.1.68	mdhcpdisover	[RFC2730]
224.0.1.69	MMP-bundle-discovery1	[Malkin]
224.0.1.70	MMP-bundle-discovery2	[Malkin]
224.0.1.71	XYPOINT DGPS Data Feed	[Green]
224.0.1.72	GilatSkySurfer	[Gal]
224.0.1.73	SharesLive	[Rowatt]
224.0.1.74	NorthernData	[Sheers]
224.0.1.75	SIP	[Schulzrinne]
224.0.1.76	IAPP	[Moelard]
224.0.1.77	AGENTVIEW	[Iyer]
224.0.1.78	Tibco Multicast1	[Shum]
224.0.1.79	Tibco Multicast2	[Shum]
224.0.1.80	MSP	[Caves]
224.0.1.81	OTT (One-way Trip Time)	[Schwartz]
224.0.1.82	TRACKTICKER	[Novick]
224.0.1.83	dtn-mc	[Gaddie]
224.0.1.84	jini-announcement	[Scheifler]
224.0.1.85	jini-request	[Scheifler]
224.0.1.86	sde-discovery	[Aronson]
224.0.1.87	DirecPC-SI	[Dillon]
224.0.1.88	B1RMonitor	[Purkiss]
224.0.1.89	3Com-AMP3 dRMON	[Banthia]
224.0.1.90	imFtmSvc	[Bhatti]

224.0.1.91	NQDS4	[Flynn]
224.0.1.92	NQDS5	[Flynn]
224.0.1.93	NQDS6	[Flynn]
224.0.1.94	NLVL12	[Flynn]
224.0.1.95	NTDS1	[Flynn]
224.0.1.96	NTDS2	[Flynn]
224.0.1.97	NODSA	[Flynn]
224.0.1.98	NODSB	[Flynn]
224.0.1.99	NODSC	[Flynn]
224.0.1.100	NODSD	[Flynn]
224.0.1.101	NQDS4R	[Flynn]
224.0.1.102	NQDS5R	[Flynn]
224.0.1.103	NQDS6R	[Flynn]
224.0.1.104	NLVL12R	[Flynn]
224.0.1.105	NTDS1R	[Flynn]
224.0.1.106	NTDS2R	[Flynn]
224.0.1.107	NODSAR	[Flynn]
224.0.1.108	NODSBR	[Flynn]
224.0.1.109	NODSCR	[Flynn]
224.0.1.110	NODSDR	[Flynn]
224.0.1.111	MRM	[Wei]
224.0.1.112	TVE-FILE	[Blackketter]
224.0.1.113	TVE-ANNOUNCE	[Blackketter]
224.0.1.114	Mac Srv Loc	[Woodcock]
224.0.1.115	Simple Multicast	[Crowcroft]
224.0.1.116	SpectraLinkGW	[Hamilton]
224.0.1.117	dieboldmcast	[Marsh]
224.0.1.118	Tivoli Systems	[Gabriel]
224.0.1.119	pq-lic-mcast	[Sledge]
224.0.1.120	HYPERFEED	[Kreutzjans]

224.0.1.121	Pipesplatform	[Dissett]
224.0.1.122	LiebDevMgmg-DM	[Velten]
224.0.1.123	TRIBALVOICE	[Thompson]
224.0.1.124	Unassigned (Retracted 1/29/01)	
224.0.1.125	PolyCom Relay1	[Coutiere]
224.0.1.126	Infront Multi1	[Lindeman]
224.0.1.127	XRX DEVICE DISC	[Wang]
224.0.1.128	CNN	[Lynch]
224.0.1.129	PTP-primary	[Eidson]
224.0.1.130	PTP-alternate1	[Eidson]
224.0.1.131	PTP-alternate2	[Eidson]
224.0.1.132	PTP-alternate3	[Eidson]
224.0.1.133	ProCast	[Revzen]
224.0.1.134	3Com Discp	[White]
224.0.1.135	CS-Multicasting	[Stanev]
224.0.1.136	TS-MC-1	[Sveistrup]
224.0.1.137	Make Source	[Daga]
224.0.1.138	Teleborsa	[Strazzera]
224.0.1.139	SUMAConfig	[Wallach]
224.0.1.140	Unassigned	
224.0.1.141	DHCP-SERVERS	[Hall]
224.0.1.142	CN Router-LL	[Armitage]
224.0.1.143	EMWIN	[Querubin]
224.0.1.144	Alchemy Cluster	[O'Rourke]
224.0.1.145	Satcast One	[Nevell]
224.0.1.146	Satcast Two	[Nevell]
224.0.1.147	Satcast Three	[Nevell]
224.0.1.148	Intline	[Sliwinski]
224.0.1.149	8x8 Multicast	[Roper]
224.0.1.150	Unassigned	[JBP]

224.0.1.151	Intline-1	[Sliwinski]
224.0.1.152	Intline-2	[Sliwinski]
224.0.1.153	Intline-3	[Sliwinski]
224.0.1.154	Intline-4	[Sliwinski]
224.0.1.155	Intline-5	[Sliwinski]
224.0.1.156	Intline-6	[Sliwinski]
224.0.1.157	Intline-7	[Sliwinski]
224.0.1.158	Intline-8	[Sliwinski]
224.0.1.159	Intline-9	[Sliwinski]
224.0.1.160	Intline-10	[Sliwinski]
224.0.1.161	Intline-11	[Sliwinski]
224.0.1.162	Intline-12	[Sliwinski]
224.0.1.163	Intline-13	[Sliwinski]
224.0.1.164	Intline-14	[Sliwinski]
224.0.1.165	Intline-15	[Sliwinski]
224.0.1.166	marratech-cc	[Parnes]
224.0.1.167	EMS-InterDev	[Lyda]
224.0.1.168	itb301	[Rueskamp]
224.0.1.169	rtv-audio	[Adams]
224.0.1.170	rtv-video	[Adams]
224.0.1.171	HAVI-Sim	[Wasserroth]
224.0.1.172	Nokia Cluster	[O'Rourke]
224.0.1.173	host-request	[K.Thompson]
224.0.1.174	host-announce	[K.Thompson]
224.0.1.175–224.0.1.255	Unassigned	[JBP]
224.0.2.1	"rwho" Group (BSD) (unofficial)	[JBP]
224.0.2.2	SUN RPC PMAPPROC_CALLIT	[BXE1]
224.0.2.0–224.0.255.0	AD-HOC Block	
224.0.2.64–224.0.2.95	SIAC MDD Service	[Tse]
224.0.2.96–224.0.2.127	CoolCast	[Ballister]

224.0.2.128–224.0.2.191	WOZ-Garage	[Marquardt]
224.0.2.192–224.0.2.255	SIAC MDD Market Service	[Lamberg]
224.0.3.0–224.0.3.255	RFE Generic Service	[DXS3]
224.0.4.0–224.0.4.255	RFE Individual Conferences	[DXS3]
224.0.5.0–224.0.5.127	CDPD Groups	[Bob Brenner]
224.0.5.128–224.0.5.191	SIAC Market Service	[Cho]
224.0.5.192–224.0.5.255	SIAC NYSE Order PDP protocol	[Chan]
224.0.6.0–224.0.6.127	Cornell ISIS Project	[Tim Clark]
224.0.6.128–224.0.6.255	Unassigned	[IANA]
224.0.7.0–224.0.7.255	Where-Are-You	[Simpson]
224.0.8.0–224.0.8.255	INTV	[Tynan]
224.0.9.0–224.0.9.255	Invisible Worlds	[Malamud]
224.0.10.0–224.0.10.255	DLSw Groups	[Lee]
224.0.11.0–224.0.11.255	NCC.NET Audio	[Rubin]
224.0.12.0–224.0.12.63	Microsoft and MSNBC	[Blank]
224.0.13.0–224.0.13.255	UUNET PIPEX Net News	[Barber]
224.0.14.0–224.0.14.255	NLANR	[Wessels]
224.0.15.0–224.0.15.255	Hewlett Packard	[van der Meulen]
224.0.16.0–224.0.16.255	XingNet	[Uusitalo]
224.0.17.0–224.0.17.31	Mercantile & Commodity Exchange	[Gilani]
224.0.17.32–224.0.17.63	NDQMD1	[Nelson]
224.0.17.64–224.0.17.127	ODN-DTV	[Hodges]
224.0.18.0–224.0.18.255	Dow Jones	[Peng]
224.0.19.0–224.0.19.63	Walt Disney Company	[Watson]
224.0.19.64–224.0.19.95	Cal Multicast	[Moran]
224.0.19.96–224.0.19.127	SIAC Market Service	[Roy]
224.0.19.128–224.0.19.191	IIG Multicast	[Carr]
224.0.19.192–224.0.19.207	Metropol	[Crawford]
224.0.19.208–224.0.19.239	Xenoscience, Inc.	[Timm]
224.0.19.240–224.0.19.255	HYPERFEED	[Felix]

224.0.20.0–224.0.20.63	MS-IP/TV	[Wong]
224.0.20.64–224.0.20.127	Reliable Network Solutions	[Vogels]
224.0.20.128–224.0.20.143	TRACKTICKER Group	[Novick]
224.0.20.144–224.0.20.207	CNR Rebroadcast MCA	[Sautter]
224.0.21.0–224.0.21.127	Talarian MCAST	[Mendal]
224.0.22.0–224.0.22.255	WORLD MCAST	[Stewart]
224.0.252.0–224.0.252.255	Domain Scoped Group	[Fenner]
224.0.253.0–224.0.253.255	Report Group	[Fenner]
224.0.254.0–224.0.254.255	Query Group	[Fenner]
224.0.255.0–224.0.255.255	Border Routers	[Fenner]
224.1.0.0–224.1.255.255	ST Multicast Groups	[RFC1190,KS14]
224.2.0.0–224.2.255.255	SDP/SAP Block	
224.2.0.0–224.2.127.253	Multimedia Conference Calls	[SC3]
224.2.127.254	SAPv1 Announcements	[SC3]
224.2.127.255	SAPv0 Announcements (deprecated)	[SC3]
224.2.128.0–224.2.255.255	SAP Dynamic Assignments	[SC3]
224.252.0.0–224.255.255.255	DIS Transient Groups	[Joel Snyder]
225.0.0.0–231.255.255.255	Reserved	[IANA]
232.0.0.0–232.255.255.255	Source Specific Multicast	[DRC3]
233.0.0.0–233.255.255.255	GLOP Block	[RFC3180]
234.0.0.0–238.255.255.255	Reserved	[IANA]
239.0.0.0–239.255.255.255	Administratively Scoped	[IANA,RFC2365]
239.0.0.0–239.63.255.255	Reserved	[IANA]
239.64.0.0–239.127.255.255	Reserved	[IANA]
239.128.0.0–239.191.255.255	Reserved	[IANA]
239.192.0.0–239.251.255.255	Organization-Local Scope	[Meyer,RFC2365]
239.252.0.0–239.252.255.255	Site-Local Scope (reserved)	[Meyer,RFC2365]
239.253.0.0–239.253.255.255	Site-Local Scope (reserved)	[Meyer,RFC2365]
239.254.0.0–239.254.255.255	Site-Local Scope (reserved)	[Meyer,RFC2365]
239.255.0.0–239.255.255.255	Site-Local Scope	[Meyer,RFC2365]
239.255.2.2	rasadv	[Thaler]

VIRTUAL LANS (VLANS)

VLANs (Virtual Local Area Networks) are logical. Each VLAN represents a single IP subnet. VLANs are beneficial in that they may be used to isolate traffic between hosts within a switched network. VLANs allow end systems connected to physical switch ports on one or more switches to be grouped based on common communication patterns. Users needing to share information can be logically placed in the same workgroup configured as a virtual LAN. For instance, all accounting PCs used by accountants would be configured as part of the same VLAN. By grouping devices within the same VLAN only those devices within the same logical VLAN will receive traffic for that group. Communication between devices within a VLAN is referred to as Intra-VLAN. Inter-VLAN communication involves two different VLANs and is only achieved by configuring routers to forward traffic between the VLANs. We will start our discussion with a basic VLAN overview.

VLAN Overview

Virtual LANs (VLANs) allow administrators to limit traffic propagation across a switched network by grouping users based on their communication pattern regardless of their physical location in the network. VLANs logically segment the physical LANs into different subnets and use switches to forward frames only between ports within the same VLAN. Switches and switch operation were discussed in Chapter 1, "Overview of Industry Models, Standards, and TCP/IP Protocols." VLANs operate at layer 2 of the OSI model, traffic between devices belonging to the same VLAN (Intra-VLAN communication) never cross a router because they do not operate at layer three (see Figure D.1).

Because the broadcasts do not cross a router, implementing VLANs decreases broadcasts across a switched network by simulating a subnet. This improves performance and security in the network.

Although Intra-VLAN communication limits you to devices within the same VLAN, Inter-VLAN traffic can occur if you use a router to forward traffic between VLANs. If you do not configure a router to recognize and route traffic between VLANs, devices cannot communicate, receive or transmit frames to hosts in other VLANs. Because of this, VLANs can serve as a natural firewall, isolating traffic, providing a high level of security to a switched network.

FIGURE D.1
A network with three
VLANs. Stations
belonging to a VLAN
can only communicate
with hosts within the
same VLAN.

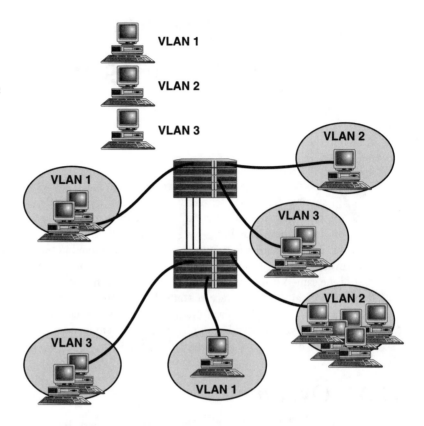

VLANs can span multiple segments within the same switch or across multiple switches. VLANs allow you to design your network more efficiently based on user traffic flow and security needs, logically segmenting traffic by projects, workgroup functions or applications regardless of the geographic location of the users.

Typically, use VLANs to provide 10/100 workgroups, server clustering, and security. You can configure VLANs either statically, assigned on a per port basis, or dynamically, using a server database associating all MAC addresses connected to a single port with the same VLAN. We will discus each one of these methods later in this appendix.

The most common and recommended method is to statically configure VLANs by port. You accomplish this by assigning each switch port to only one VLAN. All ports (and devices connected to those ports) belonging to the same VLAN share broadcasts. Vendor support for VLANs varies and is not standardized.

For example, most Cisco Catalyst switches can support up to 1,024 VLANs with 250 of them being active at one time. However, lower-end switches such as the 1900 series only support up to 64 port-based VLANs. Although this may seem like a limitation, it is highly unlikely, and definitely not recommended, that you implement this many VLANs. Each VLAN operates as a single routed subnet. That is, all ports and devices connected to these ports (regardless of their physical location) are considered to be part of the same logical subnet. If you add too many VLANs to your network, it would add more complexity to your network, requiring you to manage these VLANs.

VLANs may exist on a single switch or span across multiple switches when trunk links have been configured (trunk links and trunking protocols will be discussed later). VLANs can include stations in a single office building or span over multiple buildings while still grouping together defined communities of coworkers. Users with common job functions, such as sales or accounting, can be combined into VLANs representing these workgroups. These users do not have to be in the same geographic location. VLANs allow user end systems to be physically moved to different locations, while still maintaining their VLAN workgroup association. Application servers can also be included as a member of the VLAN associated with the users that use its resources. By grouping users and servers within the same VLAN, traffic is isolated to only those hosts and servers that need to share resources, keeping unnecessary traffic off of other VLANs.

By creating VLANs you can do the following:

- Make moves, adds, and changes of stations easier

- Reduce administrative costs involved with end station moves, adds, and changes

- Improve the control of broadcast and multicast traffic by limiting it to the ports within a single VLAN

- Provide tighter network security by allowing only Intra-VLAN communication, unless a router is providing Inter-VLAN routing

- Group servers in secured locations by placing servers in the same VLAN with users that use the resource, restricting users within another VLAN from accessing the server

VLAN Operation

Not all vendor switch products support VLANs. However, those that do include a default VLAN, known as *VLAN 1*. We will assume in our discussion that VLANs are supported. By default all switch ports on all switches automatically belong to VLAN 1. This VLAN includes all switches, ports and devices connected to these ports as belonging to a single network or subnet. If you want to subdivide your network into workgroups for the purpose of traffic isolation, you must create new VLANs.

Note

By default all ports on all VLAN supported switch products belong to one VLAN (VLAN 1). Therefore initially flooding occurs across all ports on all switches. After switch ports have been mapped to different VLANs, flooding is limited to the VLAN from which the frame originated.

The process is as follows: create new VLANs, and then statically map ports out of VLAN 1 into the new VLAN or let VLAN membership and assignment be dynamic. The creation and configuration of VLANs is dicussed later in this chapter. After the VLANs are created and the members are identified communication between devices across the switched VLAN network is limited to Intra-VLAN communication. Only those devices belonging to the same VLAN are able to communicate with each other. Inter-VLAN communication requires a router.

There are two methods of assigning VLAN memberships, Static or Dynamic. Static VLANs are port-based and require manual configuration, whereas dynamic VLANs follow the MAC address of the end system. The most common and recommended method of assigning VLAN memberships is static. Network administrators are free to choose the method that best suits their needs. The two VLAN membership options are as follows:

- **Static**—Static VLANs are port-based VLANs. An administrator assigns a VLAN to a port. All devices connected to the port belong to the VLAN configured for the port. VLAN membership follows the port assignment. Static VLANs are the most common and recommended method of defining VLANs.

- **Dynamic**—Ports on a switch automatically determine end host VLAN assignments based of their source MAC address. Dynamic VLAN assignment requires a server running the VMPS (VLAN Membership Policy Server). The VMPS service uses a locally stored database to dole out VLAN information. This database stores maps MAC addresses to VLANs. The switch detects new devices attached to a port, and immediately consults the VMPS server downloading the appropriate VLAN information. VLAN membership is not based on switch port, but follows each individual host's MAC address (see Figure D.2).

Static VLANs are the most common and recommended method of defining VLANs. By default all switch ports belong to a single VLAN, VLAN 1. Whether you decide to implement VLANs on your network, this VLAN exists, providing a single default virtual LAN and management domain across all switches on the network.

If you do decide to create additional VLANs on your network, I recommend that you leave switch ports, such as Fast Ethernet trunk ports, inter-switch links, and management ports (for example the Console port) in the default VLAN 1. By maintaining critical ports in VLAN 1, you can access and manage switches through this virtual subnet, providing a single management domain without requiring a router.

Note

Most vendors base their default switch settings on the assumption that you will be managing your switched network through VLAN1.

FIGURE D.2

Dynamic VLAN creation requires a VMPS server.

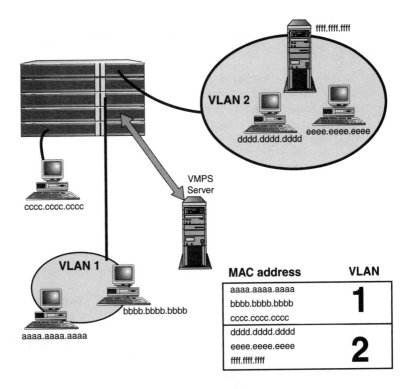

Switches identify traffic as belonging to a specific VLAN by using frame tags or frame encapsulation. Frame tagging is the process of embedding the VLAN ID within an Ethernet Frame. Encapsulation involves entirely enveloping datalink frames within a header and trailer. The header contains VLAN information used by switches to identify the specific VLAN this frame came from and which one it is destined for. The trailer contains a CRC used to validate the contents of the frame have not been damaged in transit. VLAN implementations vary and the type of VLAN identification method used depends on the trunking protocol or protocols implemented on the network.

Switches must be able to quickly identify traffic received through an interface as belonging to a specific VLAN and use this information to determine where this traffic is allowed to be forwarded. This VLAN information is kept within the switch's internal cache. The use of internal firmware and software embedded within their chipsets is used to identify and block VLAN traffic.

As discussed earlier, switches learn and associate source MAC addresses with switch ports when they receive a frame. In addition to mapping the MAC address to the port in their local table they record the statically configured or dynamically learned VLAN ID, making it easy for the switch to determine which ports and devices belong to which VLANs. Switches either add a frame tag or encapsulate frames with the VLAN header and trailer as they are received through an interface. VLAN IDs are removed prior to the frame's transmission out a user segment (non-trunk link segment). Trunk link segments are used to logically extend VLANs across multiple switches.

Each switch restricts frame forwarding by using the internal logic to distinguish and direct frames only to destination ports in the same VLAN as originating ports. When a frame arrives on a port, the switch forwards the frame only to a port that belongs to that VLAN. This limits the transmission of unicast, multicast, and broadcast traffic. Flooded traffic originating from a particular VLAN is only transmitted out other ports belonging to that VLAN.

Trunking Protocols

Generally speaking, a single port supports only the VLAN that it belongs to. However, VLANs need a trunk to connect two switches, servers, and routers together when traffic spans across multiple switches. Trunks are special connections that allow traffic for multiple VLANs and their associated VLAN IDs to be preserved and recognized (see Figure D.3).

FIGURE D.3

Trunk links are point-to-point physical connections between switches or switch to router. Trunk links are used to transport all VLAN traffic.

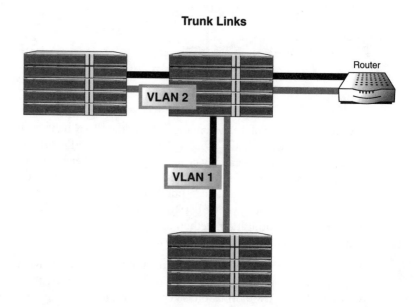

Trunk Links

For a VLAN or multiple VLANs defined on one switch to be recognized and linked to the same VLAN on other switches or routers, you need to configure some type of trunking protocol. There are four types of trunking protocols (see figure D.4):

- ISL (Cisco proprietary Fast Ethernet)

- 802.1Q (IEEE 802.3 trunking protocol)

- 802.10 (FDDI)

- ATM LANE (LAN Emulation)

FIGURE D.4

Different network technologies require different trunking protocols.

Trunking Protocols

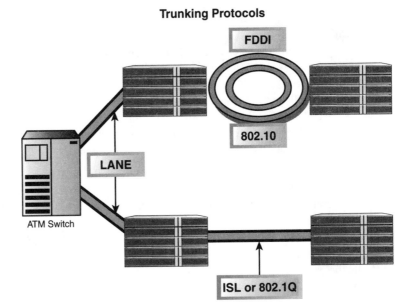

A physical connection between switches has to exist prior to configuring the link as a trunk segment. The physical link type determines the trunking protocol used. For instance, if your connection uses FDDI, the trunking protocol supported across this link is 802.10 (referring to the VLAN encapsulation across this link). There are two trunking protocol options for Fast or Gigabit Ethernet inter-switch links, the IEEE 802.1Q and Cisco's proprietary protocol, ISL (Inter-Switch Link).

The last trunking protocol alternative is ATM (Asynchronous Transfer Mode) LANE (LAN Emulation), which allows you to emulate a broadcast-based LAN environment over an ATM network providing a logical link between VLANs defined on local LAN segments on either side of this ATM network.

Trunking protocols are required to recognize and maintain VLAN information as traffic goes between switches, routers, and servers. Trunk links are point-to-point connections between switches, or switch to router. Devices connected to the same trunk link must agree on the trunking protocol. Multiple trunking protocols may be implemented within a network based on the network type used to facilitate the trunk.

All trunking protocols must either perform frame encapsulation or frame tagging to identify traffic as belonging to a particular VLAN and accomplish VLAN switching. VLAN identifiers are added as frames enter ports, maintained across trunk links and removed prior to transmission out a non-trunk link segment. This is true even with port-to-port communication within a single switch configured for multiple VLANs. The VLAN ID allows VLAN switching devices to make forwarding decisions based on the VLAN to port mapping. Each VLAN upon creation is assigned a number, such as VLAN 2 or 3, and so on. Switches use the VLAN IDs to forward a frame to the interface that matches.

VLAN identification is a key element used by switches to facilitate frame forwarding. VLAN IDs are added to frames as they enter a switch port. These IDs are only used by switches, routers, and servers connected to trunk links and are completely transparent to end users. VLAN identification assignment has the following qualities:

- Performed by port transceiver. Each port on the switch has an embedded transmitter/receiver (referred to as a transceiver) that adds the VLAN ID upon frame reception and strips it off when a frame is transmitted out a user port (see Figure D.5).

FIGURE D.5

VLAN identification is added by the transceiver upon entry into the switch. Trunk links carry VLAN traffic between switches and routers. The VLAN ID is removed prior to transmission out user segments.

VLAN Identification

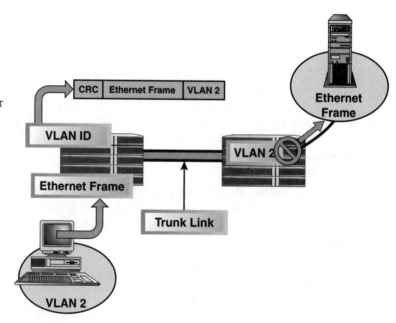

- Appears transparent to end hosts. A switch only uses VLAN IDs internally or across trunk links, not out user ports.

- Effective between any device connected directly to a trunk link, such as switches, routers, or servers that have network interface cards and drivers that are aware of the trunking protocol being implemented.

VLAN Trunking Protocol (VTP)

The VTP (VLAN Trunking Protocol) allows an administrator to distribute and manage VLANs across a switched network consisting of similar or dissimilar trunking protocols. VTP is a client-server based protocol, with VTP server switches controlling the creation, deletion, and modification of VLANs within VTP domains and VTP clients (switches) within the domains receiving VTP information from servers. This allows switches using multiple trunking protocols, such as Fast Ethernet ISL or 802.1Q, ATM LANE, and FDDI, to be managed transparently as a group defined as a single management domain.

Note

VTP (VLAN Trunking Protocol) allows an administrator to manage multiple VLANs in one domain.

VTP uses multicast advertisements to convey VLAN configuration information to all connected switches belonging to the same management domain in the network. VTP essentially provides a single point of VLAN management across mixed media trunk links using different encapsulation types. Switches forward VTP multicast advertisements only across trunking ports, never out a user segment. The dynamic nature of VTP makes managing multiple VLANs easy by reducing some of the manual configuration needs of the network.

Devices transmit VTP advertisements across trunk links only. VTP cuts down on misconfigurations and configuration inconsistencies problems, such as multiple VLAN names or incorrect VLAN-types. You can make all VLAN modifications from one central device and all other devices learn the modifications.

A VTP domain consists of one VTP switch (referred to as VTP server) controlling the creation, modification, deletion, and synchronization of VLANs on interconnected VTP client switches belonging to the same VTP domain. You configure a switch to be only in one VTP domain.

Note

VTP operates at layer two of the OSI Model. This messaging system protocol maintains VLAN configuration consistency. The VTP domain server distributes and synchronizes VLAN information with client switches within its domain.

By default, switches do not belong to any VTP domain, but will automatically join the first domain when it receives an advertisement from over a trunk link, or until you configure a management domain. To implement VTP on a switch's network, you enable the VTP protocol by configuring the VTP domain and mode on all switches (see Figure D.6).

VTP Modes

VTP modes identify the role a switch assumes within a VTP domain. When a VTP domain is defined the switch's role within the domain must be specified. The VTP mode (or role) determines whether a switch will serve as the central management point for the domain (server), learn from the central VTP switch (client), or act independently (transparent) of other domains. VTP switches can operate in one of three modes (see Figure D.6):

- Server

- Client

- Transparent

In figure D.6, there are two VTP domains, 1 and 2. Each domain has a VTP server and one client. The VTP servers in each domain serve as the central management point for the creation, deletion, and modification of VLANs for its domain. Clients within each domain will dynamically learn of VLAN changes from the server within their same domain. Transparent switches operate independently of other domains. Transparent mode switches simply pass VLAN changes between servers and clients of other domains, ignoring the changes.

FIGURE D.6
Two VTP domains, Domain 1 and 2. One Transparent VTP switch passing VTP information between the domain servers and clients.

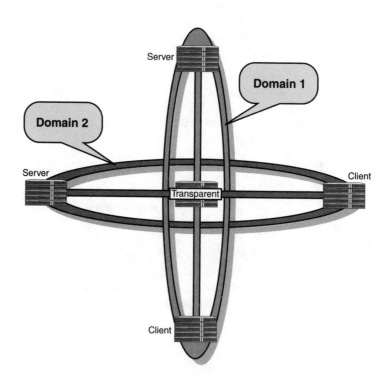

VTP Domains

Table D.1 gives a description of the three different VTP modes and their functions.

TABLE D.1   VTP Modes

VTP Mode	Function
Server	When a VTP domain is defined, this is the default switch mode. There should only be one server in a domain to avoid conflicts. Administrators can create, delete, and modify VLANs from a VTP server. Sends and forwards VLAN updates as multicast advertisements to clients. Transmits advertisements every five minutes by default or when a VLAN configuration has occurred. Synchronizes VLAN information using revision numbers to identify and ensure the appropriate updates are made by client switches. Switches receiving updates with a higher revision number overwrite VLAN information previously learned with a lower revision number.
Client	All other switches within the same domain name as the VTP server switch should be configured as clients. Receives VTP updates from the VTP server. Cannot use to create, delete, or modify VLAN configurations. Synchronizes with VTP server in the same domain.
Transparent	Used to configure backbone switches to forward VTP advertisements for domain clients and servers, but ignores VTP advertisements and updates. Operates independently of any domain. VLAN configuration defined on a transparent switch is not learned or propagated to any other VTP device. Administrators can create, delete and modify VLANs on transparent VTP switches. Forwards VTP advertisements for clients and servers from other VTP domains. Does not synchronize with any VTP domain servers.

When in VTP server mode, an administrator can create, modify, and delete VLANs. When you make a change to the VLAN configuration on the VTP server, changes are advertised to all client switches in the same VTP domain. Transparent mode switches provide the forwarding of VTP advertisements on behalf of VTP clients and servers in other domains, but these advertisements do not affect them. When in VTP client mode, a device accepts configuration changes from the VTP server for the domain, but cannot create, change, or delete VLANs. If a VLAN is created or deleted on the server these changes are automatically learned by all clients in the domain (see Figure D.7).

FIGURE D.7

The administrator on the VTP server creates VLAN 3 and deletes VLAN 2. All VTP client switches dynamically learn of these changes, adding the new VLAN 3 and deleting VLAN 2.

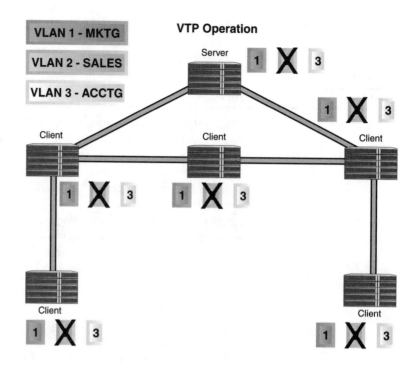

Client mode switches synchronize their VLAN configurations with the latest messages received from servers in the same domain. However, when in transparent mode, a switch does not create VTP advertisements or synchronize its VLAN configuration with messages received from switches in any domains. In this mode, it can create, delete, and modify VLANs, but the changes do not propagate to other switches in the domain, they affect only the local switch.

Note
VTP switches can operate in one of three modes: server, client, or transparent.

VLAN Configuration

After you've determined which VLANs you need to create and which switches and users will be associated with those VLANs, you can start the configuration process. You have four steps for VLAN configuration:

1. Create VLANs. The number of VLANs supported on a switch depends on the vendor. If VTP has been enabled, you can only perform this step at the VTP server switch. All other clients within that VTP domain will learn about new or deleted VLANs.

2. Enable trunking on switch links and define the appropriate trunking protocol.

3. Assign VLANs to ports or enable dynamic VLAN assignment by configuring a VMPS server. After you create VLANs, you must specify which ports on each switch will belong to that VLAN. VLANs have no meaning without associating the user ports to each subnet. Because each switch may have different port densities you must perform this step at each switch. This information cannot be learned via the VTP protocol. When you manually assign VLANs to switch ports, it is known as port-based or static VLAN membership. Any device that is physically attached to this port will belong to the VLAN mapped to that port.

    If inter-VLAN communication is desired then an additional step must be performed.

4. Physically connect a router to the switched network and configure the interface as a trunk link supporting the appropriate trunking protocol and assign the layer three network address for the subnet. Routers provide the layer 3 connection between layer 2 VLAN subnets. Without a router somewhere in the mix communication would be limited to Intra-VLAN only.

Although the specific configuration commands used to create and implement VLANs varies by vendor the basic process is the same as detailed previously. Please refer to your vendor's documentation for configuration instructions.

APPENDIX E

SUBNETTING

Registered Public IP addresses are assigned to organizations and individuals by ARIN (American Registry for Internet Numbers) allowing them to participate on the Internet. The address assigned represents the network address of the company or individual and falls in one of three main categories, Class A, B, or C, depending on the size of the network and the number of hosts. A single network address treats the network and all hosts within it as a single non-routed network. This is not realistic because most companies large and small have broken up their networks into smaller more manageable pieces called subnets. With a single 32-bit network address, bits need to be borrowed to obtain subnet addresses. The process of subdividing IP addresses into subnets is referred to as subnetting. We discussed IP addressing and subnetting in detail in Chapter 2, "IP and IP Addressing." The following tables show examples of Class A, B, and C subnetting.

Tables E.1, E.2, and E.3 include extended subnet masks, represented by a slash and then a number, decimal, and in hexadecimal. Also each table shows the number of subnets and hosts available based on the address class and bits masked beyond the classful mask. Each table is structured the same to make it an easy subnetting reference tool. The first row starts with the standard classful mask represented in bits. For example, a Class C standard mask is 24 bits in length, so the first value would be /24. The Class B standard mask is 16 bits (or /16) and Class A standard masks are always 8 bits (or /8). Each subsequent column shows the extended mask incremented one bit more than the previous up to the maximum value of 32 bits. The second row, labeled mask, shows the masked bits in decimal values. The third and fourth rows list the number of subnets and hosts based on the subnetted bits. The fifth row shows the mask in hexadecimal. The last row shows the binary values of the subnetted bits.

TABLE E.1 Class C Subnet Reference

Bits	Mask	Number of Subnets	Number of Hosts	Mask in Hex in Binary	4th Byte
/24	255.255.255.0	0	254	FF.FF.FF.00	0000 0000
/25	255.255.255.128	0	126	FF.FF.FF.80	1000 0000
/26	255.255.255.192	2	62	FF.FF.FF.C0	1100 0000
/27	255.255.255.224	6	30	FF.FF.FF.E0	1110 0000
/28	255.255.255.240	14	14	FF.FF.FF.F0	1111 0000

TABLE E.1   Continued

Bits	Mask	Number of Subnets	Number of Hosts	Mask in Hex	4th Byte in Binary
/29	255.255.255.248	30	6	FF.FF.FF.F8	1111 1000
/30	255.255.255.252	62	2	FF.FF.FF.FC	1111 1100
/31	255.255.255.254	126	0	FF.FF.FF.FE	1111 1110
/32	255.255.255.255	254	0	FF.FF.FF.FF	1111 1111

TABLE E.2   Class B Subnet Reference

Bits	Mask	Number of Subnets	Number of Hosts	Mask in Hex	3rd and 4th Byte in Binary
/16	255.255.0.0	0	65,534	FF.FF.00.00	0000 0000.0000 0000
/17	255.255.128.0	0	32,766	FF.FF.80.00	1000 0000.0000 0000
/18	255.255.192.0	2	16,382	FF.FF.C0.00	1100 0000.0000 0000
/19	255.255.224.0	6	8,190	FF.FF.E0.00	1110 0000.0000 0000
/20	255.255.240.0	14	4,094	FF.FF.F0.00	1111 0000.0000 0000
/21	255.255.248.0	30	2,046	FF.FF.F8.00	1111 1000.0000 0000
/22	255.255.252.0	62	1,022	FF.FF.FC.00	1111 1100.0000 0000
/23	255.255.254.0	126	510	FF.FF.FE.00	1111 1110.0000 0000
/24	255.255.255.0	254	254	FF.FF.FF.00	1111 1111.0000 0000
/25	255.255.255.128	510	126	FF.FF.FF.80	1111 1111.1000 0000
/26	255.255.255.192	1,022	62	FF.FF.FF.C0	1111 1111.1100 0000
/27	255.255.255.224	2,046	30	FF.FF.FF.E0	1111 1111.1110 0000
/28	255.255.255.240	4,094	14	FF.FF.FF.F0	1111 1111.1111 0000
/29	255.255.255.248	8,190	6	FF.FF.FF.F8	1111 1111.1111 1000
/30	255.255.255.252	16,382	2	FF.FF.FF.FC	1111 1111.1111 1100
/31	255.255.255.254	32,766	0	FF.FF.FF.FC	1111 1111.1111 1110
/32	255.255.255.255	65,534	0	FF.FF.FF.FF	1111 1111.1111 1111

TABLE E.3 Class A Subnet Reference

Bits	Mask	Number of Subnets	Number of Hosts	Mask in Hex	2nd, 3rd, and 4th Bytes in Binary
/8	255.0.0.0	0	16,777,214	FF.00.00.00	0000 0000.0000 0000.0000 0000
/9	255.128.0.0	0	8,388,606	FF.80.00.00	1000 0000.0000 0000.0000 0000
/10	255.192.0.0	2	4,194,302	FF.C0.00.00	1100 0000.0000 0000.0000 0000
/11	255.224.0.0	6	2,097,150	FF.E0.00.00	1110 0000.0000 0000.0000 0000
/12	255.240.0.0	14	1,048,574	FF.F0.00.00	1111 0000.0000 0000.0000 0000
/13	255.248.0.0	30	524,286	FF.F8.00.00	1111 1000.0000 0000.0000 0000
/14	255.252.0.0	62	262,142	FF.FC.00.00	1111 1100.0000 0000.0000 0000
/15	255.254.0.0	126	131,070	FF.FE.00.00	1111 1110.0000 0000.0000 0000
/16	255.255.0.0	254	65,534	FF.FF.00.00	1111 1111.0000 0000.0000 0000
/17	255.255.128.0	510	32,766	FF.FF.80.00	1111 1111.1000 0000.0000 0000
/18	255.255.192.0	1,022	16,382	FF.FF.C0.00	1111 1111.1100 0000.0000 0000
/19	255.255.224.0	2,046	8,190	FF.FF.E0.00	1111 1111.1110 0000.0000 0000
/20	255.255.240.0	4,094	4,094	FF.FF.F0.00	1111 1111.1111 0000.0000 0000
/21	255.255.248.0	8,190	2,046	FF.FF.F8.00	1111 1111.1111 1000.0000 0000
/22	255.255.252.0	16,382	1024	FF.FF.FC.00	1111 1111.1111 1100.0000 0000
/23	255.255.254.0	32,766	510	FF.FF.FC.00	1111 1111.1111 1110.0000 0000
/24	255.255.255.0	65,534	254	FF.FF.FF.00	1111 1111.1111 1111.0000 0000
/25	255.255.255.128	131,070	126	FF.FF.FF.80	1111 1111.1111 1111.1000 0000
/26	255.255.255.192	262,142	62	FF.FF.FF.C0	1111 1111.1111 1111.1100 0000
/27	255.255.255.224	524,286	30	FF.FF.FF.E0	1111 1111.1111 1111.1110 0000
/28	255.255.255.240	1,048,574	14	FF.FF.FF.F0	1111 1111.1111 1111.1111 0000
/29	255.255.255.248	2,097,150	6	FF.FF.FF.F8	1111 1111.1111 1111.1111 1000
/30	255.255.255.252	4,192,302	2	FF.FF.FF.FC	1111 1111.1111 1111.1111 1100
/31	255.255.255.254	8,388,606	0	FF.FF.FF.FE	1111 1111.1111 1111.1111 1110
/32	255.255.255.255	16,777,216	0	FF.FF.FF.FF	1111 1111.1111 1111. 1111 1111.

APPENDIX F

GLOSSARY OF TERMS

NUMERIC

1BASE5   Implementing the IEEE 802.3 standard using 1Mbps transmission on a baseband medium with a maximum segment length of 500 meters.

10BASE2   Implementing the IEEE 802.3 (Ethernet) standard using 10Mbps transmission on a baseband medium with a maximum segment length of 185 meters.

10BASE5   Implementing the IEEE 802.3 (Ethernet) standard using 10Mbps transmission on a baseband medium with a maximum segment length of 500 meters.

10BASET   Implementing the IEEE 802.3 (Ethernet) standard using 10Mbps transmission on a baseband medium. This standard enables attaching AUI-compatible devices to 24 gauge, unshielded twisted-pair cable, rather than the usual coaxial media. The maximum distance limitation of each segment is 100 meters.

100BASEFX   Implementing the IEEE 802.3 (Ethernet) standard using 100Mbps transmission on a baseband medium, using multi-mode fiber-optic cable. The maximum distance limitation for 100BaseFX multimode fiber is 412 meters for half-duplex and 2km when configured in full-duplex mode. Distances greater than 2kms are achieved when implemented over single mode fiber.

100BASET   Implementing the IEEE 802.3 (Ethernet) standard using 100Mbps transmission on a baseband medium, using UTP wiring. The maximum distance limitation of UTP is 100 meters.

100BASET4   Implementing the IEEE 802.3 (Ethernet) standard using 100Mbps transmission on a baseband medium, and using four pairs of Category 3,4, or 5 UTP wiring. The maximum distance limitation of each segment is 100 meters.

100BASE-Tx   Implementing the IEEE 802.3 (Ethernet) standard using 100Mbps transmission on a baseband medium. This standard enables attaching AUI-compatible devices to 24 gauge, unshielded twisted-pair cable, rather than the usual coaxial media. The maximum distance limitation of each segment is 100 meters.

100BASEX   Fast Ethernet specification using 100Mbps transmission, which refers to the 100BASEFX and 100BASETX standards for Fast Ethernet over fiber-optic cabling.

100VG-AnyLAN   100Mbps Fast Ethernet and Token-Ring media technology that uses four pairs of Category 3,4, or 5 UTP cabling.

A

ABR   Area border router. A router located on the border of two or more OSPF areas. It connects those areas to the backbone network.

AC   Access control. DLC byte on the IEEE 802.5 token-ring network that contains the token indicator and frame priority information.

access list   List kept by routers to control access to or from the router for a number of services.

access method   The means by which network devices access the network.

access server   Processor connecting asynchronous devices to a LAN or WAN through emulation software.

ACK   Acknowledge. Network packet that acknowledges the receipt of data.

acknowledgement   Notification sent from one network device to another acknowledging that a particular event has occurred.

active monitor   Computer on a token ring acting as a controller for the ring. It regulates the token and other aspects of performance.

address   Data structure for identifying a unique entity.

address mapping   Technique for different protocols to inter-operate by translating addresses from one format to another.

address resolution   Method for resolving differences between computer addressing schemes.

adjacency   Relationship between selected neighboring routers and end nodes for exchanging information.

ADSP   AppleTalk Data-Stream Protocol. Protocol that establishes and maintains full-duplex communication between two AppleTalk sockets.

advertising   The process in which a service makes its presence known on a network. Provided through a LAN-based multicast.

agent   Software that processes queries and returns replies.

algorithm   A defined rule or process for arriving at a solution to a problem.

all-routes explorer packet   Explorer packet that travels the entire SRB network, following all possible paths to a destination.

AMI   Alternative mark inversion (T1 lines). A pulse transmission T1 line coding scheme using alternate polarities in the pulse train.

ANSI   American National Standards Institute. An industry-supported organization that helps to develop trade and communications standards.

API   Applications program interface. The programming interface corresponding to the boundary between protocol layers. It specifies the functions and data used by one program module to access another.

AppleTalk   A series of communications protocols designed by Apple Computer, Inc.

application layer   Layer 7 of the OSI Reference Model, which provides services to application processes outside the OSI model. These can include e-mail, file transfer, and terminal emulation.

architecture   Refers to how a system is designed and how its components connect and operate with each other.

ARCnet   Baseband token-passing network from the Datapoint Corporation. It can communicate amongst up to 255 stations at 2.5Mbps.

area   A set of network segments and their attached devices.

ARP   Address resolution protocol. Used within TCP/IP to find a node's DLC address from its IP address. Interpreted in the TCP/IP suite. Can also be interpreted in the Banyan VINES PI suite.

ARPANET   Advanced Research Projects Agency Network. A packet-switching network established in 1969.

AS   Autonomous system. A collection of networks under a common administration. They share a common routing strategy.

ASBR   Autonomous system boundary router. An ABR located between an OSPF autonomous system and a non-OSPF network.

ASCII   American Standard Code for Information Interchange. Provides mapping between numeric codes and graphical characters. Used universally for PC and non-IBM mainframe applications.

asynchronous transmission   Method of data transmission enabling characters to be sent at irregular intervals. This is done by preceding each character with a start bit and following it with a stop bit. One common application is to communicate with modems and printers.

ATM   Asynchronous Transfer Mode (Cell Relay). Standard that defines a set of network services for transmitting data for high-speed LANs and WANs. Consists of a fixed-length cell of 53 octets (bytes), 5 of which are used for control functions and 48 of which are used for data.

AUI   Attachment unit interface. A drop cable for Ethernet between the station and transceiver.

AutoSPID   Automatic service profile identifier. A feature of a terminal adapter; it downloads SPID information from a compatible switch.

availability   The amount of time a network is operational.

B

B8ZS   Bipolar, with eight zero substitution. The line encoding method developed by AT&T and used on T1 circuits, ensuring that T1's "1s density" rule is enforced. This rule requires that the average number of 1s in the data be at least 12.5% (one in eight) and that no more than 15 consecutive 0s exist in a T1 data stream (because 1s are required to keep the sender and the receiver in synchronization).

B channel   Bearer channel. A 64Kbps channel that is end-user data.

backbone   The backbone is the part of the communications network that carries the heaviest traffic. It is a basis for the design of the whole network service.

background task   A secondary job that is performed while the user performs a primary task, such as a network server carrying out the duties of the network (controlling communications) while the users are running applications (such as word processors) in the foreground.

bandwidth   The amount of data that can be moved through a particular communications link.

bandwidth domain   All devices that share the same bandwidth.

bandwidth reservation   A process of assigning bandwidth to users and applications served by a given network. It gives priority to different traffic flows based on how critical and delay-sensitive they are.

baseband   A transmission technique that sends data bits without using a higher carrier frequency. The entire bandwidth of the transmission medium is used by one signal.

baud rate   A measure of the signaling speed in data communications. It specifies the number of signal elements that can be transmitted each second. For most purposes, at slow speeds, a baud rate is the same as the speed in bits per second.

BDR   Backup designated router. In OSPF, a backup to the DR.

beacon   A token-ring packet that signals a serious failure on the ring.

BECN   Backward Explicit Congestion Notification (frame relay). The sixth bit in the second octet of the frame relay header. It is used to inform a subscriber device of congestion in the backward direction.

BGP   Border gateway protocol. BGP, as defined in RFC 1771, enables the user to create loop-free, interdomain routing between autonomous systems.

binary   A numbering system using 1s and 0s (1=on, 0=off).

BIOS   Basic input/output system. A set of routines that work with the hardware to support the transfer of information between elements of the system. These include memory, disks, and the monitor.

bit   A binary digit used in the binary numbering system. It can be 0 or 1.

bit rate   The speed at which bits are transmitted, commonly expressed in bits per second (bps).

BNC   Bayonet Network Connector. A standardized coaxial cable connector; used for ARCNET networks and Thin Ethernet ("Cheapernet") cables.

BOOTP   Boot protocol. A protocol within TCP/IP used for downloading initial programs into networked stations. Interpreted in the TCP/IP PI suite.

BPDU   Bridge protocol data unit. A Spanning-Tree protocol packet sent out at configurable intervals to exchange information with bridges in the network.

bps   Bits per second.

breakout box   A test device used to view the signals in an RS-232, a V.35, or other interface. The breakout box is used to diagnose problems with the interface.

bridge   A device used to connect two separate networks into one extended network. Bridges forward only packets that are meant for the other network.

broadband   A transmission technique that sends data bits encoded within a much higher radio-frequency carrier signal. The transmission medium can be shared by many simultaneous signals because each of them uses only a portion of the available bandwidth.

broadcast   (1) A message directed to all stations on a network or collection of networks. (2) A destination address that designates all stations.

buffer   A software program, storage space in RAM, or a separate device used to store data. For example, the Sniffer Network Analyzer's capture buffer serves as a temporary storage space for captured network data until it can be analyzed or saved to disk.

bursty traffic   Data communications term that refers to an uneven pattern of data transmission.

bus   A common physical signal path composed of wires or other media, across which signals can be sent from one part of a computer to another. Also known as a highway.

bus topology   A linear LAN architecture in which transmissions from network stations propagate the link of the medium and are received by all other stations.

byte   A series of consecutive binary digits operated on as a unit.

C

CA   Certificate Authority. A third party that validates identities and creates digital certificates.

caching   A form of replication in which information learned during the previous transaction is used to process later transactions.

capture   The process by which the Sniffer analysis application records network traffic for interpretation. Generally speaking, this interpretation takes place during the display. However, the Expert Sniffer analysis application can simultaneously capture and interpret network traffic.

category cabling   Consists of five grades of UTP cabling described in the EIA/TIA-586 standard.

CBT or Core Based Trees   CBT is a sparse mode multicast routing protocol that uses a single shared tree to deliver multicast messages between members of multicast groups regardless of their location.

CCITT   Consultative Committee for International Telegraphy and Telephony. A member of the International Telecommunications Union (ITU) that is a specialized body within the United Nations. It sponsors a number of standards dealing with data communications networks, telephone switching standards, terminals, and digital systems.

channel   A communications path.

channel-attached   Refers to the attachment of devices directly by data channels to a computer.

channelized E1   Access link operating at 2.048Mbps.

channelized T1   Access link operating at 1.544Mbps.

CHAP   Challenge handshake authentication protocol. Security feature supported on lines with PPP encapsulation that helps prevent unauthorized access.

chat script   A group of three chat strings (Setup, Listen, and Disconnect) that controls communication parameters for an asynchronous device.

chat string   A Unix-style command/response sequence of characters downloaded to a serial device to control the device.

CIDR   Classless interdomain routing. A mechanism that helps alleviate the problem of exhaustion of IP addresses.

CIR   Committed information rate. The largest number of bits per second that a frame relay network agrees to carry over a PVC. CIR is assigned at the time of subscription to the frame relay service.

circuit   A communications path between two or more points.

circuit switching   A switching system in which a dedicated physical circuit path must exist between sender and receiver for the duration of the call.

classful routing protocols   Routing protocols that do not transmit information about the prefix length. Classful routing protocols do not understand subnetting.

classless routing protocols   Routing protocols that include prefix length with routing updates. Classless routing protocols understand subnetting.

CLI   Command-line interface. An interface that enables the user to interact with the operating system by entering commands and optional arguments.

client   (1) A module that uses the services of another module—for example, the Session layer is a client of the Transport layer. (2) A PC or workstation that accesses services or applications from another server PC or workstation.

CODEC   Coder-decoder. A device that often uses PCM in transforming analog signals into a digital bit stream and digital signals into analog.

collision   In Ethernet, the result of two nodes transmitting simultaneously. The frames from each device collide and are damaged when they meet on the physical media.

collision domain   In Ethernet, the network area in which frames that have collided are propagated.

community   In SNMP, a logical group of managed devices and NMSs in the same administrative domain.

community string   A text string that acts as a password and is used to authenticate messages sent between a management station and a router containing an SNMP agent.

compression   The reduction of the bandwidth or bits necessary to encode information.

concentrator   A central point for connecting several individual stations to a network ring. Commonly found on FDDI networks.

connectionless   Data transfer that occurs without the existence of a virtual circuit.

connection-oriented   Data transfer that requires the establishment of a virtual circuit.

convergence   The speed and capability of a group of internetworking devices running a specific routing protocol to arrive at a consistent understanding of the topology of an internetwork after a change in that topology.

core layer   Layer in a hierarchical network that provides optimal transport between sites.

CPU   Central processing unit. The main processor in a device, such as a computer or router.

CRC   Cyclic redundancy check. A check-word, typically 2 or 4 bytes at the end of a frame, that is used to detect errors in the data portion of the frame.

CSMA/CA   Carrier Sense Multiple Access with Collision Avoidance. Random access or contention-based control technique. The algorithm used in LocalTalk networks that controls transmission.

CSMA/CD   Carrier Sense Multiple Access with Collision Detection. Random access or contention-based control technique. The algorithm used by IEEE 802.3 and Ethernet networks that controls transmission.

CSU   Channel service unit. An interface to a common carrier's transmission facilities that ensures digital signals placed on the line are shaped and timed correctly. Often it is combined with a data service unit (DSU).

custom queuing   A method of queuing used to guarantee bandwidth for traffic by assigning queue space based on port number, protocol, or other criteria.

cut-through packet switching   A packet-switching approach that streams data through a switch so that the leading edge of the packet exits the switch at the output port before the packet finishes entering the input port.

D

D Channel   Data channel used for signaling between the switching equipment and the customer's equipment. This channel is not used for carrying user data.

DAC   Dual attachment concentrator. A concentrator offering two connections to the FDDI network, capable of accommodating the FDDI dual ring and other ports for the connection of other concentrators or FDDI stations.

DAS   Dual attachment station. An FDDI station offering two connections to the FDDI dual counter-rotating ring.

datagram   A logical grouping of information sensed as a Network layer unit over a transmission medium without prior establishment of a virtual circuit.

Data Link layer   Layer 2 of the OSI Reference Model, which provides reliable transit of data across a physical link.

DB-9   A 9-pin standardized connector used in personal computers for a token-ring network connection (female), serial I/O port (male), and RGBI output. Also used for LocalTalk.

DB-15   A 15-pin standardized connector used at the transceiver, the drop cable, and the station of IEEE 802.3 or Ethernet network components.

DB-25   A 25-pin standardized connector used in personal computers for parallel output ports (female connector on IBM PC chassis) or for serial I/O ports (male connector on IBM PC chassis).

DCE   Data circuit-terminating equipment (also called data communications equipment). On a serial communications link, it is the device that connects the DTEs into the communication line or channel.

DDP   Datagram delivery protocol. Adds to the services of the underlying link access protocol by including an internetwork of interconnected AppleTalk networks, with a provision to address packets to sockets within a node. Interpreted in the AppleTalk PT suite.

DDR   Dial-on-demand-routing. A technique in which a Cisco router can automatically initiate and close a circuit-switched session as transmitting stations demand.

DE   Discard eligibility. The seventh bit of the second octet of the frame relay header. A value of 1 in the DE bit indicates that the frame is eligible for discard by a congested network.

decapsulation   The unwrapping of data from a particular protocol header.

DECnet   DECnet is a proprietary network environment following Digital Equipment Corporation's DNA architecture. DECnet and DNA predate the OSI model.

decryption   The restoring of data to its original, unencrypted state.

dedicated LAN   Network segment allocated to a single device.

dedicated line   A line reserved for transmissions, rather than being switched as transmission is required.

default route   A routing table entry used to direct frames for which the next hop is not explicitly listed in the routing table.

default router   The router to which frames are directed when a next hop is not explicitly listed in the routing table.

delay   The time between the beginning of the transaction by a sender and the first response received by the sender.

Delay-sensitive traffic   Traffic requiring timeliness of delivery and that varies its rate accordingly.

Dense mode   Dense mode multicasting routing protocols flood multicast datagrams. When active multicast members are sparsely located with only a few active subnets (perhaps with only one host in the multicast group) and a limited amount of bandwidth. DVMRP, MOSPF and PIM-DM are all examples of dense mode multicast protocols.

destination address   The part of a message indicating for whom the message is intended.

DHCP   Dynamic Host Configuration Protocol. Enables IP addresses to be allocated dynamically so that addresses can be reused after hosts no longer need them.

dial-up line   A communications circuit established by a switched-circuit connection using the telephone network.

Differential Services or DiffServ   DiffServ is a QoS protocol that provides priority-based traffic forwarding. DiffServ uses the Differential Service field bits within the IP header to classify traffic and then prioritizes this traffic within output queues.

DIP switch   Dual in-line package switch. A switch attached to a printed circuit board. It usually requires a small screwdriver to change it. Two settings exist—on and off. Printed circuit boards usually have "banks" of multiple DIP switches that are used to configure the board in a semi-permanent way.

DISC   Disconnect. An LLC non-data frame indicating that the connection established by an earlier SABM or SABME is to be broken.

display   The process in which the Sniffer analyzer interprets the traffic recorded during capture. During display, the analyzer decodes the layers of protocol in the recorded frames and displays them as English abbreviations or summaries.

distance vector routing algorithm   Class of routing algorithms calling for each router to send some or all of its routing table to its neighbors.

Distribution layer   The layer in a hierarchical network that provides policy-based connectivity.

DLC   Data Link Control. The lowest protocol layer within the transmitted network frame. Its fields typically include the source address, the destination address, and sometimes additional control information.

DLCI   Data Link connection identifier. A 10-bit number used by the frame relay protocol that identifies a virtual circuit.

DM Disconnected Mode. An LLC message acknowledging that a previously established connection has been broken.

DNA Digital Network Architecture is a proprietary network model developed by Digital Equipment Corporation for its DECnet Phase IV environment.

DNS Domain name service. A protocol within TCP/IP used for discovering information about resources using a database distributed among different name servers. Interpreted in the TCP/IP PI suite.

DoD Department of Defense. The United States DoD was a major proponent in the development of the TCP/IP protocol suite.

DR Designated router. An OSPF router generating LSAs for a multi-access network.

DS0 Digital signal level 0 (T1 lines). A single 64Kbps channel in a DS1 signal. See also *DS1* and *DS3*.

DS1 Digital signal level 1 (T1 lines). Basic digital signal for transmission over T1 facilities. The DS1 signal consists of 24 channels at 64Kbps (called DS0, or Digital signal level 0, channels), plus 8Kbps used for synchronization and signaling—for a total bandwidth of 1,544Kbps.

DS3 Digital signal level 3 (T3 lines). Specification for transmitting digital signals at 44.736Mbps.

DSAP Destination service access point. The LLC SAP for the protocol expected to be used by the destination station in decoding the frame data.

DSL Digital Subscriber Line. Technology used between the customer premise and service provider using higher frequency ranges to enable higher bandwidth capacity over standard copper wires.

DSU Data service unit. A device that connects terminal equipment to digital communications lines. See also *CSU*.

DTE Data terminal equipment. A generic term used to describe the host or end-user machine on a serial communications link.

DUAL Diffusing update algorithm. A convergence algorithm used in enhanced IGRP, which provides loop-free operation throughout a route computation.

duplex A characteristic of data transmission, either full- or half-duplex. Full-duplex permits simultaneous two-way communication. Half-duplex means only one side can talk at a time.

DVMRP Distance Vector Multicast Routing Protocol. DVMRP is a protocol for routing multicast datagrams through an internetwork.

dynamic routing Routing that automatically adjusts the network topology or traffic changes.

E

E1   A digital transmission link with a capacity of 2.048Mbps (CCITT version of T1). E1 circuits are the European standard equivalent of a T1.

EBCDIC   Extended Binary Coded Decimal Interchange Code. Mapping between numeric codes and graphical characters used for IBM mainframe computers and communications protocols defined by IBM.

Echo   (1) A request/response protocol within XNS used to verify the existence of a host. (2) A protocol within AppleTalk that enables any node to send a datagram to any other node and to receive an echoed copy of that packet in return to verify the existence of that node or to make round-trip delay measurements. Interpreted in the AppleTalk PI suite. (3) A protocol transmitted by a Net RPC frame in Banyan VINES.

ED   An end delimiter is used to signify the end of a datagram transmission or end of a bit sequence. Token-Ring networks use this to mark the end of a datagram.

EGP   Exterior Gateway Protocol. A protocol within TCP/IP used in exchanging routing information among gateways belonging to either the same or different systems.

EIA   Electronic Industries Association. A standard organization specializing in the electrical and functional characteristics of interface equipment.

EIA/TIA-232   Repl rs232.

EIGRP   Extended Interior Gateway Routing Protocol. EIGRP is an enhanced version of IGRP and is a suite of Cisco routing protocols used in TCP/IP and OSI internetworks.

encapsulation   The wrapping of data in a particular protocol header.

encryption   Applying a specific algorithm to data to alter the appearance of the data and make it incomprehensible to those who are not authorized to see the information.

Error   A protocol within XNS by which a station reports receiving and discarding a defective packet. Interpreted in the XNS PI suite.

error rate   In data transmission, the ratio of the number of incorrect elements transmitted to the total number of elements transmitted.

ES   ES or end system is a term used to describe an end device, such as a workstation or host.

ESF   Extended Superframe Format (T1). A modification of the DS1 format that uses the 193rd bit to signal line problems.

Ethernet   A CSMA/CD network standard originally developed by Xerox; similar to (and often used interchangeably with) the IFFE 802.3 standard.

Ethertype   A 2-byte protocol-type code in Ethernet frames used by several manufacturers but independent of the IEEE 802.3 standard.

event   A network message that indicates irregularities in operation in physical elements of a network.

expansion   Running a compressed data set through an algorithm that restores the data set to its original size.

explorer packet   The packet generated by an end station trying to find its way through an SRB network.

exterior gateway protocol   An internetwork protocol used to change routing information between autonomous systems.

F

Fast Ethernet   Includes any number of 100Mbps Ethernet specifications, at a speed 10 times faster than the 10BaseT Ethernet specification.

FC   Frame control. On a token-ring network, the DLC byte that contains the frame's type.

FCS   Frame Check sequence. Similar to a CRC (Cyclic Redundancy Check). Used to detect damage to a datagram or its contents.

FDDI   Fiber distributed data interface. An ANSI/ISO standard that defines a 100Mbps LAN over a fiber-optic medium using a timed token over a dual ring of trees.

FE   Framing error. An error that occurs because of incorrect framing of data units transmitted. In asynchronous transmission, this is usually due to a deviation in the stop bit cell.

FECN   Forward explicit congestion notification (frame relay). The fifth bit in the second octet of the frame relay header. Used to inform a subscriber device of congestion in the forward direction.

FEP   Front-end processor. Sits in front of a computer and is designed to handle the telecommunications burden, so the computer can concentrate on handling the processing burden.

fiber-optic cable   A cable that conducts modulated light transmission.

filter   The Sniffer analysis application uses several varieties of filters, including capture filters that determine which arriving frames the analyzer discards and which it retains. The Sniffer also uses display filters that determine which frames in the capture buffer will be displayed. Eliminating a frame from a display with a display filter does not remove the frame from memory.

firewall   An access server or router designated as a buffer between any connections from public networks to a given private network. A firewall router ensures the security of the private network.

flash update   A routing update sent asynchronously in response to a change in the network topology.

floating static route   A static route that has a higher administrative distance than a dynamically-learned route, so that it can be overridden by dynamically-learned routing information.

flooding   A technique used by bridges and switches in which traffic received on an interface is then sent out over all the interfaces of the device, except the interface from which the information was originally received.

flow control   Hardware or software mechanisms used in data communications to turn off transmission when the receiving workstation is incapable of storing the data it is receiving. Refers to various methods of regulating the flow of data during a conversation. Buffers are an example of flow control.

fragmentation   The process of breaking a packet into smaller units when transmitting over a network that can't support a packet of the original size.

frame   The multibyte unit of data transmitted at one time by a station on the network. It is synonymous with the term packet.

frame check sequence (FCS)   In bit-oriented protocols, a 16-bit field added to the end of a frame that contains transmission error-checking information.

Frame Relay   A streamlined access protocol commonly used for LAN interconnectivity.

FRMR   Frame reject. An LLC command or response indicating that a previous frame had a bad format and is being rejected. The FRMR frame contains five bytes of data that explain why the previous frame was bad.

Front-end processor   Also known as an *FEP*. Sits in front of a computer and is designed to handle the telecommunications burden so the computer can concentrate on handling the processing burden.

FS   Frame status. A byte appended to a token-ring network frame following the CRC. It contains the Address Recognized and Frame Copied bits.

FTP   File transfer protocol. (1) A protocol based on TCP/IP for reliable file transfer. Interpreted in the TCP/IP PI suite. (2) A protocol transmitted by a Net RPC frame in Banyan VINES.

full-duplex   The capability to have simultaneous data transmission between a sending and receiving station.

full mesh   A network in which devices have been organized in a mesh topology, with each network node having a virtual or physical circuit connecting to every other network node.

functional address   A limited broadcast destination address for IEEE 802.5 token-ring networks. Individual bits in the address specify attributes that stations eligible to receive the frame should have. Similar to multicast address.

G

gateway   A computer that connects two different networks. Usually, this means two different kinds of networks. In TCP/IP terminology, however, a gateway connects two separately administered subnetworks, which might or might not be running the same networking protocols.

GNS   Get Nearest Server. Request packet sent by a client on an IPX network to locate the nearest active server of a particular type.

GUI   Graphical user interface; pronounced "goo-ey." An operating system or environment that displays options onscreen as icons or picture symbols.

H

handshaking   The electrical exchange of predetermined signals when a connection is made between two devices carrying data. Computers must *handshake* through a procedure of *greeting* the opposite device.

HDLC   High-level data link control. A standard bit-oriented protocol developed by the International Standards Organization (ISO). In HDLC, control information is always placed in the same position. Specific bit patterns used for control differ dramatically from those used to represent data, minimizing errors. Many internetworking companies (such as Cisco and Vitalink) have developed proprietary versions of HDLC that the Sniffer Internetwork analysis application can decode.

header   The beginning portion of a message that contains the destination address, source address, message-numbering, and other information. The header helps direct the message along its journey. Different protocols implement headers in different ways.

heartbeat   On Ethernet, the SQE signal generated by the transceiver at the end of a transmitted frame to check the SQE circuitry. See *SQE TEST*.

hop   A term used in routing. A hop is one data link. A path to the final destination on a net is a series of hops away from the origin. Each hop has a cost associated with it, enabling the calculation of a least cost path.

hop count   A routing metric used to measure the distance between a source and its destination.

host   A computer system on a network.

host number   The part of an IP address that designates which node on the subnetwork is being addressed.

hub   A concentrator and repeater for the network. Generally speaking, a hub is a central point for wiring or computing in a network.

I

IARP   Inverse Address Resolution Protocol. IARP enables a frame relay station to discover the protocol address corresponding to a given hardware address.

ICMP   Internet Control Message Protocol. A protocol within TCP/IP mainly used to report errors in datagram transmission. Interpreted in the TCP/IP PI suite.

ID   Identification.

IEEE   Institute of Electrical and Electronics Engineers, Inc. Standards documents are available from them at 345 East 47th Street, New York, NY 10017.

IETF   Internet Engineering Taskforce. A taskforce of more than 80 groups responsible for developing Internet standards.

I-Frame   Information frame. An LLC, HDLC, or SDLC frame type used to send sequenced data that must be acknowledged.

IGMP   Internet Group Management Protocol. IGMP is used to keep neighboring multicast routers informed of the host group memberships present on a particular local network.

IGP   Interior Gateway Protocol. Internet protocol used to exchange routing information within an autonomous system.

IGRP   Interior Gateway Routing Protocol. Cisco routing protocol designed for campus-wide use, as opposed to wide-area use.

Interface   (1) A connection between two devices or systems. (2) A network connection in routing terminology. (3) A shared boundary in telephony. (4) The boundary between adjacent layers of the OSI model.

Internet   The largest global internetwork, which connects thousands of networks worldwide.

Internetwork   A collection of one or more networks with different protocols and connecting devices.

intranet   A network that is internal to an organization, based on Web technology.

IntServ or Integrated Services   IntServ is a QoS architecture supporting service-level routing. RSVP is the major protocol within the IS Integrated Services (also known as IntServ) model. RSVP is reservation based, where host applications or ingress routers must reserve resources end to end prior to communication commencing between end systems.

I/O   Input/Output. The part of a computer system or the activity that is primarily dedicated to the passing of information into or out of the central processing unit or memory.

IP   Internet Protocol. The lowest-layer protocol under TCP/IP that is responsible for end-to-end forwarding and long packet fragmentation control. Interpreted in the TCP/IP PI suite. A similar protocol is interpreted in the Banyan VINES PI. See also *IPX* and *ISO*.

IP address   32-bit address assigned to hosts using TCP/IP. Sometimes called an Internet address.

IP multicast   Routing technique enabling IP traffic to be sent from one source to several destinations, or from many sources to many destinations.

IPX   Internet packet exchange. Novell's implementation of Xerox Internet Datagram Protocol. Interpreted in the Novell NetWare PI suite.

IP tunnel   IP tunnels are used to encapsulate datagrams within IP to carry them through an IP network. An IP tunnel consists of two routers (not necessarily on the same physical segment) that serve as entry and exit points of the tunnel. Traffic sent to the entry router of the IP tunnel performs encapsulation, whereas the exit router de-encapsulates datagrams. An example of its use is to logically connect multicast islands together, encapsulating this traffic within a unicast IP datagram allowing multicast traffic to be carried through a non-multicast enabled network or networks.

IS   (1) International Standard. (2) The final phase for an ISO protocol definition. At this point, the protocol is specified and guaranteed not to change. (3) Intermediate System. An OSI term for a system that originates and terminates traffic and that also forwards traffic to other systems. (4) Information System.

ISDN   Integrated Services Digital Network. A digital telephone technology that combines voice and data services on a single circuit.

IS-IS   The IS-IS routing protocol was originally designed by ISO for its CLNS (Connectionless Network Services). IS-IS relies on CLNP (Connectionless Network Protocol) for network layer addressing and delivery of datagrams. Enhanced support for the routing of IP datagrams resulted in the name change from IS-IS to Integrated IS-IS. Integrated IS-IS supports pure CLNP, pure IP, or integrated networks. IS-IS routing domains consist of three main entities; end systems, level 1, and level 2 routers.

ISL   Inter-switch link. Cisco protocol maintaining VLAN information as traffic flows between switches and routers.

ISO   (1) International Organization for Standardization (or International Standards Organization). (2) A consortium that is establishing a set of networking protocols. (3) The protocols standardized by that group.

ISP   Internet service provider.

ITU-T   International Telecommunications Union Telecommunication Standardization Sector. International body that sets worldwide standards for telecommunications technologies.

J–K

Kbps   Kilobytes per second.

keepalive interval   The time between each keepalive message sent by a network device.

keepalive message   Message sent by one network to another informing it that the circuit between the two is still alive.

L

Level 1   Level 1 or L1 routers are IS-IS routers that perform routing within and between areas within a domain.

Level 2   Level 2 or L2 routers are IS-IS routers that perform routing within and between domains.

LAN   Local area network. The hardware and software used to connect computers in a limited geographical area.

LANE   LAN emulation. Enables an ATM network to function as a LAN backbone.

LAP   Link Access Protocol. The logical-layer protocol for AppleTalk. It exists in two variants: ELAP (for Ethernet) and LLAP (for LocalTalk networks). Interpreted in the AppleTalk PI.

LAPB   Link Access Protocol Balanced. A subset of HDLC.

LAPD   Link Access Protocol-D. A link control protocol based on HDLC that is related to ISDN.

LAT   Local Area Transport. The DECnet protocol that handles multiplexed terminal (keyboard and screen) traffic to and from timesharing hosts. Interpreted in the DECnet PI suite.

latency   (1) The delay between the time a device requests access to a network and the time it is allowed to transmit. (2) The delay between the time a device receives a frame and the time the frame can be forwarded out the destination port.

leased line   A telephone line rented for exclusive continuous use. Commonly used to connect LANs remote from one another. The same as a leased circuit, dedicated circuit, or leased channel.

link   Network communications channel consisting of a transmission or circuit path and all the related equipment between a sender and a receiver. Often used in reference to a WAN connection.

link protocol   The set of rules by which a logical data link is set up and by which data transfers across the link. Includes formatting of the data.

Link state routing protocol   Also known as Shortest Path First Algorithm. Examples of Link state protocols are NLSP and OSBP. Link state routing protocols maintain topology maps, offer faster convergence, and send updates only when changes occur on the network.

LLC   Logical Link Control. A protocol that provides connection control and multiplexing to subsequent embedded protocols; standardized as IEEE 802.2 and ISO/DIS 8802/2.

LMI   Local Management Interface. An access signaling protocol defined for frame relay circuits. LMI carries information on the status of permanent virtual circuits between the network and a subscriber device. Additions to LMI can include multicasting, global addressing, and flow control.

load balancing   The capability of a router to distribute traffic over all its network ports that are the same distance from the destination address. This helps increase effective network bandwidth.

local explorer packet   A packet generated by an end system in an SRB network to find a host connected to the local ring.

LOOP   Loopback. A protocol under Ethernet for sending diagnostic probe messages.

LSA   Link State advertisements are sent by routers to advertise routes and link status information. OSPF routers send these types of advertisements.

LSB   Least significant bit. The lowest-order (usually rightmost) bit of a binary number.

M

MAC   Medium Access Control. The protocol layer that describes network management frames sent on the 802.5 token-ring. Most MAC frames are handled transparently by the network adapter.

MAC address   Standardized Data Link layer address required of every device or port connected to a LAN. Also known as a MAC layer address, hardware address, or physical address.

MAN   Metropolitan-area network. A network spanning a metropolitan area.

managed device   A network device that can be managed by a network management protocol.

Manchester encoding   A data encoding technique that uses a transition at the middle of each bit period that serves as a clock and also as data.

MAU   Multiple access unit (also known as a Medium attachment unit). The wiring concentrator or transceiver used for attaching stations connected to the network.

MB   Megabyte.

Mbone   Multicast Backbone. Mbone is an Internet multicast testing group established in 1992. Mbone basically consists of a collection of networks and routers referred to as multicast islands, connected by IP tunnels.

MBps   Megabytes per second.

mesh   A network topology in which devices are organized in a segmented manner with many interconnections placed between network nodes.

MIC   Media interface connector. An optical fiber connector pair that links the fiber media to the FDDI node or another cable.

mirroring   Synchronizing two disks on a file server.

modem   A contraction of modulate and demodulate. A conversion device installed in pairs at each end of an analog communications line. The modulator part of the modem codes digital information onto an analog signal by varying the frequency of the carrier signal. The demodulator part extracts digital information from a modulated carrier signal.

MOP   Maintenance Operations Protocol. A protocol under DECnet for remote testing and problem diagnosis.

MOSPF   Multicast OSPF is a dense mode multicast routing protocol that runs on top of OSPF to build shortest path trees from source to multicast group members across OSPF areas.

MPLS   Multi-Protocol Label Switching is a QoS protocol. MPLS-enabled devices identify and assign labels to traffic prioritizing forwarding based on these labels. Labels provide indicators to next hop devices as to how to forward the traffic. Labels are added upon entry into the MPLS network and removed upon exit.

MSB   Most significant bit. The highest-order bit of a binary number, not including the sign bit.

MTBF   Mean time between failure. The average time between failures of a device.

MTU   Maximum transmission unit. The maximum packet size, in bytes, that a particular interface can handle.

MTU Discovery   A function enabling software to discover and use the largest frame size that will travel over the network without requiring fragmentation.

multicast   (1) A message directed to a group of stations on a network or collection of networks (contrast with broadcast). (2) A destination address that designates such a subset.

multiplexing   Sending several signals over a single line and separating them at the other end.

N

NAK   Negative acknowledgment. A response from the recipient of data to the sender of that data that indicates the transmission was unsuccessful (that is, the data was corrupted by transmission errors).

NBMA   Non-broadcast multi-access. A multi-access network that does not support broadcasting or in which broadcasting is not feasible.

NCP   NetWare Core Protocol. Novell's Application layer protocol for the exchange of commands and data between file servers and workstations. Interpreted in the Novell NetWare PI suite.

NDS   Network Directory Services. NDS is a Novell application that operates with NCP to manage network resources.

NetBEUI   NetBIOS Basic Extended User Interface. A programming specification for NetBIOS.

NetBIOS   Network Basic Input/Output System. (1) A protocol implemented by the PC LAN program to support symbolically named stations and the exchange of arbitrary data. (2) The programming interface (API) used to send and receive NetBIOS messages. Several different and incompatible implementations of NetBIOS exist, each with a separate API—for example, in the IBM and Novell suites.

NetWare   The networking system designed by Novell, Inc., and the protocols used therein.

network   A collection of computers, printers, switches, routers, and other devices that are capable of communicating with each other over a transmission medium.

network address   A Network layer address referring to a logical network device; also known as a protocol address.

network layer   Layer 3 of the OSI Reference Model. It provides connectivity and path selection between two end systems.

network management   Systems that help maintain or troubleshoot a network.

network management protocol   The protocol that management entities within NMSs use to communicate with agents in managed devices.

network topology   The geography of a network. Examples of network topologies include ring, bus, and star.

NFS   Network file system. A protocol developed by Sun Microsystems for requests and responses to a networked file server.

NLM   NetWare Loadable Module. An individual program that can be loaded into memory and function as part of the NetWare NOS.

NLSP   NetWare Link Services Protocol. NLSP is a Link state protocol that improves the performance, reliability, scalability, and manageability of IPX traffic in large-scale LAN-WAN internetworks.

NNI   The Network-to-Network Interface defines ATM network-to-network connections.

nodes   Points on a network where service is provided or used, or where communications channels are interconnected. Node is sometimes used interchangeably with the term workstation.

non-local traffic   Traffic needing to travel to different network segments.

NOS   Network operating system. A term used to refer to distributed filesystems.

N(R)   Receive sequence number. An LLC or HDLC field for information frames indicating the sequence number of the next frame expected; all frames before N(R) are thus implicitly acknowledged.

N(S)   Send sequence number. An LLC or HDLC field for information frames that indicates the sequence number of the current frame within the connection.

NSAP   Network service access point addresses (or NSAPs) are divided into two parts; IDP (initial domain part) and DSP. The combination of these defines the location of the point of entry for the device's network layer. The IDP refers to the domain to which a device belongs. The IDP itself also contains two parts, the AFI and the IDI. The AFI (Authority and Format Identifier) specifies the authority assigning the address to the domain whereas the IDI (Initial Domain Identifier) specifies general information about the domain. The DSP (Domain Specific Part) contains the specific address of the domain to which a particular device belongs

NT1   Network Termination 1. In ISDN, a device providing the interface between customer premises equipment and central office switching equipment.

NTP/SNTP   Network Time Protocol/Simple Network Time Protocol. NTP or SNTP provides the mechanisms to synchronize time distribution in the Internet.

Null modem   Cross-pinned cable used for DTE to DTE.

NVRAM   Non-volatile RAM. RAM that retains its contents when a unit is powered off.

O

octet   String of eight bits; synonymous with byte.

ODI   Open Data-Link Interface. A Novell specification providing a standardized interface for NICs (network interface cards), enabling multiple protocols to use a single NIC.

OSI   Open systems interconnection. A generalized model of layered architecture for the interconnection of systems.

OSPF   Open Shortest Path First. A Link state IGP routing algorithm proposed to succeed RIP on the Internet.

Overhead   Information that provides support for computing processes but is not an intrinsic part of the data or operation.

P

packet   Multibyte unit of data transmitted at one time by a station on the network. Synonymous with the term frame.

packet switching   Method for sending data in packets through a network to a remote location. Data is subdivided into individual packets, each with its own identification and carrying the destination address. Packets then can be sent by different routes and reassembled in sequence by the packet ID.

PAD   Packet assembler disassembler. Computer on an X.25 network that enables asynchronous terminals to use the synchronous X.25 network by packaging asynchronous traffic into packets.

PAP   Password Authentication Protocol. Used by the PPP (Point to Point Protocol) to provide a simple method of authentication. PAP passwords are clear text only, not encrypted.

parallel interface   An interface that permits parallel transmission (or simultaneous transmission of the bits making up a character or byte) either over separate channels or on different carrier frequencies of the same channel.

parity bit   A binary bit appended to an array of bits to make the sum of the bits always odd or always even. Used with a parity check for detecting errors in transmitted binary data.

parity check   A process for detecting whether bits of data have been altered during transmission of that data.

partial mesh   A network in which devices are organized in a mesh topology, with some network nodes organized in a full mesh, but with others that are connected to only one or two other nodes in the network.

PAT   Port address translation. Cisco feature that enables the translation of private addresses into registered IP addresses by using port numbers.

patch panel   A device in which temporary connections can be made between incoming and outgoing lines. Used for modifying or reconfiguring a communications system or for connecting test instruments (such as the Sniffer Network Analyzer) to specific lines.

path control layer   Layer 3 in the SNA architectural model. Performs sequencing services related to proper data reassembly.

payload   The portion of a frame that contains the upper-layer information (data).

PC   Personal computer.

PDU   Protocol data unit. The data delivered as a single unit between peer processes on different computers. An OSI term for information at any layer in the OSI model.

PDV   Path delay value. The total round-trip propagation delay in an Ethernet network.

PGL   Peer Group Leader. Within a PNNI routing domain, PGLs are elected. The PGL is responsible for synchronizing and disseminating PNNI route information.

PHB   Per hop behavior or PHBs dictate how packets will be handled, that is, the type of service level applied when a datagram is forwarded. PHBs vary based on the differential code point set within the IP header.

Physical layer   Layer 1 of the OSI Reference Model. Concerned with the mechanical and electrical aspects of maintaining links between end systems.

pilot   A pilot of a network is a scaled-down prototype used to demonstrate basic functions; used most often for smaller networks.

PIM-DM   Protocol Independent Multicast-Dense Mode may run on top of any regular routing protocol and therefore offers a more flexible solution to multicasting across diverse networks. Uses the flooding and pruning to build multicast trees between source and group members.

PIM-SM   Protocol Independent Multicast-Sparse Mode routers may construct a single shared multicast trees through a central point (router) of reference in the network, referred to as the rendezvous point or separate multicast trees per a receivers request. The RP serves as the hub of all multicast forwarding.

Ping   A TCP/IP tool supplied with TCP/IP Distributed Sniffer System. Ping is a diagnostic utility that sends ICMP Echo Request messages to a specific IP address on the network.

PNNI   The Private Network to Network also referred to as the Private Network to Node Interface is defined within the ATM Forum af-pnni-0055.000 specification. PNNI is a protocol used to pass data between ATM switched networks.

policy routing   A routing scheme that forwards packets to specific interfaces based on user-configured policies.

POP   Point of Presence. ISPs maintain one or more connections to the Internet, referred to as a POP. This connection allows the ISP to provide access to the Internet for downstream clients.

port   The physical access point to a computer, multiplexer, device, or network where signals can be sent or received.

PPP   Point-to-Point Protocol (RFC 1331). PPP is a link-level protocol that bypasses X.25 for communication between systems that are directly connected, running any of a variety of protocols directly over HDLC.

pps   Packets per second. A measurement of throughput and performance of networks and networking devices.

preamble   A fixed data pattern transmitted before each frame to allow receiver synchronization and recognition of the start of a frame.

Presentation layer   The Presentation layer is the sixth layer of the OSI model (ISO 8823). It controls the formats of screens and files. Control codes, special graphics, and character sets work in this layer.

PRI   Primary rate interface. ISDN interface to primary rate access.

priority queuing   A method of queuing used to guarantee bandwidth for traffic by assigning space based on protocol, port number, or other criteria. Priority queuing has four levels: low, normal, medium, and high. The high queue is emptied first.

private addresses   Reserved IP addresses to be used internally only. They include: 10.0.0.0–10.255.255.255, 172.16.0.0–172.31.255.255, and 192.168.0.0–192.168.255.255.

process switching   An operation that provides full write evaluation and per-packet load balancing across parallel WAN links. It involves the transmission of entire frames to the route for CPU, where they are repackaged for delivery to or from a WAN interface, with the router making a route selection for each packet.

protocol   A specific set of rules, procedures, or conventions governing the format and timing of data transmission between two devices.

protocol stack   A set of related communications protocols that operate together and address communication at the seven layers of the OSI Reference Model.

prototype   A prototype of a network involves implementing a portion of the network to prove that its design meets the requirements used for larger networks.

provisioning   Defining the type of WAN, including the specifications and options.

proxy   An entity that stands in for another entity in the interest of efficiency.

proxy ARP   Proxy Address Resolution Protocol. A variation of the ARP protocol in which an intermediate device sends an ARP response on behalf of an end node to the requesting host.

Pruning   Multicast routers use a method called pruning to remove non-active subnets from multicast trees.

PTSE   PNNI state topology elements are route entries describing individual link state information. PSTEs are carried within PSTP (PNNI state topology packets) and are used to build a topology database. PNNI routers use the topology database to calculate routes to any given destination throughout the PNNI routing domain.

PTSP   PNNI state topology packets carry PNNI route updates. PTSPs consist of a series of PTSEs (PNNI State Topology Elements) describing individual link state information. From these updates the topology database is built giving PNNI peers within a group a complete map used to calculate routes to any given destination throughout the PNNI routing domain.

PUP   PARC Universal Packet. A type of Ethernet packet formerly used at the Xerox Corporation's Palo Alto Research Center. Interpreted in the XNS/MS-Net and the TCP/IP PIs but not included in their protocol diagrams because it's no longer in regular use.

PVC   Permanent virtual circuit. A unique, predefined logical path between two endpoints of a network. Used by frame relay.

Q

query   A message inquiring about the value of a variable or set of variables.

queue   (1) A list of elements, in order, waiting to be processed. (2) In routing, a backlog of packets waiting to be forwarded.

QoS   Quality of Service. A measure of performance for a transmission system reflecting its transmission quality.

R

RAM   Random access memory. Memory that can be read and written by a microprocessor.

RARP   Reverse Address Resolution Protocol. A protocol within TCP/IP used for finding a node's IP address, given its DLC address. Interpreted in the TCP/IP PI suite.

Rate-sensitive traffic   Traffic that is willing to give up timeliness for guaranteed rate.

reassembly   Putting an IP datagram together again at its destination, after it has been fragmented.

redistribution   Distributing routing information discovered through one routing protocol in the update messages of another routing protocol.

redundancy   Duplication of devices, connections, or services, so that in case of failure, these can perform the work of the ones that failed.

REJ   Reject. An LLC frame type that requests retransmission of previously sent frames.

reliability   The ratio of expected to received keepalives from a link. If this is a high ratio, the line is reliable.

REM   Ring error monitor. A station on the 802.5 token-ring network that collects MAC layer error messages from the other stations.

RP   Rendezvous Point. The RP serves as the hub of all multicast forwarding within a PIM-SM distribution tree.

repeater   A device inserted at intervals along a circuit to boost, amplify, and regenerate the signal being transmitted.

response time   The amount of time to receive a response to a request for a service from the network system.

RFC   Request For Comment. Designation used in DoD/TCP protocol research and development.

RG-58   The designation for 50-ohm coaxial cables used by Cheapernet (thin Ethernet).

RG-59   The designation for 75-ohm coaxial cables used by PC Network (broadband).

RG-62   The designation for 93-ohm coaxial cables used by ARCNET.

RII   Routing information indicator. If the first bit in the source address field of a token-ring frame is 1, the data field begins with routing information. Interpreted by the token-ring or Ethernet Sniffer analysis application independent of other PIs.

ring   A connection of two or more stations in a logically circular topology. Information is passed sequentially between active stations.

ring topology   A network topology that consists of a series of repeaters connected to one another by unidirectional transmission links to form a single closed loop. Each station on the network connects to the network at a repeater. Ring topologies are most often organized in a closed-loop star.

RIP   Routing Information Protocol. A protocol within the XNS and TCP/IP families used to exchange routing information among gateways. Interpreted in the XNS PT suite and TCP/IP PI suite.

RISC   Reduced instruction set computer. A type of microprocessor design that focuses on rapid and efficient processing of a relatively small set of instructions.

RJ-45   The designation for the eight-wire modular connectors used in 10BASE-T networks. It is similar to, but wider than, the standard (RJ-11) telephone modular connectors.

RMON   Remote Monitoring Management Information Base (MIB). Uses SNMP and standard MIB design to provide multivendor interoperability between monitoring products and management stations.

RNR   Receive Not Ready. An LLC and HDLC command or response indicating that transmission is blocked.

ROM   Read-only memory. Memory that can be read by the microprocessor but not written.

route   A path through an internetwork.

route summarization   The consolidation of the advertised addresses in a routing table. This reduces the number of routes in the routing table, the routing update traffic, and the overall or router overhead.

routed protocol   A protocol that can be routed by a router. A routed protocol contains enough Network layer addressing information for user traffic to be directed from one network to another network. Routed protocols define the format and use of the fields within a packet.

router   An internetwork-linking device operating at the Network layer (ISO layer 3).

routing   The process of finding a path to a destination host. Routing can be complex in larger networks because of the many potential intermediate destinations that a package might travel through before reaching its destination host.

routing domain   A group of end systems and intermediate systems operating under the same set of administrative rules.

routing metric   A standard of measurement, such as a path length, that is used by routing algorithms to determine the optimal path to the destination. This information is stored in routing tables. Metrics include communication cost, bandwidth, hop count, delay, path cost, MTU, and reliability.

routing protocol   A routing protocol supports a routed protocol by providing mechanisms for sharing routing information. Routing protocol messages move between the routers. A routing protocol enables the routers to communicate with other routers to update and maintain routing tables. Routing protocol messages do not carry end-user traffic from network to network. A routing protocol uses the routed protocol to pass information between routers.

routing table   A table stored in a router or some other internetworking device that keeps track of routes to particular network destinations and metrics associated with those routes.

routing update   A message sent from a router to indicate network reachability and associated cost of information. Typically sent at regular intervals after change occurs in the network topology.

RPC   Remote Procedure Call. A protocol for activating functions on a remote station and retrieving the result. Interpreted in the Sun PI suite. A similar protocol exists in Xerox XNS.

RPL   Remote Program Load. A protocol used by IBM on the IEEE 802.5 token-ring network to download initial programs into networked stations. Interpreted in the IBM PI suite.

RPS   Ring parameter server. A station on a token-ring network that maintains MAC layer information about the LAN configuration, such as ring numbers and physical location identifiers.

RR   Receive ready. An LLC non-data frame indicating readiness to receive data from the other station.

RS232 or RS-232C   Recommended Standard 232. EIA standard defining electrical characteristics of the signals in the cables that connect a DTE and a DCE.

RSVP   RSVP is the major protocol within the IS Integrated Services (also known as IntServ) model. RSVP is reservation-based, where host applications or ingress routers must reserve resources end-to-end prior to communication commencing between end systems. RSVP allows destination hosts to reserve resources along the path between source and destination providing QoS end to end.

RTMP   Routing Maintenance Protocol. Used in AppleTalk networks to enable internetwork routers to dynamically discover routes to the various networks of an internetwork. A node that is not a router uses a subset of RTMP (the RTMP stub) to determine the number of the network to which it is connected and the node IDs of routers on its network. Interpreted in the AppleTalk protocol interpreter.

S

S (S Frame)   Supervisory. An LLC, HDLC, or SDLC frame type used for control functions.

SABM   Set asynchronous balanced mode. An LLC non-data frame requesting the establishment of a connection over which numbered information frames can be sent.

SABME   Set asynchronous balanced mode (extended). SABM with two more bytes in the control field. Used in LAPB.

SAC   Single attachment concentrator. A concentrator that offers one S port for attachment to the FDDI network and M ports for the attachment of stations or other concentrators.

SAP   Service access point. (1) A small number used by convention, or established by a standards group, that defines the format of subsequent LLC data; a means of demultiplexing alternative protocols supported by LLC. (2) Service Advertising Protocol. Used by NetWare servers to broadcast the names and locations of servers and to send a specific response to any station that queries it.

SD   Start delimiters are used to signify the beginning of a datagram transmission or beginning of a bit sequence.

SDLC   Synchronous Data Link Control. An older serial communications protocol that was the model for LLC and with which it shares many features.

security management   One of five categories of network management defined by ISO for management of the OSI networks. Subsystems within these control access to various network services.

segment   (1) A section of any network that is bounded by routers, bridges, or switches. (2) In a LAN using a bus topology, a continuous electrical circuit often connected to other segments with repeaters. (3) In the TCP specification, a single Transport layer unit of information.

serial interface   An interface that requires serial transmission, or the transfer of information in which the bits composing a character are sent sequentially. Implies only a single transmission channel.

server   A node or software program that provides services to clients.

Session   Name for the Session layer protocol in the 1SO series, interpreted in the ISO PI suite.

Session layer   Layer 5 of the OSI Reference Model. This layer establishes, manages, and terminates sessions between applications, and manages data exchange between Presentation layer entities.

shielded cable   A cable that has a layer of shielded insulation to reduce electromagnetic interference.

silicon switching   A type of switching in which an incoming packet matches an entry in the silicon switching cache located in the SSE of the SSP module.

simplex   The capability for data transmission in only one direction between a sending station and a receiving station.

single-route packet   A packet in an SRB network that follows only one specific path to its destination.

sliding window flow control   A method of flow control in which a receiver gives a transmitter permission to transmit data until a window is full. When the window is full, the transmitter must stop transmitting until the receiver advertises a larger window.

SLIP   Serial Line Internet Protocol. Standard protocol for point-to-point serial connections using a variation of TCP/IP.

SMB   Server message block. A message type used by the IBM PC LAN program to make requests from a user station to a server and receive replies. Many of the functions are similar to those made by an application program to DOS or to OS/2 running on a single computer.

SMDS   Switched multi-megabit data service. A packet-switched, datagram-based WAN networking technology.

SMT   Station management. Provides ring management, connection management, and frame services for an FDDI ring.

SMTP   Simple Mail Transfer Protocol. A protocol within TCP/IP for reliable exchange of electronic mail messages. Interpreted in the TCP/IP PI suite.

SNA   (1) Systems Network Architecture. A set of protocols used by IBM for network communications, particularly with mainframe computers. Interpreted in the IBM PI suite. (2) Sniffer Network Analyzer. Network General's network analyzer that attaches to a network to monitor, record, analyze, and interpret network transmissions. Monitoring and analysis functions are separate menu-driven activities that provide high-level analysis and troubleshooting for complex local and wide-area network installations.

SNAP   Subnetwork Access Protocol (sometimes called Subnetwork Access Convergence Protocol). An extension to IEEE 802.2 LLC that permits a station to have multiple Network layer protocols. The protocol specifies that DSAP and SSAP addresses must be AA hex. A field subsequent to SSAP identifies one specific protocol. Interpreted in the TCP/IP PI suite and the AppleTalk PI suite.

SNMP Simple Network Management Protocol. Interpreted in the TCP/IP suite.

SNRM Set normal response mode. Places a secondary station in a mode that precludes it from sending unsolicited frames. The primary station controls all message flow. Used in SDLC.

SNRME Set normal response mode (extended). SNRM with two more bytes in the control field. Used in SDLC.

socket A logically addressable entity or service within a node, serving as a more precise identification of sender or recipient.

socket pair A socket pair consists of source and destination logical network layer addresses and upper layer udp or tcp ports. The source network layer address and port combined with the destination's network layer address and port provide a unique communication channel.

SOHO A small office or home office.

source address The part of a message that indicates from whom the message came.

spanning tree A method of creating a loop-free logical topology on an extended LAN. Formation of a spanning tree topology for transmission of messages across bridges is based on the industry-standard spanning tree algorithm defined in IEEE 802.id.

Spanning-Tree algorithm An algorithm used to create a spanning tree.

Spanning-Tree protocol A bridge protocol that utilizes the spanning-tree algorithm. This enables a learning bridge to dynamically work around the loops in a network topology by creating a spanning tree. Bridges exchange BPDU messages with other bridges to detect loops. They then remove loops by shutting down selected bridge interfaces.

Sparse mode Sparse mode multicast routing protocols assume that members are distributed and bandwidth is not plentiful and therefore tries to avoid wasting resources by building a multicast delivery tree, adding and pruning branches (subnets) as members join or leave multicast groups. CBT and PIM-SM are examples of sparse mode multicast routing protocols.

SPF The shortest path first. A routing algorithm used by routing protocols, such as OSPF to determine the shortest path to all networks and subnets througout an area.

SPID Service profile identifier. A number that some service providers use to define the services to which an ISDN device subscribes.

split horizon A routing rule that states a router can't send routing information about a network out of the same interface from which it learned that information.

SPX Sequential Packet Exchange. Novell's version of the Xerox protocol called SPP. Interpreted in the Novell NetWare PI suite.

SQE Signal quality error. The 802.3/Ethernet collision signal from the transceiver.

SQE TEST The SQE signal generated by the transceiver at the end of a transmitted frame to check the SQE circuitry. Also known as heartbeat in Ethernet.

SQL Structured Query Language. Used to access databases.

SQL server   A server that understands Structured Query Language.

SR/TLB   Source-route translational bridging. A method of bridging in which source route stations can communicate with two transparent bridge stations with the help of an intermediate bridge that translates between the two bridge protocols.

SSAP   Source service access point. The LLC SAP for the protocol used by the originating station.

SSE   Silicon switching engine. A routing and switching mechanism that compares the Data Link or Network layer header of an incoming packet to a silicon switching cache, determines the appropriate action, and forwards the packet to the proper interface. It can perform switching independently of the system processor.

SSP   (1) Silicon switch processor. A high-performance silicon switch for Cisco 7000 series routers that provides distributed processing and control for interface processors. (2) Switch-to-switch protocol. A protocol specified in the DLSw standard that routers used to establish DLSw connections, forward data, locate resources, and handle flow control and error recovery.

S/T Interface   In ISDN, the connection between a BRI interface and an NT1 device.

static route   Route that is explicitly configured and entered into the routing table.

store and forward packet switching   A packet switching technique in which frames are fully buffered and processed before being forwarded out the appropriate port. This includes calculating the CRC and checking the destination address. Bridges and switches using this method verify the frame prior to forwarding it. If a frame has been damaged, that frame is not forwarded. Store and forward devices isolate collision domains.

STP   Shielded twisted pair. A two-pair wiring medium used in a variety of network implementations. See also *Spanning-Tree protocol*.

stub area   An OSPF area that carries a default route, intra-area routes, and inter-area routes, but does not carry external routes.

stub network   A part of an internetwork that can be reached by only one path.

SUA   Stored upstream address. The network address of a token-ring station's nearest upstream neighbor. Texas Instruments calls this the UNA.

subinterface   One of a number of virtual interfaces on a single physical interface.

subnet   A term used to denote any networking technology that makes all nodes connected to it appear to be one hop away. In other words, the user of the subnet can communicate directly to all other nodes on the subnet. A collection of subnets together with a routing or network layer combine to form a network.

subnet address   A portion of an IP address that is specified as the subnetwork by the subnet mask.

subnet mask   A 32-bit number associated with an IP address; each bit in the subnet mask indicates how to interpret the corresponding bit in the IP address.

SVC   Switched virtual circuit. A virtual circuit set up on demand, as in the case of a dial-up telephone line or an X.25 call.

switch   (1) A network device the filters, forwards, and floods frames based on the destination address of each frame. (2) An electronic or mechanical device that enables a connection to be established as necessary and terminated when there is no longer a session to support.

symptom   An abnormal or unusual network event indicative of a possible network problem.

SYN   (1) The synchronized bit in a TCP segment; used to indicate that the segment is a SYN segment. (2) The first segment sent by the TCP protocol; used to synchronize the two ends of a connection in preparation for opening a connection.

synchronous transmission   A method of data transfer in which information is transmitted in blocks (frames) of bits separated by equal time intervals.

Syslog   A service that receives messages from applications on the local host or from remote hosts that have been configured to forward messages.

T

T1   A digital transmission link with a capacity of 1.544Mbps. T1 is a U.S. standard.

T3   A digital transmission link with a capacity of 44.736Mbps. T3 is a U.S. standard.

TA   Terminal adapter.

TACACS   Terminal Access Controller Access Control System. An authentication protocol that provides remote access authentication and related services, such as event logging. Uses user passwords.

TCP   Transmission Control Protocol. The connection-oriented byte-stream protocol within TCP/IP that provides reliable end-to-end communication by using sequenced data sent by IP. Interpreted in the TCP/IP PI suite.

TCP/IP   Transmission Control Protocol/Internet Program. A suite of networking protocols developed originally by the U.S. government for ARPANET and now used by several LAN manufacturers. The individual TCP/IP protocols are listed separately in this glossary.

Telnet   Protocol for transmitting character-oriented terminal (keyboard and screen) data. Interpreted in the TCP/IP suite.

terminal   A simple device, such as a computer, at which data can be entered or retrieved from the network.

terminator   A resistive connector used to terminate the end of a cable or an unused tap into its characteristic impedance. The terminator prevents interference-causing signal reflections from the ends of the cable.

TFTP   Trivial File Transfer Protocol. A protocol within TCP/IP used to exchange files between networked stations. Interpreted in the TCP/IP PI suite.

throughput   The quantity of data successfully transferred between nodes per unit of time, usually seconds.

THT   Token holding timer. The maximum length of time a station holding the token can initiate asynchronous transmissions. The THT is initialized with the value corresponding to the difference between the arrival of the token and the TTRT (FDDI).

TIA   Telecommunications Industry Association. An organization that facilitates the standardization of physical layer technologies.

token   A small message used in some networks to represent the permission to transmit; it is passed from station to station in a predefined sequence.

token bus   A type of LAN in which all stations can hear what any station transmits and in which permission to transmit is represented by a token sent from station to station.

token-ring   A ring-shaped LAN in which each station can directly hear transmissions from only its immediate neighbor. Permission to transmit is granted by a token that circulates around the ring.

topology   The physical arrangement of network nodes and media within an enterprise networking structure.

ToS   Type of service. A field in an IP datagram that indicates how the datagram should be handled.

traffic shaping   The use of queues to limit searches that can congest a network. Data is buffered and then sent into the network in regulated amounts, ensuring that traffic will fit within the promised traffic envelope for the particular connection.

translational bridging   Bridging between networks with dissimilar MAC sublayer protocols.

transparent bridging   A bridging scheme in which bridges pass frames one hop at a time based on tables associating end nodes with bridge ports. Often used in the Ethernet network.

Transport layer   Layer 4 of the OSI Reference Model. The transport layer is responsible for reliable network communication between end nodes. It implements flow and error control and often uses virtual circuits to ensure reliable data delivery.

trap   A message sent by an SNMP agent to an NMS, console, or terminal indicating the occurrence of a significant event.

tree topology   A LAN topology similar to a bus topology. Tree networks contain branches with multiple nodes.

TSR   Terminate and Stay Resident. A DOS program that, once loaded into RAM, remains there in the background until unloaded or power is shut off.

TTL   Time to live. A field in an IP header that indicates how long a packet is considered valid.

tunneling   An architecture that provides a virtual data link connection between two similar networks through a foreign network.

twisted pair   A relatively low-speed transmission medium consisting of two insulated wires arranged in a regular spiral pattern. The wires can be shielded or unshielded.

U

UA   Unnumbered acknowledgment. An LLC frame that acknowledges a previous SABME or DISC request.

UDP   User Datagram Protocol. A protocol within TCP/IP for sending unsequenced data frames not otherwise interpreted by TCP/IP.

UI   Unnumbered information. An LLC, HDLC, or SDLC frame type used to send data without sequence numbers.

U Interface   The connection between an NT1 device and the ISD network.

UNA   Upstream neighbor address. The network address of a token-ring station's nearest upstream neighbor. IBM calls this the SUA.

UNI   User-to-Network interface. An ATM forum specification defining an interoperability standard for the interface between ATM-based products located in a private network and ATM switches located in the public carrier networks.

unicast   A message sent to a single network destination.

unicast address   An address that specifies a single network device.

Unix   A popular portable operating system written by AT&T.

utilization   The percentage of the total capacity of a network segment.

UTP   Unshielded twisted pair. A four-pair wire medium used in a variety of networks. UTP does not require a fixed spacing between connections.

V

V.24   An ITU-T standard for Physical layer interfaces between DTE and DCE.

V.25bis   An ITU specification that describes procedures for call setup and teardown over the DTE-DCE interface in a PSDN.

V.32   An ITU-T standard serial-line protocol for bi-directional data transmission.

V.32bis   An ITU-T standard that extends V.32 to speeds of up to 14.4Kbps.

V.34   An ITU-T standard that specifies a serial-line protocol.

V.35   A CCITT wideband interface recommendation for WANs.

VC   Virtual circuit. A logical circuit created to ensure reliable communication between two network devices. A virtual circuit can be either permanent or switched and is used in frame relay and X.25. In ATM, virtual circuits are called virtual channels.

VCI   VCIs or Virtual Circuit Identifiers are used in conjunction with virtual path identifiers to uniquely identify logical circuits used to forward ATM cells to their intended destination. Some VPI/VCI values (also known as pairs) are well-known and reserved for specific purposes such as VPI=0/VCI=18, which is used for PNNI route information exchange.

VINES   Virtual Network Software. The networking operating system developed by Banyan Systems, Inc., and the protocols used therein. Notable components are StreetTalk and Net RPC.

VIP   Virtual interface processor.

virtual circuit   A communications link that appears to be a dedicated point-to-point circuit.

VLAN   Virtual LAN. A logical, rather than physical, grouping of devices. Devices are grouped using switch management software so that they can communicate as if they were attached to the same wire, when in fact they might be located on a number of different physical LAN segments.

VLSM   Variable length subnet mask. The capability to specify a different subnet mask for the same network number on different subnets. VLSM can help optimize available address space.

VPI   VPIs or Virtual Path Identifiers are usedin conjunction with virtual circuit identifiers to uniquely identify logical circuits used to forward ATM cells to their intended destination. Some VPI/VCI values (also known as pairs) are well-known and reserved for specific purposes such as VPI=0/VCI=18 which is used for PNNI route information exchange.

VPN   Virtual private network. Enables IP traffic to travel securely over a public TCP/IP network by encrypting all traffic from one network to another. A VPN uses tunneling to encrypt all information at the IP level.

VT   Virtual terminal. An entity that is part of the Application layer protocol and enables an application to interact with a terminal in a consistent manner independent of the terminal characteristics.

W

WAN   Wide area network. A collection of LANs, or stations and hosts, extending over a wide area that can be connected via common carrier or private lines. Typically, transmission speeds are lower on a WAN than on a LAN.

WFQ   Weighted fair queuing. A method of queuing that prioritizes low-volume traffic over high-volume traffic to ensure satisfactory response time for common user applications.

wildcard mask   A 32-bit quantity used in conjunction with an IP address to determine which bits in an IP address should be ignored when comparing that address with another IP address. A wildcard mask is specified when setting up access lists.

window   The number of data segments the sender is allowed to have outstanding without receiving an acknowledgment.

windowing   A method to control the amount of information transferred end to end, using different window sizes.

WINS   Windows Internet Naming Service. Enables clients on different IP subnets to register dynamically and browse the network without sending broadcasts.

workgroup   A collection of workstations and servers on a LAN designed to communicate and exchange data with one another.

WWW   World Wide Web. A large network of Internet servers providing hypertext and other services to terminals running client applications.

WWW browser   A GUI-based hypertext client application, used to access hypertext documents and other services located on remote servers throughout the WWW and Internet.

X–Y

X.25   A CCITT recommendation that defines the standard communications interface for access to packet-switched networks.

XID   Exchange identification. An LLC unnumbered frame type used to negotiate which LLC services will be used during a connection.

XDR   The External Data Representation protocol was developed by Sun Microsystems, Inc. to provide presentation layer services to its NFS architecture.

XNS   Xerox Network Systems. A family of protocols standardized by Xerox, particularly the Internet Transport Protocols.

X Window   Protocol for the management of high-resolution color windows at workstations. Originated by MIT, DEC, and IBM, and subsequently transferred to a consortium of vendors and developers.

Z

ZIP   Zone Information Protocol. Used in AppleTalk to maintain an internetwork-wide mapping of networks to zone names. ZIP is used by the Name Binding Protocol (NBP) to determine which networks belong to a given zone. Interpreted in the AppleTalk PI suite.

Zone   In AppleTalk networks, a set of one or more nodes within an internetwork.

APPENDIX G

ANSWERS TO QUESTIONS

Chapter 1

1. Application, Presentation, Session, Transport, Network, Data Link, and Physical.

2. The Network layer.

3. The Transport layer.

4. Bridges and switches function at layer 2 of the OSI model, the data link. They use MAC addresses (or layer 2) to forward data.

5. Ethernet_II, Ethernet_802.3, Ethernet_802.2, and Ethernet_SNAP.

6. TCP and UDP.

7. CSMA/CD—Carrier Sense Multiple Access with Collision Detection.

8. Token passing.

9. TX, FX, and T4.

10. FDDI.

Chapter 2

1. Class A, B, C, D, and E.

2. Logical addressing, connectionless packet delivery, and fragmentation and reassembly.

3. Class D.

4. 255.0.0.0.

5. 131 (128+2+1).

6. 6 subnets and 30 hosts.

7. 255.255.255.224.

8. 510 subnets and 126 hosts.

9. 6 bits = 62 hosts.

10. 12 bits would provide 2,046 hosts.

11. Static NAT is a one-to-one translation of inside private to outside registered addresses.

12. Dynamic NAT is the translation of many inside private addresses to one or more outside registered addresses.

Chapter 3

1. Directly connected interfaces, static, default and dynamic routing protocols.

2. Default router or default route.

3. Hops.

4. Interior gateway routing protocols are routing protocols that exist within an AS. IGP protocols, such as RIP, OSPF, and IS-IS, are used to keep track of routes to networks and subnets within a company's internetwork. Multiple IGPs (or routing protocols) may be implemented within a single organization. IGPs are best suited for intradomain routing.

5. EGP protocols, of which the most popular is BGP, are used to route between and across different AS'. EGPs are not designed for use within an AS. These routing protocols exchange route information necessary to forward traffic across the Internet. EGP protocols do not concern themselves with the IGP protocols within AS'.

6. AS' typically represent a single organization's internetwork, consisting of multiple internal routing domains (IGPs). However, some protocols, such as IGRP and EIGRP, use AS numbers to define their routing domain uniquely.

7. A routing domain represents a collection of networks, subnets, and routers running the same routing protocol. Within a single AS there may be multiple routing protocols (or routing domains). All devices sharing the same routing protocol and exchanging route information are said to be part of the same routing domain. Routers running more than one routing protocol are members of multiple routing domains.

8. Count to infinity, holddown, split horizon, and poison reverse.

9. Bandwidth and delay.

10. Link state routers must discover and form neighbor relationships with other routers on the same segment. This is done by exchanging hello messages. From these hello messages the adjacency database or neighbor table is built.

Chapter 4

1. IP RIP is a Distance Vector routing protocol.

2. RIP v1 and v2 use hops as their metric value.

3. RIP-enabled routers broadcast the contents of their entire route table through periodic route updates sent every 30 seconds.

4. RIP is limited to 25 route entries within each route update it broadcasts. If there are more than 25 entries, multiple broadcasts must be sent.

5. 15 hops is the maximum distance a datagram can traverse. Any value greater than 15 is considered unreachable.

6. RIP v2 supports: authentication of RIP updates, VLSM and multicasts.

7. The purpose of authentication is to allow RIP v2 routers to discriminate between authorized and unauthorized routers prior to exchanging route information. Only routers sharing the same passwords are authorized to exchange RIP updates.

8. Classless routing is supported through the inclusion of VLSMs (Variable Length Subnet Masks) within route updates. Because the mask is included, RIP v2 understands subnetting and can forward datagrams between hosts within a subdivided network.

9. RIP employs count to infinity, split horizon, and holddowns to avoid routing loops in the network.

10. RIP v2, with its enhanced features of authentication, VLSM, and multicasting, was introduced to solve some of the limitations of its predecessor, RIP v1. However, it still maintained some of the main disadvantages of RIP v1, such as periodic broadcasts, sending out its entire table, and a distance limitation of 15 hops. Other more sophisticated routing protocols like OSPF and EIGRP were introduced supporting multicasts, faster convergence, and enhanced metrics. These routing protocols were adopted by organizations instead of RIP v2.

Chapter 5

1. Bandwidth, delay, reliability, and load.

2. 255.

3. IGRP enabled routers transmit route updates every 90 seconds.

4. EIGRP offers support for multiprotocol. It can build and maintain route information for three different protocols—IP, IPX, and AppleTalk—simultaneously.

5. Successor routes are considered to be the best path to a destination and are placed in the route table. Feasible successor routes are backup routes. When the successor route fails or becomes unavailable the feasible is promoted to successor and placed in the route table.

6. Adjacency, Topology, and Forwarding databases.

7. Update, hello, query, and reply packets.

8. Bandwidth and delay.

9. EIGRP is considered a classless protocol because it supports subnetting through the inclusion of subnet masks within its updates.

10. EIGRP routers exchange hello messages to announce their presence and learn about their local neighbors. Hello messages are used to build and maintain the adjacency table.

Chapter 6

1. Link State.

2. Bandwidth.

3. All OSPF routers build and maintain three separate databases, referred to as Adjacency, Link State, and Forwarding. The Adjacency database is built through the exchange of hello messages. This database is used to keep track of OSPF neighbor routers attached to the same segment. The Link State database holds the topology map of all networks and subnets throughout the area. The Link State database is built through the exchange of route updates and is used to derive the Forwarding database, which in essence is the route table. The Forwarding database is built after the SPF algorithm is run against the Link State database.

4. Down, init, two-Way, exstart, exchange, loading, and full. An OSPF router passes through six states as it transitions from a non-participant to participant as an OSPF router within an area. Routers considered to be in the down state are not yet participants in OSPF. A router enters the init state when the router sends out its initial hello message announcing its presence on the local segment. The two-way state is achieved when a router receives hello and learns about neighbor OSPF routers on the same segment. In this state the Adjacency database is built. In the exstart state all routers on local segments become slaves to the Designated Router (master). OSPF routers exchange route information in the exchange state, building the Link State database. The loading state is used to request more information regarding a route, not received during the exchange state to complete the Link State database. The last state, full, occurs when the forwarding table has been built and convergence is achieved. This is the only state in which the router can forward datagrams.

5. 224.0.0.5.

6. Type 1 (router link) and Type 2 (network link). Type 1 advertisements are sent by all routers to the Designated Router and Backup Designated describing the directly connected networks and the state of the interfaces connected to these networks. Type 2 advertisements are sent by the DR to all OSPF routers to identify all routers connected to local network.

7. ABR (Area Border Router).

8. ASBR (Autonomous System Boundary Router).

9. Area 0 (also known as the Backbone).

10. A stub area is any area that has only one way in and one way out of Area 0.

Chapter 7

1. The current version of BGP is version 4.

2. TCP port 179.

3. IBGP and EBGP.

4. The AS number.

5. External.

6. Route reflection.

7. Open.

8. Notification.

9. A confederation is a smaller subset AS contained within another AS.

10. Stub, multi-homed, and transit.

Chapter 8

1. CLNP (Connectionless Network Protocol).

2. Adjacency, Link State, Route.

3. CSNP and PSNP. CSNP messages carry a complete set of LSP updates. PSNP messages only carry a partial list of LSP updates and are used by IS devices to request missing or more recent update information.

4. ES (end system), L1 (level 1 router), L2 (level 2 router). ESs do not route. L1s are limited to routing within an area. L2 routers may route within and between areas.

5. Priority or MAC address. The IS device with the highest priority or if priorities are equal the highest MAC address is elected as the designated router (IS device) for that segment.

6. When set, the OL bit indicates that the sending device does not have enough memory. Receivers will not send datagrams through this device for forwarding until this bit has been cleared.

7. The Hello Message.

8. The Default metric.

9. CLNP.

10. IP.

Chapter 9

1. Hello, PTSP, PTSE Ack, Database Summary, PTSE Request. Hello messages are exchanged between peers to form adjacencies. PTSPs are update messages used to exchange new or modified route information. PTSE Acks are sent in response to PTSP and database summary messages to acknowledge the receipt of PTSE route information included within these updates. Database summary messages are sent upon initial link state database exchange when a system comes online. PTSE requests are messages that may be sent to request specific route update information from a neighbor.

2. PNNI signaling and PNNI routing.

3. Peer group.

4. Hello (PNNI type 1).

5. 53 byte cell.

6. PGL (peer group leader).

7. UNI or the User to Network Interface is a signaling protocol that enables the establishment of communications between ESs and private switches or private switches and public switches.

8. A DTL (Designated Transit List) specifies the desired path (identifying systems and links within its group and group IDs of other peer groups) this system intends to use to reach the destination.

9. Systems enter the two-way state when hello messages have been successfully received by neighbors on both sides of a link. At this point neighbor systems are considered adjacent and learn remote node and port IDs of its neighbors.

10. The crankback feature allows an end system to choose an alternate path for data delivery when a previously chosen path is unavailable due to failures or lack of resources.

Chapter 10

1. The precedence, ToS, and reserved.

2. They serve to prioritize datagram delivery based on a perceived level of importance.

3. Query, error, or reply messages.

4. Path Setup, Resv Setup, Path Tear, Resv Tear, Path Error, Resv Error, and Resv Confirm.

5. Admission control is a function performed by routers or forwarding devices allowing them to accept or reject resource requests based on the availability of resources.

6. Classification, scheduling, admission control, and the RSVP protocol.

7. RSVP (ReSerVation Protocol), DiffServ (Differential Services), and MPLS (Multi-Protocol label Switching).

8. Type 3 (destination unreachable) and 5 (redirect).

9. MPLS.

10. IntServ, through the use of the RSVP protocol.

11. To manage output queues and prioritize traffic flows.

Chapter 11

1. All Systems on this subnet 224.0.0.1.

2. IGMP.

3. Member report (type 0x12 IGMP v1 or 0x16 IGMP v2).

4. MBONE is a virtual network providing a test bed for multicasting over the Internet.

5. Dense mode.

6. Sparse mode.

7. DVMRP, MOSPF and PIM-DM.

8. PIM-SM and CBT.

9. PIM-SM and CBT.

10. pim-sm.

INDEX

Numbers

A

G – H

GCAC (Generic Call Admission Control), 309
general query messages, 344
Gigabit Ethernet, 27
group addresses, 346

HA (hardware address), 394
half-duplex mode, 10
HDLC (High-Level Data Link Control), 36
header checksum, 47
headers, 123, 227, 264-265
    common, 227
    open message, 227-228
    update message, 228-229
heartbeat, 22
hello interval, 201
hello messages, 246-247, 302, 304
hello packets, 163-164, 199-200
    BDR (backup designated router), 202
    deal interval field, 202
    DR (designated router), 202
    hello interval field, 201
    neighbor field, 202
    network mask field, 201
    options field, 201
    router priority ID field, 201-202
HLDC (high-level data link control), 394
hold time field, 266
holddown timers, 112, 129, 148-149
hop count, 154
hops, 101
host precedence violation message, 324
host unreachable for ToS message, 323
hosts, 83
    bits, 62
    ranges, 63, 65
    ranges , 66
    subnets, 59

I

I (Init) bit, 203
IAB (Internet Architecture Board), 394
IAC (interpret as command), 394
IANA (Internet Assigned Number Authority), 394
IBGP (Interior Border Gateway Protocol), 231-232
ICMP (Internet Control Message Protocol), 323-324, 394
ID length field, 265
IDI (Initial Domain Identifier), 263
IDRP (Interdomain Routing Protocol), 394
IEEE (Institute of Electrical and Electronics Engineers), 15, 394
IEEE 802.1Q trunking protocol, 423
IESG (Internet Engineering Steering Group), 394
IETF (Internet Engineering Task Force), 394
IGMP (Internet Group Management Protocol), 342, 394
    checksum, 345
    group address, 346
    header, 343

    maximum response time, 345
    message types, 343-345
IGP (Interior Gateway Protocol), 98-99, 234, 394
IGRP (Interior Gateway Routing Protocol), 394
    configuring networks in, 166
    enabling route process in, 166
    load balancing, 150-151
    metrics, 144-148
    overview, 142-144
    packets, 151-152
    request packets, 152
    timers, 148-149
    update packets, 153-154
IHL (Internet Header Length), 44
init router state, 185-186
Initial Domain Identifier (IDI), 263
initial sequence number (ISN), 394
Institute of Electrical and Electronics Engineers (IEEE), 15, 394
Integrated Services Digital Network (ISDN), 394
inter-area advertisements, 181
Inter-Switch Link (ISL) trunking protocol, 423
Interdomain Routing Protocol (IDRP), 394
Interior Border Gateway Protocol (IBGP), 231-232
Interior Gateway Protocol. *See* IGP
Interior Gateway Routing Protocol. *See* IGRP
interior routes, 152
Intermediate System to Intermediate System Protocol. *See* IS-IS
internal routers, 191
international code designator, 295
International Standards Organization (ISO), 239, 394
Internet, 37
Internet Architecture Board (IAB), 394
Internet Assigned Number Authority (IANA), 394
Internet Control Message Protocol (ICMP), 323-324, 394
Internet Engineering Steering Group (IESG), 394
Internet Group Management Protocol. *See* IGMP
Internet Header Length (IHL), 44
Internet Protocol. *See* IP
Internet Research Task Force (IRTF), 394
Internet Service Provider (ISP), 394
Internet Society (ISOC), 394
Internetwork Packet Exchange (IPX), 40, 394
interpret as command (IAC), 394
intra-area advertisements, 180
intranets, 37
IntServ (Integrated Services), 327-330
invalid timers, 128, 148-149
IP (Internet Protocol), 394
    best effort delivery, 317-318
    overview, 39
    Tos (Type of Service), 318-323
IP addressing, 125
    address classes, 51-56, 340
    and ASNs (Autonomous System numbers), 218
    assigning in, 431
    Class A (Slash 8) addresses, 51-57
    Class B (Slash 16) addresses, 51-57
    Class C (Slash 24) addresses, 51-57
    Class D addresses, 52-55, 340
    Class E addresses, 52-55, 340
    dynamic, 41

T